CHEAP EATS GUIDE TO EUROPE 1995

KATIE WOOD was born and educated in Edinburgh. She read Communications then English at university and worked as a freelance journalist before specializing in travel. Author of many guidebooks, she has made a name for herself both in Britain and internationally for her practical, down-to-earth approach, and the quality of her research.

Katie Wood continues to write freelance for, among others, the *Scotsman*. She is the Travel Editor of the *Daily Express* in Scotland and, north of the border she has her own TV travel programme on the independent network – 'Scottish Passport'. She is a fellow of the Royal Geographical Society, undertaking specialist travel consultancy work for airlines, tour operators and tourist boards.

Married with two children, Katie Wood's home base is near Perth, Scotland.

Also by Katie Wood

Europe by Train 1995
Cheap Sleep Guide to Europe 1995
The 1995 Globetrotter's Bible
Traveller's Scotland (Mainstream)

With Ken Welsh

The Hitch-hiker's Guide to Europe 1995

CHEAP EATS GUIDE TO EUROPE 1995

Katie Wood

Researcher Craig Aitken

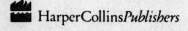 HarperCollins*Publishers*

HarperCollins*Publishers*
77–85 Fulham Palace Road,
Hammersmith, London W6 8JB

Published by HarperCollins*Publishers* 1994
9 8 7 6 5 4 3 2 1

Copyright © Katie Wood 1994

Whilst every effort has been made to ensure
accuracy throughout this work, the turbulent
nature of the international travel industry
is such that the author and publishers cannot
be held liable for changes which occur after
the time of writing.

The Author asserts the moral right to
be identified as the author of this work

A catalogue record for this book is
available from the British Library

ISBN 0 00 638380 7

Set in Linotron Meridien by
Rowland Phototypesetting Ltd
Bury St Edmunds, Suffolk

Printed in Great Britain by
HarperCollinsManufacturing Glasgow

CONTENTS

INTRODUCTION

If you're travelling on any sort of a budget – and let's face it, who isn't these days? – then you're sure to experience at least once the 'Bisto Kids' syndrome. This is familiar to anyone who has Inter-Railed, hitched, cycled or otherwise tried to see Europe cheaply, and is caused by a combination of an empty stomach and an even emptier pocket. Sufferers of the syndrome can be spotted standing dolefully outside restaurants, sniffing the delicious aromas wafting out, and shaking their heads glumly as they realize the only thing they can afford on the menu is a starter – between the two of them.

This book aims to save you from becoming one of these 'Bisto Kids', by recommending cheap restaurants and cafés throughout Europe, many of them serving the local cuisine. After all, if you visit a country hoping to sample its culture, including its cooking, it can be very frustrating to find that your budget limits you to the ubiquitous fast-food burger bars and pizza joints that you can find at home. There *are* cheap, local eateries, even in the most bustling and tourist-orientated of cities – it's just a matter of knowing where to look.

The most obvious option when eating out in a restaurant is simply to order *à la carte* (from the menu). However, it is worth remembering that in many countries it is common for restaurants to offer special set menus which allow you to eat a two- or three-course meal for a fraction of the cost of eating *à la carte*. Lunchtime set menus can be especially good value as they are usually aimed not at tourists, but at local workers looking for a decent, reasonably priced meal. Another cheap eating option available in several countries under a variety of names is the dish-of-the-day: a main course being sold at a knockdown price. Depending upon your appetite, and the asking price, all-you-can-eat buffets (found mainly in Scandinavia) can also be good value for money. Listings in this guide are based upon taking advantage of cheap eating possibilities like the above: eating out in the restaurants recommended can be more expensive than the figures quoted if you choose to eat *à la carte*.

Cafés (in the continental sense rather than the British-style cafeteria) may offer reasonably priced snacks and light meals, but bear in mind that the price can vary quite dramatically depending upon precisely *where* you eat. In France, for example, if is almost always more expensive to eat (or drink) outside at the tables than standing at the bar.

Vegetarians, of course, have special problems travelling in Europe. *Cheap Eats* aims to help by recommending restaurants that serve vegetarian food, by assessing how well (or how badly) vegetarians are catered for in different countries, and by pointing out national or local dishes which are suitable for vegetarians. The latter is very important because, whereas most countries' cuisines rely heavily on meat or fish, there are usually a few national or local specialities which are meat-free, and which chefs will usually be willing to prepare on request. This can help vegetarians avoid one common source of arguments with meat-eating companions. This occurs when the carnivore has found a nice little restaurant serving local food at reasonable prices, and the herbivore cannot see anything suitable on the menu. The latter then faces the choice of continuing the search with an increasingly bad-tempered companion, or giving in and trying hard to make a bread roll and a coffee last an hour while the other tucks in. Vegetarian options will also be a godsend for those of you concerned about the risk of stomach upsets from dodgy meat and seafood, and may be of interest to anyone watching their pennies as vegetarian meals are generally cheaper than meals with meat or fish.

If you cannot afford to eat out (or in the case of vegetarians just cannot find anything suitable) *Cheap Eats* will help by recommending conveniently located markets and supermarkets. Remember that buying fresh produce from the local market, and home-produced rather than imported brands from the supermarket, makes the most sense; not just because it usually gives you the best value for money (imported foodstuffs and drinks can easily cost twice the price of similar goods produced in the country), but also because of the contribution this can make to the economy of the country or, in the case of markets, the region you are visiting.

However many cheap restaurants you find, or however much you save by buying from markets and supermarkets, you can still use up your spending money rapidly buying drinks; not just alcohol, but also soft drinks, and tea and coffee. To save money, always carry a bottle of water to quench your thirst. Where the water is safe to drink you can simply fill a plastic bottle or cycling bottle with fresh water whenever the opportunity arises; otherwise buy some bottled water. Either way, you will be able to relax and enjoy a beer or coffee rather than guzzling it in one go.

The *Cheap Eats* guide gives you information on eating in twenty-eight countries. A general introduction covers matters such as average prices for a meal, and for various foodstuffs and drinks, as well as national and regional specialities to look out for, details of normal shopping hours, supermarket chains, etc. There then follows more detailed information on cities, with lists of specific restaurants where you can get meals which, by local standards, are both inexpensive and good value for money (the two do not always go together), and information on the spots to do your own shopping.

If you come across your own real 'find' that isn't mentioned in the book, then do let me know so other travellers can benefit. New restaurants and eateries are springing up all the time. Of course I'd also like to know if any of the places mentioned have stopped offering value for money, or if they've lowered their standards and are no longer worth a visit. You've been asking me to produce this guide for ages, so I hope you get good use from it – bon appetit!

KATIE WOOD
Perth
December 1994

AUSTRIA

Eating cheaply isn't easy in Austria, there's no getting away from it. You can find yourself paying 200AS (£11; $16.50) just for a main course, although the average price is lower. It is possible to eat well on a budget, however, as long as you know where to look and avoid the little extras that can practically double your bill. A glass of wine can cost anything from 17–35AS (£1–2; $1.50–3.00), but can sometimes work out cheaper than mineral water. Save money by asking for tap water, which is perfectly safe to drink. Some restaurants may also bring you dips or bread and butter when you sit down. Beware, these aren't free and you can be charged 20AS (£1.10; $1.65) for each tiny slice of bread; you may also be charged for each portion of butter. Another extra to watch for is the *gedeck*, a table charge, which can sometimes be added on. The most expensive places to eat are generally traditional restaurants. Look instead for *gasthöfe*, *gasthäuser* or *beisl*, which are basically inns serving inexpensive meals, often traditional Austrian food. The major cities also have Chinese, Indian and sometimes Italian and Greek restaurants, where food is generally cheaper. Look for *Kaffeekonditorei*, which are coffee and chocolate shops, often selling snacks and light meals at low prices. Cheap chains to look for are Nordsee and Wienerwald. If breakfast is included with your accommodation then make the most of it. You are likely to get a choice of breads, cheeses, meats and preserves, which will help see you through the day.

Austrian cuisine may not be renowned, but it can be very tasty and is certainly filling. Traditionally it has combined eastern and western influences, so you will often find Hungarian goulash soup, Italian pastas and German sausage and sauerkraut on the same menu. Soups tend to be clear meat soups with *nockerl* (dumplings), such as *grießnockerlsuppe* (clear soup with semolina dumplings) or *markknödelsuppe* (clear soup with bone marrow dumplings). They may sound a little heavy, but the dumplings are quite light and fluffy. Main courses rely heavily on meat, particularly beef, veal and pork. Look for *Wiener schnitzel* (breaded veal cutlet), *tafelspitz* (boiled beef and vegetables) and *backhuhn* (fried and breaded chicken). These are usually eaten with potatoes and salad. Your best chance of trying these traditional dishes is to eat your main meal at lunch time, when many restaurants offer special cheaper menus.

Desserts must be the high point of any Austrian meal. There's the famous apple strudel of course, much lighter and tastier than the versions you'll find at home, as well as a wide variety of sweet dumplings, pancakes and noodles. These may be served with fruit, jam or *topfen* (a light, creamy cottage cheese), as well as cream. Try *topfenknödel* (cottage cheese dumplings), *marmeladepalatschinken* (pancakes and jam) or *buchteln* (noodles and vanilla cream).

Austrian wines have recovered from the 'anti-freeze' scandal that once beset them, and there are several good whites and reds to choose from. Names to watch for are *Klosterneuburger* (white) and *Volauer* (a red), but given the high prices you may well decide to stick to beer. No brewery really dominates the national market – instead there are many local breweries such as Graz's Gösser, Salzburg's Stiegl and Innsbruck's Adam, which produce a range of beers, from the pale *Hell* brews, through *Pilsners* to the dark *Dunkels* and the powerful *Bock* beers. There are several popular spirits, most notably schnapps, and local brandies, which should be treated with respect.

If you've got a sweet tooth, Austria will seem like paradise, as its most famous culinary tradition has to be coffee and cakes, both of which are delicious. It is expensive though, with a cup of coffee costing from 24–35AS (£1.30–2.00; $2–3), and cakes and pastries 30–40AS (£1.65–2.20; $2.50–3.30). You'll find a huge array of cakes and pastries on offer, so forget about calorie counting. Look out for the famous *sachertorte* from Vienna, a rich chocolate cake with apricot filling, or unusual and delicious poppy-seed cakes. You'll find coffee houses all over Austria, particularly in Vienna where they dominate life. Locals tend to have 'their' coffee house, even 'their' table where they might sit every day. The most famous coffee houses are more expensive than cafés, but provided you order something you can sit for as long as you want. Don't ask for 'a coffee', by the way, as there are loads of different types and the waiter will just give you a blank look. Some varieties to look for are *mokka*, small, strong and black; *melange*, a larger cup with milk; and *einspänner*, a glass of black coffee with whipped cream. Coffee is always served with a glass of water, so this helps you to make it last.

Austria has long been spoken of as a vegetarian nightmare, since the diet features so much meat. However, things are changing, and if there aren't many specialist vegetarian restaurants at least more and more places are offering a veggie choice on the menu. Moreover chefs are often happy to provide a special veggie dish if requested. Chains to look out for are Wrenkh and Wienerwald where there's always a meat-free selection.

Shopping in Austria is easy enough, as there are plenty of supermarkets, as well as open-air markets, like the superb Naschmarkt in Vienna. You'll find plenty of delicious breads, cheeses, sausages, pastries and fruit in Konsum, Sparmarkt, Billa and (especially) Julius Meinl stores. The discount chain Höfer is not so good for fresh produce.

Graz

LOCAL SPECIALITIES

Wurzelfleisch	a stew
Sterz	a dish made of buckwheat or corn
Huhn	chicken

In addition to the famous Gösser brand, other local beers to look out for are Puntigam and Reininghaus.

CHEAP EATERIES
Cheap meals are relatively easy to find in Graz as many restaurants rely more on the custom of the large student population than tourists. There are lots of cheap eateries clustered around the university – about ten minutes' walk from the city centre.
Two-course meals for under 65AS (£3.50; $5.25)

University Mensa, Zinzendorfgasse (junction with Leechgasse). Vegetarian (*Vollwert*) meals prepared on request. Open Mon.–Fri. 11 a.m.–2 p.m.

Two-course meals from 65–90AS (£3.50–5.00; $5.25–7.50)

Gastwirtschaft Wartburgasse, Halbärthgasse 4. Plenty of vegetarian options available. Open Mon.–Fri. 9 a.m.–1 a.m.
Mangold, Griesgasse 11. Vegetarian restaurant. Open Mon.–Fri. 11 a.m.–8 p.m., Sat. 11 a.m.–4 p.m.
Calafati, Lissagasse 2. Chinese restaurant. Open daily 11.30 a.m.–3 p.m. and 5.30–11.30 p.m.
Zotter, Glacisstraße 25. Open Tues.–Fri. 7.15 a.m.–8 p.m., weekends 9 a.m.–8 p.m.
Haring, Mehlplatz 4 (tel. 82 32 18). Open Mon.–Fri. 10 a.m.–1 a.m., weekends 6 p.m.–1 a.m.

Two-course meals from 90–125AS (£5–7; $7.50–10.50)

Hotel Straßer, Eggenburger Gürtel 11. Recommended dish: *Wiener Schnitzel* (veal cutlet fried in breadcrumbs). Open daily 6–9.30 p.m.

Gambrinuskeller, Prokopigasse 1 (tel. 81 01 81). Specializes in grilled meat dishes. Open Mon.–Fri. 9 a.m.–midnight, Sat. 9.30 a.m.–3 p.m.

Rosenkavalier, Europaplatz 3 (tel. 91 12 81). Open daily 6.30 a.m.–11 p.m.

Zur Goldenen Pastete, Sporgasse 28 (tel. 82 34 16). Open Mon.–Fri. 11 a.m.–midnight.

Two-course meals from 125–180AS (£7–10; $10.50–15.00)

Landhaus-Keller, Schmiedgasse 9 (tel. 83 02 76). Open Mon.–Sat. 11 a.m.–midnight.

S'Milchmariandl, Richard-Wagner-Gasse 31 (tel. 34400). Open Mon.–Sat. 11.30 a.m.–midnight, closed Sun.

Innsbruck

LOCAL SPECIALITIES

Knödel	a light dumpling
Tiroler knödel mit gröstl	large dumplings with pieces of bacon, in a beef and potato stew
Germknödel	a dessert dumpling stuffed with plum jam, sprinkled with poppy seeds and sugar, and covered with melted butter
Kaminwurz	thinly sliced smoked sausage
Polenta	a cornmeal mixture served with mushroom sauce or strong cheese

Another popular Tyrolean dish is an omelette filled with cranberries.
   Wines to look for are St Maddalener (red) and Silvaner (white). In addition to Forst Pilsner there is a range of beers produced by the Adam and Kaiser breweries.

CHEAP EATERIES
As a rule, the restaurants along and just off Maria-Theresian-Straße are overpriced for what you get. For better value head across the River Inn from the town centre to the eateries on and around Innstraße.

Two-course meals for under 65AS (£3.50; $5.25)

University Mensa, Herzog-Sigmund-Ufer 15 (2nd floor). Open Mon.–Fri. 11 a.m.–2 p.m.
Hortnagl, Burggraben 4–6. Self-service. Open Mon.–Fri. 10.30 a.m.–6 p.m., Sat. 10.30 a.m.–1 p.m.
China-Restaurant Asia, Angerzellgasse 10. Chinese restaurant with a cheap lunchtime set menu. Open daily 11.30 a.m.–2.30 p.m. and 6 p.m.–midnight.
China-Restaurant Canton, Maria-Theresian-Straße 37 (tel. 58 53 69). Another Chinese restaurant with a cheap lunchtime set menu. Open daily 11.30 a.m.–2.30 p.m. and 5.30–11.30 p.m.

Two-course meals from 65–90AS (£3.50–5.50; $5.25–7.50)

Al Dente, Meranerstraße 7 (tel. 58 49 47). Pasta dishes. Open Mon.–Sat. 11 a.m.–10.30 p.m., Sun. 11 a.m.–9.30 p.m.
Zach, Gilmstraße 3 (tel. 58 39 20). Open Mon.–Fri. 7.30 a.m.–10 p.m., Sat. 7.30 a.m.–3 p.m.

Two-course meals from 90–125AS (£5–7; $7.50–10.50)

Philippine Vegetarische Küche, Müllerstraße 9. Vegetarian restaurant. English menu available. Open Mon.–Sat. 11.30 a.m.–2 p.m. and 6–10.30 p.m.
Country-Life, Maria-Theresien-Straße 9. Vegetarian restaurant. Open Mon.–Thurs. 11.30 a.m.–7 p.m., Fri. 11.30 a.m.–3 p.m.
Wienerwald, Museumstraße 24 and Maria-Theresien-Straße 12. Open daily 10 a.m.–midnight.
Johannes-Stüberl, Innrain 42a (tel. 58 94 32). Open Mon.–Sat. 9 a.m.–midnight, Sun. 11 a.m.–midnight.

Two-course meals from 125–180AS (£7–10; $10.50–15.00)

Gasthof Riese Haymon, Haymongasse 4 (tel. 58 98 37). Open daily 11 a.m.–9 p.m.
Löwenhaus, Rennweg 5 (tel. 58 54 79). Open daily 9 a.m.–midnight.

SHOPPING
● Supermarkets

M-preis, opposite the train station Konsum and Hofer, on Museumstrasse. Open Mon.–Fri. 8 a.m.–6 p.m., Sat. 8 a.m.–noon.

Julius Meinl, Maximilianstraße and Marktgraben.

You can also buy food at Kaufhaus Tyrol, Maria Theresien 33 (tel. 58 14 01), Innsbruck's largest department store. It's open Mon.–Fri. 8.30 a.m.–6.30 p.m., Sat. 8.30 a.m.–12.30 p.m. (5 p.m. on the first Saturday in the month).

● **Markets**
There is an indoor market in the Markthalle, Herzog-Sigmund-Ufer 1. It's open Mon.–Fri. 8 a.m.–6 p.m., Sat. 8 a.m.–noon.

Salzburg

LOCAL SPECIALITIES

Salzburger Nockerl	a huge fluffy omelette
Salzburger Knoblauchsuppe	a strong garlic soup
Buchteln	dessert noodles with vanilla cream
Pofesen	sweet stuffed roll fritters
Stiegl Paracelsus	the dark beer that is the most famous of a range of beers brewed by the Stiegl brewery

CHEAP EATERIES
Two-course meals for under 65AS (£3.50; $5.25)

Michael Haydn Stube, Mirabellplatz 1 (in the Aicher Passage). Vegetarian options available. Open Mon.–Fri. 11 a.m.–7.30 p.m.

Two-course meals from 65–90AS (£3.50–5.00; $5.25–7.50)

Blaue Gans, Getreidegasse 43 (tel. 84 24 91). Open daily except Wed. 11 a.m.–midnight.
Pizzeria Peperone, Gaisbergstraße 12 (tel. 64 14 68). Open Mon.–Sat. 11 a.m.–2 p.m. and 6–11 p.m.

Two-course meals from 90–125AS (£5–7; $7.50–10.50)

Humboldtstube, Gstättengasse 6 (tel. 84 31 71). Open daily 11–2 a.m.

Wienerwald, Griesgasse 31 (tel. 84 34 70). Vegetarian options available. Open daily 10−1 a.m.

Hofer's Schnellimbiss, Judengasse 10 (tel. 84 13 44). Italian and Austrian dishes. Open daily 9 a.m.−6.30 p.m. (until 10 p.m. during the festival).

Café Mozart, Getreidegasse 22 (tel. 84 37 46). Open daily 9 a.m.−10 p.m.

Priesterhausstube, Priesterhausgasse 12 (tel. 87 83 17). Open daily 11.30 a.m.−11 p.m.

Yuen, Getreidegasse 24 (tel. 84 37 70). Chinese restaurant. Open daily 11.30 a.m.−11 p.m.

Two-course meals from 125−180AS (£7−10; $10.50−15.00)

Paracelsus Stub'n, Kaigasse 8 (tel. 84 32 77). Recommended dishes: *Gulaschsuppe* (goulash soup) and *Wienerschnitzel mit Kartoffeln* (veal cutlet with potatoes). Recommended drink: *Stiegl Paracelsus*. Open daily 11 a.m.−2 a.m.

Beverly, Griesgasse 29 (tel. 84 34 24). Vegetarian options available. Open daily 11 a.m.−10 p.m.

Sternbräu, Griesgasse 23 (tel. 84 21 40). Extensive menu with lots of Austrian specialities and vegetarian dishes. Open daily 8 a.m.−11 p.m.

SHOPPING

It's easy to put together a picnic in Salzburg as many of the Old Town squares have stalls selling fresh produce from Mon.−Sat.

● Supermarkets

Julius Meinl, in Kiesel Passage on St Julian Straße, a five-minute walk from the train station in the direction of the town centre.

Hofer, at the junction of Schallmooser Hauptstraße and Franz-Josef Straße. Open Mon.−Fri. 8 a.m.−6 p.m., Sat. 7.30 a.m.−noon. A short distance down Schallmooser Hauptstraße are Julius Meinl and Konsum. These stores are very handy if you are staying at the youth hostel in Glockengasse.

Kaufhaus Forum, opposite Hauptbahnhof (tel. 50536). Open Mon.−Fri. 9 a.m.−5.30 p.m., Sat. 9 a.m.−noon (4 p.m. on the first Saturday of the month).

FURTHER INFORMATION

The tourist office is at Mozartplatz 5 (tel. 71712). Open daily in summer 8 a.m.−8 p.m., winter 9 a.m.−6 p.m.

Vienna

LOCAL SPECIALITIES

Serbische Bohnensuppe	a spicy, bean-based soup
Ungärische Gulaschsuppe	beef stew with paprika and spices
Wiener schnitzel	veal cutlet fried in breadcrumbs
Sachertorte	a rich chocolate cake

CHEAP EATERIES

For evening dining, the general rule is that the further you get from the centre, the cheaper the restaurant is likely to be, especially once you get outside the *Ring*. However, as long as you avoid the over-priced restaurants along and just off Kärntnerstraße, you won't find a great deal of difference between the special lunchtime deals on offer at restaurants inside the *Ring* compared to those outside. Within the *Ring*, the area around the Votivkirche and the Schottentor U-bahn station has the greatest concentration of reasonably priced eateries.

Two-course meals for under 65AS (£3.50; $5.25)

University mensas. No student ID required. At: Universitätsstraße 7 (7th floor) (tel. 43 45 94), open Mon.–Fri. 8 a.m.–7 p.m.; Johannesgasse 8 (tel. 512 9470), open Mon.–Fri. 7.30 a.m.– 3 p.m.; Oskar Kokoschka-Platz 2 (tel. 730 0954), open Mon.–Thurs. 9 a.m.–6 p.m., Fri. 9 a.m.–3 p.m.; Schillerplatz 2 (tel. 58 81 61 38), open Mon.–Fri. 8.30 a.m.–5 p.m.; Karlsplatz 13 (tel. 56 65 02), open Mon.–Fri. 11 a.m.–2.30 p.m.; Ebendor-ferstraße 8 (tel. 408 3587), open Mon.–Fri. 11.30 a.m.–2 p.m.
Weidinger, Danhausergasse 3 (tel. 506 5697), open Mon.–Fri. 10 a.m.–11 p.m.

Two-course meals from 65–90AS (£3.50–5.00; $5.25–7.50)

Bierteufl, Ungargasse 5 (tel. 712 6503). Huge selection of beers. Open Mon.–Fri. 10 a.m.–1 a.m., Sat. 4 p.m.–1 a.m., Sun. and public holidays 5 p.m.–1 a.m.
Weinhaus Wild, Radetzkyplatz 1 (tel. 712 5750). Open daily 8 a.m.–11 p.m.
Spatzennest, Ulrichsplatz 1 (tel. 526 1659). Open Sun.–Thurs. 10 a.m.–midnight.
Käuzchen, Gardegasse 8 (tel. 526 4866). Open daily 8 a.m.–2 a.m. (Sun. until 4 a.m.).

Schnitzelwirt, Neubaugasse 52 (tel. 93 37 71). Open Mon.–Fri. 11 a.m.–11 p.m., Sat. 10 a.m.–2.30 p.m. and 5 p.m.–11 p.m.

Zur Stadt Brünn, Strozzigasse 36 (tel. 42 03 88). Open Tues.–Sat. 10 a.m.–midnight, Sun. and public holidays 10 a.m.–3 p.m.

Waldviertler Eck, Pfeilgasse 27 (junction with Albertgasse) (tel. 42 32 93). Open Mon.–Thurs. 9 a.m.–11 p.m., Fri. 9 a.m.–3 p.m.

Wrenkh, Bauernmarkt 10 (tel. 533 1526). Vegetarian restaurant. Open Mon.–Sat. 11 a.m.–midnight.

Two-course meals from 90–125AS (£5–7; $7.50–10.50)

Stadt Krems, Zieglergasse 37 (tel. 93 72 00). Open daily 11 a.m.–2 p.m. and 6 p.m.–midnight.

Smutny, Elisabethstraße 8 (tel. 587 1356). Open daily 10 a.m.–midnight.

Levante, Wallnerstraße 2 (tel. 533 2326). Turkish cuisine predominates. Plenty of vegetarian dishes. Recommended dish: *Levante-Platte* (an assortment of Turkish specialities). Open daily 11.30 a.m.–11.30 p.m.

Jahrhundert Beisl, Floriangasse 37 (tel. 218 0152). Recommended dish: *gulasch*. Open Thurs.–Tues. 8 p.m.–midnight.

Schweizerhaus, Volksprater 116 (tel. 218 0152). Recommended dish: *Schweinsteize* (grilled pork with mustard and horseradish). Open Mar.–Nov. daily 10 a.m.–midnight.

Two-course meals from 125–180AS (£7–10; $10.50–15.00)

Altes Fassl, Ziegelofengasse 37 (tel. 55 42 98). Open Tues.–Sat. 6 p.m.–1 a.m., Sun. noon–3 p.m. and 6 p.m.–1 a.m.

Pizzeria Ristorante Sardegna, Servitengasse 14 (tel. 319 7733). Italian restaurant. Plenty of vegetarian options. Open Tues.–Sun. 11.30 a.m.–2.30 p.m. and 6–11.30 p.m.

Zu den 3 Hacken, Singerstraße 28 (tel. 512 5895). English menu available. Open Mon.–Fri. 9 a.m.–midnight, Sat. 9 a.m.–3 p.m.

Siddhartha, Fleischmarkt 16 (tel. 513 1197). Vegetarian restaurant. Open daily 11.30 a.m.–3 p.m. and 6–11 p.m.

Figlmüller, Wollzeile 5 (tel. 512 6177). Open daily 11 a.m.–10.30 p.m.

SHOPPING
● Markets

The city's main market is the Naschmarkt on Wienzeile (open Mon.–Fri. 6 a.m.–6.30 p.m., Sat. 6 a.m.–1 p.m.). Other markets operate on Rochusmarkt, Brunnenmarkt, Brunnengasse, Niederhofstraße and Landstraßer Haupstraße.

● **Supermarkets**
The Lugner City complex by the Burgasse/Stadthalle U-bahn
station (a short walk from the Westbahnhof) contains branches of
several of the main Austrian supermarket chains. Billa on Singerstraße, and Julius Meinl and Löwa on Hoher Markt are convenient
for shopping whilst touring the city centre.

FURTHER INFORMATION
As well as useful information on a range of other subjects, the
pamphlet 'Vienna Youth Scene' (free from Tourist Offices) has a
section containing suggestions for cheap eating.

BELGIUM

Belgian cuisine has always been rather overshadowed by that of neighbouring France, which is a shame, as it is excellent and varied. Unfortunately, it also tends to be rather expensive, but as long as you know which of the many restaurants, cafés and bars to head for, you should be able to choose from plenty of tasty dishes.

A two-course meal in a restaurant at night can cost over 800F (£16; $24), often 1,000F (£20; $30), so it's best to eat your main meal at lunchtime when the Belgians eat theirs. Bars and cafés serve basic dishes, such as omelettes, for around 200F (£4; $6), and if you look out for the *plat du jour* (dish of the day), you should spend no more than 300F (£6; $9). A more expensive *menu du jour* is often available at night. A service charge of 16%, and VAT (TVA in Belgium) of 19%, are always included. Menus are usually written in both French and Flemish, but many people speak English too, so you shouldn't get stuck. A cup of coffee in a café costs 50F (£1; $1.50).

There are many speciality Belgian dishes and you're sure to be able to try at least some of these during your stay. In the south particularly, rich sauces made with butter, cream, herbs, even beer, are common. You'll also find filling soups and the famous *Ardennes pâté* and smoked ham. Seafood dishes (*caricoles*) abound, especially mussels, and are better value than meat dishes. Every region has its own speciality dishes such as *carbonnades flamandes* (beef stewed in beer), *poulet waterzooi* (chicken and vegetables stewed in a tasty sauce), steamed hops, *moules et frites* and pheasant stew. Delicious waffles can be found everywhere, served with fruit, cream or jam. Reasonably priced tourist menus are widely available and will give you your best chance to sample local dishes. Eateries offering these display a sign consisting of the letter 'T' within an oval ring.

There are the usual fast-food burger joints in Belgium, the majority belonging to the national Quick chain, but for cheap food on the run, use the street stalls like the locals. *Friture* stands, which you'll find everywhere, sell delicious long, thin chips (*frites*), nothing like their stodgy British equivalents, for around 50–70F (£1–1.40; $1.50–2.10). You can have them with salt, mayonnaise or a host of other dressings, for which there's a small extra charge, and they're served in huge paper cones. If you thought the British have chips with everything, just wait till you get to Belgium! Other street stalls sell waffles, which are cheap and delicious, and sausages and kebabs.

Belgium is a chocoholic's dream, producing what are arguably the finest chocolates in the world. One of the best names to look out for is Leonidas, a chain of shops which offer the cheapest deluxe chocs around, while another well-known name is Godiva. You'll also find plenty of rich cakes, pastries and fruit tarts, very similar to those in France.

If it's a drink you're after, then you'll be spoiled for choice. Any bar will offer at least 40 different types of beer (La Houblonnière in Brussels has 100, Dulle Griet in Ghent a staggering 250), and there are actually over 400 brands brewed around the country. The most common beers are Pilsner-type brews such as Stella Artois, Maes and Jupiler which you can find anywhere. There are also plenty of speciality beers to try, the best known being *Lambic*, a type of beer which is fermented by contact with the yeast in the air. A variation on *Lambic* beer is *Gueuze* which is brewed in the bottle. Lambic beers are often flavoured by the addition of fruit or sugars; *kriek*, for example, is flavoured with cherries and *faro* with sugar. A real Belgian speciality are the rich, dark beers brewed by Trappist monks, with names like *Chimay*, *Affligem*, *Westmalle* and *Corsendonk*. Whereas you will normally pay around 45F (£0.90; $1.35) for a glass of beer in a bar, Trappist beers are more expensive. However, they are also stronger than ordinary beers (the suffix 6, 8 or 12 after the name, relates to the strength of the brew).

The Belgians usually drink French wine, which can be bought for around 100F (£2; $3) per bottle in a local store, though you will pay almost as much for a glass of wine to accompany a meal (typically about 80F (£1.60; $2.40). Any of the usual spirits (there is no national speciality) will cost 60F (£1.20; $1.80) a measure.

Breakfast tends to be of the continental, croissant-and-coffee variety, although hotels may serve a larger self-service spread, which includes yoghurt, cheese and cold meats. Vegetarians in particular should take advantage of this if they get the opportunity, as it is difficult to eat a varied veggie diet in Belgium, especially if you don't eat eggs. However you'll always be able to get snacks and sandwiches – plus of course the ubiquitous *frites*, and we list several specialist vegetarian restaurants, as well as ethnic eateries. Picnics won't be a problem, as there are lots of well-stocked supermarkets and grocery shops.

Supermarket chains to look out for are Grand-Bazaar (GB), Delhaize and Nopri. Another chain you will see frequently is Aldi: although these stores can be very cheap, they have been criticized in the past for the dubious quality of some of their products. On the whole prices are higher than in the UK – typically by about 20–25% – though fresh fruit and vegetables are slightly cheaper. Many shops are closed on Monday morning, but are otherwise open from 9 a.m.–5.30 p.m., sometimes shutting earlier on Saturday.

Antwerp

The area around Grote Markt has plenty of restaurants and bars but can be expensive. Cheaper food can be found near the university, at Prinsstraat, and along Oudekoornmarkt (for cheap Greek eateries) and the Jewish district around Pelikaanstrasse.

CHEAP EATERIES
Two-course meals under 300F (£6; $9)

Atlantis, Korte Nieuwestraat 6 (tel. 234 0517). Vegetarian restaurant. Open Mon. and Wed.–Fri. noon–2 p.m. and 5–9.30 p.m.; Sat. and Sun. 5–9.30 p.m.

Two-course meals from 300–400F (£6–8; $9–12)

Pizzeria Toni, Grote Markt (opposite the Stadhuis) (tel. 226 0300). Italian restaurant.
De Ware Jacob, Vlasmarkt 19. Open Mon.–Sat. 5 p.m.–2 a.m.
De Spiegel, Oude Koornmarkt 34 (tel. 233 8661). Some vegetarian options. Open Wed.–Thurs. noon–9 p.m.; Fri.–Sun. noon–midnight.
Elixir, Steenhouwersvest 57 (tel. 231 7321). Vegetarian restaurant. Open Mon.–Sat. noon–2 p.m. (also 6–8 p.m. Fri.–Sat.).
De Goede Aarde, Hendrik Conscience Straat 64 (tel. 230 1162). Vegetarian restaurant. Open Mon.–Fri. noon–2 p.m. and 6–8.30 p.m., Sat. noon–2 p.m.

Two-course meals from 400–500F (£8–10; $12–15)

Charisma, Vleminck Veld 27 (tel. 233 8409). Vegetarian dishes available. Open 6–9 p.m.
De Schorpioen, Dolfinstraat 49 (tel. 236 8567). Open noon–2 p.m. and 6–10 p.m.

SHOPPING
GB, on Schoenmarkt. Open Mon.–Thurs. 9 a.m.–8 p.m.; Fri. 9 a.m.–9 p.m.; Sat. 9 a.m.–8 p.m.

Bruges

There is no particularly cheap area in the city centre. However, when it comes to evening dining the restaurants bordering on the canals are usually best avoided as they tend to be a good deal more expensive than restaurants elsewhere, though the difference is less noticeable at lunchtime, when most restaurants offer specially priced set menus. Basically, it makes sense to eat your main meal in the middle of the day.

LOCAL SPECIALITIES
Seafood is very popular here and you may also find Flemish leek and bacon pie (a sort of rich quiche), and Flanders sweet loaf, a rich loaf made with milk and sugar.

CHEAP EATERIES
Two-course meals under 300F (£6; $9)

De Breton Crêperie, Ezelstraat 4 (tel. 34 54 25). Open daily except Tues.

The Fox, Philipstockstraat 19 (tel. 33 23 28). Closed Fri. evening.

Gran Kaffee de Passage, Dweerstraat 26 (tel. 35 02 32). Open daily.

The Lotus, Wapenmakerstraat 5. Vegetarian restaurant. Open daily mid-Aug.–July, 10 a.m.–2 p.m.

Cavalier, Kuipersstraat 25 (tel. 33 02 07). Recommended dish: *waterzooi* (chicken and vegetable stew). Open daily.

Zen, Beenhouwersstraat 117 (tel. 33 67 02). Vegetarian restaurant. Open Mon.–Sat.

Song Hua, Burgstraat 2 (tel. 22 18 48). Chinese restaurant. Open daily.

Selfi, Steenstraat 58 (tel. 33 50 68). Self-service restaurant. Open daily.

Two-course meals from 300–400F (£6–8; $9–12)

Martino, 't Zand 23 (tel. 33 41 48). Recommended dish: *mosselen* (mussels). Open daily in summer, closed on Mondays in winter.

Lautrec, Sint-Amandstraat 5 (tel. 33 76 10). Open daily except Wed.

't Mozarthuys, Huidenvettersplein 1 (tel. 33 45 30). Open daily except Mon.

't Minnewater, Wijngaardstraat 28 (tel. 33 57 46). Open daily.

Belle Epoque, Zuidzandstraat 43 (tel. 33 18 72). Open daily.

Two-course meals from 400–500F (£8–10; $12–15)

't Koffieboontje, Hallestraat 4 (tel. 33 80 27). Open daily.
De Beurze, Markt 22 (tel. 33 50 79). Open daily except Tues.
Breydel-De Coninck, Breidelstraat 24 (tel. 33 97 46). Recommended dish: *mosselen* (mussels). Open Thurs.–Mon. and Tues. lunchtimes; closed during June.
La Taverne Brugeoise, Markt 27 (tel. 33 21 32). Specializes in seafood dishes. Open daily in summer; closed on Wednesdays in winter.
Papageno, Vlamingstraat 36 (tel. 33 14 75). Open daily except Wed. Closed for first two weeks of July.

SHOPPING
● **Markets**

On Wednesday on Burg (8 a.m.–12.30 p.m.), and Sat. on 't Zand and Beursplein (both 8 a.m.–12.30 p.m.).

● **Supermarkets**

Nopri, Noordzanstraat 4. Open Mon.–Thurs. 9 a.m.–6.30 p.m.; Fri. 9 a.m.–5 p.m.; Sat. 9 a.m.–6.30 p.m.

FURTHER INFORMATION
The hotel and restaurant guide available free from the local Tourist office lists a selection of local eateries and gives an indication as to how much you can expect to pay for a meal in the establishments listed.

Brussels

Eating cheaply in the centre of Brussels is far from easy. The only real concentration of reasonably priced eateries is around the Gare du Midi, where ethnic restaurants (Greek especially) abound, but this is a depressing district even in daytime, and can be quite intimidating at night. As a rule, restaurants on and just off the Grand'Place tend to be particularly pricey.

LOCAL SPECIALITIES

Poulet à la brabançonne	chicken with Belgian endives
lapin à la Gueuze	rabbit in a beer sauce
ballekens à la Marolienne	veal and pork meatballs with tomato sauce
kip-kap or *bloedpens*	a cold meat dish
stoemp et saucisses	mashed potatoes with vegetables and sausages

Sweet specialities include fruit or rice tarts, and *pain à la Grecque* and *speculoos*, which are delicious types of biscuit.

SPECIAL EVENTS AND FESTIVALS

Brussels holds several annual festivals where Belgian food is available. At the end of June is the 'Fête des Francs–Bourgeois', late September the 'Fêtes Bruegeliennes', and at the end of October there's a food fair, 'Salon de l'alimentation et des articles ménagers'. If you're there in the winter, you can also visit the traditional Christmas market, held on the second weekend of December.

CHEAP EATERIES

Two-course meals under 300F (£6; $9)

Le Maçon, rue Joseph Staellert 87 (tel. 343 8937). Open daily.

Paon Royal, rue du Vieux-Marché-aux-Grains 6 (tel. 513 0868). Open Tues.–Thurs. 8 a.m.–9 p.m., Fri.–Sat. 8 a.m.–11 p.m.

La Cuccagna, chaussée de Wavre 39 (tel. 513 3110). Open daily noon–2 a.m.

't Kelderke, Grand'Place 15 (tel. 513 7344). Open daily noon–2 a.m.

Buffet Primeur, rue du Marché-aux-Herbes 78–80 (tel. 511 5693). Open daily.

La Stella Fontainas, Marché au Charbon 91 (tel. 512 2952). Open Mon.–Sat. noon–2 p.m. and 7–11 p.m.

Two-course meals from 300–400F (£6–8; $9–12)

Le Savarin, rue des Bouchers 7 (tel. 511 7483). Open Mon.–Sat. noon–3 p.m. and 6–11.45 p.m.

Shanti, avenue Adolphe Buyl 68 (tel. 649 4096). Vegetarian restaurant. Open daily Sept.–July; Aug. open Tues.–Sat.

La Rose, rue du Marché-aux-Herbes 97 (tel. 512 5266). Closed Sun. evening and Mon., open all other days 11.30 a.m.–9.30 p.m.

El Yasmine, chaussée d'Ixelles 234 (tel. 647 5181). Moroccan and

Tunisian dishes. Open Mon.–Fri. noon–2.30 p.m. and 7–11 p.m.; Sat. 7–11 p.m.

L'Ecole Buissonière, rue de Traversière 13 (tel. 217 0165). Open Mon.–Fri. noon–2.30 p.m. and 6.30–10 p.m.

La Tsampa, rue de Livourne 109 (tel. 647 0367). Vegetarian restaurant. Open Mon.–Fri. noon–2 p.m. and 6.30–9.30 p.m.; Sat. noon–2 p.m. only.

Sin-Ya, rue au Beurre 40 (tel. 512 3331). Chinese restaurant. Open daily noon–3 p.m. and 6–11 p.m.

Two-course meals from 400–500F (£8–10; $12–15)

Leon de Bruxelles, blvd du Centenaire 20 (tel. 478 7267). Recommended dishes: *moules* (mussels) and *waterzooi* (chicken and vegetables stewed in a sauce). Open daily noon–midnight.

Le Grand Café, blvd Anspach 78. Open daily 7 a.m.–midnight (Fri.–Sat. until 1 a.m.).

Chez Leon, rue des Bouchers 18–20 (tel. 511 2508). Recommended dish: *moules* (mussels). Open daily noon–1 a.m.

Le Paradoxe, chaussée d'Ixelles 329 (tel. 649 8981). Vegetarian restaurant. Open Mon.–Sat. noon–2 p.m. and 7–10 p.m.

Shanghai, rue des Bouchers 25–27 (tel. 511 2508). Chinese restaurant. Open daily noon–3 p.m. and 6–11.45 p.m.

La Capannina, Petite rue au Beurre 12 (tel. 512 0545). Italian restaurant. Closed from mid-July–mid-Aug., otherwise open daily.

SHOPPING
● Markets
On place Ste Catherine (daily, 7 a.m.–5 p.m.); place Emile Bockstael (Sat. 7 a.m.–2 p.m.); place de la Chapelle (daily 7 a.m.–2 p.m.); and, beside the railway tracks, close to blvd du Midi, the Sunday Casbah sells a wide range of Middle-Eastern and North African foodstuffs (6 a.m.–1 p.m.)

● Supermarkets

GB, City 2 shopping complex on rue Neuve (daily, 10 a.m.–7 p.m., open Fri. until 8 p.m.). Also at rue de la Vierge Noire (daily 9 a.m.–7.50 p.m., Fri. until 8.50 p.m.).

FURTHER INFORMATION
Brochures on food can be found at Ondah, place de Louvain 4 (tel. 210 1711).

Ghent

LOCAL SPECIALITIES

Ghent specialities to look out for include *waterzooi* (chicken – or sometimes fish – and vegetables in sauce), rabbit with prunes, green eel, jugged hare, and mutton ragout. You can also try delicious almond bread or rye bread with currants, and a local gin, *Bruggeman*.

CHEAP EATERIES

Two-course meals under 200F (£4; $6)

Overpoort, Overpoortstraat (near the junction with Citadellaan). University mensa. Student ID sometimes requested. Open Mon.–Fri. 10.30 a.m.–2.30 p.m.

Two-course meals from 200–300F (£4–6; $6–9)

De Appeleir, Citadellaan 47 (tel. 221 6733). Good choice of vegetarian dishes available. Open Sun.–Fri. 11.30 a.m.–2 p.m. and 5.30–8 p.m.; Sat. 11.30 a.m.–2.30 p.m.
Capricorn, Vrijdagmarkt 3 (tel. 25 03 05). Open daily until midnight.
Erasmus, Mageleinstraat 4 (tel. 25 19 04). Open daily until midnight.
De Poelje Bistro, Botermarkt 7 (tel. 23 83 26). Closed for two weeks in Nov., otherwise open Thurs.–Tues. until 9 p.m.
De Blauwe Bloem, Hooiaard 5 (tel. 25 56 22). Vegetarian restaurant. Open Mon.–Fri. until 2 p.m.

Two-course meals from 300–400F (£6–8; $9–12)

Carlos Quinto, Kammerstraat 20 (tel. 25 59 29). Open daily.
Buddhasbelly, Hoogpoort 30 (tel. 25 17 32). Vegetarian restaurant. Open Mon.–Sat., closed on public holidays.
Maximiliaan, Mageleinstraat 43 (tel. 24 08 66). Open daily until 7 p.m.
Pistacchio, Brabantdam 134 (tel. 25 66 80). Open daily until 7 p.m.

Two-course meals from 400–500F (£8–10; $12–15)

Sol, Zwart Zustersstraat 16 (tel. 25 06 50). Closed for three weeks in Aug.; otherwise open Mon.–Fri.

De Gouden Pauw, Vrijdagmarkt 66–67 (tel. 25 56 47). Closed first three weeks in Aug.; otherwise open daily except Tues.

Pascalino, Botermarkt 11 (tel. 25 36 57). Closed mid-June–mid-July; otherwise open daily.

SHOPPING
● **Markets**

Groentenmarkt, open Mon.–Fri. 7 a.m.–1 p.m.; Sat. 7 a.m.–7 p.m.

Vrijdagmarkt, Fri. 7 a.m.–1 p.m.; Sat. 1–5 p.m.

● **Supermarkets**

Nopri, Hoogpoort 40–44 (tel. 25 05 92).

Unic, Sint-Jacobs Nieuwsstraat 119 (tel. 25 18 20); Poel 22 (tel. 24 34 00).

Ayuno, Baudelokaai 18 (tel. 33 32 61). Vegetarian groceries.

GB, by Gent-Dampoort train station.

FURTHER INFORMATION
The hotel and restaurant guide available free from the local Tourist Office lists a selection of local restaurants with details of opening hours and a guide to prices.

BULGARIA

There is a variety of affordable options for eating out in Bulgaria. *Mehanás* are basically places for drinking, but some do provide cheap, decent food – especially simple fare like salads and grilled meat dishes. Prices for meals in a *mehaná* tend to be £1.50–2.50 ($2.25–3.75), more expensive than those sold in the cheapest of the genuine eateries – the self-service *Autoservis* where two courses will typically cost about £0.80 ($1.20). The problem with eating in an *Autoservis* is that the quality of the food often leaves a lot to be desired. A more appealing option for really cheap eating is a vegetarian *restoránt*: most of the main towns have at least one of these, and you usually get an acceptable meal for just a fraction more than you would pay in an *Autoservis*. Meals in an ordinary Bulgarian *restoránt* are inexpensive – generally about £2–3 ($3.00–4.50) for two courses – and the step up in quality from the *Autoservis* is usually immense. However, you will invariably do even better in an old-style inn (*han* or *hanche*) where the food is usually excellent, and the range of options (including speciality dishes) much wider than in a *restoránt*. A typical two course meal in one of these eateries will cost about £4 ($6). A *han* or *hanche* is the best place to head for if you want to sample Bulgarian cuisine at its best (which can be very good indeed) as the pricier restaurants attached to the large hotels tend to offer international dishes rather than Bulgarian cooking.

The Bulgarians seldom use anything other than fresh ingredients in their cuisine – a cuisine which shows many similarities with that of neighbouring Turkey, with many shared dishes, common use of slow roasting and slow stewing as means of preparing meats; and the inclusion of yoghurt in many popular dishes.

Main meals usually start with soup (*súpa*). *Póstna súpa* (vegetable) and *súpa s meso* (consommé) figure prominently on menus, as does the Bulgarian speciality *tarator* (cold yoghurt and cucumber soup).

Salads (*saláti*) are served either as starters, or as accompaniments to a main course. Foremost amongst these is the *shopska saláti* (cucumber, onion, pepper, tomato and cheese) though you will also see the aubergine, pepper and tomato salad *kypolou* frequently.

Apart from the vegetarian restaurants mentioned above, vegetarians can get by rather well in ordinary restaurants as there is quite a good range of popular meat-free dishes, common amongst which are *gyuvech zarzabat* (vegetable stew); *parzheni yaitsá s pyure ot spanak* (fried eggs with spinach puree); *mish-mash* (scrambled

eggs with peppers and tomatoes); and *parzheni tikvichki* (fried courgettes) and *parzheni chúshki* (fried peppers). The real beauty of these
dishes (with the exception of *gyuvech zarzabat*) is that they can all
be prepared quickly, and so few chefs will object to making them
on request (nor the usual standby – an omelette).

Grilled meat dishes such as *kyufteta* (meatballs), *shishcheta* (pieces
of meat on a skewer) and *kebapcheta* (small sausages) are of obvious
Turkish origin, though here you will find them prepared with pork
as well as lamb. The same is true of the various kinds of *gyuvech*
(meat baked with vegetables – typically aubergine); *musaka* (a
baked dish of alternating layers of meat and vegetables); *kebap*
(braised and spiced meat); and of the *sarmi* (vegetables – most often
cabbage or vine leaves – filled with minced meat, vegetables and
herbs). With regard to stuffed vegetables, mention must be made of
Imam Bayaldu, a Bulgarian variation on the famous Turkish stuffed
aubergine dish. Offal such as kidney, liver and heart is popular,
especially in the Rhodope region on the Greek border, where offal
frequently appears in stews: this is highly uncommon in the
country as a whole, though there are offal-based specialities like
drob sarma (lamb's liver with eggs and rice).

Along the Black Sea coast you will find fish (*ríba*) such as *kalkan*
(turbot), *skumriya* (mackerel) and *kefal* (grey mullet) on restaurant
menus, whereas in the interior carp (*sharan*) or trout (*pastarva*) are
most common. Seafish and freshwater fish alike tend to be served
simply fried or grilled. Although fish dishes work out more expensive than meat dishes they are still very good value, unless you go
for really exotic fish like *chiga* (sterlet) or *esetra* (sturgeon).

Fresh fruit, rice pudding (*mlyako s orez*) and *krem-karamel* are
fairly standard offerings in the desserts section of restaurant menus,
to which might be added the likes of *baklava* or *revane* (two of the
most popular of a range of pastry-and-syrup concoctions).

If you want something sweet, however, you will invariably have
a much wider choice of pastries, cakes (*torta*) and *banitsa* (pancakes
– with savoury as well as sweet fillings) in a patisserie, where you
can also buy *lokum* (Turkish delight).

Patisseries also serve coffee (*kafé*) – usually Turkish-style (*tursko*)
with the remains of the ground coffee at the bottom of a small cup.
Request *kafé s mlyáko* if you want your coffee white, *shvárts* if you
would prefer it black. In contrast to coffee which is very popular,
tea is rarely drunk in Bulgaria.

The *kebapcheta*, *kebap* and *shishcheta* mentioned above are favourite street snacks as well as main courses. Rivalling these in popularity are *banitsa* – a pastry or pancake, usually filled with cheese,
but sometimes with meat or spinach. Another common street snack

is the celebrated Bulgarian yoghurt (*kisselo mlyáko*) which is sold by the glassful.

Shopping is relatively straightforward, with most main towns offering both a market (*hali*) and a conveniently located supermarket (*Gastronom* or *Magazin*). Supermarkets are sparsely stocked compared to those in Western Europe, but you should have no problem picking up basics such as milk, bread, cheese, yoghurt and cooked meat, though markets are your best bet for fresh fruit, vegetables and farm goods. Prices for foodstuffs produced in Bulgaria are cheap, though you can expect to pay dearly for anything imported from Western Europe.

The choice of beer (*bíra*) brewed in Bulgaria is relatively poor, but at least the home-produced beers are very cheap, so if you happen to like what is on offer you will do rather nicely. An alternative sometimes available is an imported beer (typically Austrian or German), but you can expect to pay around £1.50 ($2.25) for a half-litre bottle of one of these.

In stark contrast to beer drinkers, wine drinkers are very well catered for, with Bulgarian wines enjoying an excellent reputation internationally. *Cabarnet*, *Melnik*, and *Gamza* are but three of the fine reds; *Tamyanka*, *Misket* and *Chardonnay* a few examples of the equally palatable whites. A bottle of wine to accompany a restaurant meal costs around £2.50–3.00 ($3.75–4.50), though you can usually buy the same wine for about half that price in a local store.

Bulgarian spirits are sold very cheaply, though again you can expect to pay dearly for anything imported from Western Europe. Home produced favourites include the aniseed-flavoured *mastika* and *raki*, and a range of fruit-based brandies, most common of which is *slivova* (distilled from plums). As an alternative to paying over the odds for a Western brand, vodka drinkers can opt for Russian (*Ruska*) vodka which is relatively widespread and inexpensive.

Sofia

CHEAP EATERIES
Two-course meals for under £1 ($1.50).

Autoservis, blvd Vitosha 5/7.
Autoservis, Graf Ignatiev 32/34.

Two-course meals from £2.00–2.50 ($3.00–3.75)

Bulgarska Gozba, blvd Vitosha 34. Good choice of Bulgarian dishes.

Rozhen, blvd Vitosha 74. Also offers a good selection from Bulgaria's cuisine.

King, Denkoglu 38 (tel. 81 39 69). English spoken. Recommended dish: *falafel* (one of several dishes suitable for vegetarians). Open daily 9 a.m.–2 a.m.

Pizzeria Venezia, Benkovski 12 (tel. 87 63 64). Pizza and other Italian dishes. Inexpensive Czech beer. Open daily, noon–1 a.m.

Rubin, pl. Sveta Nedelya. Grilled meat dishes predominate.

Koprivshtitsa, blvd Vitosha 1/3 (beneath the arcade). Good choice of Bulgarian dishes.

Kitai, Shipla 6 (tel. 46 51 29). Chinese dishes. Open daily noon–2.30 p.m. and 6–10.30 p.m.

Two-course meals from £3.00–3.50 ($4.50–5.25).

Budapest, Rakovski 145 (tel. 87 27 50). Hungarian dishes. Recommended dish: *goulash*. Open daily noon–11 p.m.

Two-course meals from £4.50–6.50 ($6.75–9.75)

Vietnam, blvd G. Kirkov 1. Mainly Vietnamese cuisine, but with other East Asian dishes.

Krim, Dobrudja 2 (tel. 87 01 31). Russian restaurant.

SHOPPING
There are markets on ul Georgi Kirkov and ul Hristo Smirnenski, and the ZUM department store on Largo has a supermarket in the basement.

CROATIA AND SLOVENIA

Eating out in Croatian or Slovenian restaurants (*restoran* or *restavracija*) is relatively inexpensive. Along the Adriatic Coast or around Lake Bled a two-course meal with wine or a beer typically costs about £3.50–5.00 ($5.25–7.50); anywhere else, including the two capitals, £2.50–4.00 ($3.75–6.00) the norm. It is possible to cut costs slightly by eating in a *krčma* (old-style inn), though these are not particularly common. A more likely option is a self-service *Expres Restoran* as these are widespread in both countries. The food in these can be surprisingly good, and comes very cheaply: two courses will usually cost around £1 ($1.50).

The cuisines of Croatia and Slovenia have been subjected to a diverse range of influences over the centuries. Germanic input is readily apparent (especially in the case of Slovenia), though in the parts of these countries closest to Hungary you can also find dishes of obvious Hungarian origin. Furthermore the existence of the likes of pizza and pasta dishes along the coastal strip of both countries is a legacy of the large communities of ethnic Italians who once lived in these parts. More recently Serbian dishes such as *pljeskavica*, *čevapčiči* and *ražnjici* (see below) have all become firm favourites in Croatia and Slovenia (see the introduction to the chapter on Serbia for further information on Serbian dishes).

Soups (*supa* or *juha*) such as *juha od povrča* (vegetable), *pileča juha* (chicken), *pasulj* (thick bean soup with bits of bacon and sausage) and *govedja juha* (beef soup) are common throughout both countries; in addition, there are various kinds of fish soup (*riblja corba*) prepared along the coast. A speciality of inland Croatia is the thick *manistra od bobiča* made from beans and maize.

By far the most famous starter (*predjela*) is *pršut* (Dalmatian smoked ham), though this is pricey in comparison to more humble offerings like *kajgana* (scrambled eggs) or *pašteta* (paté).

Not surprisingly, fish (*riba*) and shellfish dishes are much favoured along the coast. Red mullet (*barbun*), bream (*zubatac*), sardines (*sardele*) and squid (*lignji*) are all common, and usually prepared simply by grilling, though the Dalmatian speciality *brodet* is a stew of mixed fish with rice. The most popular freshwater fish found in the interior is trout (*pastrmka*), again most often served grilled. It should be noted that seafood dishes are usually sold by weight (the variations this can cause from prices stated on menus is a common source of misunderstanding when it comes to settling up). On the whole, seafood dishes work out more expensive than meat ones, but tend nevertheless to be good value for what you get.

The diverse influences which have helped shape the Croatian and Slovenian cuisines are most obvious in the realm of meat (*meso*) and poultry dishes. Beef (*govedjina*), veal (*teletina*), pork (*svinjetina*), lamb (*jagnjetina*) and chicken (*piletina*) are popular in both countries, especially pork and veal which appear as all kinds of different *odrezak* (chops and cutlets), including *snicla* (breaded cutlets – in effect a Wiener Schnitzel). The Slovenes are especially fond of sausages (*klobase*), which, like many other dishes in Slovenia, are often served with that most Germanic of accompaniments, *sauerkraut* (pickled cabbage – known here as *kiseli kupus*); in Croatia, chips (*pomfrit*) are much more common. *Pohovano pile* (chicken fried in breadcrumbs) and *gulas* (goulash – usually very good) are of clear Hungarian origin. You can almost guarantee finding at least one of the three Serbian grilled meat dishes mentioned above (*pljeskavica*, *ražnjici* and *čevapčiči*) on any restaurant menu. *Pljeskavica* are best described as beefburgers, though for taste and quality they usually compare very favourably with the British product. *Ražnjici* are small pieces of meat grilled on a skewer; *čevapčiči* small spicy sausages or meatballs cooked in the same manner. A *mešano meso* (mixed grill) often combines all three, together with a pork cutlet, liver and onions.

Vegetarians fare better along the coast, where there is always a good choice of suitable pasta dishes and pizzas, than in the interior where (with the exception of the two capitals) veggie dishes are more difficult to find. Here, unless the menu includes traditional meat-free dishes like *gibanica* (cheese pie) or *gljive na žaru* (grilled mushrooms) you may have to try requesting scrambled eggs (*kajgana*), a large portion of salad (*salata*), or an omelette made with cheese (*sir*), mushrooms (*gljive*, or *pecurke* or *šampinjons*) or assorted vegetables (*povrče*).

Fresh fruits (*voče*), stewed fruits (*kompot*) and ice cream (*sladoled*) are fairly standard on most restaurant menus. In Slovenia and certain parts of Croatia you can find the flaky, fruit-filled pastry *strudla* (very similar to Austrian *strudel*, and just as good, but much cheaper) typically filled with either apples (*sa jabukama*) or cherries (*sa tresnjama*). Slovenia offers its own speciality: *struklji* (a cheese-filled pastry). Fruit-filled pancakes known as *palačinke* are also reasonably common in both countries.

The most popular of takeaway snacks is the flaky pastry *burek*, which comes filled with cheese, meat, potato or spinach. Sausages are commonly sold as street snacks, as are the *pljeskavica*, *ražnjica* and *čevapčiči* described above. One snack likely to be of particular interest to vegetarians is *kukuruz* (grilled corn on the cob).

Cakes and ice cream, both of which the Slovenes and Croats devour avidly, may be purchased from the *slastičarnice* which are dotted all over town centres.

Shopping is straightforward in both countries. There are regular markets and centrally located supermarkets (sometimes attached to department stores) in all the main towns. Most likely you will stumble across these as you wander around, but the local Tourist Office will point you in the right direction if you want to find either quickly. In any case, provided you remember that shopping hours are normally Mon.–Fri. 8 a.m.–7 p.m.; Sat. 8 a.m.–5 p.m. (smaller shops may close from noon–3 p.m.) you will never be short of food, as even in small towns there are always plenty of food shops. Prices for foodstuffs produced in Slovenia or Croatia are very cheap, though you can expect to pay dearly for anything imported from Germany, Austria or Italy.

The same is true of beer (*pivo*), with locally produced beers (*domače pivo*) being much cheaper than imported brands. Depending on where you happen to be drinking, a Slovene or Croat beer will cost something in the region of £0.40–1.00 ($0.60–1.50); in the same establishment imported beers will probably cost £1.50–2.30 ($2.25–3.50). Slovene and Croat beers are very good in any case; a bonus being that few breweries adulterate their product with chemicals. Most are light, Pilsner-type beers but it is possible to find the occasional dark *crno pivo*. The best known beers are Slovenia's Union and Zlatorog and Croatia's Karlovacko, but there is no shortage of fine local beers to try as you travel around.

Croatian and (especially) Slovene wines (*vino*) are much better known abroad than their beers. Slovenia's main claim to fame is its *rizlings* – *Renski* and *Laski* in particular. Croatian production includes fine whites (*bijelo vino*) like Kaštelet and Grk and equally drinkable reds (*crno vino*) such as Dingač and Babič. The overall quality is very good indeed, and a bottle (*flaša*) of local wine (*domače vino*) costs very little to buy even in restaurants where you can expect to pay £1.00–2.50 ($1.50–3.75) per bottle.

The most popular spirits are *šljivovica* (plum brandy) and *vinjak* (brandy), though the very strong *lozovača* brandy enjoys great popularity along the coastal strip between Split and Dubrovnik. The same area also produces *maraskino* (from Zadar) which, in contrast to the sharp, bitter-tasting spirits mentioned above, is a sweet, smooth cherry-based liqueur (Zadar also produces a similar drink based on apricots). Spirits are cheap to buy at about £0.35 ($0.50) for a decent measure in a bar, £1.50–2.20 ($2.25–3.25) per bottle in a local store.

Coffee (*kafa*) is normally served espresso (black), but sometimes cappuccino. If you want it with milk request your coffee *sa mlekom*: the same goes for tea (*čaj*) which again is usually served without milk.

Dubrovnik

Prior to the outbreak of war the Croatian city of Dubrovnik was Yugoslavia's prime tourist destination and local restaurant prices were much higher on average than elsewhere in the country. Drinks also tended to be pricey, and it could be an expensive mistake to order where prices were not listed on the menu, or without checking prices first. At the time of writing, Dubrovnik was still in the war zone, so the following suggestions are old favourites, and the prices are those charged in the summer of 1991. Even assuming that tourists do head back to Dubrovnik in 1995 there is no guarantee that these establishments will be in operation, far less what prices they will be charging.

In 1991 the seafood restaurants along ulica Prijeko were expensive by local standards – typically about £4–5 ($6.00–7.50) per head for a couple of courses. The Konoba Moby Dick offered more for your money than most, but as a general rule restaurants at the western end of the street offered better value than the others. For about £3–4 ($4.50–6.00) you could have a two-course meal in the Konoba Cavtat on Od Puča, the Višnjica on Miha Pracata, or the Konoba Primorka at Nikole Tesle 8 – all offering seafood and Croatian specialities. Slightly cheaper meals were available in the Café-Restaurant Gruž on Gruška Obala, the Jug at Izmedju Polača 6, and the Spaghetti Club on Gundulićeva Poljana (the latter offered a very good range of pizzas). The cheapest option of all was the Expres Restorant at Lucarica 2 where a two-course meal cost about £2.20 ($3.30), but the rather poor quality of the food meant eating there was a bit of a false economy.

To put together a picnic there was a choice of shopping at the markets on Gundulićeva Poljana or by the shore in Gruz (both operated Mon.–Sat.); in one of the supermarkets along Od Puča; the mini-market by the city's west gate; or the supermarket attached to the department store in Gruž.

Split

CHEAP EATERIES
Two-course meals under £1 ($1.50)

Index, Ujevičeva 8. Student canteen.
Burek, Ilegalaca 13. Open daily 7 a.m.–10 p.m.

Two-course meals around £1.20–1.50 ($1.80–2.25)

Bastion, Marmontova 10. Open daily 7 a.m.–9 p.m.
Pivnica Pizzeria, Veselina Masleše (upstairs in the Koteks shopping mall). Pizza, pasta and Croatian meat dishes.

Two-course meals around £2.50 ($3.75)

Ero Restaurant, Marmontova 3.
Prenočište Srebena Vrata. Inside the palace's east gate.

SHOPPING
There is a market on Hrvojeva, and a supermarket in the Koteks shopping centre on Veselina Masleše.

Zagreb

Eating cheaply is no problem in Zagreb as there are a number of centrally located self-service eateries and restaurants. For a particularly good choice of Croatian specialities try the restaurants along ulica Tkalčičeva – expect to pay about £4 ($6) for two courses.

CHEAP EATERIES
Three-course meals around £0.60 ($0.90)

Studentski Centar, Savska cesta 25. Student ID required.

Two-course meals under £1 ($1.50)

Splendid Expres, Trg Zrinjskoga 15. Open daily 6 a.m.–10 p.m.
Mosor, Jurišičeva 2.
Astoria, Draškovičeva 15.

Two-course meals from £1.00–1.50 ($1.50–2.25)

Medulic, Meduličeva 2. Good range of vegetarian options, including pizzas.
Kamenita Vrata, Kamenita 2a. Pizzeria. Open until 1 a.m.

Two-course meals from £1.50–2.50 ($2.25–3.75)

Hotel Central. Opposite the train station.
Stari Fijaker, Mesnička 6.

SHOPPING
The Dolac market is just off Trg Republike, and there is a super-market, Nama, in the department store on Trg Republike.

THE CZECH LANDS & SLOVAKIA

For centuries the cuisines of these two countries were subjected to two vastly different influences. Whereas Slovak cuisine was influenced by that of the Hungarians who ruled over the country the greatest input into Czech cuisine came from the ethnic Germans who, until relatively recently, lived in great numbers in the Czech Lands. Consequently it is only to be expected that the two styles of cooking should be quite distinct, and the differences are readily apparent: even where two dishes appear superficially the same, the different techniques used in preparation often betray the cook's Czech or Slovak origins to anyone familiar with both cuisines (Slovaks, for example, employ more spices in their cooking). However, for reasons which are too complex and politically contentious to go into here, the food on offer in eateries across the two countries might lead visitors to believe that the Czechs and Slovaks possessed a unified cuisine, as wherever you go you can expect to find the Germanic-influenced Czech cooking dominating menus. Hopefully this situation will change in the near future so that visitors will have ample opportunity to sample traditional Slovak cooking in the country's eateries.

The cheapest cooked meals can be bought in a *bufet*, most of which are self-service (*samoobsluha*) establishments in which food is consumed standing at high tables. *Bufets* are intended to provide quick meals and snacks for local workers, and so are easy to find in any town centre. It would be difficult to recommend eating in *bufets* other than for very quick meals and snacks as the limited choice of food rarely reaches the quality of even the most basic restaurants; the surroundings are often very drab; and, outside of Prague, they are not that much cheaper than restaurants. Meat dishes, such as the very popular *guláš* (nothing like the original Hungarian dish) can be particularly bad value in a *bufet*, with small servings of typically poor quality meat and very basic accompaniments costing £0.35–0.50 ($0.50–0.75). If you are looking for a quick meal it makes more sense to order soup (*polievka*) (which is usually quite palatable) followed by some combination of the different salads (*salat*) and small open sandwiches (*chlebíčky*) displayed. The composition of the various *chlebíčky* will be obvious (normally ham or salami, mayonnaise, and a few salad vegetables), but the same cannot be said of the salads. Most contain small flecks of meat so that options for vegetarians are limited to pea and pepper (*feferonkový*) and egg and mayonnaise (*vajíckový*) salads. As it is unusual for salad displays to be labelled, vegetarians will have to ask if these are available.

Restaurants (*restaurace* or *reštaurácia*) offer higher quality food and a wider choice than *bufets*. Czech and Slovak restaurants exist either as establishments in their own right, or attached to hotels, pubs (*pivnice*) or wine cellars (*vinárna* or *vináreň*). How much you are likely to pay depends on where you happen to be. In Prague a meal of soup, a main course and a beer will cost about £2.50—4.00 ($3.75—6.00) in one of the cheaper local restaurants, but in smaller cities such as Pilsen, České Budějovice, Brno, Olomouc, Košice and even Bratislava £1.50—3.00 ($2.25—4.50) is the norm. The best deals, however, are to be had in small towns on the tourist trail, where the same meal will generally cost only £1—2 ($1.50—3.00). It is normal practice to have the day's menu (*jidelní lístek* or *jedálny lístok*) displayed outside, so you can get a fair idea of what you are likely to pay before you set foot inside the door. This is important in Prague, where a minority of restaurants (unfortunately quite a sizeable minority) will try to cheat you out of (relatively) large sums of money. This issue is dealt with in the Prague section because it is a problem peculiar to the Czech capital, and not something that is widely practised throughout the Czech Lands and Slovakia.

Few nationalities display the same fondness for soup (*polievka* or *polévky*) as the Czechs and Slovaks. Most common are potato (*bramborová* or *zemiaková*) and vegetable (*zelininová*), but beef (*hovězí* or *hovädzia*), chicken (*kuře* or *kurča*), pea (*hrachová*) and lentil (*čočková* or *šošovicová*) all feature regularly on menus.

Most restaurants will offer a basic choice of hors d'oeuvres such as cold meats or salami (*salám* or *saláma*) and a variety of salads, the most common of which are those based on cucumber (*okurka* or *uhorka*) and tomato (*rajče* or *rajčina*). One very palatable starter which is quite widely available is the famous Prague ham (*Pražská šunka*), often served with pickled gherkins (*kyselá okurka*).

Meat (*maso* or *mäso*) consumption in both countries is relatively high by European standards, with pork (*vepřové* or *bravčové*) and beef (*hovĕčí* or *hovädzie*) being the two favourites. The preparation of meat dishes is one of the highpoints of both cuisines since both nationalities have accumulated a vast number of different cooking techniques and accompaniments over the years. Nevertheless, some of the most popular dishes are very simple affairs, and this is certainly the case with pork cutlets fried in breadcrumbs (*vepřové řízek* or *bravčový rezeň*) and beef or pork served with gravy, potatoes and small dumplings (*knedliky* or *knedle*) – dishes which are almost guaranteed to feature on restaurant menus (albeit with the possible substitution of the flour and potato croquettes known as *halusky* for dumplings in Slovakia). Some guidebooks would have you believe there is little more to offer by way of meat dishes in these countries – which is utter nonsense, as a glance at the meat section of even a very basic menu will show. Even if you are not sure exactly what you are getting, at least you can always avoid the dishes mentioned above should you so wish.

Poultry and fowl have their own section on menus. The most common dishes are those prepared from chicken (*kuře* or *kurča*), but for a speciality dish in this field watch out for roast duck (*kachna* or *kačica*).

Fish (*ryby*) dishes are also confined to a separate section on restaurant menus. If you were only going to be in the Czech Lands or Slovakia for a few days it would be easy to recommend eating nothing but fish for the duration of your stay. This might seem contradictory in view of my praise for meat dishes, but fish dishes which would cost a lot of money at home can be sampled here at unbelievably low prices. Trout (*pstruh*) is quite common in both countries, most often served simply fried or cooked in butter. Similar in price to trout, carp (*kapr* or *kapor*) is even better value considering what you pay for it outside the Czech Lands and Slovakia. Like meat, carp is prepared in many different ways and served with a variety of accompaniments. Much of the two countries' supplies come from the carp ponds of South Bohemia, and in this region carp is very cheap: a decent portion with accompaniments will cost about £0.80–1.20 ($1.20–1.80) in an average hotel restaurant. Outside of South Bohemia you can usually count on finding carp on at least one restaurant menu (typically a hotel restaurant) even in small Czech towns, but as stocks often run out you may be disappointed if you want carp in the evening or on Sundays. In Slovakia carp is rarely found outside of hotel restaurants in the more popular tourist areas, apart from a few speciality fish restaurants in Bratislava. With the exception of Prague eateries and speciality fish restaurants, a typical carp dish bought anywhere outside South Bohemia will cost in the region of £1.50–3.00 ($2.25–4.50).

With the emphasis so heavily on meat and fish, vegetarians will struggle to find suitable restaurant meals. Do not be taken in by the *bezmasa* (literally 'without meat') section which is a feature of most menus; on the whole this will include dishes where meat is only a minor ingredient. Indeed, outside of Prague (where some restaurants offer a small selection of vegetarian dishes), and the larger towns where you may have a choice of pizzas, you will usually have to content yourself with salads, dumplings and egg (*knedliky s vejce*) or omelettes (*omeleta*) made with peas (*hrášky*), tomatoes (*rajče* or *rajčina*) or cheese (*syr*), all of which, even if they are not on the menu, will invariably be prepared on request.

The choice of desserts on restaurant menus is normally slim, but there are always a few decent options for rounding off a meal. Worth looking out for are *palačinky* (pancakes filled with chocolate) and fruit dumplings (*ovocné knedliky* or *ovocnie knedle*) which are made with a variety of fruits. Fresh fruit and cream combinations are usually of a high standard, and you can more or less count on finding at least one on any menu. Ice cream (*zmrzlina*) is almost certain to appear as well, but this is a more dicey proposition as the quality varies widely.

Street snacks are popular in both countries, especially *párek* or *párok* (thin sausages) and *smažený syr* or *vyprážený syr* (cheese fried in breadcrumbs). Sometimes a slice of ham is cooked with the cheese in which case the suffix *se šunkou* will be added. *Bramborák* (fried potato pancakes with small bits of bacon or salami) are a Czech favourite, whilst the Slovaks are very fond of *langoše* (basically a piece of fried dough smothered in garlic). Vegetarians should note that snacks such as fried cheese and *langoše* are almost always fried in animal fat.

Fortunately for vegetarians there is a fairly good choice of food available from local shops, and from the markets that are a common feature of many town centres. Even in small towns there are supermarkets, though these may be located on the fringe of the historic centre rather than inside it (bear in mind that many of the old towns are very small indeed – you will rarely be more than a ten-minute walk from one of the local supermarkets). In medium-sized towns such as České Budějovice, Hrádec Kralové and Olomouc, as well as in the larger cities, you will invariably find a supermarket attached to the PRIOR department stores, most of which are conveniently and centrally located in the main shopping areas. *Potraviny* is an all embracing term which covers shops selling a range of foodstuffs all the way up from a small general store to a supermarket, which can make it difficult when it is the latter you are looking for. Normal shopping hours are Mon.–Fri. 9 a.m.– 6 p.m.; Sat. 9 a.m.–noon. Visitors will find food prices very low: 500g of bread (*chléb*) costs about £0.15 ($0.22); a half-litre of milk (*mléko* or *mlieko*) about £0.12 ($0.18); a 250g pot of Czech or Slovak yoghurt (*jogurt*) £0.09–0.15 ($0.13–0.22) (imported brands are much dearer); whilst even imported fruits such as bananas (*banán*) are cheaper than at home.

Czech and Slovak bread is particularly good, and available either from supermarkets and general stores or from a bakery (*pečivo*). Especially worth trying is *kmínový chléb* (bread with caraway seeds).

Both nationalities are very fond of cakes and pastries, with the result that a cake shop (*cukrárna* or *cukráreň*) is never difficult to find in any town centre. Overall standards are high but several places are especially worthy of mention: Bratislava, South Moravia and South Bohemia. Cakes are inexpensive everywhere, with a large cake (or slice of cake) seldom costing more than £0.20 ($0.30), even in Prague.

Ice cream (*zmrzlina*) is extremely popular in both countries – even in winter. A cornet with one small scoop typically costs £0.05–0.10 ($0.07–0.15). Although the quality of the product can vary greatly, it is fair to say you will get more good than bad. Ice cream is sold in outlets as diverse as souvenir shops and cake shops, but one of the characteristic features of Czech and Slovak town centres is that of cornets being dispensed out of windows by someone sitting in a tiny space with only the ice cream machine for company.

Average levels of alcohol consumption in both the Czech Lands and Slovakia are amongst the highest in the world. Beer (*pivo*) is by far the most popular drink in the Czech Lands, with wine (*vino*) and spirits (*destiláty*) consumption relatively low. In contrast, although beer consumption in Slovakia is at a respectable level, wine and, especially, spirits are more popular.

Czech beers are considered to be amongst the finest to be found anywhere. All but a handful of beers – be they light-coloured or the less common dark beers – are brewed using the process of top fermentation developed in the city of Pilsen in 1842. One of the great beauties of Czech beers (and indeed of Slovak beers) is that they are brewed using only natural products, and so are totally free of the chemical additives found in many beers. The most famous Czech brands are *Plzeňský Prazdroj* and *Budvar*, brewed in the cities of Pilsen and České Budějovice respectively. Do not despair if you try these first and find you like neither of them; somewhat strangely both are lighter than the majority of Czech beers, and there are plenty of those to sample as you make your way around the country. Beer is very cheap. A half-litre of draught beer will cost about £0.40–0.50 ($0.60–0.75) in a Prague restaurant, and about £0.25 ($0.37) in a restaurant elsewhere. Buying a similar measure in a pub anywhere will cost £0.15–0.20 ($0.22–0.30), about the same as you will pay for a half-litre bottle in a local store.

One of the most pleasant aspects of wine drinking in these countries is that even highly regarded local wines can be bought for as little as £2.00–3.50 ($3.00–5.25) in a restaurant, £1–2 ($1.50–3.00) in a shop. The most important vineyards are in Southern Slovakia, followed by those of Southern Moravia near the Austrian border. Whereas these two areas are known for their whites the very small area of Bohemian wine production around Melnik is best known for the red *Ludmila*.

Vodka and rum are the best-selling spirits in both countries, followed by the plum brandy known as *slivovice*. More unusual spirits are the Slovak *borovička* (distilled from pine trees) and the Czech *Becherovka* (a combination of many different herbs). Prices are very low: a 70cl bottle of *Becherovka* costs about £2.30 ($3.50), slightly more than for a bottle of Czech or Slovak produced vodka, rum or *slivovice*.

Coffee (*káva*) is typically served Turkish-style (*turecká*): a small cup of strong black coffee with the remains of the ground coffee in the bottom of the cup. *Viděnská Káva* (Vienna coffee) is served with whipped cream – admittedly it is not quite as good as you will find in Austria, but then it is nowhere near the price you will be asked to pay there so it's well worth trying once. If you request tea (*čaj*) you will normally be given a cup, a teabag and a pot of boiling water so you can make it as strong or as weak as you like. If you want milk (*mléko* or *mlieko*) you will probably have to ask for it as neither the Czechs nor the Slovaks are in the habit of adding milk to their tea.

Bratislava

LOCAL SPECIALITIES
Cakes and pastries are particularly good in the Slovak capital.

CHEAP EATERIES
Two-course meals from £1.00–1.75 ($1.50–2.60)

Perugia Reštaurácia, Ventúrska. Mainly Italian-style dishes. Open Mon.–Sat. 11 a.m.–10 p.m.
Vegetariánska Jedáleň, Laurinská 6. Vegetarian cafeteria. Open daily 11 a.m.–8 p.m. (Fri. and Sat. until 9 p.m.)
Pizzeria, Spitálska 31 (tel. 57353). Open Mon.–Sat. 10 a.m.–10.30 p.m., Sun. 3–10 p.m.
Diétna Reštaurácia, Laurinská 8 (down the alley) (tel. 33 36 58). Self-service. Recommended dishes: *Pečené kurča s ryžou* (roast chicken with rice) and *ryžový nákyp* (rice pudding). Open lunchtimes Mon.–Fri. only.

Two-course meals from £1.50–3.00 ($2.25–4.50)

Slovenská Reštaurácia, Štúrova 3 (over the Luxor cafeteria).
English menu available. Open Mon.–Fri. 11 a.m.–3 p.m. and
5.30–10 p.m.; Sat. 11 a.m.–4 p.m.
Kavarieň Amadeus, Obchodná 68. Open daily 10 a.m.–11 p.m.
Reštaurácia Pod Baštou, Baštou Băstova ul. 3 (tel. 33 17 65). Open
daily 11 a.m.–midnight.
Terno, Dom Odievania (4th floor), Námestie SNP 29 (tel. 33 47
92). Open Mon. 10 a.m.–7 p.m., Tues.–Fri. 8 a.m.–7 p.m., Sat.
8 a.m.–1 p.m.

Two-course meals from £3–5 ($4.50–7.50)

U zlatého kapra, Prepoštská. Speciality fish restaurant.
Astor Reštaurácia, Žilinská (junction with Šankova) (tel. 21 43 12).
Open Mon.–Fri. 11 a.m.–11 p.m., weekends noon–11 p.m.

Two-course meals from £6–10 ($9–15)

Arkadia, Beblavé 3 (tel. 33 56 50). Open daily noon–11 p.m.

SHOPPING
● **Supermarket**
The PRIOR supermarket is just off Kyjevské námestie.

● **Market**
The covered market (*tržnica*) lies across the street from the Dom
Odborov.

Pilsen

LOCAL SPECIALITIES
Plzeňský Prazdroj (Pilsener Urquell) and Gambrinus beers.

CHEAP EATERIES
Two-course meals from £2–3 ($3.00–4.50)

Restaurace Prazdroj, U Prazdroje. Brewery-owned beer hall, right
by the brewery.
U Senku, Riegrova (junction with Sedláčkova). Open Mon.–Fri.
10 a.m.–10.30 p.m.; Sat. 10 a.m.–9 p.m.; Sun. 11 a.m.–6 p.m.

Two-course meals from £2.50–4.00 ($3.75–6.00)

Hotel Central, náměsti Republiky. Restaurant open daily 6.30 a.m.–
10 p.m.

SHOPPING
● **Supermarkets**

PRIOR: set back off Americká třída near the main train station.
Vamil: on the opposite side of Americká třída, a short distance away
from PRIOR.

Prague

Despite claims to the contrary, it is still possible to eat out very
cheaply in the Czech capital as there is no shortage of restaurants
where you can get a two-course meal for £2.50–3.50 ($3.75–5.25).
However, the relatively widespread practice in all categories of restaurants of cheating foreign customers can give the impression that
dining out is much more expensive than it actually should be. At
its crudest, customers are defrauded simply by overcharging for the
dishes ordered, or by adding a few extra items to the bill (an old
favourite in quite a few European countries). More common, however, despite the fact that almost all restaurants display a menu
outside, is the practice of not showing you a menu once you are
inside but instead offering you a number of options verbally once
the staff have established which language you speak. In some cases
this is a genuine attempt to save you struggling with the menu,
but where the aim is to cheat you it is not unusual to be paying
four or five times the price of very similar (or even identical) dishes
on the menu. Should you persist in asking to see the menu, another
trick is to present you with a specially prepared menu on which
basic dishes are charged at extortionate prices. Once you have
accepted a verbal offer or ordered from the specially prepared menu
you have no comeback, so always look for a menu posted outside
so that you can get some rough idea of what the cost of a main
course is likely to be. If you suspect that staff are trying to cheat
you, simply leave and take your custom elsewhere: it is worth
remembering that the number of restaurants which will try to trick
you is small in comparison to those which will not.

LOCAL SPECIALITIES
Pražská šunka (Prague ham) and beers brewed by the *Smichovské*
(*Staropramen 12°* amongst others) and *Braník* breweries. *Flek 13°* is
a strong, dark beer sold only in U Fleků on Kremencova.

CHEAP EATERIES
Two-course meals from £2.50–3.00 ($3.75–4.50)

U Zlatých Andělů, Celetná 31. English menu available with some
vegetarian options. Open daily 11 a.m.–11 p.m.
Cafe FX, Břlehradská 120. Vegetarian café. Open daily 11 a.m.–
5 a.m.
Slovanska Hospada, Na Přikope 22 (tel. 25 12 10). Open Mon.–Sat.
11 a.m.–10 p.m.
V Soudim dvoře, Karmelitská 19. Open daily 10 a.m.–11 p.m.

Two-course meals from £2.50–4.00 ($3.75–6.00)

U Čerta, Nerudova 6. English menu available. Open daily 11 a.m.–
11 p.m.
U Purkmistra, Vodickova 26 (tel. 26 00 05). Open daily 11 a.m.–
11 p.m.
U svatého Tomáše, Letenská 12. *Branik 12°* on tap. Restaurant open
11 a.m.–4 p.m. and 6–10.30 p.m. daily.
U Supá, Celetná 22. *Branik 14°* on tap. Open Mon.–Sat. 11 a.m.–
11 p.m.; Sun. 11 a.m.–10 p.m.
Regent, Karmelitská 20. German menu available. Small choice of
vegetarian dishes. Serves *Staropramen 12°*. Open daily 10 a.m.–
1 p.m.
Krušovická pivnice, Široká 20. Open daily 11 a.m.–11 p.m.
Černý Kůň, Vodicková 36 (tel. 22 41 53). Open daily 11 a.m.–
11 p.m.
U Palečka, Nitranská 22 (tel. 25 13 00). Open daily 11 a.m.–
midnight.

Two-course meals from £3.50–5.00 ($5.25–7.50)

U cerveneho raka, Karlova 20. Fine range of fish specialities. Open
daily noon–11 p.m.
ve Stare Radnice, Loretánská 1. English menu available. Open daily
10 a.m.–10 p.m.

Two-course meals from £6–8 ($9–12)

U prince, Staroměstské náměstí 29. Menu in several languages just inside the door. Best reserved ahead for lunchtime and evening meals. Open daily 10 a.m.–midnight.

SHOPPING
● **Supermarkets**

Pomona, Václavské náměstí 52. Open Mon.–Fri. 7 a.m.–9 p.m.; Sat. 9 a.m.–2 p.m.; Sun. noon–9 p.m.

Casa Pascual, Narodni třída 27. Open Mon.–Fri. 8 a.m.–7 p.m.; Sat. 8 a.m.–1 p.m.

MAZ/PRIOR supermarket in basement of the department store on Národni třída.

DENMARK

The brochure produced by the Danish Tourist Board states that 'For a Dane eating is living'. That may not be quite the case, but there is certainly an enormous variety of restaurants and eateries available. It's also the only Scandinavian country where it is easy to get a drink and there are a great many bars, cafés and inns.

However, eating out can be an expensive business and traditional Danish restaurants in particular are not only rather thin on the ground but many are likely to be out of the budget traveller's price range. A two-course evening meal could easily cost 200DKr (£20; $30), although if you stick to the lunchtime *Dagens Ret* (dish of the day) the price can drop to 60−80DKr (£6−8; $9−12). A service charge of 15% is nearly always included. A glass of beer or wine will cost a minimum of 20DKr (£2; $3), a cup of coffee in a café is 14DKr (£1.40; $2.10), and a loaf of bread costs around 12DKr (£1.20; $1.80).

Don't worry though, this doesn't mean that you won't be able to sample the national cuisine, you just need to know where to look. There are certainly quite a number of speciality dishes to try. The most famous of these is *smørrebrød*, which are lavish open sandwiches and can be found in restaurant buffets, cafés and take-away shops. The Danes eat them as snacks and for lunch, and they consist of a slice of brown bread covered with fish, meat or cheese and garnished with a variety of pickles and salads. The price varies enormously depending on the topping; in takeaway shops you can pay from 10−40DKr (£1−4; $1.50−6.00). Buy your *smørrebrød* early in the day, as most shops selling it close by about 2 p.m.

Another Danish lunchtime favourite are sausages (*pølser*). You'll find a huge variety of these available on hot-dog stands, at very reasonable prices. The Danes love fast food, so you'll find stands like this everywhere. By the way, lunch generally starts at about noon in Denmark and lasts until 2 p.m.

A boon for the hungry budget traveller is the Danish tradition of fixed-price, all-you-can-eat buffets, where you can sample a large variety of hot and cold fish and meat dishes, as well as various salads. Although these are really only a viable option for lunch (*frokost*), as prices climb in the evening, they're worth trying at least once. Look out too for restaurants offering the *Dan Menu*, which is a fixed-price tourist menu, usually available at lunchtime. Dinner (*aftensmad*), which in Denmark is eaten between about 6−9 p.m., is the opportunity for the budget traveller to try one of the many ethnic and international restaurants in Denmark, as they offer the best value during the evening.

If you've got a sweet tooth, then you'll want to sample the famous Danish pastries. These are much lighter and less sugary than the type you buy in Britain, and they're cheap and filling at around 6DKr (£0.60; $0.90).

Breakfast (*morgenmad*) is a substantial meal in Denmark and offers a good opportunity to stock up. Almost all hotels and youth hostels will offer a self-service buffet of boiled eggs, cereal, yoghurt, bread and rolls, cheese, cold meats and tea or coffee, for around 40DKr (£4; $6).

Other Danish specialities to look out for are: *hakkebøf* (a sort of hamburger), regarded as the Danish national dish, and served with fried onions, boiled potatoes and pickled cucumbers and beetroot; *frikadeller* (a pork rissole); *flaeskesteg* (pork served with red cabbage, potatoes and brown sauce); *stegt flaesk* (sliced pork, fried and served with boiled potatoes and parsley sauce); *stegt rødspaette*, which is fried plaice served the same way; and *aeggekage* (omelette with bacon and chives). You'll also find lots of different types of herring, and delicious ice cream, which is served in cones filled with several flavours of ice cream and topped with cream and jam. The favourite Danish drink is beer, either *Carlsberg* or *Tuborg*, and it is also worth trying *akvavit*, a potato-based schnapps, but beware: it's not only expensive, it's extremely potent!

Since Danish cuisine is based very much on meat and fish, vegetarians will be limited in the traditional dishes they can try; cheese *smørrebrød*, salad at buffets, and pastries. Since picnicking is such a popular Danish pastime, however, you won't feel too out of place buying your own provisions in the supermarket. The Danish breakfast also offers plenty of choice and many of the ethnic restaurants will easily accommodate you, so you won't go hungry.

If you're going to put together your own meal, the main supermarkets to look out for are Brugsen, Irma, Netto and Aldi. Most Danes speak excellent English so shopping won't be a problem.

Århus

LOCAL SPECIALITIES
Beers produced by the Ceres brewery.

SPECIAL EVENTS AND FESTIVALS

Guided tours of the Ceres brewery (Wed. at 2 p.m.) finish up with a few glasses of beer. Free tickets for the tours are available from the Tourist Office.

CHEAP EATERIES
Two-course meals under 50DKr (£5; $7.50)

Kulturgyngen, Mejlgade 53 (tel. 86 19 22 55). Vegetarian options available. Open Mon.–Sat. 10 a.m.–9 p.m.

Pizzeria Roma, Frederiksgade 19 (tel. 86 19 60 56). Italian restaurant. Open Mon.–Sat. noon–11 p.m.; Sun. 2–11 p.m.

Husets Restaurant, Vester Allé 15 (tel. 86 12 27 95). Open Mon.–Fri. noon–9 p.m.

Café Englen, Studsgade 3 (tel. 86 13 06 44). Open daily 10 a.m.–1 a.m.

Two-course meals from 50–70DKr (£5–7; $7.50–10.50)

Shanghai, Guldsmedgade 2 (tel. 86 13 00 47). Chinese restaurant. Open daily noon–11 p.m.

Colosseum, Skolegade 33 (tel. 86 12 42 45). Italian restaurant. Open daily 4.30–11 p.m.

DSB Restaurant, Hovedbanegården (tel. 86 12 02 26). Open daily 11.30 a.m.–11 p.m.

Kasba, Vestergade 50 (tel. 86 20 21 82). Algerian restaurant. Vegetarian dishes available. Open Mon.–Wed. 11.30 a.m.–2 p.m. and 5–11 p.m.; Thurs.–Fri. 11.30 a.m.–2 p.m. and 5 p.m.–midnight; Sat. 5 p.m.–midnight; Sun. 5–11 p.m.

Two-course meals from 70–100DKr (£7–10; $10.50–15.00)

Restaurant No. 7, Vestergade 7 (tel. 86 76 01 66). Plenty of vegetarian options. Open Mon.–Fri. noon–11 p.m.; Sat. 5–11 p.m.

Guldhornet, Banegårdspladsen 10 (tel. 86 12 02 62). Open daily 10 a.m.–midnight.

Kapadokya, Klostergade 32 (tel. 86 20 94 95). Turkish restaurant offering an all-you-can-eat buffet. Open Tues.–Sun. 1–11 p.m.

SHOPPING
● **Market**

On Ingerslev Boulevard in front of the theatre (Bispetorv), Wed. and Sat. from 7 a.m.–2 p.m.

● **Supermarkets**

Brugsen. Branches at Søndergade 72; Vesterbro Torv 1; and at the
  junction of Jaegergårdsgade and Godthåbsgade. Open
  Mon.–Thurs. 9 a.m.–5.30 p.m.; Fri. 9 a.m.–8 p.m.; Sat. 9 a.m.–
  1 p.m. (extended opening on the first Saturday of every month).
Føtex. Branches at Frederiks Allé 22–24; Guldsmedgade 3–9; and
  Bruuensgade 55.
DSB Supermarket. At the train station. Open 8 a.m.–midnight.

Copenhagen

LOCAL SPECIALITIES
Beers brewed by the Carlsberg and Tuborg breweries.

SPECIAL EVENTS AND FESTIVALS
Both the Carlsberg brewery at Ny Carlsbergvej 140 and the Tuborg
brewery at Strandvejen 54 offer free guided tours (Carlsberg:
Mon.–Fri. at 11 a.m. and 2 p.m.; Tuborg: Mon.–Fri. at 10 a.m.,
12.30 p.m. and 2 p.m.) with some free drinks at the end. Check
details with the Tourist Office – the Tuborg brewery may be closing
down in the near future.

CHEAP EATERIES
Restaurants along Strøget, on Nyhavn, and close to Tivoli tend to
be expensive. There are reasonably priced eateries scattered all over
the city centre, but Vesterbrogade and the area around Grabrodre-
torv offer the most choice.
Two-course meals under 50DKr (£5; $7.50)

Den Grone Kælder, Klarehoderne 10. Vegetarian restaurant. Open
  Mon.–Sat. 11 a.m.–9 p.m.
Bananrepublikken A/S, Nørrebrogade 13 (tel. 31 39 79 21). Open
  daily 11 a.m.–2 a.m.
Kreta, Nørrebrogade 2. Greek restaurant.
Kashmir, Nørrebrogade 35 (tel. 35 37 54 71). Indian Restaurant.
  Open daily 11 a.m.–11 p.m.
Riz Raz, Kompagnistræde 20. Vegetarian dishes with a Mediter-
  ranean influence. Open daily 11.30 a.m.–midnight.
Govindas, Nørre Farimagsgade 82. Hare Krishna-run vegetarian
  restaurant. Open Mon.–Sat.

Two-course meals from 50–70DKr (£5–7; $7.50–10.50)

Floras Kaffebar, Blågardsgåde 27 (tel. 31 39 00 18). Open Mon.–Sat. 10 a.m.–2 a.m.; Sun. 11 a.m.–midnight.

Nyhavns Fægekro, Nyhavn 5 (tel. 33 12 15 88). Specializes in fish dishes. Open daily 11.30 a.m.–4 p.m. and 5–11.30 p.m.

India Palace, Hans Christian Andersen Blvd 13 (tel. 33 91 04 08 / 33 91 44 08). Indian restaurant. Open daily 11 a.m.–midnight.

Alexanders Pizza, Kannikestræde 5 (tel. 33 12 55 36). Open Sun.–Thurs. noon–10 p.m.; Fri.–Sat. noon–11.30 p.m.

El Greco, Skindergade 20 (tel. 33 32 93 44). Greek restaurant. Open daily 11 a.m.–midnight.

København Cafeen, Badstuestræde 10 (tel. 33 32 80 81). Open daily 11.30 a.m.–10 p.m.

Quattro Fontane, Guldbergsgade 3 (tel. 31 39 39 31). Italian restaurant. Open daily 4 p.m.–midnight.

Greens, Grønnegade 12–14 (tel. 33 15 16 90). Vegetarian restaurant with vegan options. Open daily 11.30 a.m.– 9.30 p.m.

Two-course meals from 70–100DKr (£7–10; $10.50–15.00)

Spisehuset, Rådhusstræde 13 (tel. 33 14 52 70). Open daily noon–3 p.m. and 5–11 p.m.

Shezan, Viktoriagade 22 (tel. 31 24 78 88). Pakistani restaurant. Open daily 11.30 a.m.–11.30 p.m.

Pak Ka, Dronningens Tværgade 30 (tel. 33 15 16 07). Chinese restaurant. Open daily 11 a.m.–midnight.

SHOPPING
● **Markets**

There is a market on Israels Plads near the Nørreport station (Mon.–Fri. 7 a.m.–6 p.m.; Sat. 7 a.m.–2 p.m.), and an abundance of fruit stalls along Strøget.

● **Supermarkets**

Opening hours are generally Mon.–Fri. 9 a.m.–7 p.m.; Sat. 9 a.m.– 2 p.m.

Brugsen, Nørre Voldgade and Axeltorv.
Irma, Vesterbrogade and Ostergade.
Netto, Nørre Voldgade.
Fakta, Landemærket.

FURTHER INFORMATION
Neon Guiden, a monthly supplement to the *Ekstra Bladet* newspaper, contains a wealth of information on prices and special deals in many local eateries. Another good source of information on cheap eating possibilities is USE IT at Rådhusstræde 13 (tel. 33 15 65 18).

Odense

LOCAL SPECIALITIES
As you might expect on an island, fish dishes are very popular – look out for smoked eel, marinated herring and smoked salmon. Restaurants may also serve *Funen Omelettes*, which are open omelettes served with sliced bacon and chives. Another speciality is smoked cheese sprinkled with caraway seeds.

CHEAP EATERIES
Two-course meals under 50DKr (£5; $7.50)

Prior Café, Fisketorvet 2–4 (tel. 66 12 74 94). Self-service restaurant. Open Mon.–Fri. 8 a.m.–6 p.m.; Sat. 8 a.m.–2 p.m.
Café Skt. Gertrud, Jernbanegade 8 (tel. 65 91 33 02). Open daily 10 a.m.–12.45 a.m.
Føtex Verehus, Vesterbro 39 (tel. 66 14 22 88), and Middelfartvej 125 (tel. 66 16 73 55). Supermarket cafeterias. Open Mon. and Thurs. 9 a.m.–7 p.m.; Tues. and Wed. 9 a.m.–6 p.m.; Fri. 9 a.m.–8 p.m.; Sat. 9 a.m.–2 p.m. (5 p.m. on first Sat. of the month).

Two-course meals from 50–70DKr (£5–7; $7.50–10.50)

Målet, Jernbanegade 17 (tel. 66 17 82 41). Open Mon.–Sat. 11 a.m.–10 p.m.; Sun. 2–10 p.m.
Mona Lisa, Brandts Passage 9–11 (tel. 65 91 50 11). Italian dishes. Open Mon.–Sat. noon–midnight.
Pizzeria Ristorante Italiano, Vesterbrogade 9 (tel. 66 11 04 06). Italian restaurant.

Two-course meals from 70–100DKr (£7–10; $10.50–15.00)

Air Pub, Kongensgade 41 (tel. 66 14 66 08). Open Mon.–Thurs. 10 a.m.–midnight; Fri. and Sat. 10–2 a.m.
Den Grimme Aelling, Hans Jensens Stræde 1 (tel. 65 91 70 30).

Open Mon.–Sat. noon–2.30 p.m. and 5.30–10 p.m.; Sun. noon–2.30 p.m.

Den Gamle Kro, Overgade 23 (tel. 66 12 14 33). Recommended dish: *Funen Omelette*. Open Mon.–Sat. 11 a.m.–10.30 p.m.; Sun. 11 a.m.–9.30 p.m.

SHOPPING
● **Market**

Sortebrødre Torv, Wed. and Sat. early morning until noon.

● **Supermarkets**

Brugsen, Vestergade 76. Open Mon.–Wed. 8.30 a.m.–6 p.m.; Thurs. and Fri. 8.30 a.m.–7 p.m.; Sat. 8 a.m.–4 p.m.

Obs!, Rosengårdscentret, Ørbaekvej 75. Open Mon., Thurs. and Fri. 9 a.m.–8 p.m.; Tues. and Wed. 9 a.m.–5.30 p.m.; Sat. 8 a.m.–2 p.m. (5 p.m. on the first Saturday of the month).

Føtex, Vesterbro 39–51. Open Mon. and Thurs. 9 a.m.–7 p.m.; Tues. and Wed. 9 a.m.–6 p.m.; Fri. 9 a.m.–8 p.m.; Sat. 9 a.m.–2 p.m. (5 p.m. on the first Saturday of the month).

Bilka, Niels Bohrs Allé 150. Open Mon., Thurs. and Fri. 9 a.m.–8 p.m.; Tues. 9 a.m.–5.30 p.m.; Wed. 9 a.m.–6 p.m.; Sat. 8 a.m.–2 p.m. (5 p.m. on the first Saturday of the month).

FINLAND

Finnish food is an interesting combination of Scandinavian, Baltic, Eastern and Western cuisines. Finns set great store by using fresh, local ingredients and preparing dishes in simple, traditional ways. Unfortunately it is also very expensive and there's not much chance of a budget traveller getting to sample unusual dishes like smoked reindeer, elk, or bear, every day. It's all too easy to pay 100M (£12.35; $18.50) for lunch alone, so check prices beforehand. Restaurants (*ravintola*) specializing in Finnish cuisine are also rather thin on the ground and tend to be particularly pricey.

Having said that, don't think you'll have to exist on hamburgers and picnics alone. If you have your main meal at lunchtime you'll be able to try a selection of hot and cold Finnish dishes at the traditional buffet – *voileipäpöytä* (or *smörgåsbord*). This will be at a fixed price of around 65–85M (£8.00–10.50; $12.00–15.75); you can eat as much as you want and a service charge is always included.

If your accommodation includes breakfast, stock up then, as it's usually a large meal. Traditionally served between 6.30 a.m.–10 a.m., it consists of a selection of herring, eggs, cereals, yoghurt, cheese, salami and breads, washed down with gallons of coffee.

Cheap meals are also available at *baari* (snackbars), *kahvilas* (cafeterias), *grilli* (fast-food stands), standard fast-food chains, or in department store restaurants and cafeterias. Don't expect to get a drink in the *baari* though, as they're unlicensed and will only serve the very mildest beer. *Baari* also tend to close at about 5 p.m.–6 p.m. A half-litre of draught beer typically costs around 20–25M (£2.50–3.10; $3.75–4.60) in any licensed establishment, a glass of wine roughly the same; there's a heavy tax on alcohol and this pushes the price up. A cup of tea in a café will cost 7–10M (£0.85–1.25; $1.25–$1.90), coffee slightly less; and a loaf of bread, anything from 8–16M (£1–2; $1.50–3.00).

Finnish cooking features good quality, fresh produce. Fish is very popular, particularly salmon (*loti*), white fish, pike, bream and slightly salted Baltic herring (*silli*). From mid-July to September, you can try fresh crayfish (*rapuja*) which is then in season, and in the autumn delicious wild mushrooms. Some buffet specialities to look out for are *sillisalaatli* (herring salad); smoked *poronliha* (reindeer); *kesakeitto*, fresh vegetable soup with milk; or *kalakukko*, a hot fish and pork pie with salt baked potatoes. You may also find *karjalanpurakka* (rice and potato pastries), *lanttulaatikko* (turnip casserole) and *paistetut sienet* (fried wild mushrooms). The Finns tend to eat four meals a day, so lunch, the main meal, is usually eaten between 11 a.m. and 1 p.m. Dinner then follows at 4 p.m.– 7 p.m. and supper from 7 p.m.–midnight. Other Finnish staples are dark rye bread (*ruisleipä*), local cheeses such as *romadur*, and lots of unusual and delicious wild berries like loganberries, brambleberries, blueberries and yellow cloudberries from Lapland. These may be served alone, with pancakes, or even made into soups, and are plentiful in summer. Eat your main meal at lunchtime, as it will be cheaper then, and head for street stalls, university cafés (*mensas*) and pizzerias at other times. A favourite Finnish street-snack to watch out for are *litapurakkas* (hot doughnuts filled with meat and rice). Some large hotels offer bargain breakfasts to non-residents, so these are well worth investigating.

Pilma (sour milk) and *kalja* (non-alcoholic beer) are commonly drunk here. For something stronger you'll need to head for an ALKO, the state-controlled off-licence chain; these are open Mon.–Thurs. 10 a.m.–5 p.m., Fri. 10 a.m.–6 p.m. year round, and also Saturday 9 a.m.–2 p.m. June–August. Here you'll find many different types of schnapps (*jalovina*), the most popular of which are *koskenkorva* and *Finlandia vodka*, as well as liqueurs from almost every edible wild berry. Even wines are made from whitecurrants and fruit. Beer (*olut*) comes in three different categories, from *Olut IV*, the strongest and most expensive, to *Olut I*, which is virtually non-alcoholic. (It should be noted that it is an offence to drink a strong beer in a public place). The favourite Finnish hot drink is coffee, of which they drink enormous quantities. It's very good and much better than the tea, which isn't a typical beverage here.

Vegetarians won't have an easy time of it in Finland, as traditional dishes consist primarily of fish and meat. Supermarkets are well stocked for picnics, however, and there are also open-air markets and ethnic restaurants. Some veggie salads and dishes should be available on buffet tables, but you may not feel particularly full afterwards. Make sure you eat well at breakfast to see you through the day.

When doing your own food shopping, you'll find plenty of well-stocked supermarkets; the chains to look for are Alepo and Valintalo. Large department stores often have good food halls, in addition to in-store cafés, and kiosks will stock some essentials. You'll be glad to know that buying or ordering food won't be difficult, as most Finns speak good English. Supermarket opening hours are generally Mon.–Fri. 9 a.m.–5 p.m.; Sat. 9 a.m.–noon, but in the cities opening hours may be longer, and may include a Sunday opening during the summer.

Helsinki

SPECIAL EVENTS AND FESTIVALS
If you like fish you might like to visit the Herring Market, which is held every year during the first week in October. There is also an annual festival of regional food, when areas like Lapland promote their own cuisine; it's held every June.

CHEAP EATERIES
Two-course meals under 25M (£3; $4.50)

Student mensas. At Aleksanterinkatu 5 and Hallituskatu 11–13. Both open Mon.–Sat. during termtime; one or other is open the same days in summer. Student ID may be required.

Two-course meals from 25–40M (£3–5; $4.50–7.50)

Palace Café, Eteleränta 20 (2nd floor). Open Mon.–Fri. 7 a.m.– 3 p.m.
Ani, Telakkakatu 2 (tel. 66 50 22). Turkish restaurant with an all-you-can-eat lunchtime buffet.
Café Caraveo, Pohjoinen Makasiinikatu 1 (tel. 65 55 07).
Russian Fast Food, Kauppahalli. Open Mon.–Fri. 8 a.m.–5 p.m.; Sat. 8 a.m.–2 p.m.

Two-course meals from 40–56M (£5–7; $7.50–10.50)

Café Engel, Aleksanterinkatu 26. Recommended dish: lasagna.
Kappeli, Eteläesplanadi 1. Open daily 9 a.m.–4 a.m.
Green Way, Kaisaniemenkatu 1. Vegetarian restaurant. Open Mon.–Fri. 11 a.m.–6 p.m.; Sat. 11 a.m.–4 p.m. (throughout July closes 2 p.m. on Sat.)
Houne ja Keittiö, Huvilakatu 28. Open Mon.–Fri.
Omenapuu, Keskuskatu 6 (tel. 63 02 05). Open daily 11 a.m.– 1 a.m.
Kasvisravintola, Korkeavuorenkatu 3 (tel. 17 92 12). Vegetarian restaurant. Open Mon.–Fri. 11 a.m.–6 p.m.; weekends noon–6 p.m.
Sukhothai, Runeberginkatu 32 (tel. 44 67 74). Thai restaurant. Open Mon.–Fri. 11 a.m.–midnight; Sat. 1–10 p.m.; Sun. 1– 9 p.m.

Two-course meals from 56–80M (£7–10; $10.50–15.00)

Pikku Italia, Aleksanterinkatu 9 (KLUUVI shopping centre) (tel. 63 72 00). Italian restaurant.

Aurinkotuuli, Lapinlahdenkatu 25 (tel. 694 2563). Vegetarian restaurant. Closed July; otherwise open Mon.–Fri. 11 a.m.–6 p.m.; Sat. noon–4 p.m.

Kuu, Töölönkatu 27 (tel. 44 33 08). Good value Finnish dishes.

SHOPPING
● **Markets**
On Kauppatori (June–Aug. 7 a.m.–2 p.m. and 4–8 p.m.; Sept.–July 7 a.m.–2 p.m. only) and in the Kauppahalli nearby (open Mon.–Fri. 8 a.m.–5 p.m.; Sat. 8 a.m.–2 p.m.).

● **Supermarkets**
Alepa, Anttila, Valintatalo and Säästäri are the names you will see most often in central Helsinki. Their branches in Tunneli near the train station are especially convenient due to their longer opening hours (generally Mon.–Sat. 10 a.m.–10 p.m.; Sun. noon–10 p.m.). In addition to the supermarket chains, Stockmann's department store at Pohjoisesplanadi 41 has a fine food hall.

FURTHER INFORMATION
Helsinki This Week, a brochure available free from the Tourist Office, is a useful source of information on local restaurants and cafés.

Turku

SPECIAL EVENTS AND FESTIVALS
The word *turku* means market place and there are several markets throughout the year when traditional foodstuffs are available. These are:

Manun Markkinat (Manu's market)	May
Heikin Markkinat (Heikki's market)	September
Silakkamarkkinat (Herring market)	October
Joulumarkkinat (Traditional Christmas market)	November/December

CHEAP EATERIES
Two-course meals under 40M (£5; $7.50)

Gadolinia, in the Åbo Akademi on Henrikenkatu. Student mensa. Student ID may be requested. Open Mon.–Fri. 9 a.m.–2.30 p.m.; Sat. 10.30 a.m.–2 p.m.

Tolmuset, Hämeenkatu 8. Open Mon.–Fri. 7.30 a.m.–6 p.m.

Verso, Linnankatu 3 (1st floor). Vegetarian restaurant. Discount for students. Open year round Mon.–Fri. 11 a.m.–5 p.m., and, from Sept.–May on Sat. noon–5 p.m.

Dennis Pizzeria, Linnankatu 17 (tel. 51 14 40). Open Mon.–Thurs. 11 a.m.–11 p.m.; Fri.–Sat. 11 a.m.–midnight; Sun. 1–11 p.m.

Mien Tay, Kellonsoittajankatu 3–7 (tel. 33 50 59). Vietnamese and Chinese dishes.

Two-course meals from 40–56M (£5–7; $7.50–10.50)

Basilica Bar and Brasserie, Scandic Hotel, Matkustajasatama (tel. 30 26 00). Open daily 11 a.m.–11 p.m.

Green Way, Yliopistonkatu 28 (tel. 51 65 66). Vegetarian restaurant. Open Mon.–Fri. 11 a.m.–5.30 p.m.; Sat. 11 a.m.–4 p.m.

Torre, Yliopistonkatu 30 (tel. 51 54 12). Open Mon.–Thurs. 11 a.m.–11 p.m.; Fri.–Sat. 11 a.m.–midnight; Sun. noon–11 p.m.

Two-course meals from 56–80M (£7–10; $10.50–15.00)

Brahen Kellari, Puolalankatu 1 (tel. 32 54 00).

Calamare, Linnankatu 32 (tel. 33 63 00). Seafood restaurant.

Simply Wonderful, Yliopistonkatu 33. Indian vegetarian dishes. Open Mon.–Fri. 11 a.m.–4 p.m.; Sat. 11 a.m.–3 p.m.

SHOPPING
● Markets

On Kauppatori (Mon.–Sat. 8 a.m.–2 p.m.) and in the Kauppahalli on Eerikinkatu (open Mon.–Fri. 8 a.m.–5 p.m.; Sat. 8 a.m.–2 p.m.).

● Supermarkets

Anttila, Brahenkatu 8 (tel. 33 12 00). Open Mon.–Fri. 9 a.m.–8 p.m.; Sat. 8 a.m.–6 p.m.

CM Citymarket, Kupittaa, Uudenmaantie 17 (tel. 33 66 55). Open Mon.–Fri. 9 a.m.–8 p.m., Sat. 9 a.m.–6 p.m.

Stockmann, Hansa Shopping Centre (near Kauppatori). Department store with a fine food hall. Open Mon.–Fri. 9 a.m.–8 p.m.; Sat. 9 a.m.–6 p.m.

FRANCE

In gourmet circles France is said to possess one of the world's great cuisines. The French certainly take their food very seriously and the consummate skill each woman (and man!) displays in shopping, combined with the great reverence with which even the simplest meals are planned and prepared is a lesson to us all. French restaurants in Britain tend to capitalize on the reputation of their cuisine by serving over-priced, minuscule portions that send you hurrying to the nearest chip shop to fill up afterwards. Happily this is seldom the case in France, for provided you know where to look you can find small, family-run restaurants and bistros that offer really good food at low prices.

Lunch in France used to be the main meal of the day, lasting from around noon to 2.30 p.m. These days, dinner is fast becoming more important, particularly in the cities, but you can still find excellent, filling lunches for as little as 45–80F (£5.30–9.40; $8–14). Look for the signs *menu du jour* or *menu fixe*, both of which denote a two- or three-course, fixed-price menu at well below à la carte prices. The *carte*, by the way, is the complete menu of the house, which gives you a wider choice of selections. Some fixed-price menus include a glass of wine as well, just look for *boissons compris* or BC. Another good bet is the *plat du jour* (dish of the day), which is often excellent value at 30–60F (£3.50–7.00; $5.25–10.50). A service charge of 15% is usually included in the price (*service compris*) as is VAT (TVA). If you're watching the pennies, then make lunch your main meal, as prices tend to rise in the evening. Restaurants open only between 12–2.30 p.m. and 7–10 p.m., so if you want to eat outside those hours you'll have to go to a *brasserie* or *bistro*. These are often modest but lively, offering quick meals at slightly lower prices than restaurants. Bistros generally serve traditional farmhouse meals, brasseries much lighter fare. They're particularly good if you only want one course in the evening, as restaurateurs can be quite snooty if you enter their establishment seeking anything other than a total gastronomic experience. The traditional French 'blow-out', incidentally, would consist of an aperitif, an *entrée* (starter), the *plat* (main course), salad, cheese, dessert, fruit, coffee and a *digestif* – not a meal to be rushed.

As you might expect in a country where meals are practically an art form, snacks aren't really part of French life. Cafés offer a limited range of snacks, such as *croque-monsieurs* (cheese-and-ham toasted sandwiches), omelettes and sandwiches (generally French bread with paté, cheese or ham), and these can cost from 18–30F (£2.10–3.50; $3.25–5.25). Cafés also vary their charges depending on where you sit; prices can rise by 30% if you sit outside on the pavement, rather than stand inside at the bar (*comptoir*). A cup of coffee, for example, can vary from 5F (£0.60; $0.90), right up to 12F (£1.40; $2.10), depending on where you sit. On the other hand, you can stay in a café for as long as you like and they're often a good choice for breakfast if it isn't included in the price of your hotel room.

Breakfast is traditionally a very simple meal of coffee and either a croissant with jam, or a *pain au chocolat* (similar to a croissant but filled with chocolate). If you simply ask for a coffee (*un café*) you'll get an espresso, small, black and strong, while a *café crème* will get you the same but served with a jug of hot milk. If you prefer to drink it very milky, ask for *un café au lait*. Tea (*thé*), isn't a common drink here and tends to be served without milk or lemon, but the hot chocolate (*chocolat chaud*) is delicious. A glass of wine or beer in a café can vary from 9–15F (£1.05–1.75; $1.60–2.60).

The price of bread varies from 3.50F (£0.40; $0.60) for a baguette, to 6–8F (£0.70–0.95; $1.00–$1.40) for a loaf.

If you thought French cookery was all rich sauces and garlic then you'll be in for a surprise, as every region has its own distinctive dishes and way of cooking. Cooking in Normandy is based on its excellent dairy products, while in Provence it takes on a Mediterranean tone, using olives and fine herbs. There are also local names for famous dishes like *coq au vin* and fish stew (*bouillabaisse*). Simple dishes like *steak frites* (steak and chips), *tripes* (tripe cooked in herbs) and *rognons* (kidneys) can be found everywhere. Watch out for *cheval* though, it's horse, and if you're squeamish you might also wish to avoid *cuisses de grenouille* (frogs' legs) and *escargots* (snails). Meat, even liver, is served much rarer than in Britain, usually *saignant* – bleeding. If you prefer it well cooked ask for *bien cuit*, well done, or *très cuit*, extra well done.

Other typical French foods to look out for are the huge variety of bread, patés, pastries and cheese. As well as the ever popular *baguettes* and *croissants*, you'll find wonderful, crusty, unbleached *pain de campagne*, brown *pain complet* and *pain de seigle*, a rye bread. There are hundreds of varieties of patés, from rough *pâté de campagne*, made with pork, to smooth *pâté de foie*, made from goose liver. Cheeses are a real treat, over 400 of them in all, ranging from strongly flavoured blues like *Roquefort* to delicate goats' cheeses (*fromages de chevre*).

You can spend many a happy hour sampling France's huge selection of wines. All supermarkets will sell cheap red and white table

wines (*vin de table* or *vin ordinaire*) which can cost as little as 10F
(£1.20; $1.80) a bottle, more in a restaurant, where house wine is
generally served in a quarter-litre carafe (*un quart*). In areas like
Bordeaux this can be very good, but often it's little more than
plonk. For just a few francs more you can try really good wines –
look for the sign AOC or AC (*Appellation d'Origine Controleé*) on the
label, which denotes that the wine will have passed stringent con-
trols and should be of a certain standard. Watch the prices in restaurants though as anything other than table wine can have a huge
mark-up. If you see the sign *dégustation* (tasting), make the most
of it, as it means you can taste the wine with no obligation to buy.
Ask the local tourist office about properties which offer tours of
the vineyards and free tastings. The French also drink quite a lot
of beer (*bière*), both home-produced brews and imported brands
from Belgium and Germany. Alsace is by far the most important
region in terms of beer production, though the northern city of Lille
boasts the Pelforth brewery, which in addition to the light-coloured
beers favoured in France, also produces a dark (*brun*) beer. Cider
(*cidre*) is a popular drink in Normandy and Brittany. The main
spirits drunk in France are *Cognac* and *Armagnac* brandies, and the
aniseed-based *Ricard*.

For a country that prides itself on its inventive approach to food,
you'd think that France would offer vegetarians more choice than
anywhere else. Not a bit of it. In fact in some restaurants you'll be
treated with nothing short of contempt. The delights of the set
menu are virtually always non-veggie, and you may find you have
to order a plate of vegetables *à la carte* in order to eat at all, especially
if you don't eat eggs. Watch out for the soups, too, as there's a
good chance that meat stock has been used. There are specialist
vegetarian restaurants around, however, and while they tend to
be a bit unimaginative, you may find that preferable to dealing
with snooty restaurateurs.

The good thing about France is that there's a huge array of well-
stocked supermarkets, specialist shops and open-air markets. In fact
food shopping is a national pastime and a French picnic a feast in
itself. You'll find small *boulangeries* (bakeries) and *pâtisseries* (pastry
shops) everywhere, selling mouthwatering bread, rolls, exotic
cakes, pastries and fruit tarts. Go early in the day as they tend to
sell out. Look out for *charcuteries* as well, which, while their name
means pork butcher, actually sell all types of cooked meats, patés,
pies, quiches and even salads. *Epiceries* are general groceries and
you may also find *fromageries* (cheese shops) and *crèmeries*, which
sell dairy products.

If you want fresh fruit or vegetables, then head for the local open-air markets (*marchés*), where the produce is usually good quality and fairly cheap. Supermarkets are well worth a visit as they usually offer very good quality and great choice of produce. They're the best place to buy the wine to go with your picnic; look for branches of Monoprix, Uniprix, Prisunic, Protin or Felix.

Avignon

LOCAL SPECIALITIES

Avignon is part of Provence, so you'll find many of the same dishes here as in Marseille and Nice: *ratatouille; soupe au pistou* and *bouilla-baisse*. The area is noted for its aromatic herbs: sage, thyme, basil and rosemary are much in evidence, as are olives and fresh veg-etables, particularly tomatoes. Lamb, beef and all types of fish are popular. Look out too for:

tapenade	purée of olives
fruits confits	fruit preserved in sugar
moules marinières	mussles cooked in wine
truffes	truffles
aubergines à la bohemienne	aubergines and tomatoes cooked in olive oil and seasoned with parsley
miel	honey
papalines d'Avignon	a pastry made with chocolate and liqueur

CHEAP EATERIES
Two-course meals under 50F (£6; $9)

Café Flunch, blvd Raspail 11 (tel. 90 86 06 23). Open daily 11 a.m.–10 p.m.

Oanh, rue de la Bonneterie 31b (tel. 90 85 81 04). Vietnamese restaurant. Recommended dish: *crevettes Xao Lang* (shrimp with red curry noodles and vegetables). Open daily 11 a.m.–2 p.m. and 6–11 p.m.

Taché d'Encre, rue des Teinturiers 22 (tel. 90 85 46 03). Open Tues.–Sat. noon–2 p.m. and 7.30 p.m.–midnight; Sun.–Mon. 7.30 p.m.–midnight.

La Ferigoulo, rue Rempart du Rhône 10 (tel. 90 82 10 28). Closed Sun. evening and Mon.

Le Saboly, place Saboly 4 (tel. 90 85 58 93). Open daily.

Two-course meals from 50–68F (£6–8; $9–12)

Le Pain Bis, rue Armand de Pontmartin 6. Organic meals. Vegetarian dishes predominate. Open July–Aug. daily noon–2.30 p.m. and 7.30–midnight; Sept.–June daily noon–2.30 p.m. and 7.30–11 p.m.
Le Médaillon, rue Grivolas 4 (tel. 90 82 19 20). Closed on Sun., except during the festival.
Le Table de Patrick, rue du Chapeau Rouge 22 (tel. 90 82 66 99). Closed on Sun.
Le Pavillon d'Or, rue Carnot 4 (tel. 90 82 06 76). Vietnamese and Chinese dishes. Open daily.

Two-course meals from 68–85F (£8–10; $12–15)

Au Petit Nice, pl. de l'Horloge 14 (tel. 90 86 07 52). Closed Sun. in winter.
La Dolce Vita, pl. de la Principale 4 (tel. 90 86 12 12). Regional and Italian dishes. Open Tues.–Sun. noon–3 p.m. and 7–11 p.m.
Le Tournesol, rue Bonneterie 64 (tel. 90 14 00 31). Polynesian dishes. Open daily.

SHOPPING
● **Markets**

Les Halles, place Pie (open Tues.–Sun. 8 a.m.–1 p.m.)
Porte Magnanen (outside the walls). Sat. and Sun.
Pl. des Carmes. Organic produce. Thurs. morning.

● **Supermarket**

Codec, rue de la République. Open Mon.–Sat. 9 a.m.–7.15 p.m.

FURTHER INFORMATION
As well as a range of other useful information, the *Guide Pratique*, available free from the Tourist Office, includes a restaurant guide which gives an idea of how much you can expect to pay in many local restaurants, and the types of food on offer.

Bordeaux

There are clusters of cheap restaurants around pl. du Général Serrail (especially rue des Augustins) and pl. St-Michel. The latter area, however, is best avoided at night. For information on university restaurants contact CROUS at rue du Hamel 18 (tel. 56 33 86 86).

LOCAL SPECIALITIES
Think of Bordeaux and you think of wine, particularly red wine. (Wine-tasting tours of nearby vineyards are available, though they're expensive. Just ask at the tourist office.) Here you'll find well-known names like *Graves*, *St-Émilion* and *Medoc*, as well as other regional wines which aren't only for drinking but also feature strongly in local cuisine. Most famous of these is *sauce à la bordelaise*, used in a variety of dishes and made from red wine, bone marrow, shallots and tarragon. Also worth watching out for are confits of duck and goose and lots of mushrooms.

agneau de pré-salé	salt-marsh lamb
lamproie	lamprey eel

CHEAP EATERIES
Two-course meals under 50F (£6; $9)

Flunch, cours de l'Intendance 4−6 (tel. 56 48 28 38). Open daily 11 a.m.−11 p.m.
Cambo, rue Porte-Dijeaux 68 (tel. 56 44 15 37). Open Mon.−Sat. 10 a.m.−10 p.m. Closed for two weeks in August.
La Chine, rue St-Rémi 54 (tel. 56 79 13 24). Chinese restaurant. Open daily noon−2 p.m. and 7−9 p.m.
Brasserie Asiatique, rue de Castillon 6−8 (tel. 56 79 09 21). Thai and Chinese dishes. Open Mon.−Sat. 11.45 a.m.−2.30 p.m. and 6.45−10.30 p.m.

Two-course meals from 50−68F (£6−8; $9−12)

Café des Arts, cours Victor Hugo 138 (tel. 56 91 78 46). Open daily 11 a.m.−12.45 a.m.
Bistro Romain, cours de l'Intendance 65−67 (tel. 56 44 93 33). Open daily 11.30 a.m.−2 a.m.
L'Athenée, rue des Trois Conils 44 (tel. 56 52 18 18). Open

Mon.–Fri. noon–2 p.m. and 8–10.30 p.m.; Sat. noon–2 p.m.

Two-course meals from 68–85F (£8–10; $12–15)

Le Basque, rue du Chai-des-Farines 10 (tel. 56 48 53 54). Open
Tues.–Sat. noon–1.45 p.m. and 7.30–10 p.m.; Sun.
noon–1.45 p.m. Closed for four weeks June–July.
Le Médoc, cours du Médoc 66 (tel. 56 39 47 04). Open Mon.–Sat.
7.30 a.m.–10 p.m. Closed last two weeks of Aug.
L'Aquitain, rue Ste-Catherine 177–179 (tel. 56 81 17 63). Open
daily 7.30 a.m.–11 p.m.

SHOPPING
● **Markets**

Marche des Capuchins, off cours de la Marne. Open Mon.–Sat.
6 a.m.–1 p.m.
Pl. de la Ferme de Richemont, on cours Victor Hugo. Open
Mon.–Sat. 6 a.m.–1 p.m.
Pl. des Grands Hommes.

● **Supermarket**

Auchan, Centre Meriodock, rue Claude Bonnier. Open Mon.–Sat.
8.30 a.m.–10 p.m.

FURTHER INFORMATION
The leaflet *Quelques Grandes Tables Restaurants, Brasseries et Cafés de
Bordeaux* (free from the Tourist Office) contains information on
average prices, opening hours, and the type of cuisine on offer at
a selection of local restaurants.

Dieppe

LOCAL SPECIALITIES

soupe de poisson	fish soup
harengs marinés	marinated herring
maquereaux marinés	marinated mackerel
marmite dieppoise	fish and shellfish chowder
sole dieppoise	sole with white wine, cream and shellfish

SPECIAL EVENTS AND FESTIVALS
Dieppe hosts the 'Foire aux Moules' (Mussels Festival) around 20
June, and the famous 'Fête du Hareng et de la Coquille' (Herring
and Scallop Festival) in mid-November.

CHEAP EATERIES
Two-course meals under 50F (£6; $9)

Les Ecamias, quai Henri IV 129 (tel. 35 84 46 67). Open daily except
  Mon.
Pizzeria de l'Europe, rue d'Ecosse 57–61 (tel. 35 84 37 76).

Two-course meals from 50–68F (£6–8; $9–12)

Le Celtic, quai Henri IV 95 (tel. 35 84 58 50).
L'Orange Bleue, quai Henri IV 101 (tel. 35 84 49 02).

Two-course meals from 68–85F (£8–10; $9–15)

Le Grand Bleu, blvd Clemenceau 25 (tel. 35 82 63 68).
Pontoise, rue Thiers 10 (tel. 35 84 14 57).
Au Grand Duquesne, place St-Jacques 15 (tel. 35 84 21 51).
Les Vapeurs, arcades de la Poissonnerie 21 (tel. 35 84 66 90).

SHOPPING
● **Market**

Pl. National. Open Tues. and Thurs. mornings, and Sat. morning–
  late afternoon.

● **Supermarkets**
Prisunic and Shopi both have stores in the main pedestrian area of
the Grande Rue and rue de la Barre.

Dijon

Average prices in local restaurants are higher than is usual for
France, with the result that meals for under 50F, or in the 50–70F
price range are harder to find than normal. The largest concentration of cheaper eateries is in the area around rue de la Musette,
but even here the choice is far from extensive.

LOCAL SPECIALITIES

moutarde de Dijon	Dijon mustard
jambon persillé	jellied ham with parsley
boeuf bourguignon	beef stewed with red wine, onions and mushrooms
coq au vin	chicken cooked in wine
escargots	snails – served fresh, or cooked (often with garlic butter
pain d'épices	bread baked with honey and spices
cassis	blackcurrant liqueur
Nuits St Georges	one of the most highly regarded of the famous Burgundian red wines

CHEAP EATERIES
Two-course meals under 25F (£3; $4.50)

University Mensas at: rue du Dr Maret 3; blvd Mansart 6; and rue du Recteur-Bouchard 6. Student ID required. All are open 11.30 a.m.–1.15 p.m. and 6.45–7.15 p.m. year round.

Two-course meals under 50F (£6; $9)

La Théière, rue Verrerie 6 (tel. 80 31 82 94). Open Mon.–Sat. noon–3 p.m.
Le Potimaron, av. de l'Ouche 4 (tel. 80 43 38 07). Some vegetarian options. Open Mon.–Sat.

Two-course meals from 50–68F (£6–8; $9–12)

Au Bec Fin, rue Jeannin 47 (tel. 80 66 17 77). Open Mon.–Fri. 12–1.30 p.m. and 7.30–10.30 p.m.; Sat. 7.30–10.30 p.m.
La Soupière, av. Marechal Foch 15–17 (Hôtel Climat de France). Open daily noon–2 p.m. and 7–10.30 p.m.
La Vie Saine, rue de la Musette 27–29 (tel. 80 30 15 10). Vegetarian restaurant. Open Mon.–Sat. noon–2 p.m.
Thai, rue Monge 44 (tel. 80 30 49 88). Thai restaurant.

Two-course meals from 68–85F (£8–10; $12–15)

Au Moulin à Vent, Place François Fude 8 (tel. 80 30 81 43). Recommended dish: *boeuf bourguignon*. Open Tues.–Sat. noon–2 p.m. and 7–10 p.m.

La Tosca, rue de la Liberté 94 (tel. 80 30 79 88). Mainly Italian
dishes. Open daily.
Le Grand Mandarin de Côte d'Or, rue Devosge 53 (tel. 80 73 56
55). Chinese restaurant.

SHOPPING
● **Markets**

Les Halles (covered market) and on the surrounding streets: rue
Bannelier; rue Quentin; rue C.-Ramey; and rue Odebert (Tues.,
Fri. and Sat. 6 a.m.–noon).

● **Supermarkets**

Nouvelles Galeries, rue de la Liberté 41.
Prisunic, rue Piron 11. Open Mon.–Sat. 9 a.m.–7.15 p.m.

Lyon

The greatest concentration of restaurants is in Vieux-Lyon (*5ème
arrondissement*), though average prices here are slightly higher than
in the *1er* and *2ème arrondissements*, both of which also offer a wide
choice of restaurants. The Cordeliers-République part of the *2ème
arrondissement* is a particularly good spot to look for meals around
50F. Around pl. des Terreaux in the *1er arrondissement* are most of
the remaining *bouchons* – small restaurants serving regional specialities (usually at reasonable prices).

For information on university canteens contact CROUS at rue
de la Madelaine 59 (tel. 78 80 13 13).

LOCAL SPECIALITIES
Pork and offal feature prominently in the cuisine of Lyon and the
Rhône valley.

tripes à la lyonnaise	tripe with onions and vinegar
tablier de sapeur	a special kind of tripe
Jesus	a liver sausage
salade Lyonnaise	eggs, bacon and fried bread, served with lettuce and tomatoes

rosette	salami
Bleu de Bresse	cheese
cervelle de canut	a curd cheese
Ardèche	chestnuts
Montelimar nougat	nougat
tarte Lyonnaise	a flan with kirsch and almonds
St Etienne	chocolates
Beaujolais and *Côtes du Rhône*	two of the most notable wines produced in the Rhône Valley

CHEAP EATERIES
Two-course meals under 50F (£6; $9)

Le Rubis, rue Ste-Catherine 9 (tel. 78 28 33 12). Chinese and Vietnamese dishes. Closed Sun. evening.

Le P'Tit Comte, rue Auguste-Comte 17 (tel. 72 41 06 09). Closed at weekends and for two weeks in Aug.

Country Rock, quai des Célestins 1 (tel. 78 37 41 80). Open daily.

Le Patisson, rue du Port-du-Temple 17 (tel. 72 81 41 71). Vegetarian restaurant. Closed Fri. evening, Sat. lunchtime and all day Sun.

Le Comptoir de Bœuf, pl. Neuve-St-Jean 3 (tel. 78 92 82 35). Closed Sun.

Two-course meals from 50–68F (£6–8; $9–12)

Le Bouchon de Fourvière, rue de la Quarantaine 9 (tel. 72 41 85 02). Closed weekends and throughout Aug.

Le Cabaretier, rue de la Fronde 6 (tel. 78 42 38 11). Closed Sun. Oct.–Apr.

La Tosca, rue Mercière 51 (tel. 78 37 24 65). Italian restaurant. Closed Sun. lunchtime.

Les Trois Tonneaux, rue des Marroniers 4 (tel. 78 37 34 72). Closed Sun. and throughout Aug.

Two-course meals from 68–85F (£8–10; $12–15)

Le Bouchon Fleuri, rue des Trois-Maries 4 (tel. 78 42 60 76). Open daily.

La Moulinère, rue Thomassin 1 (tel. 78 37 90 80). Belgian and French dishes. Open daily.

Les Adrets, rue du Bœuf 30 (tel. 78 38 24 30). Closed weekends.

SHOPPING
● **Markets**

Quai St Antoine. Open Tues.–Sun. 7.30 a.m.–12.30 p.m.
Blvd de la Croix Rousse. Open Tues.–Sun. 7.30 a.m.–12.30 p.m.
Les Halles, cours Lafayette 102. Open Tues.–Sat. 7 a.m.–noon and
3 p.m.–7 p.m.; Sun. 7 a.m.–noon.

● **Supermarkets**

Monoprix, rue Gambetta (junction with rue de Brest). Open
Mon.–Sat. 8.45 a.m.–7.15 p.m.
Grand Bazar, rue de la République (pl. des Cordeliers). Open
Mon.–Sat. 8.45 a.m.–12.30 p.m. and 3–8 p.m.
Maréchal Central, rue de la Plantière (junction with rue Lanterne).
Open Mon.–Sat. 8 a.m.–12.30 p.m. and 3–8 p.m.
Intermarché, in the Part-Dieu shopping centre.
Carrefour. Opposite the youth hostel.

FURTHER INFORMATION
The Tourist Office publishes the free *Hôtels, Restaurants Nocturne*
guide, which includes information on how much you can expect
to pay at a selection of local restaurants.

Marseilles

The North African quarter of the city (located roughly between La
Canebière, the train station and the Porte d'Aix) contains a multitude of cheap, (mainly) North African restaurants, whilst La Canebière and the Vieux Port area offer a good selection of restaurants
serving French dishes at reasonable prices. Unfortunately, neither
district is to be recommended for evening dining: the North African
quarter is best avoided totally after dark, and La Canebière and
the Vieux Port can be unsafe after about 9 p.m. (avoid the small
side-streets even before that time). The area around pl. Jean-Jaurès
and cours Julien (a part of town popular with local students) not
only offers a decent choice of inexpensive French and ethnic restaurants but has the bonus of being trouble-free in the evening.
   For information on university restaurants, contact CROUS at rue
du 141ème 42 R.I.A. (tel. 91 95 90 06).

LOCAL SPECIALITIES

bourride   a creamy fish soup
pieds-et-pacquets   a tripe dish
bouillabaisse   fish (of any type) stewed with a variety of
                      ingredients (typically: seafood, spices and orange
                      peel)

CHEAP EATERIES
Two-course meals under 50F (£6; $9)

Le Mondial, rue Tilsit 68. Recommended dish: *steak frites* (steak
   with chips). Open Sept.–July Mon.–Fri. noon–2 p.m. and 7–
   10 p.m.
Des Allées–Sampiero III, La Canebière 91 (tel. 91 62 36 08 / 91
   50 42 75). Specializes in grilled fish dishes. Open daily.
Buffet Marseille, in Gare St-Charles, 1 Square Narvick (tel. 91 50
   10 60). Recommended dish: *pieds-et-pacquets*. Open daily.

Two-course meals from 50–68F (£6–8; $9–12)

Country Life, rue Venture 14 (tel. 91 54 16 44). Vegetarian restaurant. Open Mon.–Fri. 11.30 a.m.–2.30 p.m. and 7.30–
   9.30 p.m.
La Flamiche, rue de la Paix 16 (tel. 91 33 00 74) Recommended
   dish: *soupe de poisson* (fish soup). Open Mon.–Fri. noon–2 p.m.
   and 7–10 p.m.; Sat. 7–10 p.m.
La Dent Creuse, rue Sénac 14 (tel. 91 42 05 67). Closed Sat. and
   Sun. lunchtimes, and Mon. evening.
Le Jardin d'à Côté, cours Julien 65. Open daily noon–2.30 p.m.
   and 8 p.m.–1 a.m.

Two-course meals from 68–85F (£8–10; $12–15)

Auberge du Vieux Moulin, rue de Provence 12 (tel. 91 49 37 55).
   Closed Wed. and Sun. evenings.
Chez Noël, La Canebière 174 (tel. 91 42 17 22). Dishes from
   Provence and Italy. Closed Mon.
Racasse-Dauphin, quai de Rive-neuve 6 (tel. 91 33 11 53 / 91 33
   17 25). Recommended dish: *bouillabaisse*. Open Fri.–Wed.
   noon–2 p.m. and 7–11 p.m.

SHOPPING
● Markets
On pl. Sébastopol; pl. Jean-Jaurès; and av. du Prado. All open Mon.–Sat. mornings.

● Supermarkets

Monoprix, La Canebière 59. Open Mon.–Sat, 9 a.m.–6 p.m.
Nouvelles Galeries. In the Centre Bourse shopping centre off La Canebière. Open Mon.–Sat. 9 a.m.–7 p.m.
Timi, rue de la République 14–16. Open Mon.–Sat. 7.30 a.m.–1.30 p.m. and 3–7 p.m.

FURTHER INFORMATION
The *Marseille hôtels & restaurants* guide available free from the Tourist Office lists a selection of local restaurants, complete with a guide to how much you can expect to pay for a meal in each restaurant.

Nice

The largest concentration of restaurants (in all price categories) is in Vieux Nice, but there is also a decent selection of reasonably priced establishments near the train station, around rue de Belgique, rue d'Alsace-Lorraine, and rue d'Angleterre.

For a full list of student restaurants and cafeterias contact CROUS at av. des Fleurs 18 (tel. 93 96 73 73).

LOCAL SPECIALITIES
The local cuisine is strongly influenced by the proximity of the sea, and of Italy. The widespread availability of meat-free pasta dishes, plus several vegetable-based local specialities, means that vegetarians have more options than in most French cities.

soupe au pistou	vegetable soup flavoured with basil
salade niçoise	salad with French beans, olives and egg
gnocchi	potato pasta
ratatouille niçoise	the famous vegetable stew
pissaladière	a tart of fried onions, anchovies and black olives
tourte de blea	spinach beet tart

socca	a fried pancake made with chickpea flour, which may be cooked with breadcrumbs and grated cheese
fougasse	a local bread
pan bagnat	a roll filled with tuna, salad, olives and anchovies (a favourite snack in Nice)
Bellet and *Côtes de Provence*	two local wines

CHEAP EATERIES
Two-course meals for under 38F (£4.50; $6.75)

Restaurant Université, av. Robert Schumann 3 (tel. 93 97 10 20). Open Sept.–June daily 11.30 a.m.–1.30 p.m. and 6–8 p.m.
Montebello, av. Valrose 96 (tel. 93 52 56 59). University cafeteria. Open Sept.–mid-Aug. daily 11.30 a.m.–1.30 p.m. and 6–8 p.m.
Cafétéria Flunch, av. Thiers (by the train station). Open daily 11 a.m.–midnight.

Two-course meals from 38–50F (£4.50–6.00; $6.75–9.00)

Restaurant de Paris, rue d'Angleterre 28 (tel. 93 88 99 88). Recommended dish: *tarte aux pommes chantilly* (apple tart with whipped cream). Open Dec.–Oct. daily 11.30 a.m.–2.30 p.m. and 7 p.m.–midnight.
La Buffeteria, av. Notre Dame 28 (tel. 93 92 30 54). Self-service restaurant. French and Italian dishes. Open daily until 5 p.m.

Two-course meals from 50–68F (£6–8; $9–12)

Le Säetone, rue d'Alsace-Lorraine 8. Recommended dishes: *soupe au pistou* and *salade niçoise*. Open Tues.–Sat. 11.30 a.m.–2 p.m. and 6–10 p.m.
Via Veneto, rue d'Angleterre 37/b (tel. 93 82 02 10). Open Mon.–Sat. 7–11 p.m.
Voyageurs Nissart, rue d'Alsace-Lorraine 19 (tel. 93 82 19 60). Recommended dish: *ratatouille*. Open Tues.–Sun. Closed Jan. and July.
Au Soleil, rue d'Italie 7/b (tel. 93 88 77 74). Recommended dish: *soupe au pistou*. Open daily.
La Nissarda, rue Gubernatis 17 (tel. 93 85 26 29). Closed Sun. and Aug.

Two-course meals from 68–85F (£8–10; $12–15)

Le Faubourg Montmartre, rue Pertinax 32. Recommended dish: *bouillabaisse* (fish stew). Open daily 1–3 p.m. and 5 p.m.–midnight.

Bar du Donjon, Parc du Château de Nice (tel. 93 26 19 70). Recommended dishes: *salade niçoise* and *gigot d'agneau* (lamb chops). Closed when it rains.

Tosello, rue Ste Réparate 8 (tel. 93 62 10 20). Regional and Italian dishes. Open daily.

Le California, rue de Belgique 5 (tel. 93 88 75 69). Recommended dish: *ratatouille*. Open daily.

SHOPPING
● **Markets**

pl. St François (fish market). Open daily, early morning till noon.
Cours Saleya. Open Tues.–Sun. early morning till noon.
Av. Malausséna. Open daily from early morning till noon.

● **Supermarkets**

Prisunic, rue Jean Médecin 42. Open Mon.–Thurs. and Sat. 8.30 a.m.—8 p.m.; Fri. 8.30 a.m.–9 p.m.
Casino, rue Deudon. Open Mon.–Sat. 8.30 a.m.–8 p.m.

FURTHER INFORMATION
Nice Restaurants, available free from the Tourist Office, contains a price guide to a small selection of some of the city's cheaper restaurants.

Paris

Although you can find reasonably priced restaurants in any of the various administrative districts (*arrondissements*) of central Paris, average prices are higher in the 8*ème* (Champs-Élysées), 14*ème* (Montparnasse), and 18*ème* (Montmartre – see below) *arrondissements*, with the result that your choice of restaurants serving meals in the 50–68F (£5–7; $7.50–10.50) price range is much more restricted than elsewhere in the city centre. For the widest choice of restaurants serving inexpensive French food, the 5*ème arrondissement* (Le Quartier Latin) surpasses other districts, though restaurants along blvd St-Michel (Boul'Mich) are usually overpriced (as are the Greek and Turkish eateries scattered around the Latin Quarter). In contrast to many European cities, ethnic restaurants in Paris tend to be more expensive (and poorer value for money) than those offering the national cuisine. Partial exceptions to this rule are the kosher restaurants of the 3*ème* and 4*ème arrondissements* (Le Marais), and North African restaurants, of which there are particularly large concentrations in the 9*ème* and 10*ème arrondissements*. However, parts of these districts, and all of the 18*ème arrondissement* (Montmartre), are best avoided at night unless you are part of a group (even then it is advisable to stay clear of le Pigalle, Anvers and Barbès-Rochechouart metro stations).

University restaurants offer three-course meals for around 25F (£3; $4.50). For information contact CROUS at av. Georges-Bernanos 39, 5*ème* (tel. 40 51 37 10).

CHEAP EATERIES
Two-course meals under 50F (£6; $9)

La Dame Tartine, rue Bisemiche 2 (tel. 42 77 32 22). Métro: Rambuteau. Open daily, noon–11.30 p.m.

Chez Marianne, rue des Hôspitalières St-Gervais 2 (tel. 42 72 18 86). Métro: St-Paul. East European and Middle-Eastern dishes. Recommended dish: *pierogi* (stuffed cabbage leaves). Open Sat.–Thurs. 11 a.m.–midnight.

L'Apostrophe, rue de la Montagne Ste-Geneviève 34 (tel. 43 54 10 93). Métro: Maubert-Mutualité. Open Tues.–Sat. noon–2 p.m. and 7–10 p.m.

Orestias, rue Grégoire-de-Tours 4 (tel. 43 54 62 01). Métro: Odéon. Open Mon.–Sat. noon–2.30 p.m. and 6.30–11.30 p.m.

Kiotori, rue Monsieur le Prince 61 (tel. 43 54 48 44). Métro: Odéon or Luxembourg. Open Mon.–Sat. noon–2.30 p.m. and 7–11 p.m.

Sampieru Corsu, rue de l'Amiral Roussin 12. Métro: Cambronne. Open Mon.–Fri. noon–2 p.m. and 7–9.30 p.m.

Naturesto, av des Champs-Élysées (in the Galerie Point Show) (tel. 42 56 49 01). Métro: Franklin D. Roosevelt. Vegetarian restaurant. Open Mon.–Fri. noon–3 p.m.

Anarkali, pl. Gustave Toudouze 4 (tel. 48 78 11 48). Métro: St-Georges. Indian restaurant. Open Tues.–Sun. noon–2.30 p.m. and 7 p.m.–12.30 a.m. (closed Sun. in winter).

Occitanie, rue Oberkampf 96 (tel. 48 06 46 98). Métro: St-Maur. Specializes in dishes from the South of France. Open Mon.–Fri. noon–2 p.m. and 7–10.30 p.m.; Sat. 7–10.30 p.m. Closed mid-July–mid-Aug.

Au Trou Normand, rue Jean-Pierre Timbaud 9 (tel. 48 05 80 23).

Métro: Oberkampf. Open Mon.–Fri. noon–2.30 p.m. and 7.30–11 p.m.; Sat. 7.30–11 p.m. Closed Aug.

Two-course meals from 50–68F (£6–8; $9–12)

Au Petit Ramoneur, rue St-Denis 74 (tel. 42 36 39 24). Métro: Les Halles. Open Mon.–Sat. 11.30 a.m.–2.30 p.m. and 6.30–9.30 p.m.; Sun. 11.30 a.m.–2.30 p.m.

L'Incroyable, rue de Richelieu 26 (tel. 42 96 24 64). Métro: Palais-Royal. Open Feb.–late Dec. Tues.–Fri. 11.45 a.m.–2.15 p.m. and 6.30–9 p.m.; Sat. and Mon. 11.45 a.m.–2.15 p.m.

Au Clair de Lune, rue Tiquetonne 27 (tel. 42 33 59 10). Métro: Etienne-Marcel. French and Algerian dishes. Recommended dish: *couscous*. Recommended drinks: *Royal Smahab* and *Sidi Brabim* (two Algerian wines). Open daily, noon–3 p.m. and 7.30–11 p.m.

L'Arbre Aux Sabots, rue Simon Leclerc 3 (tel. 42 71 10 24). Métro: Rambuteau. Open Mon.–Fri. noon till midnight.

Perraudin, rue St-Jacques 157 (tel. 46 33 15 75). Métro: Luxembourg. Recommended dish: *Sauté d'agneau aux flageolets* (lamb with white beans). Open Tues.–Fri. noon–2.15 p.m. and 7.30–10.15 p.m.; Mon. and Sat. 7.30–10.15 p.m.

Café La Volcan, rue Thouin 10 (tel. 46 33 38 33). Métro: Cardinal Lemoine. Greek restaurant. Open daily noon–2 p.m. and 7–11.30 p.m.

Le Petit Vatel, rue Lobineau 5 (tel. 43 54 28 49). Métro: Odéon or Mabillon. Vegetarian options available. Open Mon.–Fri. noon–3 p.m. and 7 p.m.– midnight; Sat. noon–1 a.m.; Sun. 7 p.m.–midnight.

La Croque au Sel, rue St-Dominique 131 (tel. 47 05 23 53). Métro: Ecole Militaire. Open Mon.–Fri. noon–2 p.m. and 7–10.30 p.m.; Sat. 7–10.30 p.m.

L'Aubergade, rue La Boétie 122 (tel. 42 25 10 60). Métro: Franklin D. Roosevelt. Open Mon.–Fri. 10 a.m.–3 p.m. and 6–11 p.m.; Sat. 6–11 p.m.

Paris-Dakar, rue du Faubourg St-Martin 95 (tel. 42 08 16 64). Métro: Gare de l'Est. Senegalese restaurant. Open daily noon–4 p.m. and 7 p.m.–midnight.

Au Petit Keller, rue Keller 13 (tel. 47 00 12 97). Métro: Ledru-Rollin. Open Mon.–Fri. noon–2.30 p.m. and 7–11 p.m.

Au Rendez-Vous des Camionneurs, rue des Plantes 34 (tel. 45 40 43 36). Métro: Alésia. Open Mon.–Fri. 12.45–2.45 p.m. and 6–9.30 p.m.

Le Jerobam, rue Didot 72 (tel. 45 39 39 13). Métro: Alésia. Recom-

mended dish: *tarine de poisson aux olives et citron confit* (fish stew
with olives and lemon preserve). Open Tues.–Sat. noon–2 p.m.
and 7–10 p.m.; Mon. noon–2 p.m.

Aquarius Café, rue de Gergovie 40 (tel. 45 42 10 29). Métro: Pernety. Vegetarian restaurant. Open Mon.–Sat. noon–2.30 p.m.
and 7–10.30 p.m.

Two-course meals from 68–85F (£8–10; $12–15)

Les Arquebusiers, rue des Arquebusiers 12 (tel. 48 87 94 12).
Métro: Sebastian-Froissart. Open Tues.–Fri. 11 a.m.–3.30 p.m.
and 7 p.m.–1.30 a.m.; Sat. 7 p.m.–1.30 a.m.; Sun.–Mon.
11 a.m.–3.30 p.m.

La Cambeuse, rue Casimir Delavigne 8 (tel. 43 26 48 84). Métro:
Odéon. Recommended dishes: *soupe a l'oignon* (onion soup) and
coq au vin (chicken cooked in wine). Open Mon.–Sat.
noon–2 p.m. and 5–11 p.m.

Au Babylone, rue de Babylone 13 (tel. 45 48 72 73). Métro: Sèvres-
Babylone. Recommended dish: *gigot d'agneau* (lamb chop). Open
Mon.–Sat. 11.30 a.m.–2.30 p.m. and 7.30–11 p.m. Closed
Aug.

Le Berbère, rue de Gergovie 50 (tel. 45 42 10 29). Métro: Pernety.
Moroccan restaurant. Recommended dish: *couscous*. Open
Mon.–Sat. noon–2.30 p.m. and 7–10.30 p.m.

Two-course meals from 85–100F (£10–12; $15–18)

Lescure, rue de Mondovi 7 (tel. 42 60 18 91). Métro: Concorde.
Open Mon.–Fri. noon–2.15 p.m. and 7–10 p.m.; Sat.
noon–2.15 p.m. Closed Aug.

Chez Lena et Mimille, rue Tournefort 32 (tel. 47 07 72 47). Métro:
Censier Daubenton. Open Wed.–Mon. noon–2 p.m. and 7.30–
11 p.m.

Aux Délices de Széchuen, av. Duquesne 40 (junction with av. Bre-
teuil). Métro: St-François-Xavier. Chinese and French dishes.
Recommended dishes: *poulet sauté champignon noir* (chicken with
black mushrooms) and *salade de meduse* (jellyfish salad). Open
Tues.–Sun. noon–2.30 p.m. and 7 p.m.–10.30 p.m.

Dynastie Thai, rue La Boétie 101. Métro: St-Philippe du Roule. Thai
restaurant. Open daily noon–2.30 p.m. and 7–11.30 p.m.

À la Banane Ivoirienne, rue de la Forge-Royale 10 (tel. 43 70 49
90). Métro: Faidherbe-Chaligny. West African specialities. Open
Tues.–Sat. 7 p.m.–midnight.

SHOPPING
● Markets
Most *arrondissements* host at least one market a week. Those listed below are merely some of the most convenient. For a complete list ask the Tourist Office for a copy of *Les Marchés de Paris*.

rue Mouffetard (near the junction with blvd du Port-Royal), *5ème arrondissement*. Open daily 9 a.m.–1 p.m. and 4–7 p.m.

Marché Biologique. On the section of blvd Raspail between rue de Rennes and rue Cherche-Midi, *6ème arrondissement*. Lots of organic produce. Open Sun. 7 a.m.–1.30 p.m.

rue Clér, between av. de la Motte-Picquet and rue de Grenelle, *7ème arrondissement*. Open Tues.—Sat. early morning till early afternoon.

Marché Europe, rue Corvetto 1, *8ème arrondissement*. Covered market, open Mon.–Sat. 8 a.m.–1.30 p.m. and 4–7 p.m.; Sun. 8 a.m.–1 p.m.

Marché St-Quentin, blvd de Magenta 85/b, *10ème arrondissement*. Covered market, open Tues.–Sat. 8 a.m.–1 p.m. and 3.30–7.30 p.m.; Sun. 8 a.m.–1 p.m.

● Supermarkets
Outside of the main tourist area between Notre-Dame and the Arc de Triomphe you are seldom far away from a supermarket, so it is just a case of asking the locals precisely where the nearest supermarket is (Monoprix and Prisunic in particular have a multitude of branches). Even in the heart of tourist Paris there is a hypermarket in the Forum des Halles (*1er arrondissement*), and a Prisunic on the Champs-Élysées which stays open until midnight.

Reims

LOCAL SPECIALITIES

champagne	the famous sparkling wine
volaille au champagne	chicken cooked in champagne

SPECIAL EVENTS AND FESTIVALS
Many of the champagne houses offer tours of the *caves* where the drink is produced, usually ending with some samples aimed at enticing you to buy a bottle or two. Advance booking is often

required, and there is usually an admission fee (typically about 15–20F (£1.80–2.40; $2.70–3.60)). For full details on which houses offer tours contact the local Tourist Office. Some of the better tours are: Pommery, pl. Général Gourard 5 (tel. 26 61 62 55) which has the virtue of being free; Mumm, rue du Champ de Mars 14 (tel. 26 49 59 70), which is interesting and ends with a glass of Cordon Rouge; and Taittinger, pl. St-Niçaise 9 (tel. 26 85 45 35) and Veuve Clicquot-Ponsardin, pl. des Droits-de-l'Homme 1 (tel. 26 40 25 42), both of which offer excellent presentations with their tours.

CHEAP EATERIES
Two-course meals under 50F (£6; $9)

Le Gaulois, pl. Drouet d'Erlon 2–4 (tel. 26 47 35 76). Open daily 8 a.m.–3 a.m.
Le Fléchambault, esplanade Fléchambault 2 (tel. 26 85 47 11). Open Mon.–Sat. 7 a.m.–9 p.m.
L'Os et l'Arête, rue du Colonel Fabien 15 (tel. 26 04 63 12). Open Tues.–Fri. and Sun. noon–2 p.m. and 6.30–10.30 p.m.; Sat. 6.30–10.30 p.m.
Le Cardinal, pl. des Martyrs de la Resistance 1 (tel. 26 40 33 19). Open Mon.–Sat. 7.30 a.m.–9 p.m.

Two-course meals from 50–68F (£6–8; $9–12)

Le Flamm'steak, rue Libergier 17 (tel. 26 47 04 06). Open daily 11 a.m.–2 p.m. and 6.30–11 p.m.
New Mandarin, rue de Thillois 31 (tel. 26 47 63 37). Chinese restaurant. Open daily.
St-Nicolas, passage du Commerce 4 (at rue de Vesle 27) (tel. 26 47 76 06). Open daily 10 a.m.–midnight, except Friday evenings.
Le Palais du Mandarin, rue Chanzy 36 (tel. 26 88 68 25). Chinese and Thai dishes. Open Wed.–Mon.

Two-course meals from 68–85F (£8–10; $12–15)

La Lorraine, pl. Drouet d'Erlon 7 (tel. 26 47 32 73). Open daily.
Pizzeria Spago, pl. Drouet d'Erlon 56 (tel. 26 88 64 12). Pizza and other Italian dishes. Open daily.
Les Quatre Saisons, rue Eugène Desteuque 47 (tel. 26 88 32 38). Open Sat.–Thurs.
Les Brisants, rue de Chativesle 13 (tel. 26 40 60 41). Open Mon.—Fri. noon–2 p.m. and 7–10.30 p.m.; Sat. 7–11 p.m.
La Moulinière, rue Berlin 4 (tel. 26 88 64 19). Recommended dish:

moules aux champagne (mussels cooked in champagne). Open daily.

SHOPPING
● **Supermarket**
Monoprix, at the junction of rue de Vesle and rue de Tallyrand. Open Mon.–Sat. 8.30 a.m.–7.30 p.m.

Rouen

For the widest selection of cheap restaurants look around the pl. du Vieux-Marché and the surrounding streets. For information on university restaurants contact CROUS at rue d'Herbouville 3 (tel. 35 98 44 50).

LOCAL SPECIALITIES

canard au sang	pressed duck
terrine de canard à la rouennaise	duck paté
caneton	duckling
galettes	pancakes stuffed with vegetables, cheese or meat
sole Normande	sole with shrimps, mussels and mushrooms
tripe à la normandaise	tripe in a spicy sauce
cidre	apple cider
calvados	a potent apple liqueur
Camembert, Livarot, Neufchâtel, and *Pont l'Eveque*	cheeses

CHEAP EATERIES
Two-course meals for under 50F (£6; $9)

Napoléon, pl. Général-de-Gaulle 29 (tel. 35 70 46 93). Closed on Sunday Nov.–May.
Flunch, rue des Carmes 60 (tel. 35 71 81 81). Self-service restaurant. Open daily 11 a.m.–10 p.m.
Les Flanders, rue des Bons-Enfants 5. Open Mon.–Fri. noon–1.30 p.m. and 7.30–9.15 p.m.; Sat. noon–1.30 p.m.

Les Chrysanthèmes, rue St-Sever 72 (tel. 35 72 89 11). Closed Sun.
  and public holidays.
Natural Vital, rue du Petit Salut 3. Vegetarian restaurant. Open
  Mon.–Sat.

Two-course meals from 50–68F (£6–8; $9–12)

Pascaline, rue de la Poterne 5 (tel. 35 89 67 44). Open daily.
Le Florence, rue de Crosne 8 (tel. 35 07 61 60). Closed Sun.
Brasserie Paul, pl. de la Cathédrale 1 (tel. 35 71 86 07). Open daily.
Brasserie du Départ, rue Verte 25 (tel. 35 71 10 11). Closed Sun.

Two-course meals from 68–85F (£8–10; $12–15)

Le Marmite, rue de Florence 3 (tel. 33 71 75 55). Open Tues.–Sat.
  noon–2 p.m. and 7–10 p.m.; Sun. noon–2 p.m.
Le Vieux Logis, rue de Joyeuse 5 (tel. 35 71 55 30). Open daily.
Le P'tit Bec, rue Eau-de-Robec 182 (tel. 35 07 63 33). Closed Sun.
Byblos, rue de Fontenelle 60 (tel. 35 15 58 58). Closed Sun. and
  for two weeks in Aug.

SHOPPING
● **Market**
Pl. du Vieux Marché. Open Tues–Wed. and Fri.–Sun. 7 a.m.–
12.30 p.m.

● **Supermarkets**

Monoprix, rue du Gros Horloge 67. Open Mon.–Sat. 9 a.m.–7 p.m.
Marché, rue de Cercle. Open Mon.–Sat. 9 a.m.–12.30 p.m. and 3–
  7.30 p.m.

FURTHER INFORMATION
The *Herbergement Restaurants Loisirs* brochure, available free from
the Tourist Office, contains a guide to prices and days of opening
at a selection of city-centre restaurants.

Strasbourg

On average, local restaurant prices are higher than in the rest of
the country, but fortunately you can usually find better value meals

in one of the many *winstub* (wine bars) which are such a distinctive feature of Strasbourg compared to other major French cities. However, both restaurants and *winstub* located around the cathedral, or in La Petite France, tend to serve meals which are overpriced even by the inflated local standards.

For information on student restaurants contact CROUS at quai du Maire-Dietrich 1 (tel. 88 36 16 91).

LOCAL SPECIALITIES
Alsatian cooking has a distinctly Germanic flavour which you won't find anywhere else in France.

tarte à l'oignon and *tarte flambée*	onion tarts made with cream and bacon
choucroute	sauerkraut with sausages
baeckeoffe	a rich meat and potato casserole

You'll also find chicken and fish cooked in *Riesling*, the best known of the Alsatian wines. Local cheeses include *Munster* and *Emmenthal*, and fruit tarts and *Kirsch soufflé* are popular desserts. Also worth trying are *Kougelhopf* and *Birewecke*, rich fruit and almond breads.

Almost all the wines from this area are white, and in addition to *Riesling*, you'll find *Sylvaner*, the wonderful, tangy *Gewürztraminer* and *Pinot Blanc*. Due to the strong German influence, beer is more popular in Alsace than in France as a whole. In fact with two of the country's main breweries located in the city — Kronenbourg and Kanterbrau — Strasbourg can claim to be the brewing capital of France.

SPECIAL EVENTS AND FESTIVALS
The suburb of Schiltigheim hosts a week-long beer festival in mid-August. At any time of year you can visit the following breweries and sample their beer, provided you contact them in advance:

Kronenbourg, route d'Oberhausbergen 68 (tel. 88 27 41 59).
Heineken France, rue St-Charles 10, Schiltigheim (tel. 88 62 90 80).
Meteor, rue du Général Lebocq 6, Hochfelden (tel. 88 71 73 73).

CHEAP EATERIES
Two-course meals under 50F (£6; $9)

Flunch Self-Service, pl. Kléber 31 (tel. 88 22 39 22). Open daily.

Au Rendez-vous des Jardiniers, blvd de Lyon 28 (tel. 88 23 17 11). Closed Sun.

Marco Polo, Ponts Couverts 5 (tel. 88 36 26 81). Italian dishes. Open daily.

Two-course meals from 50–68F (£6–8; $9–12)

Winstub La Mouche, rue Finkwiller 43 (tel. 88 36 04 18). Recommended dish: *choucroute*. Closed Sun.

Pfifferbriader, pl. du Marché-aux-Cochons-de-lait (tel. 88 32 15 43). Recommended dish: *baeckeoffe*. Closed Sun. and during Aug.

Au Petit Pecheur, pl. du Corbeau 2–3 (tel. 88 36 11 49). Recommended dish: *tarte flambée* (served in the evening only). Closed Tues. evening and Wed.

Coucou des Bois, allée David Goldschmidt 44 (tel. 88 39 76 19). Recommended dish: *tarte flambée*. Open daily.

Europ'Snack, rue du Vieux-Marché-aux-Vins 48 (tel. 88 32 75 10). Closed Sun.

Léon de Bruxelles, quai des Bateliers 38 (tel. 88 24 20 24). Belgian specialities. Recommended dish: *moules frites* (mussels with chips). Closed Mon.

Two-course meals from 68–85F (£8–10; $12–15)

Bourse, pl. de Lattre-de-Tassigny 1 (tel. 88 36 40 53). Recommended dish: *baeckeoffe*. Closed Mon. and Tues. evenings.

Au Cerf d'Or, pl. de l'Hôpital 6 (tel. 88 36 20 05). Closed Wed. evening.

A l'Oiseau de France, rue de Faubourg National 1 (tel. 88 32 18 68). Recommended dishes: *choucroute* and *baeckeoffe*. Closed Sun. outside peak season.

SHOPPING
● **Markets**

Bd de la Marne. Open Tues. and Sat. mornings.
Pl. Broglie and Quai Turckheim. Open Wed. and Fri. mornings.
Rue de Zurich. Open Wed. morning.

● **Supermarkets**

Suma, rue du 22 Novembre 33 and rue des Grandes Arcades 47. Both open Mon.–Sat. 8.30 a.m.–8 p.m.

FURTHER INFORMATION
The brochure *Strasbourg Hôtels, Restaurants* available free from the Tourist Office contains a guide to the prices, opening hours and speciality dishes of a selection of local restaurants and *winstube*.

Toulouse

Rue Alsace-Lorraine, blvd de Strasbourg, pl. Victor Hugo, rue des Filatiers, rue St-Rome, and (especially) rue du Taur offer a good selection of inexpensive eateries. For information on student restaurants contact CROUS at rue des Salenques 7 (tel. 61 21 13 61).

LOCAL SPECIALITIES
Poultry plays a very important role in the regional cuisine.

paté de foie gras	made from fattened goose livers
cassoulet	goose, kidney beans and assorted vegetables and other meats
Roquefort	a strong cheese
violet	a liqueur prepared from violets (the flower is the symbol of the city)

CHEAP EATERIES
Two-course meals under 50F (£6; $9)

Le Chawarma, rue Bayard 26 (tel. 61 62 75 44). Vegetarian restaurant. Open daily noon till midnight.
Salade Gasconne, rue du Taur 75 (tel. 61 23 90 19). Open Mon.–Fri. noon–2 p.m. and 7.30–10 p.m.; Sat. noon–2 p.m. and 7.30 p.m.–midnight.
La Ripaille, rue Bayard 72 (tel. 61 62 98 47). Open daily noon–2.30 p.m. and 6.30–11 p.m.
La Tassée, rue du Taur 15 (tel. 61 21 63 35). Open daily 11.30 a.m.–3 p.m.
Flunch, allée Jean-Jaurès 28 (tel. 61 62 05 32). Self-service restaurant. Open daily 11 a.m.–11 p.m.

Two-course meals from 50–68F (£6–8; $9–12)

Auberge Louis XIII, rue Tripière 1/b. Open Mon.–Fri. noon–2 p.m. and 7–9.45 p.m. Closed Aug.

Au Coq Hardi, rue Jules-Chalande 6. Open Mon.–Sat. noon–2 p.m. and 7–10 p.m.

Place du May, rue du May 4. Open Mon.–Sat. noon–2 p.m. and 8–11 p.m.

Benjamin, rue des Gestes 7 (tel. 61 22 92 66). Open daily noon–2 p.m. and 8–11 p.m.

Two-course meals from 68–85F (£8–10; $12–15)

Les Caves de la Maréchal, rue Jules-Chalande 3 (tel. 61 23 89 88). Open Mon. 8–10.30 p.m.; Tues.–Sat. noon–2 p.m. and 8–10.30 p.m.

Bistro des Vins, pl. St-Etienne (tel. 61 25 20 41). Open Tues.–Sat. noon–2 p.m. and 8–11 p.m.

L'Ecluse, pl. Victor Hugo 8–10 (tel. 61 29 89 00). Open daily, noon till midnight.

SHOPPING
● **Markets**

Rue Victor Hugo and pl. des Carmes. Open Tues.–Sun. mornings.
Blvd de Strasbourg. Open daily 9 a.m.–1 p.m.

● **Supermarkets**

Monoprix, rue Alsace-Lorraine 39. Open Mon.–Sat. 8.30 a.m.– 8 p.m.

Nouvelles Galeries, rue Lapeyrouse 6. Open Mon.–Sat. 8.30 a.m.– 7.30 p.m.

FURTHER INFORMATION
The *Hôtels Restaurants* brochure available free from the Tourist Office lists a selection of local restaurants, complete with a guide to opening times, and how much you can expect to pay for a meal.

GERMANY

If you like German food you cannot really go wrong in the west of the country where well-prepared meals are almost guaranteed, along with efficient and pleasant service (thankfully free of the forced niceness you can find elsewhere). While the same cannot be assured in the east of the country, the quality of both food and service is rising fast: in fact the food is usually fine, though the quality of service at present can be poor compared to the west of the country (but not in comparison to some other West European countries).

The main options for eating out are ordinary restaurants or a variety of establishments (*Gastätte, Gasthof, Gasthaus, Wirtschaft* and *Brauhaus*) which are a combination of eating and drinking place, and particularly fine venues to do either. The thrust of the cooking in the latter group of establishments is towards the sort of meals you would find in a typical German home, with prices slightly lower than you would find in a restaurant, and servings even larger than the generous amounts on offer in a restaurant. As a rule you can expect to pay about DM13–20 (£5.20–8.00; $7.80–12.00) for a two-course meal in the cheaper of the above eateries in the west; about 20–25% less in the east: excellent value for what you receive. It is always worth looking out for special fixed-menu offers as these can be even better value for money (as an example, many of Munich's eateries offer three-course lunches for DM13–16 (£5.20–6.40; $7.80–9.60)). One good option for cooked meals widely available in the west of the country are department store restaurants (such as those in the Karstadt, Kaufhof and Hertie chains) where a basic two-course meal usually costs about DM10–12 (£4.00–4.80; $6.00–7.20).

German cuisine is sometimes said to lack a great choice of soups (*suppe*), but at least there is quite a diversity amongst the national favourites. Fairly basic soups include *Erbsensuppe* (pea), *Linsensuppe* (lentil), *Hühnersuppe* (chicken) and *Ochsenschwanzensuppe* (oxtail), to which can be added two clear soups that are real German specialities – *Leberknödelsuppe* and *Fleischsuppe* (containing small dumplings made from liver and meat respectively). Other popular soups such as *Bohnensuppe* (bean), *Zwiebelsuppe* (onion) and *Gulaschsuppe* (goulash soup) are German copies of, or variants on, foreign dishes.

Starters tend to fall into one of four basic categories: paté; cold meat dishes; items served on bread (like chives or smoked salmon); or salads (*salat*) such as *Gruner Salat* (mixed greens) or *Gurkensalat* (cucumber). Outside these categories comes the sweet and sour combination *Melone mit Schinken* (melon and ham).

Beef (*Rindfleisch*), pork (*Schweinefleisch*), lamb (*Lamm*), sausage (*Wurst*), chicken (*Huhn/Hähnchen*) and game dishes all feature regularly on restaurant menus, but those based on pork are by far the most common. Pork (and less commonly veal) is used to prepare the variety of *schnitzels* (cutlets) which are such a famous part of German cuisine. The most common is the *Wiener Schnitzel* (escalope cooked in breadcrumbs), but you will also see the likes of *Zigeunerschnitzel* (cooked in paprika sauce) and the *Jägerschnitzel* (cooked with wine and mushrooms) regularly. The same is true of two other pork-based favourites: *Schweinebraten* (roast pork) and *Schweinehaxe* (knuckle of pork). Pork dishes tend to be cheaper than the less common beef variety. Virtually every region has its own way of preparing *Sauerbraten* (pickled and braised beef); another speciality worth watching out for is *Rouladen* (beef stuffed with bacon, onions, gherkins and various herbs). All over Germany you will find a wide range of sausages, but most regions have their own favourite: with the exception of Franconia, *Weisswurst* (veal or pork sausage with herbs) is the most popular in Bavaria, whereas Thuringia is associated first and foremost with the grilled *Thüringer Bratwurst*. Chicken dishes are relatively inexpensive, but game dishes can be pricey.

There are several main course accompaniments which are typically German. *Sauerkraut* (pickled green cabbage) is something most people would associate with Germany, but less well-known is *Apfelrotkohl* (red cabbage with apple). *Knödel* (small dumplings made from flour and potato) are very popular, especially in the south of the country, whilst *Spätzle* (noodles) and *Maultaschen* (similar to ravioli) are traditional Swabian accompaniments increasingly found elsewhere in the country.

Along the coastline you are often spoilt for choice as regards seafish, with the likes of *Aal* (eel), *Hering/Matjes* (herring), *Makrele* (mackerel) and *Scholle* (plaice) readily available, in addition to more unusual offerings such as *Rotbarsch* (rosefish). Away from the coast, freshwater fish – especially *Forelle* (trout) – are much more likely to feature on restaurant menus than saltwater fish. However, in the east you can get good quality seafish dishes in most towns at one of the *Gastmahl des Meeres* chain of restaurants.

How well vegetarians fare depends most of all upon which part of the country they are travelling in. Although German cuisine is heavily meat-orientated, vegetarians can get by in the west. In the east, however, they are likely to struggle. The west has an established vegetarian movement and vegetarian restaurants in all the

main towns, and the concept of vegetarianism is widely understood. The latter is particularly important, for even though ordinary
restaurants tend not to offer much that is suitable for vegetarians
it does mean that requests for a vegetarian omelette or crêpe will
get you a dish without small flecks or chunks of meat in it. The
situation in the east is vastly different. Not only is there no
vegetarian movement worth speaking of (and consequently no
specifically vegetarian restaurants), but the idea of vegetarianism
is simply not recognized, and so even where restaurant staff are
keen to please, unless you speak excellent German you may still
be disappointed by the food you receive. Even standbys such as
pizzas and pasta dishes that are widely available in the Italian restaurants of the west are not an option in the east for the simple
reason that there are (as yet) few Italian restaurants in that part of
the country.

Eis (ice cream), fresh and stewed fruits, and cheeses are the mainstays of the desserts section on most menus. The *Käseplatte* (platter
of different cheeses) is a good option if you want to sample a range
of German cheeses. Although you may find the likes of *Apfelstrudel
mit Sahne* (apple strudel with cream) or the Bavarian *Dampfnudeln*
(dumpling with vanilla sauce) on menus, if you are looking for
cakes (*kuchen*), gâteau (*torte*) or pastries (*geback*), then you would
probably do better to skip dessert and indulge yourself later in a
bakery or café.

Snacks can be bought from street vendors (*Imbiss*), or from a
variety of shops: meat-based snacks such as sausages or Munich's
Leberkase (a kind of meat loaf) from butchers' shops; pizzas or
kebabs from Italian or Turkish eateries (both rare in the east);
spit-roasted chicken from butchers' shops or from specialist outlets
like *Kochlöffel*; fish-based snacks from the Nordsee chain of shops.

Shopping is simple in Germany, as even in small towns you can
always find a supermarket as well as a host of little specialist shops.
The food halls (*lebensmittel*) within department stores such as
Kaufhof offer superb quality, whilst in the west of the country
names such as Kaiser's, Coop, Tengelmann and Kaufhalle are all
guaranteed to have good quality food, as are the less commonly
seen Mini-Mal, Rewe and Spar. The latter two have, however,
made great inroads in the east, so much so that at the time of
writing these are the two supermarket chains you are most likely
to see in that part of the country. There are also a number of reliable
names which operate locally rather than nationally such as Kupsch
around Würzburg and Nanz around Heidelberg. The west has several discount supermarket chains, such as Aldi, Norma and Penny
Markt. These can be very cheap, but you will not find much in the

way of brand names or fresh produce (none of these three keep fresh milk for example), and it is worth noting that Aldi has been much criticized for the quality of its food, especially meat and fish products. Plus, part of the group that owns Kaiser's and Tengelmann, is also billed as a discount supermarket, but you will find much more in the way of brand names in these stores. Prices are, on the whole, slightly cheaper than in the UK, though fresh fruit and vegetables are usually a good deal less expensive. Normal shopping hours are Mon.–Fri. 8 or 9 a.m.–6 p.m., Sat. 8 or 9 a.m.– 2 p.m. Most big towns also have markets at least once a week, and in some cases the larger cities have a daily indoor market held in the local *Markthalle* (ask for details at the local Tourist Office).

More than any other country in the world Germany is associated with beer (*Bier*). Statistics alone say much about the German love affair with beer: Germany has around 40% of the world's breweries (c.1,500), and more breweries than the rest of the European Community combined; Dortmund and Munich are the second and third largest brewing centres in the world; and Munich and Stuttgart are home to the two largest beer festivals in the world. There is a tremendous diversity of beers brewed in the country: pale *Hell/ Helles*; *Pils*; dark (*Dunkel*) beers; the strong *Bock* beers; beers brewed using wheat (*Weisse/Weizen*); the *Kolsch* that is a speciality of Cologne; and the *Alt* beers popular mainly around the Ruhr (Dusseldorf in particular). The vast majority of these beers (no matter what their colour) are brewed using the same bottom-fermentation process used to produce British lager (hard to believe); a technique pioneered by German brewers in Pilsen in 1842 (exceptions to this are *Kolsch* and all *Alt* and wheat beers). Whatever the brewing style, in accordance with a purity law established as long ago as 1516 in Bavaria and subsequently adopted throughout the rest of the country, no chemical substitutes are used in the brewing process. Beer is not expensive to buy in a bar – typically about DM3,00–3,50 (£1.20–1.40; $1.90–2.10) for a half-litre, and carry-outs are very cheap at only DM1,00–1,50 (£0.40–0.60; $0.60–0.90) for a half-litre bottle of all but the most expensive beers (not including deposit).

Germany is one of only a few countries where both high-quality beer and high-quality wine (*Wein*) is produced. German wines are predominantly whites as climatic conditions rule out the widespread production of reds, but *Spätburgunder* is a very palatable red worth looking out for. Much of the country's production comes from the area roughly bounded by Mannheim, Saarbrucken, Trier, Koblenz and Frankfurt-am-Main, which includes the Mosel-Saar-Ruhr, Rheingau, Nahe, Rheinpfalz and Rhein-Hessen regions.

Other important regions in the west of the country are Baden-Wurttemberg and Franconia. There are relatively few vineyards in the east of the country, though there are some fine wines produced around Meissen. Wine is quite cheap to buy with a bottle of table wine (*Tafelwein*) costing as little as DM4 (£1.60; $2.40) in a shop; a quality wine (*Qualitätswein*) may cost anything from DM8 (£3.20; $4.80).

A variation on wine found in and around Frankfurt-am-Main is *apfelwein* (apple wine – known locally as *ebbelwei/ebbelwoi*), a regional speciality in which apples are substituted for grapes in the wine-making process to produce a drink like cider.

Popular German spirits include rum (often drunk warm as *Grog*), the rye-based *Korn*, and a range of spirits distilled from fruits, the most famous of which is the cherry-based *Kirsch*. In addition to these there is also a good choice of smoother, sweeter fruit-based liqueurs.

Coffee (*Kaffee*) generally comes in one of three forms (*espresso*, *cappuccino* or *mocca*), though you may also be offered Turkish-style coffee if you are dining in a Turkish restaurant. Request *Kaffee mit milch* if you would like your coffee white. Tea (*Tee*) is increasingly popular in Germany, as are *Zitronentee* (lemon tea) and *Kräutertee/Pflanzentee* (herbal tea). Another German favourite at any time of the day is drinking chocolate (*Trinkschokolade*).

Berlin

LOCAL SPECIALITIES

Berliner Weisse	a beer brewed from wheat
Berliner Weisse mit Schuss	the above with added fruit syrup

There are a number of other Berlin beers, including Berliner Pilsner, Schultheiss, Berliner Kindl and Bürgerbräu.

CHEAP EATERIES

Berlin offers far more restaurants where you can get a couple of courses for under DM15 (£6; $9) than anywhere else in the country. The quality of food available in the capital is too often dismissed, but it is fair to say that if you want to sample some of the various ethnic cuisines to be found in Germany then Berlin is an excellent place to do so. This is especially true of the Turkish,

Greek and Italian restaurants which have long been a feature of
the west of the city.
Two-course meals under DM15 (£6; $9)

Mensa der Freie Universität. In the university complex at Hab-
elschwerdter Allee 45. DM4 (£1.60; $2.40) for two courses.
Student ID is sometimes requested. Open Mon.–Fri. 11.15 a.m.–
2.30 p.m.

Mensa TU, Hardenbergerstraße 34. Similar in price to the mensa
above. Open Mon.–Fri. 11.15 a.m.–2.30 p.m.

Die Rote Harfe, Oranienstraße 13. German cuisine. Recommended
dishes: *Allgauer Kasespätzle* (cheese noodles) and *Schweizer Schnitzel* (breaded pork cutlet), although choosing the latter dish will
take you into the DM15–20 price category.

Tegernseer Tönnchen, Mommsenstraße 34. Bavarian specialities.
Recommended dish: *Zigeunerschnitzel* (pork chop in a spicy
sauce), but this costs DM15 alone. Good value three-course fixed
menus from DM11–18 (£4.60–7.50; $6.90–11.25).

Zur Rippe, Poststraße 17. German cuisine. Recommended drink:
Berliner Weisse mit Rippenshose, a cocktail that is the house speciality.

Schwarzes Café, Kantstraße 148 (tel. 313 8038). Closed Tues.
3 a.m.–Wed. 11 a.m., otherwise open round-the-clock.

Beth Café, Tucholskystraße 40 (tel. 281 3135). Kosher restaurant.
Open Sun.–Thurs. 1–10 p.m. (closes at 8 p.m. on Mon.). Closed
Fri. and Sat.

Tiergartenquelle, Stadtbahnbogen 482 (tel. 392 7615). German cuisine. Open 6 p.m.–midnight.

Mediencafé Strada, Potsdamerstraße 131 (tel. 215 9381). Open
Mon.–Thurs. 8.30 a.m.–2 a.m.; Fri. 8.30 a.m.–3 a.m.; weekends
10 a.m.–2 a.m.

Ashoka, Grolmanstraße 51. Indian food. Plenty of vegetarian
options. Open daily 11 a.m.–midnight.

Einhorn, Wittenbergplatz 5 and Mommsenstraße 2. Two fine vegetarian restaurants, but you have to stand whilst eating. Open
until 6 p.m. daily.

Schnecken und Knoblauch, Oranienstraße 47 (tel. 614 6816). German, Italian, Arabic, seafood and vegetarian dishes.

Der Ägypter, Kantstraße 26. Egyptian cuisine, plus a good choice
of vegetarian dishes.

Two-course meals from DM15–20 (£6–8; $9–12)

La Maskera, Koburgstraße 5. Vegetarian cooking with an Italian
influence. Open daily 5 p.m.–1 a.m.

Zur Letzten Instanz, Waisenstraße 14 (tel. 242 5548). German cuisine. Open Mon.–Sat. noon–1 a.m.; Sun. noon till midnight.

Café Savigny, Grolmanstraße 51 (tel. 312 8195). Open daily 10 a.m.–2 a.m.

Atlantik-Küche, Bergmannstraße 112. Plenty of vegetarian options. Open daily 10 a.m.–2 a.m.

Osteria No. 1, Kreuzbergstraße 71 (tel. 786 9162). Italian cuisine. Best reserved ahead.

Som Tropical, Kaiser-Friedrich-Straße 40. South American dishes.

Two-course meals from DM20–30 (£8–12; $12–18)

Cour Carré, Savignyplatz 5. French cuisine. Open noon–2 a.m.

Bistro am Wittenbergplatz, Wittenbergplatz. Open Mon.–Sat. 9 a.m.–1 a.m., Sun. 10 a.m.–midnight.

Florian, Grolmanstraße 52. Serves the German equivalent of French nouvelle cuisine.

SHOPPING
● **Supermarkets**

Aldi, near Berlin Zoo train station, in the shopping complex at the junction of Hardenbergstraße and Joachimstaler Straße.

Ullrich, under the rail tracks on Hardenbergstraße.

Bilka, a short distance further along Joachimstaler Straße from Aldi.

Kaufhof des Westens (KaDeWe), the famous department store on Wittenbergplatz, with an excellent supermarket on the sixth floor.

Kaufhof, on Alexanderplatz.

Kaiser's, near Friedrichstraße train station.

Mitropa Reisemarkt, in the Friedrichstraße train station. Open Mon.–Sat. 6 a.m.–10 p.m., Sun. 8 a.m.–10 p.m.

Cologne

LOCAL SPECIALITIES

Halver Hahn	rye bread roll with Dutch cheese
Kölsch caviar	smoked black pudding served with raw onion and a roll
Himmel und Äd	mashed potatoes and apples, served with black pudding

Kölsch   a top fermented beer, brewed by some
twenty-four different local breweries

CHEAP EATERIES

There is a profusion of restaurants and cafés in the streets just back from the Rhine between the Hohenzollernbrücke and Deutzer Brücke, with the area around the Fischmarkt being the best for relatively inexpensive meals.

Two-course meals for under DM15 (£6; $9)

Universität Mensa (in the university complex of Zülpicherstraße). Open daily year round 11.30 a.m.–2 p.m. and 5.30–7.30 p.m.
Rendezvous, Zülpicherstraße. Pizzas and pasta dishes. Open Sun.–Thurs. 8 a.m.–1 a.m.; Sat. 8 a.m.–3 a.m.
Alt Köln, Trankgasse 7–9.
Brauhaus Sion, Unter Taschenmacher 5.
Früh am Dom, Am Hof 12–14.
Zur Malzmühle, Heumarkt 6.
Vanille, Zülpicherstraße 25 (tel. 21 87 79). Open Mon.–Sat. 10 a.m.–1 a.m., Sun. 11 a.m.–1 a.m.

Two-course meals from DM15–20 (£6–8; $9–12)

Peppermint, Hohenstaufenring 23 (tel. 240 1929). Open daily 7.30 p.m.–2 a.m.

SHOPPING
● **Supermarkets**
Aldi, Plus and Rewe all have stores on Eigelstein, a five-minute walk from the rear exit of the main train station.

● **Market**
Fresh farm produce is sold Mon.–Sat. on Wilhelmsplatz in the northern suburb of Nippes (only really convenient if you are staying in that area).

Dresden

LOCAL SPECIALITIES
Feldschlossen and Felsenqueller beers.

CHEAP EATERIES
As a rule you will get better value for money in the restaurants of the Neustadt.
Two-course meals under DM15 (£6; $9)

Neue Mensa, Bergstraße 47 (tel. 463 6495). Open mid-Oct.–Feb. and Apr.–June.
Restaurant Am Zwinger, Wilhofstraße 24. Part of a complex comprising a number of different eateries. Open Mon.–Sat. 7 a.m.–7 p.m.
Bierbar Am Thor, Hauptstraße 35 (tel. 51372). Open daily noon–2 a.m.
Tagesbar Der Löwe, Hauptstraße 48 (tel. 51138) Open Mon.–Sat. 10 a.m.–midnight, Sun. noon–midnight.
Restaurant 7 Schwaben, An der Augustusbrücke. Open daily 10 a.m.–midnight.
Haus Altmarkt, Altmarkt. Another complex with a choice of eateries.
Gaststätte am Gewandhaus, Am Gewandhaus. A no-smoking restaurant.
Mandarin, Gewandhausstraße 5 (tel. 496 3193). Chinese restaurant with cheap lunches. In the price category below for evening dining. Open daily 11.30 a.m.–2.30 p.m. and 5.30–11.30 p.m.
Dynamo Gastätte, Lennestraße (near the Rudolf-Harbig Stadion). Open Mon.–Sat. 11 a.m.–1 a.m.

Two-course meals from DM15–20 (£6–8; $9–12)

Szeged, Wilhofstraße 4. Hungarian specialities.
Äberlausitzer Töppl, Hauptstraße 14. Specializes in dishes from the region of Upper Lusatia.

Two-course meals from DM20–30 (£8–12; $12–18)

Kügegenhaus, Hauptstraße 13. Recommended dishes: any chicken dish. Open daily 11 a.m.–midnight.

SHOPPING
● **Market**
There is an open-air market just down from the Altmarkt in the direction of the Tourist Office. Open Mon.–Fri. 8 a.m.–5 p.m., Sat. 8 a.m.–2 p.m.

● **Supermarkets**

Spar, in the Feinkosthaus, on Prager Straße near the Tourist Office.
Karstadt, on the left hand side as you walk from the Tourist Office
  towards the Altmarkt.
Mitropa Markt, in Dresden Hauptbahnhof, open 6 a.m.–10 p.m.
  daily.

Frankfurt-am-Main

LOCAL SPECIALITIES

Rippchen mit Kraut	smoked pork with *Sauerkraut*
Handkäse mit Musik	cheese with onions and a vinaigrette
Ebbelwoi/ebbelwei	apple wine

Beers brewed by the Binding and Henninger breweries.

CHEAP EATERIES
It is possible to find reasonably cheap meals in the city centre, but
there is no obvious concentration of cheap restaurants here, so it
is very much a case of simply seeing what is on offer at individual
establishments. However, prices are slightly higher than average in
the centre of town, so you might do better by heading over the
river to the taverns of Sachsenhausen if you want traditional German fare, or out to Bockenheim if you would prefer ethnic cuisine
(Greek and Italian restaurants predominate).
Two-course meals under DM15 (£6; $9)

Universität Mensa, Bockenheimer Landstraße 120. Officially only
  open to those with a student ID issued in Hesse, but the rule is
  not always enforced.
Tomate, Fressgasse 6–8 (tel. 29 31 74). Italian cuisine. Open daily
  11.30 a.m.–1 a.m.
Club Voltaire, Hochstraße 5 (tel. 29 24 08). Open Sun.–Thurs.
  6 p.m.–1 a.m., Fri. – Sat. until 2 a.m.
Wolkenbruch, Textorstraße 26 (tel. 66 26 12). Vegetarian restaurant. No smoking. Open daily 6–11 p.m.

Two-course meals from DM15–20 (£6–8; $9–12)

Eichkatzerl, Dreieichstraße 29. Open Tues.–Sun. 3 p.m.–midnight.

Green Hill, Gutzkowstraße 43 (tel. 62 63 01). Vegetarian restaurant. Open Tues.–Sun. 6 p.m.–1 a.m., but cold dishes only after 11.50 p.m.

Aubergine, Alte Gasse 14. The DM20 lunch time menu is very good value given the quality of the food. It is much more expensive to eat here in the evening. Open until 11 p.m.

Atschel, Wallstraße 7 (tel. 61 92 01). Recommended dishes: *Handkäse mit Musik* and *Rippchen mit Kraut*. Open daily 5.30 p.m.– 1 a.m.

Two-course meals from DM20–30 (£8–12; $12–18)

Die Leiter, Kaiserhofstraße 11 (tel. 28 99 77). Open daily noon–1 a.m.

SHOPPING
There is a Kaufhof supermarket on Zeil.

Hamburg

LOCAL SPECIALITIES

Aalsuppe	eel soup
Labskaus	typically pickled corned beef, herring, mashed potato, onions, gherkins, and beetroot baked together and served with a fried egg on top

Holsten Pils is brewed in Hamburg.

CHEAP EATERIES
Near the main train station Kirchenallee has some of the cheapest restaurants in the city centre. Inexpensive restaurants in the Neustadt cluster around the Grossneumarkt. Down by the St Pauli Landungsbrücken the fish restaurants vary greatly in price from the reasonable to the very expensive.
Two-course meals under DM15 (£6; $9)

University Mensa, Schlüterstraße 7. Lunch available Mon.–Fri. for as little as DM6 (£2.50; $3.75). Student ID required.

Gröninger Braukeller, Ost-West-Straße 47 (tel. 33 13 81). Open Mon.–Fri. 11 a.m.–midnight, Sat. 5 p.m.–midnight.

Sagres, Vorsetzen 42. Portuguese cuisine. Recommended dish: swordfish (*espadarte*).

Noodles & Mehr, Schanzenstraße 2–4 (tel. 439 2840). Open Mon.–Thurs. 11 a.m.–1 a.m.; Sat. 5 p.m.–1 a.m.; Sun. 11 a.m.–11 p.m.

Piceno, Hein-Hoyer-Straße 8 (tel. 31 04 77). Italian restaurant. Recommended dish: *macaroni arabiata* (macaroni served in a spicy tomato sauce with basil and peppers).

Two-course meals from DM15–20 (£6–8; $9–12)

Fischerhaus, St-Pauli-Fischmarkt 14 (tel. 31 40 53). Specializes in fresh fish dishes. Open daily 11 a.m.–11 p.m.

But'n Dammdoor, Mittelweg 27.

Vegetarische Gastätte & Café, Alsterkaden 11a and Neuerwall 13 (tel. 34 47 03). Vegetarian restaurant. Open Mon.–Fri. 11.30 a.m.–7.30 p.m., Sat. 11.30 a.m.–5 p.m., Sun. noon–5 p.m.

The Old Spaghetti House, Gänsemarkt-Passage (off Poststraße). Mainly pasta dishes and salads.

Golden Oase, Eppendorferbaum 34. Vegan restaurant. Open Mon.–Sat. noon–10 p.m.; Sun. 10 a.m.–6 p.m.

Two-course meals from DM20–30 (£8–12; $12–18)

Alt Hamburger Aalspeicher, Deichstraße 43 (tel. 36 29 90). Recommended dishes: Aalsuppe and any of the fish dishes. Open daily noon till midnight.

SHOPPING
● **Market**

There is a market below the subway rails on Isestraße (Tues. and Fri. 9 a.m.–2 p.m.).

● **Supermarkets**

Horten, on Mönckebergstraße by the main train station

Kaufhof, on Mönckebergstraße, near Horten

Karstadt, ten minutes' walk along Mönckebergstraße from the train station

Hertie, on Jungfernsteig

Hanover

LOCAL SPECIALITIES
Beers brewed by the Herrenhauser and Lindener Gilde breweries.

CHEAP EATERIES
Two-course meals under DM15 (£6; $9)

Hannen-Fass, Knochenhauerstraße (junction with Schuhstraße).
Kröpcke, Kröpcke.
Irodian, Grosse Packhofstraße. Open Mon.–Thurs. 10.30 a.m.–midnight, Fri.–Sat. 10.30 a.m.–1.30 a.m.
Brauhaus Ernst August, Schmiedestraße 13.
Mandarin-Pavillion, Marktstraße 45. Chinese restaurant. The lunch time fixed menus are in the price category quoted above; eating à la carte will take you into the grade below.
Mövenpick, Georgstraße 35.
Hoa Binh, An der Strangreide. Vietnamese cuisine, with a good choice of vegetarian dishes.
Restaurant Marché, Galerie Luise, Luisenstraße 5. Self-service cafeteria. Open daily 11 a.m.–10 p.m.
Altstadt Café, Kramerstraße 4 (tel. 32 03 77). Pizzas and pasta dishes. Open daily from 11 a.m.

Two-course meals from DM15–20 (£6–8; $9–12)

Altdeutsche Bierstube, Lärchenstraße 4.
Bavarium, Windmuhlstraße 10. Recommended dish: *Wienerschnitzel* (pork cutlet). Open daily 11 a.m.–11 p.m.
da Claudio, Andreasstraße 2a. Italian cuisine. Open Mon.–Sat. 10 a.m.–midnight, Sun. 11 a.m.–midnight.
Klatschmohn, Lange Laube 20. Vegetarian restaurant.

SHOPPING
The market is held at the Markthalle on Karmarschstraße. There is a CO-OP supermarket at the end of the Pasarelle.

Heidelberg

LOCAL SPECIALITIES
Beers brewed by the Heidelberger Schlossquell brewery.

CHEAP EATERIES

Restaurants along Hauptstraße tend to be overpriced compared to those elsewhere in the city, even just a few blocks away. The best value city-centre meals are generally found in the student cafés and bars on the streets running off, or parallel to Hauptstraße.

Two-course meals under DM15 (£6; $9)

Universität Mensa, Marstall, Marstallstraße. Student ID usually required.

Abel's Café and Weinstube, Hauptstraße 133 (looks onto Universitätplatz) (tel. 21431). Open daily 10 a.m.–11 p.m. (Sat. until 1 a.m.).

Higher Taste, Kornmarkt 9. Vegetarian restaurant. Open daily 10.45 a.m.–6.30 p.m.

Roter Ochsen, Hauptstraße 217 (tel. 20977). Open Mon.–Sat. 5 p.m.–midnight.

Zum Sepp'l, Hauptstraße 213 (tel. 23085). Open daily 11 a.m.–midnight.

Sudpfanne, Hauptstraße 223 (tel. 23543). Open Mon.–Fri. 4 p.m.–midnight, weekends 11.30 a.m.–midnight.

Schlossquell Braustübl, Bergheimerstraße 91 (tel. 24036).

Two-course meals from DM15–20 (£6–8; $9–12)

Goldener Hecht, Steingasse 2, Am Brückentor (tel. 26984).

Wirsthaus Zum Spreisel, Neckarstaaden 66 (Hotel Hollandischer Hof). Open Sun.–Thurs. 5 p.m.–midnight; Fri.–Sat. 2 p.m.–midnight.

SHOPPING
● Markets

Rathausplatz, open Wed. and Sat. 7 a.m.–1 p.m.
Friedrich-Ebert-Platz, open Tues. and Fri. 7 a.m.–1 p.m.
Wilhelmplatz, open Mon. and Thurs. 7 a.m.–1 p.m.
Tiefburg, open Sat. 7 a.m.–1 p.m.

● Supermarkets

Nanz, at Hauptstraße numbers 17, 116 and 198.
Kaufhof, at Hauptstraße 24.
Horten, at Bergheimerstraße 1.
HL, at Bahnhofstraße 9 and Kurfursten-Anlage 4.

Leipzig

CHEAP EATERIES
Two-course meals under DM15 (£6; $9)

Universität Leipzig Mensa, off Universitätstraße. Meals around DM6 (£2.50; $3.75).
Buffet Am Hallischen Tor, Am Hallischen Tor. Self-service cafeteria, open Mon.–Fri. 7.30 a.m.–7 p.m., Sat. 8 a.m.–7 p.m.
Thüringer Hof, Burgstraße 19.
Gastmahl des Meeres, Dr-Kurt-Fischer-Straße 1. Fish and seafood dishes.
Burgkeller, Naschmarkt 1–3 (tel. 28 50 32/29 56 39).
Ostasiatisches Restaurant, Große Fleischergasse 4. Mainly Vietnamese cuisine, but with other East Asian dishes on the menu.
Kubanische Speisebar Varadero, Barfußgäßchen 8. Cuban cuisine.
Bistro Am Brühl, Am Brühl 10–12 (tel. 28 73 09). Good range of meat-free pasta dishes and salads. Open daily 11 a.m.–10 p.m.
Antiquäten Café Galerie 'Kleinod', Käthe-Kollwitz-Straße 71. Serves light meals based on soups and salads. Open daily 2– 10 p.m.
Restaurant Nudelmacher, Peterstraße. Open Mon.–Wed. and Fri.–Sat. 9 a.m.–8 p.m.; Thurs. 9 a.m.–9 p.m.; Sun. 11 a.m.– 8 p.m.

SHOPPING
There is an open-air market on Sachsenplatz (Mon.–Sat.), and a Tengelmann supermarket just off Sachsenplatz on Am Brühl.

Munich

Finding a cheap meal is relatively simple in Munich as there is no shortage of places offering two courses for under DM15. Some of the very best deals are to be found within a 5–10 minute walk of the main thoroughfare leading from the Karlstor to Marienplatz. It's best to dine out at lunchtime because many establishments offer three-course fixed menus in the DM10–15 (£4–6; $6–9) range. Amongst the many ethnic restaurants the Italian establishments tend to offer the best value for money. One cheap eating option not immediately apparent is the chain of Vincenz Murr

butchers' shops in the city which offer both snacks and more substantial fare (it would be unusual to find a butcher's shop not selling
leberkäse).

LOCAL SPECIALITIES

Leberkäse   a type of meatloaf made with beef and ham and
served in slices
Schweinebraten roast pork

Beers brewed by the Löwenbräu, Hofbräu, Paulaner, Augustiner,
Spaten and Hacker-Pschorr breweries.

SPECIAL EVENTS AND FESTIVALS
Munich is famous for its beer festivals: 'Starkbierzeit' is a festival period starting a few weeks after Ash Wednesday for which
special strong beers are produced; the 'Maibock-Anstich' takes
place in May and is another period for which special strong
beers are brewed; 'Oktoberfest' is the largest beer festival in the
world, held over a two-week period in late September and early
October.

CHEAP EATERIES
Two-course meals for under DM15 (£6; $9)

University Mensas at five locations: Arcisstraße 17; Leopoldstraße
13–15; in the main university building on Schellingstraße; at
Dachauer Straße 98b; and on the Helene-Mayer-Ring.
Gaststätte Engelsburg, Türkenstraße (junction with Schellings-
traße). Bavarian cuisine and a range of salads. Recommended
dishes: *Nürnberger Rostbratwürstl* and *Weisswürste* (two types of
sausage). Open daily 9.30 a.m.–1 a.m.
Lehrer Lämpl, Amalienstraße 81. Some vegetarian options. Open
Mon.–Fri. 10 a.m.–1 a.m., Sat. 6 p.m.–1 a.m.
Türkenhof, Türkenstraße 78. Recommended dish: *Käsespätzle*
(cheese noodles). Open daily 11 a.m.–1 a.m.
Bürgerheim, Bergmannstraße 33 (tel. 50 51 53). Bavarian cuisine.
Open daily 9 a.m.–midnight.
Atzinger, Schellingstraße 98. Very good lunchtime fixed menus.
Spatenhofkeller, Neuhauserstraße 26.
Augustinerbrau, Neuhauserstraße 16. Open daily 10.30 a.m.–
midnight.
Löwenbräukeller, Nymphenburger Straße 2. Open daily 9.30 a.m.–
1 a.m.

Mango, Rosental 3–4. Self-service vegetarian eatery. Open Mon.–Fri. 11 a.m.–7 p.m. (Thurs. until 9 p.m.), Sat. 11 a.m.– 4 p.m.

Café Oase, Amalienstraße 89. Open Mon.–Fri. 8.30 a.m.–1 a.m., weekends 9.30 a.m.–1 a.m.

Metternich, Lindwurmstraße 21. Open daily 7 a.m.–10 p.m.

Two-course meals from DM15–20 (£6–8; $9–12)

Obermaier, Truderingerstraße 306 (tel. 42 49 43). Recommended dishes: any of the *schnitzels* (veal or pork cutlets). Open Tues. 3 p.m.–midnight, otherwise daily 9 a.m.–midnight.

Beim Sendlymayr, Westenriedstraße 6. Bavarian cuisine. Open daily 11 a.m.–11 p.m.

Prinz Myshkin, Hackenstraße 2 (tel. 26 55 96). Vegetarian restaurant. Mostly Mediterranean-style cuisine, but also some Chinese- and Japanese-style dishes. Open daily 11 a.m.– 11 p.m.

Weisses Bräuhaus (Schneider), Im Tal 10. Bavarian cuisine. Recommended dish: *Schweinebraten* (roast pork). Open 9 a.m.– midnight.

Zum Bögner, Im Tal 72. Bavarian cooking. Open daily 9 a.m.– midnight.

Two-course meals from DM20–30 (£8–12; $12–18)

Vierjahreszeiten, Sebastianplatz 9 (tel. 260 9578). Vegetarian restaurant. Open Mon.–Fri. 5–11 p.m., weekends 11.30 a.m.– 11 p.m.

Werneckhof, Werneckstraße 11. French cuisine.

Zadar Grill, Theresienstraße 54. Balkan specialities.

SHOPPING
For an excellent market, visit the Viktualienmarkt just off Marienplatz and open Mon.–Fri. 6 a.m.–6.30 p.m., Sat. 6 a.m.– 12 p.m.

● Supermarkets

Tengelmann, on Schützenstraße, near the main train station.

Kaufhalle, on Neuhauserstraße, near the Karlstor Kaufhof, just off Marienplatz on Kaufingerstraße.

FURTHER INFORMATION
The *Young People's Guide to Munich*, available from the local Tourist Office, includes a selection of local eateries which are particularly popular with young locals, as well as a host of other useful information.

Potsdam

LOCAL SPECIALITIES
Rex Pils, brewed by the local Potsdam Brauerei.

CHEAP EATERIES
The greatest concentration of restaurants is to be found along Brandenburgerstraße.
Two-course meals under DM15 (£6; $9)

Gastmahl des Meeres, Brandenburgerstraße 72. Fish and seafood dishes. Open Mon.–Fri. 10 a.m.–8 p.m., weekends 11 a.m.–3 p.m.
Restaurant am Stadttor (Speisebar), Brandenburgerstraße (close to the Brandenburg Gate). The *Speisebar* is upstairs; the restaurant downstairs is more expensive. *Speisebar* open daily 11 a.m.– 9 p.m., except the second Monday of the month.

Two-course meals from DM15–20 (£6–8; $9–12)

Altes Jagdschloß, Am Jagdschloß Stern. Traditional Brandenburg dishes. Closed Thurs.
Börse, Brandenburgerstraße 36. German and East European cooking. Open Mon.–Fri. 7 a.m.–9 p.m. Last orders taken at 8 p.m.
Gaststätte Charlottenhof, Geschwitzer-Schollstraße. Open Mon.–Fri. 13.30–11 p.m., weekends 10 a.m.–11 p.m.

Two-course meals from DM20–30 (£8–12; $12–18)

Strandterrassen, Kleines Schloß, Park Babelsberg (tel. 75156). Open Wed.–Sun. noon–9 p.m.
Minsk-Nationalitätengastätte, Max-Planck-Straße 10, am Brauhausberg (tel. 23490). Byelorussian-style cooking.

SHOPPING
There is a Spar supermarket on Friedrich-Ebert-Straße, near the Hollandische Viertel.

Stuttgart

LOCAL SPECIALITIES

Gaisburger Marsch	beef, potato and *Spätzle* stew
Spätzle	chunky, fried noodles
Maultaschen	small pieces of pasta filled with meat and spinach

Beers produced by Stuttgarter Hofbräu, Dinkel Acker, Schwaben Bräu and Plochinger Waldhornbräu.

SPECIAL EVENTS AND FESTIVALS

The 'Cannstatter Volksfest' (last week of September and first week of October) is the second largest beer festival in the world.

Wine festivals include the 'Stuttgarter Weindorf' (last Friday in August to the first Sunday in September) and the 'Fellbacher Herbst' (second week of October).

CHEAP EATERIES

There is a glut of restaurants offering relatively inexpensive Swabian, German or ethnic cuisine in the city centre as a whole, but especially along Eberhardstraße.

Two-course meals under DM15 (£6; $9)

Universität Mensa, Holzgartenstraße 9–11. Meals for around DM6 (£2.50; $3.75). Student ID required. At the entrance you must get a Mensa credit card and leave a deposit of DM20.

Iden, Eberhardstraße 1 (tel. 23 59 89). Vegetarian cafeteria. Open Mon.–Fri. 11 a.m.–8 p.m. (Thurs. until 9 p.m.); Sat. 10 a.m.–4 p.m.

Block House, Eberhardstraße 10 (tel. 236 9420). Open 3 p.m.–12.30 a.m.

Weinstube Der Besen, Rosenstraße 38 (tel. 23 32 65). Good choice of Swabian dishes. Open Mon.–Fri. 3.30 p.m.–12.30 a.m., weekends 5 p.m.–12.30 a.m.

Litfass, Eberhardstraße 37 (tel. 24 30 31). Turkish and Swabian cuisine. Open daily 11.30 a.m.–5 a.m.

Weinhaus Stetter, Rosenstraße 32 (tel. 24 01 63). Wide range of Swabian specialities, and an exceptional choice of wines. Recommended dish: *Maultaschen*. Open Mon.–Fri. 3–11 p.m., weekends 10 a.m.–2 p.m.

Stuttgarter Lokalbrauerei, Calwer Straße 31 (tel. 226 1104/1244).
German and Swabian dishes, and the establishment's own beer
brewed on the premises.
Greiner-Stuben, Arnulf-Klett-Platz 1 (tel. 29 51 21). A complex of
five restaurants and cafés. The Bräustüble and the vegetarian
Greiner's Natürkuche serve meals in the DM15 price category.

Two-course meals from DM15–20 (£6–8; $9–12)

Backerschmeide, Scurwaldstraße 42. Recommended dish: *Gais-
burger Marsch.*
Klösterle, Marktstraße 71. In Bad Cannstatt.

SHOPPING
There are markets held on Marktplatz (Schillerplatz), Feuerseeplatz
and the Marktplatz in Bad Cannstatt every Tues., Thurs. and Sat.
Open from 7 a.m.–12.30 p.m.

● **Supermarkets**

Kaufhof, at Königstraße 6.
Kaufhalle, at Königstraße 23.
ALDI, in the passageway at Marienstraße 11.
Plus, on Marienstraße, a short distance uphill from ALDI.

Weimar

LOCAL SPECIALITIES

Thüringer Bratwurst	the famous Thuringian sausage, widely available from street sellers, from butchers' shops, and in restaurants
Weimarer Pils	the local beer

CHEAP EATERIES
Two-course meals under DM15 (£6; $9)

Hochschule für Architektur und Bauwesen, Marienstrasse. Mensa,
cafeteria and restaurant open daily 11 a.m.–11 p.m.
Gastmahl des Meeres, Herderplatz (tel. 4521/4721). Fish and sea-

food dishes. Open Mon.–Fri. 11 a.m.–10 p.m., weekends 11 a.m.–3 p.m.

Weimarhalle, Karl-Liebknecht-Straße 3 (tel. 2341). Open daily 9 a.m.–11 p.m.

Scharfe Ecke, Eisfeld 2 (tel. 2430). Recommended dish: *schnitzel* (pork cutlet). Open Mon.–Fri. 5 p.m.–1 a.m., weekends 11 a.m.–1 a.m.

Scenario, Carl-August-Allee 15 (tel. 41 96 40). Pizzas and salads. Open daily for meals 11 a.m.–11 p.m.

Two-course meals from DM15–20 (£6–8; $9–12)

Alt-Weïmar, Prellerstraße 3 (tel. 2056). Open Tues.–Sun. 5 p.m.–midnight.

Elephantenkeller, Markt 19 (under the Hotel Elephant).

Two-course meals from DM20–30 (£8–12; $12–18)

Zum Weissen Schwan, Frauenplan (tel. 61715). Open daily noon–11 p.m. (Fri. and Sat. until midnight).

SHOPPING
Visit the market on the Marktplatz, Mon.–Fri. (early morning–5 p.m.), and occasionally on Saturday mornings.

● Supermarkets

REWEkonsum Markt am Theater, by the theatre.

OKAY, in a courtyard at Frauenplan 8.

Schnellkauf, on Carl-August-Allee, a short walk from the train station.

Markt im Bahnhof, in the train station. Open Mon.–Fri. 6 a.m.–8 p.m., weekends 8 a.m.–8 p.m.

Würzburg

LOCAL SPECIALITIES

Blaue zipfel	sausages cooked in a sour sauce, with bread and onion rings
Meefischli	fried small fish from the Main

| *Würzburger*
Hofbräu | the local beer |
| *Würzburger Stein* | the Franconian wine produced on the
outskirts of the city (see **Further**
Information below) |

SPECIAL EVENTS AND FESTIVALS
The region is home to several wine festivals: 'Würzburger Wein-dorf' (end of May/beginning of June); 'Burgerspital Weinfest' (late June/early July); 'Hofgarten-Weinfest' (late June/early July); and the 'Winzerfest' (September).

A beer festival takes place biannually in April (the next one will be in 1995).

CHEAP EATERIES
Two-course meals under DM15 (£6; $9)

Universität Mensa, Studentenhaus, Friedrich-Ebert-Ring (junction with Münzstraße). Officially open only to local students, though the rule is not always enforced. Meals around DM4 (£1.60; $2.40). Open mid-Oct.–mid-July Mon.–Thurs. 11 a.m.–2 p.m. and 5.30–7.30 p.m.; Fri. 11 a.m.–2 p.m.; Sat. 11.30 a.m.–2 p.m.
Metzgermeister Grill, Kaiserstraße 12. Cheap grilled dishes. No seats. Open Mon.–Sat. 10 a.m.–6 p.m.
Restaurant Karthäuser, Ludwigstraße 1 (tel. 54723). Specializes in roast chicken dishes and pizzas. Open daily 11.30 a.m.–1 a.m.
Crêperie Le Clochard, Neubaustraße 20 (tel. 12907). Specializes in crêpes, but also offers a good selection of vegetarian dishes.

Two-course meals from DM15–20 (£6–8; $9–12)

Bürgerspital Weinstuben, Theaterstraße 19 (tel. 13861). Franconian dishes and wines. Open Wed.–Mon. 9 a.m.–midnight.
Juliusspital Weinstuben, Juliuspromenade 19 (tel. 54080). Franconian dishes and wines. Open Tues.–Sun., 10 a.m.–midnight.
Wirtshaus Zum Lämmle, Marienplatz 5 (Markt) (tel. 54748). Specializes in pork dishes and Franconian regional cuisine. Open Mon.–Sat. 9 a.m.–1 a.m.

Two-course meals from DM20–30 (£8–12; $12–18)

Gasthof Russ, Wolfhartsgasse 1 (tel. 59129). Franconian and vegetarian dishes. Open daily 11 a.m.–3 p.m. and 5 p.m.–midnight.

'Mal was Anderes', Bahnhofstraße 22 (tel. 51171). Vegetarian restaurant. No smoking. Open Wed.–Mon. 11 a.m.–11 p.m.

Restaurant Würzburg (Hotel Strauss), Juliuspromenade 5 (tel. 30570). Franconian and German cuisine. Open Wed.–Mon. 7 a.m.–midnight.

SHOPPING
The market is open Mon.–Sat. on the Markt.

● Supermarkets

Kupsch, on Kaiserstraße and Domstraße
Kaufhof, just off the Markt on Schönbornstraße

FURTHER INFORMATION
Anyone particularly interested in wine should ask the local Tourist Office for a copy of the informative pamphlet *Franconia and Wine*.

GREECE

Eating out is no big deal in Greece; there's none of the ritual attached to eating here that you'll find in France or Italy. Restaurants are often basic to the point of being downright scruffy — yet often the best food is found in places like this. In fact you may well be charged extra for tablecloths and napkins in some places! This all helps to keep the prices low, and while things are more expensive than they used to be, the average price of a full meal with wine is still only around 2500dr (£6.75; $10). Do remember to keep a tab on what you're spending though, as chances are you won't be able to make head or tail of your bill (*to logariasmó*). If the establishment doesn't have a written menu (which is fairly common), ask the price before you order anything. Try to steer clear of English menus as they tend to indicate inflated tourist prices. A service charge is always included in the bill, but it's polite to leave your small change.

An *estiatorio* is perhaps the most upmarket of the Greek restaurants, serving Greek and often international cuisine. The Greek food is likely to consist of casseroles, which you order by going into the kitchen and pointing at what you want. A taverna is generally family owned and may be very simple (although some are quite sophisticated these days). The smartness of the establishment isn't necessarily a guide to the quality of the food, and if you see a run-down taverna that is well patronized by the local people do investigate as the meals may be great. Specialist tavernas also exist: *psarotavérnes* specialize in fish and tend to be pricey, while *psistariés* sell meat and poultry roasted on spits. The price of your order here is determined by the weight. Ethnic eateries are few and far between in Greece and, unlike in most other countries, they tend to be the most expensive option of all.

Breakfast is generally just a cup of coffee, although you can get bread (*psomí*), with jam (*marmeládha*) or butter with honey (*méli me voútiro*) and yoghurt at a café cum pâtisserie (*zaharoplastío*) or dairy bar (*galaktopolío*). For the rest of the day, eat late like the locals. Lunch, a large meal, is eaten between 2–3 p.m. and dinner between 9–11 p.m.

The image of Greek cuisine tends to be all *moussaká*, salad and olive oil (*horís ládhi*), but while these are certainly common, you'll be glad to discover that there's a lot more on offer than that. One feature of a Greek meal is that all the dishes you've ordered are likely to arrive together, so you can share the food between you in the traditional way. Try a selection of starters such as *tzatzíki* (a yoghurt, cucumber and garlic dip), *taramosalata* (a creamy dip of cod's roe, olive oil, lemon and garlic), *kolokithakia* (fried courgettes), *melitzanosaláta* (aubergine dip) or *saganáki* (fried cheese), and for the more adventurous *okhtapódhi* (boiled octopus) or *kalamária* (squid). Soups to look out for include *avgolemono* (egg and lemon), *faki* (lentil) and *fasolada* (bean and tomato).

Meat (*kréas*), particularly lamb (*arní*), features in a wide variety of traditional dishes. Casseroles to look for include: *moussaká* (made with minced meat, aubergines and tomato and bechamel sauces); *yiouvétsi* (lamb casserole with pasta and tomatoes); *stifado* (veal stew with onions); *yemistá* (tomatoes, courgettes or peppers stuffed with minced meat or rice); *pastitsio* (mince, macaroni and tomato pie); and *keftedhes marinati* (meatballs in sauce). By the way, don't expect a piping hot casserole — it's more likely to be lukewarm, as food is traditionally left to stand for several hours before being eaten. Meat may also be served roasted, grilled, or in kebabs. *Katsíki* is roast kid, *païdhákia*, lamb cutlets and *dolmadakia* are vine leaves stuffed with rice and minced meat. *Souvláki* (shish kebabs) are widely available from street stalls as well as tavernas.

You'd expect fish (*psaria*) to be a real bargain in Greece, particularly on the islands, but in fact it tends to be extremely expensive. Varieties such as *barbounia* (red mullet), *sardelles* (sardines), *glóssa* (sole) and *xifias* (swordfish) are available and may be grilled and served with olive oil and a lemon dressing. Cuttlefish (*soupiés*) is also popular and is served in a variety of ways: *soupiés me spanáki* (with spinach), *soupiés piláfi* (with rice), or *soupiés yiahní* (in a wine and tomato juice sauce).

Vegetarians won't have a huge choice of dishes available, but there are a few suitable Greek specialities to try. *Briám me patátes ke kolokithákia* is a potato and courgette bake, *fasolia*, oven-baked beans, and *melitzanes sto fourno* (oven-baked aubergines). *Gigantes* (butter beans) and *barnies* (okra) may also be cooked in a tomato sauce. For snacks from street stalls or as a starter, order *spanakópitta* (spinach pie) and *tyrópitta* (cheese pie). *Horiátiki* is the ubiquitous *Greek salad*, which consists of tomatoes, cucumber, olives, cabbage or lettuce, and crumbly, salty *feta* cheese.

Greek yoghurt (*yiaóurti*) is thick, creamy and delicious and there are many more cheeses available than *feta*. Look for *kasséri* (creamy and mild, similar to Cheddar), *kefalotiri* (hard cheese, usually grated like parmesan), *graviéra* (similar to Gruyere), and *manouri* and *mizithra* (soft, unsalted white cheeses).

Desserts (*glyka*) aren't an important part of a Greek meal, and are most likely to be served in tourist joints, but you will find plenty of delicious fruit (*frouta*), as well as yoghurt and sometimes ice cream (*pagoto*). Yellow peaches from Veria and Noussa are good, as are water melons (*karpoúzi*), grapes (*fistíkia*) and melon (*pepóni*). Pastries tend to be extremely sweet and sticky, and are often made with honey: *baklavá* is a wicked confection of layers of filo pastry, chopped almonds and spices all drenched in syrup. Other desserts you may come across are: *halva* (baked sweet semolina); *rizogalo* (rice pudding); *loukoumadhes* (puffs of batter with honey and cinnamon), and *galaktoboúreko* (a sweet custard pie). All of these can be bought at a *zaharoplastío*.

Greek wines can be very good, particularly those from the North like *Boutari*, *Tsantali* and *Cambas*, which are all bottled varieties. The famous local wine is *Retsina*, which is available straight from the barrel or in bottles. It is made by adding quantities of pine resin to wine during fermentation, giving the wine a distinctive flavour that has to grow on you. Non-resinated wines are becoming increasingly popular. They can be sweet (*ghlikó*), semi-sweet (*imighlikó*), or sparkling. A glass of wine should cost around 400–500dr (£1.10–1.35; $1.60–2.00). Beer (*bira*) is usually available as imported lager, but Greek brands like *Hellas* are worth trying for a change.

The traditional aperitif is *oúzo*, a clear, aniseed-based spirit which you mix with water until it turns cloudy. Take it easy though, this is potent stuff. The Greeks generally eat *mezédhes* with their *oúzo*: bite-sized pieces of cheese, tomato, olives and even octopus. You can buy *oúzo* in coffee houses or *kafenía* (which are generally all-male preserves), in bars or *oúzerí*, which specialize in *oúzo* and *mezédhes*. After dinner try a glass of *Metaxa* brandy or the Greeks' favourite drink, coffee (*kafés*). This is similar to Turkish coffee and is served from a brass pot called a *briki*. It comes either *varis ghlykos* (strong and sweet), *métrios* (medium strength with a little sugar), *skétos* (without sugar), or *ghlykós vrastos* (very sweet). If you prefer instant coffee you should ask for Nescafé, or try a cool *kafés frappé* (an iced instant coffee). A cup of coffee will cost around 150–350dr (£0.40–1.00; $0.60–1.50), with the Greek variety being the cheapest.

There are plenty of open-air markets and small shops in Greece where you can buy fresh fruit, vegetables, bread and cheese. Look for the signs *pantopolio* (grocer), *artopiio* (baker) and *oporopolio* (greengrocer). A loaf of bread will cost around 100–200dr (£0.25–0.50; $0.40–0.75). Supermarkets are less common and chains are generally only found in Athens. The best-known names are Vassilopoulos, Marinopoulos, Skiavenitis, Metro and Tresco. Shopping hours tend to be somewhat erratic: roughly speaking shops are open from 9 a.m.–2 p.m. on Mon., Wed. and Sat., and between

9 a.m.–1.30 p.m. and 5.30–8.30 p.m. on Tues., Thurs. and Fri. Don't forget the *souvláki* (shish kebab) stalls or *yíros* (doner kebabs) either, but do take as much care as you can about what you're eating – tummy bugs are all too common for tourists. Drink bottled water and use it to wash any fruit and veg you may buy.

Athens

As you might expect, Athens has plenty of cheap restaurants and tavernas, as well as a number of ethnic outlets which can offer a change from Greek food, though these tend to be pricey. Unusually for Greece, it also has a couple of exclusively vegetarian restaurants. The Pláka is the best known area of Athens for eateries, but it can get overcrowded. If you're willing to make a short journey for your meals, go instead to Exárhia, Pangráti or Méts, where you'll find more authentic cuisine, fewer crowds and better prices.

CHEAP EATERIES
Two-course meals under 1850dr (£5; $7.50)

Taverna Bairaktaris, Platia Monastiraki 2 (tel. 321 3036). Open daily 7 a.m.–2 a.m.

Eden, Lissiou 12 (junction with Minissikleous) (tel. 324 8858). Vegetarian restaurant. Recommended dishes: *moussaká* and *lasagne* (both made with tofu). Open daily, noon until midnight.

Taverna Platanos, Diogenous 4 (tel. 322 0666). Open Mon.–Sat. 12.20–4.30 p.m. and 8 p.m.–midnight.

O Kostis, Kydathineon 18 (tel. 322 9636). Recommended dishes: *moussaká* and *keftedes*. Open daily noon–1 a.m.

Taverna Theophilos, Vakhou 1 (tel. 322 3901). Recommended dish: *giouvetsi* (veal with rice). Open Tues.–Sat. 8 p.m.–1 a.m.

Gardhenia, Zíni 31. Open Mon.–Fri. noon–10 p.m.; weekends noon–6 p.m.

Tsekouras, Tripodon 3. Recommended dish: *souvláki* (shish kebab). Open Thurs.–Tues. 7 p.m.–midnight.

Syntrivani, Filellinon 5 (tel. 322 4502 / 325 3226). Open 8.30 a.m.–11.30 p.m.

Taverna Kostoyiannis, Zaimi 37 (tel. 822 0624). Open Mon.–Sat. 7 p.m.–2 a.m.

Caravitis, Pafsaniou 4. Open daily 8.30 a.m.–2 a.m.

Taverna Strofi, Rovertou Galli 25 (tel. 921 4130). Open Mon.–Sat., evenings only.

Two-course meals from 1850–2600dr (£5–7; $7.50–10.50)

Menesis, Márkou Moussoúrou 3, Mets (tel. 922 7684). Open Mon.–Sat. evenings only.
To Xani, Adrianou 138. Open daily Feb.–Nov. evenings only.
Possidon, Kapnikareas 35 (tel. 322 3822). Recommended dish: *oktopódhi* (octopus).
Taverna Piccolino, Sotiros 26 (junction with Kidatheneon) (tel. 324 5592). Greek and Italian dishes.
Golden Flower, Nikis 30 (tel. 323 0113). Chinese/Korean dishes. Open Mon.–Sat. noon–4 p.m. and 7 p.m.–midnight; Sun. 7 p.m.–midnight.
Taverna Poulakis, Panos 6 (tel. 321 3222). Open daily noon–midnight. Typical taverna.
Corfu, Kriezotou 6 (tel. 361 3011). Open Mon.–Fri. noon–midnight, and Sat. noon–5 p.m. Well-established restaurant, serving traditional Greek food.
Fruitopia, Soultani 12, Exhárhia. Open evenings only, closed during Aug. Vegetarian restaurant.
Rodia Taverna, Aristipou 44 (tel. 722 9883). Open Mon.–Sat. until 2 a.m.

Two-course meals from 2650–3700dr (£7–10; $10.50–15.00)

Al Convento, Anapíron Polémou 4–6 (tel. 723 9163). Open daily. Italian restaurant.
Prunier, Ipsilándou 63 (tel. 722 7379). Open daily. French restaurant.
Taverna Xinos, Angelou Geronta 4 (tel. 322 1065).
Café Aeridies, Markou Avriliou 3 (tel. 322 6266).
Michiko, Kidatheneon 27 (tel. 322 0980). Japanese restaurant. Open daily 12.30–2.30 p.m. and 6.30 p.m.–midnight.

SHOPPING
The food hall of the Minion Department Store, 28 Oktovriou Street, is open from 9 a.m.–5 p.m. on Mon. and Wed.; 10 a.m.–7 p.m. on Tues., Thurs. and Fri.; and 8.30 a.m.–3.30 p.m. on Saturday.

● Markets
There are several open-air markets in Athens where you can get fruit and vegetables. The largest is in the centre of the city, on Athinas Street near Omonia Square. It's open Mon. and Wed. 9 a.m.–4.30 p.m.; Tues. 9 a.m.–6 p.m.; Thurs. 9.30 a.m.–6.30 p.m.; Fri. 9.30 a.m.–7 p.m.; and Sat. 8.30 a.m.– 4.30 p.m.

● **Supermarkets**

Mapinopoylos on Kanari Street
A. B. Vasilopoulos on Stadioy Street

Corfu Town

Tourist ghettos are hard to avoid in Corfu. You'll see a plethora of places selling fish and chips or shepherd's pie. Avoid these and make for traditional tavernas, where you'll be able to try Greek and Corfiot specialities.

LOCAL SPECIALITIES
Island dishes to look out for include:

sofrito	veal in a white wine and herb sauce, served with rice or fried potatoes
pastitsada	beef in a spicy tomato sauce, served with macaroni
bourdetto	fish stewed in tomato sauce, seasoned with paprika
bianco	fish stewed with potatoes, herbs, black pepper and lemon juice

Other specialities feature charcoal grills of lamb, beef or fish, sprinkled with oregano. You can also get *mandolato nougat* and *kumquat* liqueur.

CHEAP EATERIES
Two-course meals under 1850dr (£5; $7.50)

To Nautikon, N. Theotaki 150 (tel. 30009). Recommended dish: *moussáka*. Open daily Apr.–Oct. noon–midnight.
Restaurant Aegli, Spianada (tel. 31949).
Pizza Pete, Arseniou 19 (tel. 22301). Open daily Apr.–Oct. 10 a.m.–midnight. Pizzas predominate, but there are usually a few vegetarian options amongst the other dishes.
Rex, Kapodistriou (tel. 39649). Traditional Greek eaterie.
Yisdhakis, Solomóu 20. Open daily. Authentic Greek restaurant.
Hrissi Kardhia, Sevastianoú 44. Open daily 10 a.m.–4 p.m., 7 p.m.–midnight.
Orestis, Stratiyoú 78. (tel. 35664). Open daily. Specializes in seafood.

Café Corner, Agias Sofias 10 (tel. 26457). Café serving organic vegan dishes.

Two-course meals from 1850–2600dr (£5–7; $7.50–10.50)

Argo, Ethnikis Antistassis, New Port (tel. 24398/22593). Open 5 p.m.–1 a.m. Seafood restaurant.
Ciao, Vlahernon 46, Ethnikou Stadiou (tel. 26462). Italian food.
To Phanari, Mandouki Square. Meat and fish charcoal grills, also veggie options.
Averof, Prosalendou 18 (tel. 31468). Open daily. Traditional Greek cuisine.

SHOPPING

To make up your own picnic go to the open-air market, off G. Markora near the New Fortress. It is open from 7 a.m.–2 p.m. but try to get there early. For fresh fish, head for the specialist market off N. Theotaki. For British style sandwiches, salads and cakes, try Breadwinners, 51 Gilford (tel. 43832), open Mon.–Sat. from 8 a.m.–3 p.m.

● Supermarkets

Spilias, Solomou 13 (open Tues., Thurs. and Fri. 8 a.m.–1.30 p.m. and 5.30–8.30 p.m.; Mon., Wed. and Sat. 8.30 a.m.–1.45 p.m.).
Koskinas, Platia Sanrocco (open Mon.–Fri. 8 a.m.–2 p.m.).
Markato, Sanrocco Sq. (open 8 a.m.–8 p.m.).
Dhmhtra, Sanrocco Sq. (open 8 a.m.–8 p.m.).

If you're out of town look for the ENA chain, which has two outlets on the island:

National Road Lefkimmi 26, near the airport.
National Road Paleokastritsa, at Kontokali.

Shops on the island are generally open between 8.30 a.m.–1.30 p.m. and 5.30–9 p.m. on Tues., Thurs. and Fri.; and from 8.30 a.m.–2 p.m. on Mon., Wed. and Sat.

Crete

Crete is a large touristy island and the chance of finding good food at low prices varies considerably. Heraklion (Iráklion), for example, is the main port, yet restaurants, particularly good ones, are thin on the ground there. Eleftherías and Venizélou, its main squares, are generally over-priced and you'd do better to go a few streets away to F. Theodosáki, which is tatty, but contains traditional tavernas offering much better value for money. Réthimnon has a better choice, with eateries clustered around the old harbour, by the Rimóndi fountain and along Titos Petickakis St.

Haniá has plenty of restaurants close to its harbour, although they aren't much to shout about. The cheapest outlets, along with fast-food stands, can be found around Hálidhon and on Kondiláki.

Áyios Nikólaos, a real tourist trap on the north coast of the island, has plenty of restaurants, but few of them offer the cheap food that you can expect in other parts of Greece. Most eateries are around the harbour, with some cheaper outlets along Koundoúrou.

LOCAL SPECIALITIES

Dishes that you may wish to try in Crete include *kaltzounia* (sweet tarts), *staka* (fried cheese), seafood (cuttlefish and sea urchins), and for the strong of stomach: stewed goat.

SHOPPING

The best way to put together a picnic is from the local markets, small bakeries and street stalls.

Crete – Áyios Nikólaos

CHEAP EATERIES

Two-course meals under 1850dr (£5; $7.50)

Chinese Take Away, Koundarou. Cheap Chinese food.
Ciao-Ciao Pizza, 25th Martiou 4. Open noon–3 a.m.
Haris, east side of the waterfront. Open noon–3 a.m.

Two-course meals from 1850–2600dr (£5–7; $7.50–10.50)

Actaion. By the bridge. Fish dishes.

Crete – Haniá

CHEAP EATERIES
Two-course meals for under 1850dr (£5; $7.50)

Tamam, Zabeliou 59 (tel. 96080).
Pafsilipon, Sifaka 19. Traditional taverna. Veggie dishes available.
Hippopotamus Pizzeria, Sarpidóna. Serves pizza and pasta dishes.
Vasilis, Platía Sindriváni.
Karnagio, Platía Kateháki 8 (tel. 53366).
Dinos. By the harbour. Recommended dish: any seafood dish.

SHOPPING
For *souvláki* stalls and other snacks Hálidhon, 1866, and Tzanakaki offer good choices. On Dhaskaloyiánnis you'll find Singanaki, a traditional bakery.

Crete – Heraklion

CHEAP EATERIES
Two-course meals under 1850dr (£5; $7.50)

Ta Psaria. At the foot of 25th Augustou. Recommended dish: *kalamari* (squid). Open 10 a.m.–midnight.
Taverna Rizes, Hándakos. Open 6 p.m.–midnight.
Pizzeria Napoli, Eleftherías Square. Open 10 a.m.–midnight.
Taverna Giovanni. Close to Dedhálou. Italian restaurant.

SHOPPING
The open-air market is on Odhós 1866, by Venizelou Sq. It's open Mon.–Sat. from 8 a.m.–8.30 p.m. and has cheeses and sweets, as well as fruit, vegetables and meat. You'll also find *souvláki* stalls on Avgoústou, near El Greco Park.

Crete – Réthimnon

CHEAP EATERIES
Two-course meals under 1850dr (£5; $7.50)

Restaurant Apostolaki, Kalinois Siganou 10 (tel. 24401). Recommended dish: *moussáka*.
Alana's, Salaminos 11 (tel. 27737). Recommended dish: *souvláki* (shish kebab).
O Zefyros, on the Venetian harbour. Open 10–2 a.m. Seafood restaurant.
Vangela, by the Rimóndi fountain. Traditional taverna.
Stelios Soumbasakis, Nikiforou Foka 98. Traditional taverna.
Orthonas Taverna, Titos Petickakis.
Agrimi, Platía Petiháki, near the Rimóndi fountain.

SHOPPING
There are open-air markets during the week, between Moátsou and Koundouriotou, and on E. Andistásis, as well as plenty of *souvláki* stands dotted around the town. I Gaspari, Mesolongiou, is a good bakery where you can stock up on bread, cakes and pies.

Thessalonika

SPECIAL EVENTS AND FESTIVALS
If you enjoy local festivals and are in this area during the summer, you may wish to take a trip to Halkidiki for the 'Sardine Festival' which takes place in the first few days in July, or to Poligira for the 'Profitis Ilias Festival', which runs on 19 and 20 July, and where local delicacies in the form of meats and pastas are available.

CHEAP EATERIES
Two-course meals under 1850dr (£5; $8)

Ta Spata, Aristotélous 28 (tel. 23 19 66). Open 11 a.m.–midnight daily.
New Ilisia, Leontos Sofou 17 (tel. 53 69 96). Open daily 8.30 a.m.– 2 a.m.
Ta Koumbarakia, Egnatías 140. Specializes in grills and seafood. Closed Sun.

Psistaria Megas-Kotsiamanis, Olímbou 83. Specializes in grilled meat dishes.

Two-course meals from 1850–2600dr (£5–7; $7.50–10.50)

Aproöpto, L. Margaríti 11 (tel. 28 32 45). Serves some vegetarian dishes. Open Mon.–Sat. noon–midnight.
Olymbos Naoussa, Níkis 5 (tel. 27 57 15). Open Mon.–Sat. noon till midnight.
Bechtsinar, Katoúni 11 (tel. 53 11 02). Open Mon.–Sat. noon till midnight. Closed mid-July–mid-Aug.
To Sokaki, Kalapotháki 4 (tel. 22 91 84). Open Mon.–Sat. 1 p.m.– 2 a.m. Closed mid-July–mid-Aug.

Two-course meals from 2600–3700dr (£7–10; $10.50–15.00)

Limaniotis, Navárhou Vótsi 1–3. Specializes in seafood dishes. Open Mon.–Sat.
La Pignatta, Kerasoúndos 2 (Kalamariá suburb), (tel. 42 41 20). Italian dishes. Open for dinner after 8 p.m. Mon.–Sat.

SHOPPING
There are several choices for picnic supplies. The open-air market is between Aristotélous, Iraklíou and Venizélou and is open from 7.30 a.m.–3 p.m. For supermarket shopping head for the corner of Mitropoleos and Karolou Dil, where there is a Safeway, or visit Klaoudatos, a department store at the corner of Aristotélous and Ermou.

HUNGARY

Hungary is a budget eater's dream: great food, generous portions at extremely low prices. If you've been existing on bread, cheese and bottled water, now's your chance to splash out. Even though inflation here is climbing alarmingly, at the time of writing you can still eat a two-course meal for as little as £2 ($3), or experience the works in a plush tourist restaurant, complete with gypsy music, for £10 ($15).

The cheapest places of all are the self-service restaurants (*önkiszolgáló étterem*), followed by *bisztrós* and *büfe* (snack bars). At all of these you'll be able to get a limited number of hot dishes, while the *bisztrós* and *büfes* also serve things like salami rolls and pastries. You can either stand up or eat sitting down. Slightly more expensive are the *csárdas*, traditional inns which tend to specialize in certain dishes, generally eaten to the sound of gypsy music; *vendéglö* (our idea of a bistro); and *étterem*, restaurants. Many restaurants will offer a *napi menü*, a fixed-price tourist menu, offering two, sometimes three set courses at around £2–3 ($3.00–4.50). The Hungarians traditionally eat their main meal at lunchtime, usually three courses plus coffee, and eating out tends to be cheaper then than in the evening. Lunch (*ebed*) is usually eaten some time between noon and 3 p.m., and dinner (*vacsora*) between 7–10 p.m. Although tax and a service charge are included in your bill, you will be expected to tip 10% to the waiter, as well as a small amount to the musician if he plays at your table.

Coffee houses were once a central part of Hungarian culture. That's not quite the case now but you'll still be able to get a good cup of coffee in a typical local café for about £0.30 ($0.45). Look for the signs *kávé*, *eszpresszo* or *kávéház*. Coffee is nearly always drunk at breakfast (*reggeli*), along with a simple meal of bread and jam, cheese, eggs or salami. Have your breakfast in a self-service café or a *tejbár*, a stand-up milk bar serving hot drinks and pastries. Tea isn't a traditional drink here, so isn't particularly good.

One of Hungary's best known products is wine, and you can taste it extremely cheaply: a glass costs around £0.25 ($0.40), although you can pay as much as £1 ($1.50). Beer is slightly more expensive, but still excellent value at around £0.45 ($0.70) per glass, top price around £0.75 ($1.10); while a 1kg loaf of bread will cost from £0.30–0.50 ($0.45–0.75).

Mention Hungarian food and most people will think of goulash and paprika. However there's a great deal more to it than that. In fact Hungarian cuisine is often said to be the finest in Europe.

Paprika is certainly important, and comes in six strengths: from *kulonleges* (delicate), and *feledes* (semi sweet) to *eros* or *csipos* (hot). You'll always find a shaker of the hotter varieties on the table, but milder ones are generally used in cooking. At one time food tended to be cooked in lard or goose fat, and this gave it a reputation for being heavy and hard to digest. This is now changing, as chefs have taken to using lighter vegetable oils, but the food is certainly filling, making good use of dumplings, pastry, meats and cabbage.

Hungarian cuisine is particularly interesting for the unusual way it mixes and serves ingredients. *Meggyleves*, for example, is a chilled soup made from morello cherries and served with sour cream, while *keposztaleves* is a type of cabbage soup. Soups can be very substantial here: *halászlé* is a fish soup; *ujhazi tyukhusleves* a chicken broth with vegetables, and *lebbencsleves*, a soup with pasta, peppers and fried bacon.

Incidentally goulash (*gulyás*) is a soup as well, not the stew that we think. It's made with beef, paprika, tomatoes and onions. What we think of as goulash is really *pörkölt* or *tokany*, which is either pork or beef cooked in much the same way as *gulyás*, but thicker and served with sour cream and dumplings. Other popular dishes are *töltött-káposzta* (green cabbage filled with minced meat and served with a tomato sauce), *töltött-paprika* (green peppers stuffed the same way), *paprikas csirke* (paprika chicken) and *fatanyeros*, a selection of meats with salad and bacon. Common accompaniments to dishes are *galuska*, small dumplings, or noodles with cottage cheese.

Fish is also served a lot here, but not run-of-the-mill cod or haddock. Instead there's carp, pike, trout, and even giant catfish. Try *racponty* (carp baked with potatoes, peppers, tomatoes, onions and paprika, topped with sour cream), or *káposztas csuka alföldiesen* (pike cooked with sauerkraut, peppers, tomatoes, onions, herbs, cream and paprika).

Desserts are also rich and unusual. *Somlói galuska* consists of pieces of rich sponge cake, covered with chocolate sauce and rum or cream, while *rétes* is the Hungarian version of strudel (pastry filled with fruits, ground nuts and poppy seeds). Try *palacsinta* as well, which are pancakes filled with curd cheese and raisins, jam or chocolate and nuts. Noodles (*metelt* or *nudli*) may be served hot and sprinkled with nuts, poppy seeds, sugar – even ham. Traditional cheeses to try are *bakony*, similar to camembert; *palpusztai*, which is like gorgonzola; and *korozott*, a mixture of ewe cheese, butter, paprika and caraway seeds.

It's not only Hungarian food which is good: its wine (*bor*) is also worth a try and you'll find quite a lot of varieties to choose from.

The most famous is Bull's Blood of Egar (*Egri Bikavér*), a red wine considered similar to burgundy. *Egri Leányka* (Maiden of Eger), is a light white wine, while *homoki siller* is a rosé. Other rather unusual ones, like *Tokaji aszu*, come from the volcanic Tokay region and are generally quite rich and sweet (Hungarians often add mineral water to their wine). At around £1.25 ($1.90) a bottle in a shop, and £2.25 ($3.40) in a restaurant, wine is excellent value.

Beer (*sör*) is similar to lager. There are a number of imported varieties on sale, and you may find an Austro-Hungarian brand, *Dreter*. Or you can be adventurous and try *pálinka*, a clear brandy made from local fruits. The apricot version (*barack*) is the best known, but it also comes in cherry (*csersznye*), pear (*körte*), plum (*szilva*) and even walnut varieties.

Unfortunately, vegetarians will find it very difficult to sample Hungarian cuisine, as meat and fish feature in almost everything. Even the innocuous sounding bean soup contains meat, and some desserts are garnished with pork crackling or bacon. *Rántott sajt* is fried cheese, *rántott gombafejek* are fried mushrooms in breadcrumbs, and *gombapörkölt* is mushroom stew, but beware — animal fats may have been used in the cooking. Vegetables are often served as *fozolek*, which is a mixture of boiled peas, beans and carrots, mixed with a thick fat and flour sauce. One official, when asked what vegetarians could eat in Hungary said simply 'forget it', but others say that restaurants are willing to do something if required. If necessary you can always rely on the open-air markets, which have a good range of fruit and vegetables on sale. There are also the delicatessens (*csemege* and *salátbárs*) and pâtisseries (*cukrászda*). There are also street stalls that sell *kukorica* (corn on the cob), *gesztenye* (roast chestnuts) and *gofri* (waffles). In the self-service restaurants and snack bars, you will also be able to buy toasted sandwiches (*melegszendvics*) filled with cheese (*sajtos*) or mushroom paste (*gombas*). Pizza may also be available and *lángos*, a large doughnut eaten with cheese or sour cream.

The supermarket chains to look out for are ABC and Julius Meinl (the latter lost no time in expanding from its Austrian base once the Hungarian market opened up). Shopping hours are generally Mon.–Fri. 7 a.m.–7 p.m.; Sat. 7 a.m.–1 p.m.

The Hungarian language is difficult to get to grips with, and while some German and English is spoken, you may find it worthwhile investing in a phrase book if you intend to be there for any length of time.

Budapest

You certainly won't have any problem finding somewhere to eat cheaply in Budapest. There's a wide range of restaurants, snack bars and cafés available – even specialist veggie ones. Some eateries are real tourist traps, with lashings of gypsy music and high prices, but even so you shouldn't pay more than 1,200Ft (£10; $15.20). Ask for the *napi menü* which, though it exists, may not always be displayed. Each March, during the Budapest Spring Festival, restaurants and hotels will have special promotions of local food.

Note: In the addresses below the Roman numerals before the street name refer to the district of the city.

CHEAP EATERIES
Two-course meals under £5 ($7.50)

Csendes, VI, Múzeum körút 13 (tel. 117 3704). Open Mon.–Sat. noon to midnight.

Shalom Restaurant, VII, Klauzal tér 2 (tel. 122 1464). Kosher restaurant. Open daily noon–11 p.m.

Sirály, VI, Bajcsy-Zsilinszky út. 9 (tel. 122 8864 / 122 8880). English menu available. Open daily noon till midnight.

Megálló, VII, Károly körút 23. Extensive menu, available in English. Open daily 11 a.m.–11 p.m.

Tian Ma, VIII, Luther útca 1/b. Chinese restaurant. Open until 11 p.m. daily.

Vegetárium, V, Cukor útca 3 (tel. 138 3710). Vegetarian restaurant. English menu available. Open daily noon–10 p.m.

Il Treno, XII, Alkotás útca 15 (tel. 156 4251). Pizzeria. Open until 2 a.m. daily.

Two-course meals from £5–7 ($7.50–10.50)

Karpatia, V, Karolyi Mihaly útca 4–8 (tel. 117 7305). Open daily 11 a.m.–11 p.m.

Nimrod, V, Nador útca 24 (tel. 111 6098). Open daily 11.30 a.m.–11 p.m.

Kádár Étkezde, VII, Klauzal tér 9. Hungarian and Jewish dishes. Open weekdays 11.30 a.m.–3 p.m.

Aranyszarvas, I, Szarvas tér 1 (tel. 175 6451). Specializes in game dishes. Open until midnight on Sun., otherwise until 2 a.m. daily.

Prágai Vencel, VIII, Rákóczi út 57 (tel. 133 1342). Czech and Slovak dishes. Open until 11.30 p.m. daily.

Two-course meals from £7–10 ($10.50–15.00)

Kisbuda Gyöngye, III, Kenyeres utca 34 (tel. 115 2244).
Múzeum, VIII, Múzeum körút 12 (tel. 138 4221). Open daily 10–
   1 a.m.
Szindbad, V, Bajcsy-Zsilinszky útca 74 (tel. 132 2749). Open
   Mon.–Fri. noon till midnight; weekends 6 p.m.–midnight.
Aprod Csárda, V, Szondi útca 17. Open Mon.–Fri. 9 a.m.–9 p.m.;
   Sun. 9 a.m.–4.30 p.m. Closed Sat.
Acapulco, VII, Erzsébet körút 39 (tel. 122 6014). Mexican dishes.

SHOPPING
● **Supermarkets**

ABC, I, Batthyányi tér 5–7 (1st floor). Open Mon.–Fri. 7 a.m.–
   7 p.m.; Sat. 7 a.m.–1 p.m.
Non-Stop, V, Oktober 6 u. 5 and Regi Posta u. Pricier than the
   other stores, but open round-the-clock.
VI, Deák Ferenc tér 6.
V, Váci útca 1/3.
V, Ferenciek tére 1.
V, Apaczay Csere Janos út. 1.

● **Market**
At IX, Vámház körút 1–3, Fovám tér.

Eger

LOCAL SPECIALITIES

Egri bikavér	the famous Bull's Blood, a rich, red wine
Egri Leányka	'Maiden of Eger' – a white wine
Egri Olaszrizling	a white wine
Egri Tramini	a white wine

SPECIAL EVENTS AND FESTIVALS
During the 'Vintage Days' festival in September you can sample
the local wines for free at one of the numerous street stalls which
are set up around town. At other times less liberal free measures
are available at the local Wine Museum, or in the cellars of the

Szépasszony-völgy (Valley of the Beautiful Women) on the out-skirts of town.

CHEAP EATERIES
Two-course meals under £5 ($7.50)

Express, Barkoczy út. 4 (Pyrker tér) (tel. 10732). Self-service restaurant. Open 7 a.m.–8 p.m. daily.

Vörös Rák, Szent János útca 11 (tel. 12814). Self-service restaurant. Open 7 a.m.–4 p.m. daily.

Panoráma, Bajcsy-Zsilinszky útca Tömbbelsó (tel. 11927 / 11693). Recommended dish: *cigánype csenye* (pork cutlet in paprika sauce). Open daily 11 a.m.–10 p.m.

Kazamata, Pyrker tér 3 (tel. 11538). Open 10 a.m.–11 p.m. daily.

Dorner, Kossuth Lajos útca 28 (tel. 21069). Open 8 a.m.–10 p.m. daily.

HBH (Bavarian Beer House), Bajcsy-Zsilinszky útca 19 (tel. 16312). English menu available. Open daily 10 a.m.–10 p.m. (except Nov.–Mar.: closed Sun.).

Two-course meals from £5–7 ($7.50–10.50)

Amstel Beer House, Dr. Sandor I. út. 2 (tel. 16951). Open 11 a.m.–1 a.m. daily.

Vadaszkurt, Ersek út. 4 (tel. 11304). Open 8 a.m.–11 p.m. daily.

Belvarosi, Bajcsy-Zsilinszky út. 8 (tel. 11872). Open weekdays 7 a.m.–10 p.m., weekends 7 a.m.–3 p.m.

Two-course meals from £7–10 ($10.50–15.00)

Park Restaurant, Klapka út. 4 (tel. 13233). Open noon–midnight daily.

Talizman, Kossuth L. út. 19 (tel. 20883). Open noon–10 p.m. daily.

SHOPPING
● Supermarkets

Belvarosi ABC, Dr. Sandor I. út.;
Skala-Coop ABC, Katona tér 2;
Csemege–Julius Meinl, Szechenyi út. 8

There is also a supermarket on the left hand side of the street as you walk from the train station to the town centre. If you are waiting for a train connection in Füzesabony, you might want to stock up before reaching Eger at the supermarket just 100m down the main street from the train station.

● **Market**
Indoor market, near the Centrum áruház department store. Open Mon.–Fri. 6 a.m.–6 p.m.; Sat. 6 a.m.–1 p.m.; Sun. 6–10 a.m.

IRELAND

Irish cooking may not be sophisticated, but it's good value and full of character and flavour. Portions tend to be so large that it's often impossible to eat more than one course for a meal, so while prices are higher than in Britain, your money can go just as far. The average price of a two-course meal is IR£9 (£9; $13.50) with main courses costing around IR£5.50 (£5.50; $8.25). In addition many places offer special tourist menus, particularly at lunchtime and early evening, with three courses for around IR£8 (£8; $12). Best bargains of all are to be found in the numerous pubs, which often offer excellent lunchtime specials at low prices.

Major Irish cities have a large number of restaurants, pubs and ethnic places to choose from, as well as plenty of fast-food outlets like Abrekebabra, La Pizza and Supermacs, so it won't be difficult to find something to suit you. The price of a pint of beer is IR£1.65 (£1.65; $2.50), while the national brew, Guinness, is a bit more expensive. A glass of wine costs around IR£1.50 (£1.50; $2.25). If you're going to be putting together a picnic, you should expect to pay around IR£0.70 (£0.70; $1) for a loaf of bread.

Irish cuisine is not renowned for its classicism, and can still be a bit basic and stodgy; standards however are rapidly rising and, most importantly, you can be sure that you won't go hungry. Traditionally dishes have focused on potatoes and cabbage, along with meats like beef, bacon and lamb. Specialities to look out for include Irish Stew (stewed mutton and potatoes), corned beef with cabbage, and *colcannon* (potatoes cooked with cream and onion). A more unusual food is *carrageen*, an edible seaweed.

Breakfast is generally a substantial meal of fried sausage, bacon and eggs, served with strong tea (always drunk with milk) and lots of delicious soda bread, a traditional loaf made with white or brown flour and bicarbonate of soda instead of yeast. Fill yourself up here and, if you've got room, eat your main meal at lunchtime as this is when you'll get the best bargains.

Fresh ingredients and simple cooking methods are what counts in Ireland, and fish dishes are very popular, particularly in the west. Look for salmon, potted herring, lobsters and Ireland's highly rated oysters. Traditional Irish restaurants are becoming more popular these days, but if you want a change there are plenty of ethnic restaurants to choose from.

Though beer and lager are available in Ireland, the national brew, Guinness, is by far the most popular. It's commonly stated that you've never tasted Guinness until you've drunk it in Ireland, and this is most certainly true. Almost black, with a thick white head (Guinness is actually a stout beer), here it's darker, richer and creamier than anywhere else — in fact it's a meal in itself. Two similar and very popular brews are Murphys and Beamish. Many young people are drinking bottled beers these days, so you'll find plenty of these to choose from as well. Although wine (usually French or German) is available, it's not a traditional Irish drink — unlike whiskey, which is a stronger version of its Scottish cousin; Jamesons, Paddys or Powers are the names to look out for. In addition, Ireland has given its name to a sweet liqueur, Bailey's Irish Cream, which is a blend of cream and Irish whiskey and can be drunk with ice.

Hot strong tea is the order of the day here, but coffee is becoming more and more popular and can be very good. The Bewleys chain of coffee houses are excellent and also offer cakes, snacks and hot meals. Irish coffee, a relatively recent invention, is widely available and very good. It is sweet black coffee laced with whiskey and served with a layer of cream carefully poured on top, so that it looks rather like Guinness. If you're really strapped for cash it's useful to know that you don't have to ask for drinks with your meal. You will usually be brought a jug or a huge glass of water which will quench your thirst if nothing else.

While classic Irish dishes, with their emphasis on meat and fish, are not suitable for vegetarians to sample, there will be no problem at all in finding something to eat. Most restaurants, and even many pubs, offer veggie options on the menu, and if not, people are usually only too happy to make you up something special. In fact, Ireland has to be one of the best places for vegetarians to eat out, and the dishes are often more inventive than traditional ones. Even fast-food outlets tend to offer meatless dishes, and there are always lots of ethnic options.

If you want to buy food for a picnic, there are plenty of super-markets, as well as small shops like bakers and grocers. Look for supermarket chains like Quinnsworth, Roches and Dunnes. Opening hours tend to be from 9 a.m.–5.30 p.m., Mon.–Sat., although many large stores will stay open later on Thursday. A few shops are also open on Sunday. It's a good idea to buy your fruit and vegetables from street stalls or open air markets, the best of these being in Dublin. Food is usually excellent quality and very good value.

Cork

LOCAL SPECIALITIES

crubeen   pig's trotters
drisheen   black pudding
Murphy's   a thick, dark stout – slightly sweeter in taste than
             Dublin's Guinness
Beamish   another thick, dark stout

CHEAP EATERIES

Most of the city's eateries (cheap or otherwise) are clustered in the city centre. The area between Patrick Street and Paul Street has a particularly wide choice of eateries, especially along Carey's Lane and French Church Street. On average, prices are slightly higher than in Dublin, but this should not affect you unduly if you eat in the middle of the day when many restaurants offer special lunchtime deals.

Two-course meals for under IR£5 (£5; $7.50)

La Pizza, 35 Patrick Street (tel. 27 79 57). Good choice of pizzas and
    salads. Open daily 9 a.m.–midnight (Fri. and Sat. until 3 a.m.).
Kelly's, 64 Oliver Plunkett Street (tel. 27 33 75). Recommended
    dish: shepherd's pie. Open daily noon–9 p.m.
Kyelmore Café, Merchants Quay Shopping Centre, Patrick Street.
    Open Mon.–Sat. 8 a.m.–6 p.m.
Pizza Pomodoro, 34 Patrick Street (tel. 27 28 95). Pizza and other
    Italian dishes. Open daily noon–1 a.m.

Two-course meals from IR£5–7 (£5–7; $7.50–10.50)

The Delhi Palace, 6 Washington Street (tel. 27 62 27). Indian res-
    taurant. Open daily 5.30 p.m.–12.30 a.m. and also 12.30–
    2.30 p.m. Thurs.–Sat.
Bullys, 40 Paul Street (tel. 27 35 55). Italian dishes predominate.
    Some vegetarian options. Open Mon.–Sat. noon–11.30 p.m.;
    Sun. 5–11 p.m.
Quay Co-op, 24 Sullivans Quay (tel. 31 76 60). Vegetarian res-
    taurant. Open daily 9.30 a.m.–10.30 p.m.

Two-course meals from IR£7–10 (£7–10; $10.50–15.00)

The Huguenot, French Church Street (tel. 27 33 57). Open daily.

The Green Door, 17 Academy Street (tel. 27 10 90). Vegetarian dishes available. No smoking. Open Mon.–Sat. 6 p.m.–late.

Crawford Gallery Cafe, Emmet Place (tel. 27 44 15). Open daily 12.30–2.30 p.m. and 6.30–9.30 p.m.

SHOPPING

The 'Old English Market', a covered market on Grand Parade, is the place for fresh food. It's open Mon.–Sat. 9 a.m.–5.30 p.m., and sells meat, fruit, vegetables and bread. There's a branch of Roches, the supermarket chain, in Merchants Quay Shopping Centre, Patrick Street, and a Quinnsworth store in the Paul Street Shopping Centre.

Dublin

LOCAL SPECIALITIES

Guinness has been brewed here since 1769 and you can visit the brewery's museum for an insight into the preparation of this famous drink, as well as a tasting. The Guinness Brewery Hop Store Gallery is in Crane Street (tel. 53 67 00 ext. 5238) and is open Mon.–Fri., admission IR£2 (£2; $3). Along the same lines you can also visit Irish Whiskey Corner, Bow Street (tel. 72 55 66), where Irish Distillers offer tastings, an exhibition, and tours.

CHEAP EATERIES

There are lots of restaurants, from the cheap to the very expensive, in the area around Temple Bar and Trinity College.
Two-course meals for under IR£5 (£5; $7.50)

Cellary Restaurant, 1 Fownes Street Lower (tel. 671 0362). Vegetarian restaurant. Open Mon.–Tues. 9 a.m.–10 p.m.; Wed.–Sun. 9 a.m.–late.

Beshoffs, 14 Westmoreland Street (tel. 77 67 61) and 7 Upper O'Connell Street. Fish restaurants. Recommended dish: haddock and chips. Open Mon.–Thurs. 12.30–11 p.m.; Fri.–Sat. 11.30 a.m.–11 p.m.; Sun. 11.30–3 a.m. Special teatime offer 3–5 p.m.

Switzer and Co., Grafton St (tel. 77 68 21 ext. 219). Department store with a self-service cafeteria on the 3rd floor. Open Mon.–Sat. (except public holidays) 9.30 a.m.–5.15 p.m.

It's Natural, 71 Dame Street (tel. 679 5015). Vegetarian restaurant.

Open Mon.–Thurs. 10 a.m.–8 p.m.; Fri.–Sat. 10 a.m.–12.30 a.m.
The Stag's Head, 1 Dame Court (tel. 679 3701). Pub serving meals.
Open Mon.–Fri. 12.30–3.30 p.m. and 5.30–7.30 p.m.; Sat.
12.30–2.30 p.m.

Two-course meals from IR£5–7 (£5–7; $7.50–10.50)

La Mezza Luna, 1 Temple Lane (tel. 671 2840). Italian restaurant.
Some vegetarian options. Recommended dishes: *paglia* (smoked
ham and mushrooms in a wine and cream sauce) and *fettucini
putanesca* (pasta with sausage, olives and anchovies). Open daily
12.30–10.30 p.m.
Irish Film Centre, 6 Eustace Street (tel. 667 8788). Recommended
dish: *cannelloni*. Open Sun.–Tues. 12.30–8.30 p.m.; Wed.–Sat.
12.30–11 p.m.
Kilkenny Kitchen, 6 Nassau Street (tel. 677 7066). Recommended
dish: beef and onion pie. Open Mon.–Sat. 9 a.m.–6 p.m. (Thurs.
until 9 p.m.).
Blazing Salads II, Powerscourt Townhouse Centre, William Street
South (tel. 671 9552). Vegetarian restaurant. Recommended
dishes: carrot and fennel bake, and pinto bean and vegetable
casserole served with brown rice. Open Mon.–Sat. 9 a.m.–6 p.m.
Periwinkle Seafood Bar, Powerscourt Townhouse Centre, William
Street South (tel. 679 4203). Seafood restaurant. Recommended
dish: cockle-and-mussel salad. Open Mon.–Sat. (except public
holidays) 10.30 a.m.–5 p.m.

Two-course meals from IR£7–10 (£7–10; $10.50–15.00)

101 Talbot, 100–102 Talbot Street (tel. 874 5011). Recommended
dishes: pork with avocado and strawberry dressing, and brazil
nut *ressoles* with red pepper sauce. Open Tues.–Sat. 10 a.m.–
11 p.m.; Mon. 10 a.m.–3.30 p.m.
La Cave, 28 South Anne Street (tel. 679 4409) French cuisine predominates. Recommended dishes: beef braised with Dijon mustard, and vegetable couscous. Open daily 12.30–3 p.m. and
6 p.m.–2 a.m.
Dillons, 21 Suffolk Street (tel. 77 48 04). Vegetarian dishes available.
Recommended dish: Irish stew. Open daily 8 a.m.–midnight.
Gallaghers Boxty House, 20–21 Temple Bar (tel. 77 27 62). Traditional Irish and vegetarian dishes. Recommended dishes: bacon
and cabbage boxty (one of a range of potato pancakes sold on
the premises) and Irish stew. Open daily 12.30–11.30 p.m.
Tosca, 20 Suffolk Street (tel. 679 6744). Italian restaurant. Some

vegetarian options. Open Sun.–Wed. 10.30 a.m.–midnight;
Thurs.–Sat. 10.30–1 a.m.

Brokers Restaurant, 25 Dame Street (tel. 679 3534). Extensive
menu, with some vegetarian options. Special three-course
evening set menu. Open daily 11.30 a.m.–midnight.

SHOPPING
● Markets

Moore Street Market. Meat, fruit and vegetables. Open Mon.–Sat.
9 a.m.–5 p.m.

Thomas Street Market. Fruit and vegetables. Open Fri.–Sat. 9 a.m.–
5 p.m.

● Supermarkets

Dunne's Stores. In the St Stephen's Green Shopping Centre; in the
ILAC Centre off Henry Street; and on North Earl Street. All open
Mon.–Sat. 9 a.m.–6 p.m. (Thurs. until 9 p.m.).

Galway

LOCAL SPECIALITIES
The city is famous for its seafood: salmon, trout, lobsters, crabs –
and oysters. In season, game such as woodcock, duck and partridge
often appear on menus, along with steaks, and lamb from
Connemara.

SPECIAL EVENTS AND FESTIVALS
During the last week in September there is an annual international
oyster festival. Tickets for the festival itself are expensive, but many
pubs and restaurants offer specials, such as half a dozen oysters for
IR£5 (£5; $7.50), along with Guinness or Irish coffee.

CHEAP EATERIES
Many eateries drop their prices considerably at lunchtime, or offer
special fixed-menus, so it makes sense to eat your main meal then,
rather than in the evening. Vegetarian options are available at the
vast majority of local restaurants.

Two-course meals for under IR£5 (£5; $7.50)

GBC (Galway Bakery Company), 7 Williamsgate (tel. 63087). The restaurant upstairs offers cheap lunchtime set menus. Open daily noon–11 p.m.

The Grainstore, Lower Abbeygate Street (tel. 66620). Recommended dish: stuffed aubergines. Open Mon.–Sat. 9.30 a.m.– 9 p.m. (closes 5.50 p.m. in winter).

The Sunflower Restaurant, Quay Street. Vegetarian restaurant. Recommended dish: organic vegetable stew. Open daily June– Sept. 9 a.m.–midnight; Oct.–May 11 a.m.–8 p.m.

McDonagh's, 22 Quay Street (tel. 65001). Fish and seafood dishes. Recommended dish: cod and chips. Restaurant open daily 12.30–3 p.m. and 5 p.m.–12.30 a.m. Fish-and-chip shop closed Sun., otherwise same hours as restaurant.

Kylemore Café, Eyre Square Shopping Centre. Open Mon.–Sat. 9 a.m.–6.30 p.m. (until 9 p.m. on Fri.).

The Left Bank Café, 49 Dominick Street (tel. 67791). Specializes in vegetarian and seafood dishes. Open daily 9 a.m.–9 p.m.

Two-course meals from IR£5–7 (£5–7; $7.50–10.50)

Chestnut Restaurant, 3 Eyre Square (tel. 65800/65575). Recommended dish: plaice with potatoes and vegetables. Open daily noon–10 p.m.

Seventh Heaven, Courthouse Lane (tel. 63838). Italian, Mexican, and vegetarian dishes. Open daily noon till midnight.

Lydons of Shop Street (tel. 64051). Open daily 11 a.m.–10 p.m.

Two-course meals from IR£7–10 (£7–10; $10.50–15.00)

Nimmo's. By the Spanish Arch. Recommended dish: salmon in herb sauce. Open 12.30–3 p.m. and 7 p.m.–late.

The Brasserie, Middle Street (tel. 61610). Open Mon.–Sat. 12.30– 10 p.m.

Maxwell McNamara's, Williamsgate Street (tel. 65727). Open daily 9 a.m.–10 p.m.

SHOPPING
There's a branch of Roches Stores in Eyre Square (open Mon.–Sat. 9 a.m.–5.30 p.m.; late-night shopping Fri. until 9 p.m.), and Supervalue, in the Eyre Square Shopping Centre, which is open Mon.–Sat. 9 a.m.–6.30 p.m. (until 9 p.m. on Fri.).

There's a good open-air market for fruit, vegetables, cakes and meat on Saturday morning, 8 a.m.–2 p.m. at Market Street and Lombard Street.

FURTHER INFORMATION
Two free publications available from the local Tourist Office which
include some information on eating out are the *Galway Tourist Guide*
and the *Galway – Western Tourism News.*

Limerick

CHEAP EATERIES
Two-course meals for under IR£5 (£5; $7.50)

Riverrun Restaurant, Honan's Quay. Recommended dish: chilli
with rice. Open Tues.–Sat. 10 a.m.–5.30 p.m.
Glentworth Hotel, Glentworth Street (tel. 41 38 22). Vegetarian
options available.
The Cellar, 118 O'Connell Street (tel. 41 82 86). Specializes in grills
and steaks. Open daily 8.30 a.m.–9 p.m.
Sails Restaurant, Arthurs Quay Shopping Centre (tel. 41 66 22).
Open Mon.–Sat. 9.30 a.m.–5.30 p.m.
Tea Leaf, 104 O'Connell Street (tel. 41 53 75). Offers a four-course
lunch menu for IR£5.50. Open Mon.–Sat. May–Sept. 9 a.m.–
10 p.m.; Oct.–Apr. 9 a.m.–6 p.m.

Two-course meals from IR£5–7 (£5–7; $7.50–10.50)

Mortell's Restaurant, 49 Roches Street (tel. 45457). Specializes in
seafood dishes. Open daily May–Sept. 8.30 a.m.–9 p.m.;
Oct.–Apr. 8.30 a.m.–6 p.m.
Handi Steak House, 1 Henry Street (tel. 41 15 77). Indian restaurant. Open daily noon–2.30 p.m. and 5 p.m.–12.30 a.m.
Café Vienna, 67 William Street (tel. 41 17 20). Open Mon.–Sat.
9 a.m.–6 p.m.

Two-course meals from IR£7–10 (£7–10; $10.50–15.00)

Texas Steakout, 116 O'Connell Street (tel. 41 44 40/41 03 50).
Steak, chicken, fish, and pasta dishes. Open daily, noon– 11 p.m.
Jasmine Palace, O'Connell Street Mall (tel. 41 24 84). Chinese
restaurant. Open daily 12.30 a.m.–12.30 p.m.
Restaurant de la Fountaine, 12 Upper Gerald Griffin Street (tel.
41 44 61). Open Tues.–Fri. 12.30–2.30 p.m. and 7–10 p.m.;
Mon. and Sat. 7–10 p.m.

SHOPPING

Shopping hours are Mon.–Sat. from 9.30 a.m.–5.30 p.m., late-night shopping on Thurs. and Fri. until 9 p.m. Supermarkets include Quinnsworth's in Arthurs Quay Shopping Centre, and Roche's in Sarsfield Street. There's also Spaights Shopping Centre on Henry Street. On Saturday mornings there is a fresh fruit and vegetable market in Robert Street.

ITALY

Italian food has a reputation for being tasty, cheap and filling, yet while meals can be good, prices are sometimes steep, particularly once you've added on the extra charges which inevitably appear. A bread and cover charge (*pane e coperto*) will usually add 1,500L (£0.60; $0.90) to the cost of your meal, but even in fairly modest eateries it is not uncommon to be charged 3,000L (£0.90; $1.35). Also, with service charges typically running at 10–15 per cent it is best to check the menu to see if the service charge is included (*servizio compreso*). Once you take these charges into account, you can expect to pay in the region of 12,500–17,000L (£5–7; $7.50–10.50) in one of the cheaper local restaurants. There is, however, a huge selection of eateries from which to choose, and you shouldn't have too much difficulty in eating well, whatever your budget. Food is generally excellent and varied, and relies heavily on fresh, simple ingredients like tomatoes, herbs, mushrooms and garlic. Opening hours tend to be from 12.30–2 p.m. and 7–11 p.m., although you will be able to eat later in the south. Keep an eye out for *piatti del giorno*, which are daily specials, and do remember to check your bill (*il conto*) carefully – 'mistakes' are not uncommon.

Breakfast isn't an important meal in Italy, so opt out of it at your accommodation and go instead to a bar or café for a coffee and pastries, croissants or *bombolini* (sugared doughnuts), which should cost around 2,000–3,000L (£0.80–1.20; $1.20–1.80). If you're looking for a snack, *paninoteche* (sandwich bars) sell rolls filled with salami, ham or cheese, as do *alimentari* (grocers); the cost is around 1,500–3,000L (£0.60–1.20; $0.90–1.80) per sandwich. Bars, which open from early in the morning until late at night, may sell *tramezzini*, sliced bread sandwiches, which aren't as tasty as rolls but are cheaper at around 1,000L (£0.40; $0.60).

Try not to stop for too many snacks and cups of coffee. The price of a coffee in a café can vary from 1,000–2,500L (£0.40–1.00; $0.60–1.50) while a glass of wine is 1,600–2,500L (£0.65–1.00; $1.00–1.50) and beer costs around 2,000–3,000L (£0.80–1.20; $1.20–1.80). If you want to make your own expect to pay 1,200–1,800L (£0.50–0.75; $0.75–1.10) for one of the cheaper loaves of bread in a supermarket. For takeaway hot food, look for *rosticceria* – where you can get chicken, pizzas, chips and burgers – and *pizzeria*, which serve pizzas both whole and by the slice.

The cheapest places for you to sit down and eat are *tavole calde*, snack bars with limited seating. They are followed in order of grandeur by *osterie*, simple family-run eateries; *trattorie*; and finally *ristoranti*. You will often see the sign *menu turistico*, a fixed-price tourist menu which should cost around 15,000–20,000L (£6–8; $9–12). While these *can* be good value, don't assume they're the best bet – you might end up with a second-rate meal. Always shop around first. Some *osterie* and *trattorie* may not even have a written menu, but the food can be delicious and great value. The cost of a pizza may vary from 2,000–8,000L (£0.80–3.20; $1.20–4.80) depending on where you are and what the topping is; pastas will cost around 5,000–10,000L (£2–4; $3–6). In many establishments you are expected to order two courses, but in *tavole calde* you can get away with ordering only one, so make it a filling one! Try to eat your main meal at lunchtime, as many Italians still do, when prices are usually lower.

It's hard to remember that it was only a few years ago that spaghetti bolognaise was the only Italian meal most people knew. Now, pizzas and pasta dishes are on every supermarket shelf, but don't expect the food in Italy to taste the same. For a start, pizzas are thin and crispy, admittedly disappointing if you're ravenous and expecting an American deep-pan variety, but often much tastier. They're usually cooked in traditional wood-burning ovens, that give them a distinctive taste. You should also bear in mind that regional variations in cooking styles are nearly as great as in France. The North tends to use more rice, dairy products and meat, while Southern staples are olive oil, pasta and tomatoes. Identically named dishes may contain different ingredients from region to region and even from town to town; most regions also have their own specialities, which you should make every effort to try. Umbria, for example, is noted for its use of black truffles, while the famous *panettone* (a kind of spiced cake) originates from Milan. Cooking in Piedmont has close links with France, and Alto Adige with Austria. Venice specializes in seafood, Lombardy is noted for its cheeses, and Tuscan dishes frequently contain beans and spinach. In addition, there are 200 types of pasta, and 600 different names for them. The Italians always consider the consistency of the sauce when matching it with the pasta shape. As a rule, thick sauces are best served with short, hollow or spiral varieties such as *penne* (quills), *conchiglie* (shells) or *eliche* (spirals). Thinner sauces go with long, thin pasta such as *spaghetti* or *fettucine*. Other pasta shapes to look out for include: *bucatini* (a thicker version of spaghetti, but hollow all the way through); *cannelloni* (large tubes of pasta, served stuffed with a rich filling and topped with sauce); *farfalle* (bow shapes); *lasagne* (broad pasta sheets, served between layers of meat sauce); *macaroni* (short curved tubes of hollow pasta); *pappardelle* (wide pasta ribbons), and *tagliatelle* (narrow ribbons). Pasta in the North tends to be *pasta fresca*, which is soft, usually home-made, and consists of flour, eggs and a little water. In the South it tends to be *pasta asciutta*, which is a harder, factory-produced pasta, made from flour and water.

There are four main traditional pasta sauces (salse): *Napoletana*, *Bolognese*, *Bechamel* and *Pesto*. Napoletana is a rich tomato sauce, with celery, garlic and herbs, while Bolognese sauce contains meat, wine, garlic and tomatoes. Bechamel is a white sauce, and Pesto (from Genoa) is made from basil, olive oil, pine kernels and Parmesan cheese.

Other common dishes are *pollo alla padovana* (a spicy, spit-roasted chicken); *polenta* (cornflour pudding); *pastizzada* (a meat stew), *brodetto* (fish stew from Rimini) and *calzone* (a pizza folded over, then cooked). In addition, there are 200 types of pasta, and 600 different names for them. As well as pasta and pizzas, the Italians are, of course, noted for their ice cream. This really is every bit as good as it's cracked up to be, and can be bought in *gelaterie*, specialist shops which offer a wide range of choices.

There are many delicious cheeses to try in addition to the most famous *Parmigiano* (Parmesan). *Bel paese* is smooth, mild and spreadable; *Burrini* are small cheeses with a knob of butter in the centre; *Dolcelatte* is a creamy, blue-veined cheese; *Fontina* is made from unpasteurized cows' milk; *Gorgonzola* is strong and blue-veined; *Mascarpone* is rich, sweet and creamy, and often used in desserts; *Ricotta* is a delicately flavoured cottage cheese, and *Mozzarella* is mild, soft cheese often used in cooking.

A full Italian meal would start with a choice of *antipasto*, hors d'oeuvres, sometimes a buffet with salami, cheese, olives and salads; the first course (*primo piatto*) is usually pasta or soup; the main course (*secondo piatto*) may be meat or fish, with cooked vegetables (*contorni*) or salad (*insalata*), which are ordered separately. Desserts (*dolci*) are not a strong point and tend to be either fruit, ice cream or local cheeses, although more sophisticated concoctions may sometimes be on offer, such as *tirami su* (chocolate and coffee gateau, soaked in alcohol), *cassata all Siciliano gelato* (ice cream made with Ricotta cheese from Sicily), or *zuppà inglese* (trifle).

Mention Italian wine and people automatically think of cheap plonk. Yet in fact many are world-class, particularly the reds. Try some of the better *Chiantis*, from Tuscany, and *Barolo*, a heavy red wine from Piedmont. *Verdicchio* and *Soave* are good whites and *Bardolino* is a pleasant rosé. *Secco* denotes a dry wine, *dolce*, a sweet, and *spumante*, sparkling. Local hooch will be your cheapest bet, although this will get rougher the further south you go. You'll be able to buy all the standard spirits here, and there's a good choice of liqueurs. In addition to Vermouth, brandy and *grappa* (which is made from the leftovers of the wine-making process!) are popular tipples, and you should look out too for *Amaretto* (an almond-based liqueur) and *Sambuca* (which is made from aniseed). Imported beers are expensive, so try the Italian brands *Peroni* and *Dreher* which are available in bottles. You are advised not to drink Italian tap water, so stick to the bottled varieties. Mineral waters come sparkling (*con gas* or *gassata*), or still (*senza gas*). Remember that it's always cheaper to drink standing up at the counter rather than sitting down.

Coffee in Italy is good and is generally served black and strong (*espresso*) in small cups. Milky coffee is traditionally drunk only at breakfast; ask for *caffe latte* or *cappuccino* (strong coffee with a frothy milky top and a sprinkling of cocoa powder). There are several other variations, including *caffe corretto al rhum* or *alla grappa* (with rum and brandy) and *caffe freddo* (iced coffee). If you prefer tea, remember to ask for milk, *tè con latte*, as otherwise it will be served black.

Vegetarians shouldn't have many problems eating out in Italy and will be able to try plenty of traditional foods. There is nearly always a delicious meat-free pasta or pizza dish on the menu, so you needn't look for specialist outlets. This is just as well, because ethnic eateries with veggie options are very hard to find. Restaurants are often quite happy to prepare something special for you, but do check they haven't slipped in a small amount of meat or fish as sometimes happens. Further information is available from: Associazione Vegetariana Italiana, Viale Gran Sasso 38, Milan.

Picnicking is easy, too, with plenty of breads, cheeses, salamis, ham, fruit and tomatoes to choose from. Shop in the open-air markets which can be found in every town, or the small specialist shops like *alimentari* (grocers), *panetterie* (bakers), *salumerie* (butchers) and *pasticcerie* (pastry shops). There are no particularly noteworthy supermarket chains in Italy – use the ones mentioned under each city section. Most shops are open from 8 a.m.–1 p.m., then 4–7 p.m. or 8 p.m., although the siesta is no longer so fashionable in the North. Almost all shops are closed on Sundays; there are also seasonal variations as many shops are closed on Monday mornings in the winter and Saturday afternoons in the summer. Fresh produce is generally of good quality, so you can be sure you won't go hungry. Try to learn a few Italian phrases before you go, as not many people speak English.

Bologna

LOCAL SPECIALITIES
The local cuisine focuses on handmade pasta dishes like *tagliatelle*, *lasagne*, *tortellini*, *ravioli*, and of course *spaghetti*, which is often served with the famous *Bolognese* sauce (also known as *ragu*). It's made from minced meat, onions, carrots, butter and fresh tomatoes. Look out too for meat products and salamis such as:

mortadella	a pork sausage with peppercorns
prosciutto	ham from nearby Parma
pan speziale	a cake made with honey, nuts and spices

In spring, asparagus is widely available and in autumn you can buy porcini mushrooms. The speciality cheese is a variety of parmesan, *Parmigiano-Reggiano*, and the local wine is Lambrusco, which tastes much better here than it does outside Italy.

CHEAP EATERIES
Two-course meals for under 12,500L (£5; $7.50)

Mensa Universitaria, Piazza Puntoni 1. Student ID required. Open Sept.–July, Mon.–Sat. 11.45 a.m.–2.30 p.m. and 6.45–9 p.m.
Ristorante Clorofilla, Strada Maggiore 64 (tel. 23 53 43). Vegetarian dishes predominate. Open Mon.–Sat. 11 a.m.–3 p.m. and 7 p.m.–midnight. Closed Aug.
Oggi Si Vola, Via Urbana 7 (tel. 58 53 08). Vegetarian restaurant. Open Mon.–Sat. noon–2.30 p.m. and 8–10.30 p.m.
Self Service Centro, Via Indipendenza 45 (tel. 23 42 16).
Trattoria Da Danio, Via S. Felice 50 (tel. 55 52 02). Open Mon.–Sat. noon–2.30 p.m. and 7.30–10 p.m. Closed for two weeks in Aug.
Café del Tribunale Enoteca, Via de' Ruini 1 (tel. 58 40 62). Closed Sun. and for two weeks in Aug.

Two-course meals from 12,500–17,500L (£5–7; $7.50–10.50)

Trattoria Della Santa, Via Urbana 7/F. Open Mon.–Sat. 12.30–2.30 p.m. and 7.45–10.30 p.m.
Osteria Matusel, Via Beroloni 2/2 (tel. 23 17 18).
La Taverna di Mago Merlino, Via S. Carlo 44 (tel. 24 64 01). Open 7 p.m.–1 a.m.

Two-course meals from 17,500–25,000L (£7–10; $10.50–15.00)

Antico Trattoria Roberto Spiga, Via Broccaidosse 21/a (tel. 26 00 67). Open Mon.–Sat. noon–2 p.m. and 7–10 p.m. Closed Aug.

Osteria dell'Orsa, Via Mentana 1/f (tel. 23 15 76). Open Mon.–Sat. 8 p.m.–2 a.m. Closed Aug.

Osteria del Moretto, Via S. Mamolo 5 (tel. 58 02 84). Open Mon.–Sat. 6 p.m.–2.30 a.m. (also noon–2.30 p.m. Sat.).

Hostaria S. Carlino, Via S. Carlo 16 (tel. 26 74 96). Open Mon.–Sat. 12.30–3 p.m. and 8 p.m.–2 a.m.

SHOPPING

Around Mercato delle Erbe you will find some of Bologna's finest food shops, which are at least worth exploring although some of them will be pricey. For the best ice cream, try Moline, Via delle Moline 6.

● Markets

There are many places where you can stock up on picnic food in Bologna. The best of the numerous markets are:

Mercato delle Erbe on Via Ugo Bassi
Mercato di mezzo on Via Pescherie Vecchie

Opening hours are: mornings Mon.–Sat. from 7 a.m.–1 p.m.; afternoons Mon.–Wed. 5–7 p.m., Fri. 4.30–7.30 p.m. Closed Thurs., Sat. and Sun. afternoons.

● Supermarkets

PAM, Via Marconi 28/A.
COOP, Piazza dei Martiri (Via Montebello 2).

Florence

LOCAL SPECIALITIES

pappa al pomodoro	a soup containing tomatoes, bread and basil
minestra di fagioli	white bean and garlic soup
ribollista	made with beans, bread and black cabbage
crostini	toasted bread with chicken liver paté
bruschette	bread grilled with olive oil and garlic

fagioli alla fiorentina	boiled haricot beans with pepper, salt and lemon juice
fagioli all'uccelletto	haricot beans in a tomato and herb sauce
bistecca alla fiorentina	steak with a little lemon juice, usually served *al sangue* (very rare)
arista	roast pork with rosemary
trippa alla fiorentina	tripe in tomato and cheese sauce
zuccotto	liqueur-soaked sponge and chocolate, served chilled
cantuccini di prato	almond biscuits
pecorino	a well-known local cheese

Chianti is the best known wine, but reds such as *Brunello di Montalcino* and *Vino Nobile di Montepulciano*, and whites like *Valdinievole* and *Valdichiana* are also very palatable, as is *Vin santo* (a sweet dessert wine made from dried grapes).

Florence is generally acknowledged as the ice cream capital of Italy. Foremost among the city's many ice cream shops is Vivoli at Via Isole dei Stinchi 74 (tel. 239 2334), whose ice cream is regarded as being amongst the best in the world (open Tues.–Sun. 9 a.m.– 1 a.m., closed Jan. and Aug.).

CHEAP EATERIES
It is virtually impossible to escape the tourist crowds in the historic centre of Florence, so, as you might expect, eating here can be a good deal more expensive than in the rest of the country (Venice excepted). Before ordering, be sure to check not just the prices but all the small print relating to cover and service charges as well.

Two-course meals for under 12,500L (£5; $7.50)

Mensa Universitaria, Via San Gallo 25/A. Open mid-Sept.–mid-July Mon.–Sat. noon–2.15 p.m. and 6.45–8.45 p.m. Student ID required.

Mensa San Francesco, Piazza Sant'Annunziata 2. Open Sept.–July Mon.–Fri. noon–2 p.m. Student ID required.

Ristorante Bella Cina, Via Guelfa 24. Chinese restaurant. Open daily noon–3 p.m. and 7–11 p.m.

Il Santommaso, Via Romana 80 (tel. 22 11 66). Vegetarian restaurant.

Trattoria da Benvenuto, Via dei Neri 47. Recommended dish: *braciola* (grilled veal chop). Open Mon.–Tues. and Thurs.–Sat. noon–3 p.m. and 7.15–10 p.m.

Almanacco, Via delle Ruote 30 (tel. 47 50 30). Florentine vegetarian

club. Restaurant open for lunch Tues.–Fri., and for dinner Tues.–Sat. Cheap membership available at the door.
Oltrarno Trattoria Casalinga, Via Michelozzi 9. Open Mon.–Sat. noon–3 p.m. and 7.30–9.30 p.m.
Rosticceria di Barone, Via Guelfo 40 (tel. 21 70 39). Persian cuisine. Recommended dish: *melanzano affumicaté* (smoked aubergine in sauce) – available only on Wed. Open Mon.–Fri. noon–10 p.m.; Sat. noon–9 p.m.

Two-course meals from 12,500–17,500L (£5–7; $7.50–10.50)

Trattoria da Giorgio, Via Palazzuolo 100. Open Mon.–Sat. noon–3 p.m. and 6.30–10 p.m.
La Scogliera, Via Palazzuolo 80 (tel. 21 02 57). Open Mon.–Fri. noon–3 p.m. and 7–11 p.m.
Il Giardino, Via della Scala 67 (tel. 21 31 41). Recommended dish: *tagliatelle*. Open Wed.–Mon. noon–3 p.m. and 7–10 p.m.
Trattoria da Za Za, Piazza Mercato Centrale 26 (tel. 21 54 11). Recommended dish: *tagliatelli al pesto*. Open Mon.–Sat. noon–2.30 p.m. and 7–10 p.m.

Two-course meals from 17,500–25,000L (£7–10; $10.50–15.00)

La Stazione di Zima, Via Ghibellina 70 (tel. 234 5318). Vegetarian restaurant. Open Mon. 12.30–3.30 p.m., Tues.–Fri. 12.30–3.30 p.m. and 7.30–11.30 p.m.; weekends 7.30–11.30 p.m.
Aquerello, Via Ghibellina 156 (tel. 234 0554). Recommended dish: *anitra all'arancia* (duck in orange sauce). Open Fri.–Wed. 11 a.m.–3 p.m. and 7–1 a.m.
La Maremmana, Via dei Macci 77 (tel. 24 12 26). Open Sept.–July Mon.–Sat. 12.30–3 p.m. and 7.30–10.30 p.m. Closed Aug.
Trattoria Sostanza, Via della Porcellana 25 (tel. 21 26 91). Open Mon.–Fri. noon–2.30 p.m. and 7.30–9.30 p.m. Closed Aug.
Ristorante Acqua al Due, Via dell'Acqua 2 (tel. 28 41 70). Open Tues.–Sun. 12.30–3 p.m. and 7.30 p.m.–1 a.m.

SHOPPING
The covered Mercato Centrale at Via dell'Ariosto 12 (near San Lorenzo) is open Mon.–Sat. 6.30 a.m.–1 p.m. year round, and also from 4–8.30 p.m. June–Sept. The Standa supermarket at Via Pietrapiana 1 is open Mon. 3–8 p.m.; Tues.–Sat. 8.30 a.m.–8 p.m.

Genoa (Genova)

There is a good selection of cheap restaurants in the *centro storico* (old town), but these are only to be recommended for lunchtime dining as the area is dangerous at night. Borgo Incrociati, near the Brignole train station, offers an array of inexpensive restaurants, and there are no problems as regards personal safety in this part of town.

LOCAL SPECIALITIES

pesto	a sauce prepared from ground basil, pine nuts, garlic, olive oil and parmesan cheese, which is served with pasta or added to minestrone soup
pansotti	ravioli filled with spinach and ricotta cheese, usually served with walnut sauce
zuppa di ceci	chickpea soup
burrida	fish stew
cima alla genovese	stuffed veal
polpettone	mashed potatoes and beans baked in breadcrumbs
farinata	a sort of fried pancake made from chickpeas
torta pasqualina	a pie made from spinach, cheese and eggs

CHEAP EATERIES
Two-course meals for under 12,500L (£5; $7.50)

Osteria da Colombo e Bruno, Borgo Incrociati 44. Open Sept.–July Mon.–Sat. 12.30–2.30 p.m. and 7.30–10 p.m.

Trattoria da Maria, Vico Testadoro 14 (tel. 58 10 80). Open Sun.–Thurs. noon–2 p.m. and 4.30–7 p.m.

Sa Pesta, Via Giustiniani 16 (tel. 20 86 36). Recommended dishes: *minestrone alla genovese* (with pesto added) and *farinata*. Open Sept.–July Mon.–Sat. noon–2.30 p.m.

Two-course meals from 12,500–17,500L (£5–7; $7.50–10.50)

Brera Express, Via Brera (tel. 54 32 80). Open Mon.–Fri. 11.30–2 p.m. and 7–midnight.

Kilt 2 Self-Service, Vicolo Doria. Open Mon.–Sat. 12.45–2.30 p.m.

Moody, Via XII Ottobre 8. Self-service restaurant. Open daily.

Bakari, Vicolo della Fieno 16. Vegetarian options always available.
   Open Mon.–Tues. and Thurs. noon–2.30 p.m. and 7–9.15 p.m.;
   Wed. and Fri. noon–2.30 p.m.
Luciano e Mimma, Corso M. Quadrio 4. Open Mon.–Fri.
   noon–2.30 p.m.

Milan

LOCAL SPECIALITIES

minestrone	soup, often served cold in summer
risotto alla certosina	Carthusian risotto
risotto alla milanese	saffron-flavoured risotto
costaletta alla milanese	veal cutlet, fried in breadcrumbs
ossobuco	marrow bone stew
cazzoeula	pork and vegetable stew, traditionally made in the winter
busecca	tripe
polenta pasticçiata	polenta pie with cheese sauce and white truffles
busecchina	chestnuts stewed in white wine, milk and cream
panettone	a cake made with sultanas and candied fruits
Grumello and *Sangue di Guida*	wines

CHEAP EATERIES
Two-course meals for under 12,500L (£5; $7.50)

Italy and Italy. Restaurant chain with branches at Corso Buenos
   Aires 7; Corso Venezia 7; and on Largo Carrobio.
Centro Macrobiotico, Via Larga 7 (tel. 86 68 19). Vegetarian res-
   taurant.
La Piccola Napoli, Viale Monza 13 (tel. 26 14 33 97). Open mid-
   Aug.–mid-July Tues.–Sun. 6 p.m.–3 a.m.
Mergellina, Via Molino delle Armi 48 (tel. 89 40 13 33). Open
   Sept.–July Thurs.–Mon. 11 a.m.–3 p.m. and 7 p.m.–1 a.m.;
   Wed. 7 p.m.–1 a.m.
Ciao. Restaurant chain with branches at Corso Europa 12; Via F.
   Filzi 8; and on Piazza del Duomo. Open daily noon–2.30 p.m.
   and 6.30–11 p.m.

Brek, Via Lepetit 24 and Via del Duca 5. Self-service restaurants. Open Sun.–Fri. 11.30 a.m.–3 p.m. and 6.30–10.30 p.m.

Two-course meals from 12,500–17,500L (£5–7; $7.50–10.50)

Be Bop Caffè/Ristorante, Viale Col di Lana 4 (tel. 837 6972). Open Sept.–mid-Aug. Mon.–Sat. noon–2.30 p.m. and 7.30 p.m.– 1 a.m.

Le Briciole, Via Camperio 17 (tel. 87 71 85 / 80 41 14). Open Tues.–Fri. and Sun. 12.15–2.30 p.m. and 7.15 p.m.–midnight.

Pizzeria del Nonno, Via Andrea Costa 1 (tel. 26 14 52 62). Open Tues.–Sat. noon–2.30 p.m. and 7 p.m.–12.30 a.m.; Sun. 6 p.m.– 12.30 a.m.

Spaghetteria Enoteca, Via Solferino 3. Open Sept.–July Mon.–Sat. 7.30–midnight.

Two-course meals from 17,500–25,000L (£7–10; $10.50–15.00)

Tarantella, Via le Abruzzi 35 (tel. 29 40 02 18). Open Sept.–July Sun.–Fri. noon–3 p.m. and 7–11.30 p.m.

Abele, Via Temperanza 5. Recommended dish: *risotto alla Milanese*. Open evenings only. Closed Mon.

Alfredo-Gran San Bernardo, Via Borghese 14. Specializes in local dishes. Recommended dish: *costaletta alla Milanese*. Closed Sun.

SHOPPING

There are several open-air markets in Milan: Fiera di Sinigallia, Catalafini – all day Saturday; Via Fauche or Viale Papiniano – Tues. and Sat.; Via Santa Croce – Thurs. You'll find plenty of small food shops as well, most of which will probably be closed on Sun. and Mon. afternoons. The nearest supermarkets are Standa, Via Torino 37 and Esselunga, Viale Piave 38.

If you like ice-cream you should head for Viel Gelati, Via Luca Beltrami, open Thurs.–Tues. until 2 a.m.

Naples

LOCAL SPECIALITIES

Pizza originated in Naples, and the city is still reputed to be the best place to try the dish. Some of the most popular toppings are classically simple, such as that named after the city, *alla napoletana* (with anchovies), or the two original types, *alla marina* (with tomatoes, oregano, garlic and olive oil) and *margherita* (with tomato, basil, and mozzarella cheese).

Other local specialities include:

zuppa di cozze	mussel soup
spaghetti alle vongole	spaghetti with clams, tomatoes and garlic
spaghetti alle cozze	spaghetti with mussels, tomatoes and garlic
mozzarella	a soft white cheese which becomes stringy when cooked, used in many dishes, including pizza
insalata caprese	mozzarella, tomato and basil salad
sfogliatella	a pastry filled with ricotta cheese and candied peel, eaten as a dessert or as a snack
gragnano	a red wine
lacrima christi	'Christ's tears' – a white wine which is the traditional accompaniment to seafood dishes

CHEAP EATERIES
Two-course meals for under 12,500L (£5; $7.50)

Mensa Universitaria, Via Mezzocanone. Student ID required.

Le Bistrot dell'Università, Via Sedile di Porto 51. Open Mon.–Fri. noon–4 p.m. Sept.–mid-Aug. Also open in the evening from Sept.–June, with South American cuisine on the menu.

Antica Pizzeria Da Michele, Via Cesare Sersale 1–3 (tel. 553 9204). Long established pizzeria serving only the two original types of pizza. Open Sept.–mid-Aug. 8 a.m.–10 p.m.

Trattoria Da Maria, Via Genova 115. Recommended dish: *bucatini alla puttanesca* (pasta with olives, tomatoes and capers). Open Mon.–Sat. noon–3.30 p.m. and 6.30–10 p.m. Closed last two weeks in Aug.

Trattoria Fratelli Prigiobbo, Via Portacarrese 96 (tel. 40 79 62). Recommended dish: *calamaro* (squid). Open Sept.–early Aug. Mon.–Sat. 9 a.m–11 p.m.

Trattoria alla Brace, Via Silvio Spaventa 14 (tel. 26 12 60). Open Mon.–Sat. noon till midnight.

Two-course meals from 12,500–17,500L (£5–7; $7.50–10.50)

Pizzeria Trianon da Ciro, Via Parco Margherita 27 (tel. 41 46 78). Recommended dish: *pizza Trianon* (a pizza with different toppings

on each of its four sections). Open daily noon–4 p.m. and 6 p.m.–
1 a.m. Best reserved in advance on Sat. night.
Pizzeria Port'Alba, Via Port'Alba 18 (tel. 45 97 13). Recommended
dish: *vecchia pizza Port'Alba* (pizza with four sections and four
toppings). Open Thurs.–Tues. 9 a.m.–2 a.m.
Antica Trattoria al Vicoletto, Via Camillo Cucca 52 (tel. 66 92 90).
Recommended dish: *tagliatelle al vicoletto* (with tomatoes, peppers,
aubergine and pesto). Open Sept.–July Mon.–Sat. noon–3 p.m.
and 7 p.m.–1 a.m.
Osteria Donna Teresa, Via Kerbaker 58 (tel. 556 7070). Recommended dish: *spaghetti alle vongole*. Open Sept.–July Mon.–Sat.
noon–3 p.m. and 8 p.m.–midnight.
Gopala, Corso Vittorio Emanuele 170 (tel. 41 40 11). Vegetarian
Indian restaurant. Open Tues.–Sun. 8 p.m.–midnight.
Osteria Canterbury, Via Ascensione 6 (tel. 41 35 84). Recommended dish: *penne di casa Canterbury* (pasta with aubergine,
cheese and tomato sauce). Open Sept.–July 1–3 p.m. and
8.30 p.m.–midnight.

Two-course meals from 17,500–25,000L (£7–10; $10.50–15.00)

Avellinese Da Peppino, Via Silvio Spaventa 31–35 (tel. 28 38 97).
Recommended dish: *spaghetti alle vongole*. Open daily 11 a.m.–
midnight.

SHOPPING
● **Supermarket**

Standa, Via Toledo 128 (junction with Via Roma). Open Mon.–Fri.
9 a.m.–1 p.m. and 4–7.45 p.m.; Sat. 9.10 a.m.–1 p.m.

● **Markets**
There is a general food market just off Piazza Garibaldi on Via
Suprammuro (Mon.–Sat. 8 a.m.–1.30 p.m.) and a fish market by
the Porta Nolana.

Pisa

The largest concentration of reasonably priced eateries is in the
area around Piazza Cavalieri and Piazza Dante Alighieri. Establish-

ments in the immediate vicinity of the Leaning Tower tend to be more expensive than elsewhere in the city.

LOCAL SPECIALITIES

torta di ceci/cecina   a pizza made with chickpeas

CHEAP EATERIES
Two-course meals for under 12,500L (£5; $7.50)

Mensa Universitaria, Via Martiri. Student ID required. Open mid-Sept.–mid-July Mon.–Fri. noon–2.30 p.m. and 7–9 p.m.; weekends noon–2.30 p.m.
Buffet Stazione, Piazza Stazione 12 (tel. 46319). Closed Tues.
Trattoria Da Matteo, Via l'Aroncio 46. Recommended dish: *scaloppina in umido con i funghi* (veal with mushrooms). Open Sun.–Fri. noon–3 p.m. and 7–10.30 p.m.
Pizzeria Nando, Corso Italia 103. Open Mon.–Sat. 10 a.m.–2.30 p.m. and 4–10 p.m.

Two-course meals from 12,500–17,500L (£5–7; $7.50–10.50)

Cassio, Piazza Cavallotti 14 (tel. 55 34 69). Closed at weekends.
Trattoria Stelio, Piazza Dante 11. Closed Sat. evening and Sun.

Two-course meals from 17,500–25,000L (£7–10; $10.50–15.00)

Bruno, Via L. Bianchi 12 (tel. 56 08 18). Good range of Tuscan specialities. Closed Mon. evening, all day Tues., and for two weeks in Aug.
Sergio, Lungarno Pacinotti 1 (tel. 48245). Closed Sun. and lunchtime Mon.
Da Spartaco, Piazza Vittorio Emanuele 22 (tel. 23335 / 20457). Good range of regional dishes. Closed Sun.

SHOPPING
● **Supermarket**
Next to the campsite at Viale delle Caseirne, a 5–10 minute walk from the Leaning Tower.

● **Market**
On Piazza Vettovaglio.

Rome

LOCAL SPECIALITIES
Speciality foods of the area include the classic sauces, *carbonara* (cream, bacon and egg), and *amatriciana* (bacon and tomato), served with pasta, usually spaghetti or fettucine.

Stracciatella	clear soup with egg
codadibue alla vaccinara	oxtail stuffed with onions and carrots
animelle alla griglia	grilled calf's veins
fave al guanciale	broad beans with onions and bacon

Typical cheeses are *ricotta* and *pecorino romano*.

SPECIAL EVENTS AND FESTIVALS
Local festivals where food is available include the Feast of Saint John (in June), when snails are eaten in the San Giovanni neighbourhood; and the Festa de Noantri (in July), when the streets are lit up and everyone eats out on the pavements of Trastevere.

CHEAP EATERIES
In contrast to some of the other major Italian cities, it is relatively easy to eat cheaply in Rome. Although restaurants close by prime tourist sites such as the Spanish Steps tend to be overpriced there are plenty of more reasonably priced eateries around, especially in the San Lorenzo, Testaccio, Trastevere and Campo dei Fiori districts, and along the streets just off Piazza Navona (establishments on the square generally offer poor value for money).
Two-course meals for under 12,500L (£5; $7.50)

Casa dello Studente, Via Cesare de Lollis 24 (tel. 49 02 43). Student ID required.
Bar Marco Polo, Largo S. Susanna 108 (tel. 482 4869). Self-service. Open Mon.–Sat. noon–3 p.m. and 6.30–10 p.m.
Pizzeria Baffetto, Via del Governo Vecchio 114 (tel. 686 1617). Open Mon.–Sat. 6.30 p.m.–1 a.m. Closed Sundays for fifteen days in Aug.
Osteria con Cucina de Andreis Luciano, Via Giovanni Amendola 73–75 (tel. 488 1640). Recommended dish: *pollo e pepperoni* (chicken and peppers). Open Mon.–Fri. 9 a.m.–3 p.m. and 7–9 p.m.; Sat. 11.30 a.m.–5 p.m.
Filetto di Baccalà, Largo dei Librari 88 (tel. 686 4018).

Recommended dish: *filetto di baccalà* (fried cod fillet) and *fiori di zucca* (fried courgette flowers).

Two-course meals from 12,500–17,500L (£5–7; $7.50–10.50)

Mario's, Via del Moro 53 (tel. 580 3809). Open Sept.–mid-Aug. Mon.–Sat. noon–3 p.m. and 7–11 p.m.

Pizzeria Imperiale, Largo C. Ricci 37 (tel. 678 6871). Recommended pizza: *peccato del frate* (red peppers, spicy sausage, courgettes, artichokes and olives). Open Mon.–Sat. noon–4 p.m. and 7.30 p.m.–midnight.

Centro Macrobiotico Italiano, Via della Vite 14 (3rd floor) (tel. 679 2509). Vegetarian club. Tourists with their passports are allowed one meal, for which a small surcharge is levied. Recommended dish: *cous-cous vegetale*. Open Mon.–Fri. 10 a.m.–7.30 p.m.

Ristorante La Pollorola, Piazza della Pollorola 24–25 (tel. 68 80 16 54). Recommended dish: *spaghetti alle vongole* (with clams). Open Mon.–Sat. noon–4 p.m. and 7 p.m. midnight.

Hostaria Grappolo d'Oro, Piazza della Cancelleria 80–81 (tel. 686 4118). Recommended dish: *spaghetti alle vongole* (with clams). Open Mon.–Sat. noon–4 p.m. and 7 p.m.–midnight.

L'Insalata Ricca, Largo di Chiavari 85 (tel. 654 3656). Good range of salads. Recommended dish: *insalata ricca* (mixed salad). Open Thurs.–Tues. 12.30–3 p.m. and 7–11 p.m. Closed 15–16 Aug.

Navona Notte, Via del Teatro Pace 44–46 (tel. 656 9278). Recommended dish: *cozze* (mussels). Open Thurs.–Tues. 7 p.m.–3 a.m.

Ristorante il Delfino, Corso Vittorio Emanuele II 67 (tel. 686 4053). Self-service restaurant. Open Tues.–Sun. 8 a.m.–9 p.m.

Il Gardinetto, Via del Governo Vecchio 125. Open Tues.–Sun. 12.30–3 p.m. and 7.30 p.m.–midnight.

Two-course meals from 17,500–25,000L (£7–10; $10.50–15.00)

Trattoria Da Settimio all'Arancio, Via dell'Arancio 50 (tel. 687 6119). Recommended dish: *ossobuco* (braised veal shank in sauce). Open Mon.–Sat. 1–3.30 p.m. and 7 p.m.–midnight. Closed one week in Aug.

Taverna dei Quaranta, Via Claudia 24 (tel. 700 0550). Recommended dish: *fritto misto vegetale* (fried mixed vegetables). Open noon–3 p.m. and 8 p.m.–1 a.m.

Hostaria dei Bastioni, Via Leone IV 29 (tel. 39 72 30 34). Fine range of seafood dishes. Recommended dish: *risotto alla pescatore* (rice with seafood sauce). Open Mon.–Sat. noon–3 p.m. and 7 p.m.–1.30 a.m.

Trattoria Turiddo, Via Galvani 64 (tel. 575 0447). Recommended dishes: *animelle alla griglia* (grilled calves veins) and *rigatoni con pagliata* (with lamb's intestine and tomato). Open mid-Sept.–mid-Aug. Mon.–Tues. and Thurs. 12.30–4 p.m. and 7.30 p.m.–11 p.m.; Sun. 1–2.30 p.m.

Trattoria Al Vecchio Mattatoio, Piazza Giustanini 2 (tel. 574 1382). Recommended dishes: *tonarello sugo coda* (thick spaghetti with oxtail and tomato sauce) and *arrosto misto di frattaglie* (mixed grill with liver, intestines, veins and back muscles). Open Sept.–July Wed.–Sun. 12.30–4 p.m. and 7.30–11 p.m.; Mon. 1–3 p.m.

Il Canestro, Via Luca della Robbia 47 (tel. 574 2800). Vegetarian dishes predominate. Open Mon.–Sat. 12.30–3.30 p.m. and 7.30 p.m.–12.30 a.m.

SHOPPING
● **Supermarkets**
Standa. On Viale Trastevere and on Via Cola di Rienzo.

● **Markets**
On Piazza Vittorio Emanuele II, Piazza Campo dei Fiori, and the indoor market just off Via Cola di Rienzo. Hours vary, but generally Mon.–Sat. 6 a.m.–2 p.m.

Turin (Torino)

LOCAL SPECIALITIES

agnolotti	ravioli filled with lamb and cabbage
bagna cauda	a sauce prepared from olive oil, butter, anchovies, garlic and cream, served with raw or cooked vegetables
bocca di leone	a doughnut filled with whipped cream
spumone piemontese	a thick mousse prepared with mascarpone cheese and rum
baci di dama	a pastry (literally 'lady's kisses')
lingue di gatto	literally 'cat's tongue' – another exotically named pastry

CHEAP EATERIES
Two-course meals for under 12,500L (£5; $7.50)

Trattoria Messico, Via B. Galliari 8 (tel. 650 8793). Open Mon.–Sat. noon–2 p.m. and 7–10 p.m.

Trattoria Toscana, Via Vanchiglia 2 (tel. 812 2914). Recommended dish: *bistecca di cinghiale* (wild boar steak). Open Sept.–July Sun.–Fri. noon–4.30 p.m. and 7–9.30 p.m.

Seven-Up, Via A. Doria 4. Open Tues.–Sun. noon–2.30 p.m. and 6.30–11 p.m.

Brek, Piazza Carlo Felice 22. Self-service restaurant. Open daily 11.30 a.m.–3 p.m. and 6.30–10.30 p.m.

Two-course meals from 12,500–17,500L (£5–7; $7.50–10.50)

Ristorante Taverna Fiorentina, Via Palazzo di Città 6 (tel. 54 24 12). Recommended dish: *capretto Sardo al forno* (Sardinian-style baked lamb). Open Aug.–June Sun.–Fri. noon–3 p.m. and 7–10 p.m.

Trattoria Amelia, Via dei Mercanti 6 (tel. 562 8478). Open Sun.–Fri. noon–2.30 p.m. and 6.30–9.30 p.m.

Il Punto Verde, Via Belfiore 15/F (tel. 640 4514). Vegetarian restaurant. Open Tues.–Fri.

Peppino, Via dei Mercanti 9/A. Open Mon.–Sat. noon–2.30 p.m. and 7–10 p.m.

Two-course meals from 17,500–25,000L (£7–10; $10.50–15.00)

La Tre Galline, Via Bellezia 37. Open daily noon–2.30 p.m. and 7.30–10 p.m.

SHOPPING
● **Markets**

Piazza della Repubblica. Open Mon.–Fri. 8 a.m.–1 p.m.

Mercato Rossini, Via Rossini (junction with Via Lagrange). Open Mon.–Tues. and Thurs.–Fri. 8.30 a.m.–1 p.m. and 4–7.30 p.m.; Wed. 8.30 a.m.–1 p.m.

● **Supermarket**

Metà, Via Mazzina 42. Open Mon.–Tues. and Thurs.–Sat. 8.30 a.m.–12.30 p.m. and 4–7.30 p.m.; Wed. 8.30 a.m.–12.30 p.m.

Venice

LOCAL SPECIALITIES

Once you've found a cheap place to eat there are plenty of typical Venetian dishes for you to try:

risi e bisi	thick rice and pea soup
bigoli in salsa	wholemeal spaghetti with anchovy sauce
pasta e fasioi	pasta, pork and bean soup
pasticcio di pesce	pasta baked with fish
seppie in nero	cuttlefish cooked in its own ink
pesca fritta mista	mixed fried fish
fegato di vitello alla veneziana	liver and onions Venetian-style

Baicoli is a typical biscuit of the city, and you will find the following sweets available during the Carnival (which runs for 10 days in Lent, starting on Shrove Tuesday): *fritole*, *galani* and *castagnole*. Regional wines include Tocai and Pinot (whites), and Merlot, Cabernet, Roboso and Refosco (reds).

CHEAP EATERIES

Finding good value meals is far from easy in Venice. Fixed-price tourist menus are often the best option, though what you get for your money here will rarely compare with what you might expect elsewhere in the country. Eateries around San Marco tend to be vastly overpriced, even by Venetian standards. Wherever you are be sure to check the cover charge before ordering: 3,000L (£1.20; $1.80) cover charges are far more common in Venice than in the other major cities.
Two-course meals for under 12,500L (£5; $7)

Mensa Universitaria di Ca Foscari, S. Polo 2480 on Calle del Magazen (tel. 71 80 69). Student ID required. Open Mon.–Sat. 11.45 a.m.–2.30 p.m. and 6.30–8.30 p.m.; Sun. noon–2 p.m.

Mensa Dopolavoro Ferroviario. The railway workers' canteen, near Venezia Santa Lucia train station.

Gino's, Cannaregio 158, on Lista di Spagna (tel. 71 60 72). Open Fri.–Wed. 9 a.m.–midnight.

Ristorante al Giardinetto, San Polo 2909 on Calle del Cristo. Open Tues.–Sun. noon–2 p.m. and 7–10 p.m.

Self-service Rialto, Riva del Carbon (tel. 523 7909). Open Mon.–Sat.

Da Mario, Fondamente della Malvasia Vecchia 2614 (tel. 528 5968). Open Sun.–Fri.

Trattoria alle Burcheille, Santa Croce 393 on Fondamente Burchielle (tel. 523 1342). Open Tues.–Sun. for lunch and dinner.

Leon Bianco, San Marco 4153 on Salizzata San Luca. Eat whilst standing at tall tables. Open Mon.–Sat. 8 a.m.–8 p.m.

Two-course meals from 12,500–17,500L (£5–7; $7.50–10.50)

Ristorante al Ponte, Cannaregio 2352 on Ponte Geremia (tel. 522 8609). Recommended dish: *seppie nere alla Veneziana* (cuttlefish in a sauce made with olive oil, tomatoes and white wine). Open Wed.–Mon. 11.30 a.m.–2.30 p.m. and 6.30–9.30 p.m.

Ai Promessi Sposi, Cannaregio 4367 on Calle dell'Oca (tel. 522 8609). Recommended dish: *spaghetti bigoli in salsa* (with anchovies and onions). Open Thurs.–Tues. noon–2.30 p.m. and 7–10 p.m.

Trattoria Casa Mia, Cannaregio 4430 on Calle dell'Oca (tel. 528 5590). Open Wed.–Mon. noon–3 p.m. and 6–10 p.m.

Trattoria/Pizzeria All'Anfora, Santa Croce 1223 on Lista Vecchia dei Bari (tel. 524 1342). Open Tues.–Sun. for lunch and dinner.

Rosticceria San Bartolomeo, San Marco 5424/A on Calle de la Bissa (tel. 522 3569). Recommended dish: *seppie con polenta* (cuttlefish with cornmeal pudding). Open Feb.–Dec. Tues.–Sun. 10 a.m.–2.25 p.m. and 4.50–9 p.m.

Antiche Botteselle, Via Castello 1621 on Via Garibaldi (tel. 523 7292). Open Thurs.–Tues. 8.30 a.m.–3 p.m. and 6–10 p.m.

Alla Rivetta, San Polo 1479 by the canal on Campiello dei Melone (tel. 522 4246). Open Tues.–Sun. 7 a.m.–noon and 2–9.30 p.m.

Two-course meals from 17,500–25,000L (£7–10; $10.50–15.00)

Osteria Al Mascaron, Castell 5225 on Calle Longa Santa Maria Formosa (tel. 522 5995). Recommended dish: *spaghetti alle vongolenero* (with black clams). Open mid-Jan–mid-Dec. Mon.–Sat. 11 a.m.–3 p.m. and 6–11 p.m.

Trattoria alla Rivetta, Castello 9625 on Salizzada San Provolo (tel. 528 7302). Recommended dish: *pesce fritta mista* (mixed fried seafood). Open Tues.–Sun. 10 a.m.–10 p.m. Closed Aug.

L'Arca di Noe, Cannaregio 5401 on Calle Larga Giacinto Gallina (tel. 523 8153). Vegetarian restaurant. Indian food on Wed. Open Fri.–Wed. 9 a.m.–3 p.m. and 5–11 p.m.

SHOPPING
● **Supermarkets**

Standa, Cannaregio 3660 on Strada Nova near Campo S. Felice. Open daily 8.30 a.m.–7.20 p.m.

Su. Ve, Castello 5816 on Calle del Mondo Novo off Campo Santa Maria Formosa. Open Mon.–Tues. and Thurs.–Sat. 8.45 a.m.–7 p.m.; Wed. 8.45 a.m.–1 p.m.

Mega I, Dorsoduro 3019/B on Campo Santa Margherita (the entrance between the phone booth and caffe is unsigned). Open daily 9 a.m.–1 p.m.; extended hours Thurs.–Tues. 4.30–7.30 p.m. and Sat. 4.30–7.45 p.m.

Vivo, Giudecca 203/A on Fondamente de Zittele. Open Mon.–Sat. except Wed. afternoon.

Supermarket, Dorsoduro 1492 on Fondamente Zattere. Open Mon.–Sat. 8.30 a.m.–12.30 p.m. and 3.30–7.30 p.m.; Wed. 8.30 a.m.–12.30 p.m. only.

● **Markets**

In San Polo the city's famous Mercato Rialto operates daily from 7.30 a.m.–1 p.m. Other open-air markets can be found on:

Via Garibaldi (Mon.–Sat. 8.30 a.m.–1.30 p.m.)
Campo Santa Margherita (Tues.–Sat. 8.30 a.m.–1 p.m.)
Rio Terra S. Leonardo (Mon.–Sat. 8.30 a.m.–1.30 p.m.)

Verona

LOCAL SPECIALITIES

gnocchi di patate	potato gnocchi, a heavier pasta than usual, but absolutely delicious
tortino di patate pioppini e tartufo nero	potato pie with mushrooms and black truffles – a pricey dish
maltagliati al ragu di conigilio	pasta with rabbit sauce
peara	sauce made from a blend of breadcrumbs and bone marrow, and delicious and unusual mushrooms

Wines to look out for are Valpolicella and Bardolino (red), and Soave and Bianco di Custoza (white).

SPECIAL EVENTS AND FESTIVALS
Some local festivals where you may get the chance to try food and
wine are: 'Carnevale' in February; 'Vinitaly', the wine fair in April;
and 'Festa dell'Uva', the grape fair in October.

CHEAP EATERIES
Two-course meals for under 12,500L (£5; $7.50)

Brek, Piazza Bra 20 (tel. 800 4561). Open daily 11.30 a.m.–3 p.m.
and 6.30–10 p.m. Self-service joint.
Ciao Ristorante, Via Mazzini 36 (tel. 59 46 12). Open Tues.–Sun.
11.30 a.m.–3 p.m. and 5.30–11 p.m.
Gamma, Viale del Lavoro 39 (tel. 58 37 18). Open Mon.–Sat.
7 a.m.–8 p.m.
Tavola Calda alle Sgarzerie, Corte Sgarzerie. Open Mon.–Sat.
9.30 a.m.–10.30 p.m.
Vimac, Via Roma 26 (tel. 803 3830). Open 11 a.m.–2.30 p.m. and
5–8.30 p.m. Closed Sat. afternoon and all day Sun. Self-service
restaurant.
Trattoria Al Cacciatore, Via Seminario 4 (tel. 59 42 91). Open
Mon.–Fri. 8.30 a.m.–2.30 p.m. and 6.30–10 p.m.; Sat.
noon–2.30 p.m.

Two-course meals from 12,500–17,500L (£5–7; $7.50–10.50)

Trattoria Fontanina, Piazzetta Chiavica 5 (tel. 803 1133). Open
Wed.–Sun. noon–2 p.m. and 7–9.30 p.m.; Mon. noon–2 p.m.
Il Grillo Parlante, Vicolo Seghe San Tommaso 10 (tel. 59 11 56).
Vegetarian restaurant. Open Fri.–Sun and Tues.–Wed.
noon–2 p.m. and 7.30–10 p.m. Thurs. noon–2 p.m. only.
Nuova Grottina, Via Interrato dell'Acqua Morta 38 (tel. 803 0152).
Open Fri.–Wed. 9.30 a.m.–2.30 p.m. and 6 p.m.–1 a.m.
Trattoria dal Ropeton, Via San Giovanne in Valle 46 (tel. 30040).
Open Wed.–Mon. 12.30–3 p.m. and 7.30–11 p.m.

Two-course meals from 17,500–25,000L (£7–10; $10.50–15.00)

Le Gourmet, Via XX Settembre 109 (tel. 800 6827). Open
Mon.–Sat.
La Grotta, Via Bresciana 16 (tel. 890 3865). Open Fri.–Wed.
La Pagoda, Via Fama 6 (tel. 800 1932). Open Tues.–Sun. Chinese
restaurant.

SHOPPING
● Supermarkets

PAM, Via del Mutilato 3. Open Mon.–Tues. and Thurs.–Sat.
   8.30 a.m.–7.30 p.m.; Wed. 8.30 a.m.–noon.
YMAS, Via XXIV Maggio.
ESSELUNGA, Corso Milano 96.

N.B. On Wednesdays be sure to get any shopping you need in the morning as most shops close in the afternoon.

● Market

Piazza delle Erbe, Mon.–Sat.

LUXEMBOURG

The best cheap option for a cooked meal in Luxembourg is a *menu du jour* – a fixed menu typically comprising soup, a main course and dessert – which many restaurants offer. Prices for fixed menus start about 300LF (£6; $9) in the capital, about 250LF (£5; $7.50) elsewhere in the country. Eating *à la carte* is much more expensive, with the cheapest two-course meals in the city costing 300–400LF (£6–8; $9–12); 250–300LF (£5–6; $7.50–9.00) outside the capital.

Given the small size of the Grand Duchy it is hardly surprising that its cuisine shows similarities with those of its three larger neighbours. Nevertheless there are a number of dishes which are real Lëtzebuergesch specialities, and others which are particular local favourites.

Soups fall into one of two categories: clear consommés or thicker broths. Mixed vegetable, onion, pea, lentil, chicken, and oxtail soups are all common, but it is potato soup and green bean soup which enjoy the greatest popularity.

The finest starter is the wafer thin Ardennes ham, though you can also find this served as a main course with a variety of accompaniments.

Meat-based specialities include jellied suckling pig, smoked neck of pork with broad beans and *treipen* (black pudding – usually accompanied with sausage, mashed potatoes and horse radish).

Amongst the more common accompaniments to meat-based entrées are *sauerkraut* (pickled cabbage), potato dumplings and calves' liver dumplings – all of obvious Germanic origin.

Apart from hare (which is a speciality during the hunting season) and mussels, the other main course specialities tend to incorporate freshwater fish: trout prepared in Riesling wine, pike and *friture de la Moselle* (fried mixed small fish).

Vegetarians are well catered for in Luxembourg. Most restaurants offer at least one meat-free dish, and even where this is not the case the relative absence of language difficulties coupled with restaurant staff who are invariably eager to please means that you are virtually assured something suitable in any restaurant in the country.

The most popular of Lëtzebuergesch desserts are apple cake and cheesecake. In addition to these, and desserts based on fresh fruits, there are the seasonal favourites *quetsch* (plum tarts, made in September) and *Les Pensées Brouillées* (pastries made in the period leading up to Shrovetide).

For a hearty snack you can buy *hammeschmier, zoossis-schmier* or *kachkeis schmier* in virtually any café. These consist of slices of bread piled up on a plate, topped with ham, sausage or the unique Lëtzebuergesch cheese *kachkeis*, respectively. Prices vary, but you will pay something in the region of 200–300LF (£4–6; $6–9) in most places.

Putting together a picnic lunch is simple in Luxembourg. You can usually find a supermarket even in quite small towns, though in some cases these are located on the fringes of town, with what amount to mini-markets in the centre. In larger towns supermarkets tend to be located in what are known in Luxembourg as shopping centres. Shopping hours vary, but the most common opening hours are Mon. 2–6 p.m., Tues.–Fri. 9 a.m.–noon and 2–6 p.m., Sat. 9 a.m.–noon (large supermarkets tend not to close at lunchtime). On the whole, prices are higher than in the UK (usually by about 20%), but fresh fruit and vegetables are slightly cheaper.

Luxembourg's white wines are very well regarded amongst wine drinkers. In addition to well-known still whites such as *Riesling, Pinot Blanc, Auxerrois* and *Elbing*, there are also the sparkling white *Moselle Perlé* wines. There are many inexpensive wines costing around 200LF (£4; $6) per bottle in a restaurant, or 70–100LF (£1.40–2.00; $2.10–3.00) in a local store. Over 80% of the country's production comes from the vineyards along the Moselle, and most of the towns in this area have at least one wine festival a year. Festivals take place from Easter to November, but your best chance of catching one is if you are travelling in August or September.

Luxembourg's beers deserve to be as well known as the country's wines. Breweries like Mousel, Bofferding, Diekirch, Henri Funck, Clausen and Battin turn out some fine light *pils* and dark (*donkel*) beers between them; all are brewed without any chemical additives whatsoever. A typical 0.33 litre measure costs about 35LF (£0.70; $1) in a bar; a smaller 0.25 litre measure about 28LF (£0.55; $0.85). A 0.33 litre bottle in a local shop will usually cost 20LF (£0.40; $0.60), not including the deposit.

All the usual spirits are available in Luxembourg, but imported spirits can be pricey. Home-produced spirits and liqueurs such as *Mirabelle, Kirsch* and *Prunelle* are much better value.

Luxembourg

CHEAP EATERIES
Two-course meals for under 200LF (£4; $6)

Monopol-Gare, av. de la Liberté 53 (tel. 49 09 04). Self-service cafeteria. Open Mon.–Sat. until 5 p.m.
Monopol-Ville, rue Génistre 5 (tel. 47 38 22). City-centre branch of the above. Same hours. Vegetarian menus available.

Two-course meals from 200–300LF (£4–6; $6–9)

Grennesch Stuff, rue de Trèves 1 (tel. 46 66 71). Vegetarian menu available. Closed Tues. evening, otherwise open daily until 12.30 a.m.
As Arcadas, rue Joseph Junck 29 (tel. 49 12 64). Open daily until 11 p.m.
Peking Garden, rue Philippe II 31 (tel. 47 55 51). Chinese restaurant. Vegetarian menu available. Open daily until 11 p.m.

Two-course meals from 300–400LF (£6–8; $9–12)

EMS, place de la Gare 30 (tel. 48 77 99). Recommended dishes: smoked Ardennes ham, and any of the fish dishes. Closes at noon on Sat., otherwise open daily until 12.45 a.m.
Le Gaugin, place Guillaume 8 (tel. 22 04 93). Vegetarian menu available. Open daily until 9 p.m.

Two-course meals from 400–500LF (£8–10; $12–15)

Rotisserie Ardennaise, av. du X Septembre 1 (tel. 45 09 74). Vegetarian menu available. Open Mon.–Sat. until 10 p.m.
Um Dierfgen, côte d'Eich 6 (tel. 22 61 41). Open daily until 11 p.m.

SHOPPING
There is a supermarket downstairs in the shopping centre at av. de la Gare 47.

FURTHER INFORMATION
The brochure *Hôtels Restaurants – Ville de Luxembourg*, available from the Municipal Tourist Office on place d'Armes lists a selection of restaurants in the city, complete with a guide to prices in all the restaurants included.

MOROCCO

Moroccan cuisine revolves around a number of classic dishes. Foremost amongst the soups is *harira*, a combination of small cubes of meat, lentils, beans, tomatoes and spices, which is almost guaranteed to figure on any restaurant menu. As is the case with the majority of Moroccan soups, *harira* is sufficiently thick and filling to make for a substantial snack.

Stews (*tajines*) proliferate in Moroccan cooking; they are usually based either on lamb or poultry cooked with various combinations of fruit, nuts and vegetables. The ubiquity of *tajines* on restaurant menus matches that of *harira*.

The national dish is *couscous*, typically prepared by steaming wheat semolina above a stew of lamb or chicken with garbanzo beans and assorted vegetables. In truth there is no single recipe for *couscous*, but rather a whole host of regional variations on this basic formula, including a number of fish-based *couscous* found along the coast.

Two of the highlights of Moroccan cuisine are *meshoui* and *bastilla*. The former is oven- or spit-roasted lamb; the latter, pigeon and almond baked in a thin pastry, often sprinkled with sugar and cinnamon.

For a sit-down meal the major divide falls between eateries in the *medina* and those located in the *ville nouvelle*. At the former your choice of main course tends to be restricted, since many *medina* eateries offer little more than a basic choice of *tajine* or *kebabs* (pieces of meat, and occasionally offal, grilled on a skewer). *Ville nouvelle* restaurants are more likely to serve *couscous*, *bastilla*, *meshoui*, spit-roasted chicken (*poulet rôti*), chicken with olives and lemon (*poulet aux olives et citron*) or, near the coast, fish-based dishes. In addition to these mainstream Moroccan dishes (and of course the omnipresent *tajines*) *ville nouvelle* restaurants generally fill out their menu with several examples of French cuisine.

Wherever you choose to eat, decent-sized portions are virtually assured. Eating in the *medina* is, not surprisingly, the cheapest option: a basic meal of soup, *tajine* or *kebabs*, plus a dessert usually costs in the region of 22dh (£1.60; $2.35). Depending upon what you choose, you can expect to pay up to 70dh (£5.25; $8) for a three-course meal in a typical *ville nouvelle* restaurant.

Although the thrust of Moroccan cuisine is towards meat-based dishes, vegetarians can get by. However, as in many other countries, the range of options on restaurant menus is slim. Bean-based dishes and omelettes (the latter are also sold from street stalls) are common, as is the *salade marocaine* which turns up on most menus.

There is no set way of preparing this salad, but you can expect cucumber and tomatoes, plus a few other vegetables. The situation is improved enormously if you speak French, as restaurant staff are far more likely to understand this than English, and will seldom be averse to putting together a meat-free dish on request.

The most common desserts are fresh fruit and nuts, or, to a lesser extent, the highly rated Moroccan pastries. The incredible sweetness of the latter may come as something of a shock initially; there are countless different pastries, but the main unifying theme is the presence of large amounts of honey and almonds. Most famous of all is the crescent shaped *corne de gazelle* (gazelle's horn). If you really want to try some of these pastries it is far simpler just to buy them from a patisserie or a street vendor than to rely upon finding them in a local restaurant.

Morocco enjoys such an abundance of seasonal fruit and nuts that the variety on offer can be quite astonishing: almonds, grapes, melons, apricots, peaches, plums, strawberries, cactus fruit, figs and a variety of dates. Fruit and nuts make for excellent snacks as they can be bought virtually anywhere from street sellers, but to be on the safe side fruit should always be peeled or washed in bottled water before it is eaten.

For a meat-based snack whilst exploring the *medina*, takeaway *kebabs* and *kefta* (small, spicy meatballs) can be purchased from street stalls or from many eateries. Another widely available snack possibility is the high-quality Moroccan yoghurt (*yaourt*) which is sold on many street stalls, either in cartons costing about 2–3dh (£0.14–0.21; $0.20–0.32), or in smaller measures poured into a glass.

It is reasonably easy to get an alcoholic drink in a *ville nouvelle* of one of the main towns, but you will seldom find any alcohol on sale in the *medinas*. Morocco produces a relatively small amount of wine, but the average quality is surprisingly good. If Moroccan wines are not to your taste it is no great problem as all types (and price categories) of French and Spanish wines can be found in *ville nouvelle* eateries.

Regardless of whether it is ordered as an accompaniment to a meal, or simply drunk on its own in a bar, beer is (comparatively) expensive at around 12dh (£0.85; $1.30) for a 0.33 litre bottle in a bar, and around 20–30% more in a restaurant.

Morocco's national drink is tea, first brought to the country in the eighteenth century by the English, though the Moroccan method of preparation is far removed from that of modern-day England. The Moroccans drink *thé à la menthe* (green tea with sprigs of fresh mint), to which locals tend to add about four or five teaspoonfuls of sugar.

Mineral water (*eau minerale*) is a must in Morocco as it is unwise to drink tap water. The most widely available brand names are Sidi Harazem, Sidi Ali and Oulmes. When buying a bottle always check that the seal is unbroken as some unscrupulous traders sell tourists bottles filled with tap water.

Fez

LOCAL SPECIALITIES

bastilla   pigeon and almond baked in a thin pastry (often sprinkled with sugar and cinnamon)

CHEAP EATERIES
Two-course meals under 20dh (£1.50; $2.25)

Rotisserie La Rotonde, rue Nador (tel. 62 05 89). Open daily 9 a.m.–10 p.m.

Two-course meals from 30–50dh (£2.25–3.75; $3.40–5.65)

Restaurant CTM (Hotel CTM), rue Ksar El Kbir. Recommended dish: *tajine marocaine*. Open daily 9 a.m.–10 p.m.
Restaurant des Jeunes, rue Serrajine 16 (tel. 63 49 75). Recommended dish: *tajine* and *bastilla*. Open 6 a.m.–midnight.
Restaurant Bouayad, rue Serrajine 26 (tel. 63 62 78). Recommended dish: *couscous*. Open round the clock.

Two-course meals from 50–70dh (£3.75–5.25; $5.65–8.00)

Restaurant Es Saada, av. Slaoui 42. Recommended dish: *meshoui* (spit-roasted lamb). Open 6.30 a.m.–11 p.m.
Restaurant Oued de la Bière, blvd Mohammed V 59 (tel. 62 53 24). Open noon–3 p.m. and 6 p.m.–midnight.
A la Tour d'Argent, av. Slaoui 30 (tel. 62 26 89). French restaurant. Recommended dishes: *poulet aux amandes* (chicken with almonds) and *tajine d'agneaux* (lamb *tajine*). Open noon–3 p.m. and 6–11 p.m.

SHOPPING
● **Market**
Off blvd Mohammed V, across from the Café Zanzi Bar.

Marrakesh

CHEAP EATERIES

There are several good options for a cheap meal close to the Djemâa El Fna, both on the square itself and just off the square along rue Bani Marin. In the Ville Nouvelle (Gueliz) the majority of cafés and restaurants are along, or just off, av. Mohammed V, as are most of the bars.

Two-course meals under 20dh (£1.50; $2.25)

Café-Restaurant Marocain, pl. Djemâa El Fna. Recommended dishes: beef or chicken *tajine*. Open 8 a.m.–11 p.m.
Chez Chegrouni, pl. Djemâa El Fna 4/6. Recommended dish: *soupe marocaine* and *poulet grillé* (grilled chicken).

Two-course meals from 20–30dh (£1.50–2.25; $2.25–3.40)

Café-Patisserie Toubkal, pl. Djemâa El Fna. Recommended dish: *shish kebab* with onions and peppers, and steak with chips and salad.
Café-Restaurant al-Baraka, rue Bab Agnaou. Recommended dish: *tajine à la viande* (beef *tajine*). Open 8 a.m.–11 p.m.
Restaurant Etoile de Marrakech, rue Bab Agnaou. Recommended dishes: *tajine* or *couscous*. Three-course fixed menu 25dh (£1.80; $2.60). Open 11 a.m.–11 p.m.

Two-course meals from 30–50dh (£2.25–3.75; $3.40–5.65)

Café-Restaurant-Hôtel de France, pl. Djemâa El Fna. Open 8 a.m.–midnight.
Ali, place de Foucauld. Three-course fixed menus from 40dh (£3; $4.50).

Two-course meals from 50–70dh (£3.75–5.25; $5.65–8.00)

La Taverne, blvd Zerktouni 23 (tel. 44 61 26). Excellent French three-course set menu 70dh. Open 11 a.m.–3 p.m. and 7 p.m.–midnight.
Hôtel Tazi, rue Bab Agnaou. Fixed menus 60–70dh (£4.50–5.25; $6.80–8.00). Eating à la carte you can expect to pay 100dh (£7.50; $11.30) and upwards.
Restaurant de Foucauld, pl. de Foucauld/rue el-Mouahidine (tel.

42 54 99). Under the same ownership as the Tazi, above, and similar in price. Recommended dish: *bastilla*.

SHOPPING
● **Market**
A daily fruit and vegetable market operates just outside the Bab Aghmat.

Rabat

For cheap meals in the ville nouvelle, try the area around the train station and av. Moulay Youssef, or around av. Mohammed V and av. Allal ben Abdellah (the latter is closer to the medina).

CHEAP EATERIES
Two-course meals under 20dh (£1.50; $2.25)

Le Broodjest, av. Allal ben Abdellah 78. Open daily 11 a.m.–midnight.

Two-course meals from 20–30dh (£1.50–2.25; $2.25–3.40)

El-Bahia, av. Hassan II (tel. 73 45 04). Open daily 11 a.m.–11 p.m.

Two-course meals from 30–50dh (£2.25–3.75; $3.40–5.65)

Ghazzah, rue Ghazza 3 (tel. 72 45 53). Open daily 9 a.m.–11 p.m.
La Clef (tel. 70 19 72). From the train station turn right on to av. Moulay Youssef, then take the first left. Recommended dish: *tajine pigeon* (pigeon stewed with prunes, onions and almonds). Open daily noon–4 p.m. and 7–11 p.m.

Two-course meals from 50–70dh (£3.75–5.25; $5.65–8.00)

L'Oasis, rue al Osquofiah 7 (tel. 72 05 57). Recommended dish: *bastilla*. Open daily noon–3 p.m. and 7 p.m.–10.30 p.m.
Le Fouquet's, av. Mohammed V 285 (tel. 76 80 07). Open daily 10.30 a.m.–3.30 p.m. and 6.30 p.m.–midnight.

SHOPPING
● **Market**
The covered market is between pl. du Marché and the medina.

Tangier

CHEAP EATERIES

In the medina the following streets are particularly well supplied with decent inexpensive restaurants: rue Mokhtar Ahardan, rue du Commerce and rue des Chrétiens. In the ville nouvelle there is a string of reasonably priced establishments along rue Salah Eddine el-Ayoubi.

Two-course meals under 20dh (£1.50; $2.25)

Restaurant Aladin, rue du Commerce. Recommended dishes: *harira* and *tajine de kefta*.

Two-course meals from 20–30dh (£1.50–2.25; $2.25–3.40)

Restaurant Ahlen, rue Mokhtar Ahardan 8 (tel. 93 19 54). Recommended dish: *couscous*. Open 9 a.m.–10 p.m.

Restaurant Andalus, rue du Commerce. Recommended dish: *swordfish*. No set hours.

Restaurant Africa, rue Salah Eddine el-Ayoubi 83 (tel. 93 54 36). Recommended dish: *couscous*. Filling four-course set menu only 40dh (£3; $4.50). Open 9 a.m.–12.30 a.m.

Restaurant Chez Larbi, rue Mohammed Abdou 18. Recommended dish: *tajine*. Open 11 a.m.–4 a.m.

Two-course meals from 30–50dh (£2.25–3.75; $3.40–5.65)

L'Marsa, av. d'Espagne 92 (tel. 93 23 39). Mainly Italian food, but with a selection of Moroccan specialities. Open 11 a.m.–11 p.m.

El Dorado, rue Allah ben Abdellah 21 (tel. 94 33 53). Recommended dishes: *kebap* and *couscous*. Open 11 a.m.–3 p.m. and 6.30–11 p.m.

Two-course meals from 50–70dh (£3.75–5.25; $5.65–8.00)

Restaurant Hammadi, rue de la Kasbah 2 (tel. 93 45 14). Recommended dishes: *tajine* and *couscous*. Open Mon.–Sat. noon–3 p.m. and 8 p.m.–1 a.m. (occasionally opens on Sun., same hours).

La Grenouille, rue el-Jabba el-Quatania 3 (tel. 93 62 42). Menu includes Moroccan and English dishes, but French cuisine predominates. Recommended dish: *coq au vin* (chicken in wine). Open Tues.–Sun. noon–2.30 p.m. and 7 p.m.–11 p.m.

THE NETHERLANDS

Not only is it possible to eat out reasonably cheaply in the Netherlands, but an added bonus is that you are very unlikely to receive a poorly prepared meal. If you want to keep costs as low as possible then enquire about student cafeterias in university towns as these invariably offer good, filling meals for under 10Dfl (£3.50; $5.25). Self-service restaurants in the cities are always a good bet for decent quality three-course meals in the 10−17Dfl (£3.50−6.00; $5.25−9.00) price range, and throughout the country you should be able to find local restaurants offering similar meals for 13−17Dfl (£4.50−6.00; $6.75−9.00). However, if you can afford to spend a little bit more there is a much wider choice of restaurants in the 17−23Dfl (£6−8; $9−12) price range. One very convenient restaurant option which many people overlook is train station restaurants. Although such establishments in the UK are frequently criticized, their Dutch counterparts offer good quality meals at reasonable prices: three courses will usually cost in the region of 13−19Dfl (£4.50−6.75; $6.75−10.00). If your budget stretches as far as restaurants in the 23−28Dfl (£8−10; $12−15) price range, then it is worth seeking out restaurants which are members of the Tourist Menu scheme (there are some 280 such establishments around the country − look for the blue plaque with the white fork, or ask at the local Tourist Office). Tourist Menu restaurants offer their own fixed three-course menus, but at the same rate no matter where you are (the 1994 price was 25Dfl (£8.90; $13.50)). Such menus are invariably very good value for money: eating *à la carte* in the same restaurants normally costs a good deal more than the cost of the Tourist Menu.

Bearing in mind that restaurants usually offer generous helpings of food, and that Dutch cuisine is generally filling in any case, three (or even two) courses may be too much for some people, so another possibility for keeping costs down is just to order a main course. Look out for restaurants offering a *dagschotel* (speciality dish of the day). Typical prices for meat or fish *dagschotel* are 10−15Dfl (£3.60−5.40; $5.40−8.00). Given that fish dishes are normally quite expensive, a fish-based *dagschotel* is very good value indeed (whereas meat dishes usually cost in the region of 15−25Dfl (£5.40−9.00; $8.00−13.50) fish dishes are normally priced in the 25−30Dfl (£9.00−10.75; $13.50−16.00) range).

As well as restaurants, you may also find full cooked meals in some local bars (known as *eetcafés*). The quality of food on offer will be of a similar standard to that you would expect to find in a restaurant, but prices are usually slightly lower. For the most part, however, bar food is restricted to snacks or the light lunchtime fare described below.

As is the case in most countries, the Dutch have a particular eating pattern which most people adhere to: breakfast, a light lunch in the middle of the day, and then the main meal in the evening, usually between 6–7 p.m. Because of this many restaurants do not open until early evening, but there are always plenty which are open earlier so you are in no way bound to follow the Dutch pattern.

In stark contrast to many of the countries covered in this guide, a traditional Dutch breakfast (*ontbijt*) is a hearty (if simple) affair capable of filling you up for a decent length of time. A typical breakfast spread might include a choice of different breads, hard-boiled eggs, cheese, ham, salami, jam, honey, peanut butter, chocolate spread and *appelstroep* (an apple-based syrup), from which you can take as much as you want, followed by coffee, tea or *chòcomel* (drinking chocolate, served either hot or cold).

Around lunchtime many Dutch eateries offer a *koffietafel*, best described as a re-run of breakfast with an accompanying dish such as a pie, omelette or salad, with a cup of coffee, tea or *chocomel* to follow. Another favourite at this time is *uitsmijter*: several slices of buttered bread with ham, roast beef or cheese, fried eggs and gherkins. For those who prefer something lighter, there are a wide variety of filled rolls (*broodjes*) and sandwiches (*boterham*) to choose from in most bars and cafés.

Soup is an important part of the evening meal. Most Dutch soups are thick and filling, none more so than *erwtensoep* (basically a green pea soup, but often including all manner of meats and sausages). Even the most popular of the consommé-type soups, *Groentensoep*, is full of vegetables and small meatballs.

Some of the greatest Dutch delicacies are eaten as hors d'oeuvres; examples include Limburg asparagus (May–June), fried Limburg mushrooms (often served with snails), and the celebrated *groene haring* or *nieuwe haring* (small herring caught in the first three weeks of the fishing season in May). Throughout the rest of the year herring (*haring*) and red herring (*bokking*) marinaded in vinegar are popular starters, as is smoked eel (*gerookte paling*).

Meat or poultry entrées are usually served with a sauce and accompanied either by a salad or piles of cooked vegetables such as potatoes, cauliflower, carrots, peas, and the Dutch favourite, green beans (*snijbonen*). The most famous Dutch meat dish is the meat and vegetable stew *hutspot*. In a very different vein is *rolpens met Rodekool* (spiced and pickled beef and tripe cut into thin slices, cooked in butter, and then served with apple and red cabbage).

Although you will usually be able to find at least one main course on a restaurant menu containing fish, it is nowhere near as important a feature of Dutch cuisine as one might imagine. Sole (*tong*) is the most popular, followed by turbot (*tarbot*) and plaice (*schol*).

Vegetarians are well catered for in the Netherlands. Not only are there vegetarian eateries in all the main towns, but ordinary restaurants invariably offer at least one veggie option on their menu. The virtual absence of language difficulties is a real plus; most Dutch people speak English, so it is very unusual to find a restaurant where none of the staff can understand you. One typical Dutch dish which is suitable for vegetarians is *boerenkool* (mashed potatoes with cabbage), though you should check that the dish has not been prepared with sausages (*worst*) or smoked sausages (*rookworst*), as is sometimes the case. When these have been included the suffix *met [rook]worst* is normally added, but it is best to check anyway.

The staples of the desserts section of Dutch menus are ice-cream, pastries and fresh fruit – the latter two usually being served up with a generous topping of whipped cream (*slagroom*).

Street snacks abound in the Netherlands. Mussels and mackerel rolls (*broodje mackerel*) are the two main seafood snacks on offer at most times of the year, but the real delicacy in this line is the *nieuwe haring* or *groene haring* mentioned above. These are eaten raw whilst in season. The Dutch may not have the Belgians' passion for chips (*frites* or *patat*) but you will never have to walk very far if you want some. *Fricandel* (a long, spiced sausage) and *kroketten* (deep-fried spicy meatballs) are two Dutch favourites that are sold by street vendors everywhere, as well as being mainstays of the self-service dispensaries (*automatiek*) that you will see all over the country. Prices for *automatiek* snacks vary, but 1.25–1.50Dfl (£0.45–0.55; $0.65–0.85) is the average.

Putting together a picnic couldn't be simpler. On the whole you will end up paying about the same as you would in the UK; prices for fresh fruit and vegetables are noticeably cheaper but most other items are slightly more expensive. There are always supermarkets either right in the centre of town or ten minutes' walk away at the most, and the majority of towns have a market at least once a week (usually on Saturday). The local Tourist Office (VVV) will help with details of supermarkets and markets in town. One supermarket chain which can be relied upon for good quality fresh and preserved food is Albert Heijn which has stores across the country. Another name you may see is ALDI, part of a supermarket chain that operates in several European countries. Although ALDI can be very cheap it is worth noting that in both Belgium and Germany these stores have been criticized over the years for the quality of their food, especially meat and fish products. Shopping hours are normally Mon.–Fri. 8.30 or 9 a.m.–5.30 or 6 p.m.; Sat. 8.30 or 9 a.m.–4 or 5 p.m.

Whilst most first-time visitors will know that the Netherlands is famous for its cheeses, most would be unable to name any apart from the two bestsellers: *Edam* and *Gouda*. These are just two amongst a wide variety of cheeses produced in the Netherlands, of which special mention should be made of *Leidse kaas* and *Friese kaas* (flavoured with caraway seeds and cloves respectively), and the creamy *Kernhem*. Even *Gouda* and *Edam* are available in different forms here – they can be bought either *jonge* (fresh and creamy) or *oude* (ripened – dry and strong tasting). *Gouda* and *Edam* are the two cheeses which are weighed and sold at the Friday morning cheese market in Alkmaar which is such a great tourist attraction.

Beer is the most popular of alcoholic drinks, and the major breweries are all likely to be familiar to British visitors. Amstel and Oranjeboom have been exported to the UK for several years, though neither has achieved quite the fame in the UK of Heineken or of Grolsch. If beer drinkers (in the British sense) have not been impressed with the Pilsner-type products exported to Britain, it is worth noting that both Amstel and Heineken also produce dark (*bruin*) beers, and that as in neighbouring Belgium (though to nowhere near the same extent), there is a tradition of trappist monks brewing powerful dark beers. Belgian trappist beers are common in the Netherlands: the best known of the home produced trappist beers is Koningshoeven. Trappist beers apart, beer prices are fairly standard throughout the country: usually about 3Dfl (£1.40; $1.65) for a 0.33-litre glass of pils or bruin in a bar; 1–2Dfl (£0.35–0.70; $0.55–1.10) for a half-litre bottle in a local shop (not including the deposit).

The favourite spirit is *jenever* (Dutch gin, which is different from English gin) which the Dutch have been producing and consuming for about four centuries. *Jenever* is sold either *jong* (young) or *oude* (old), the latter being smoother and less sharp in taste. A measure of *jenever* in a bar or café generally costs the same as you would pay for a beer in the same establishment. Other Dutch specialities in the spirit line are the caraway-seed flavoured *kummel* and the brandy-based *advocaat*.

Although the Dutch do not produce wine themselves imported wines are widely available in restaurants, bars and local shops, with decent quality whites and reds (usually French) selling for about 6Dfl (£2.10; $3.30) in restaurants.

Coffee (*koffie*) – taken with either fresh milk (*melk*) or *koffiemelk* (evaporated milk) – is much more popular with the Dutch than tea, but tea drinkers need not fret as tea is always served in cafés and restaurants. However, as the Dutch tend not to add anything to tea (except possibly lemon) you will have to request milk if you want it. Another drink which enjoys great popularity with the Dutch is *chocomel*, mentioned above. Coffee, tea and *chocomel* all cost about 2Dfl (£0.75; $1.10) per cup on average.

Amsterdam

LOCAL SPECIALITIES
Beers produced by the Amstel and Heineken breweries.

SPECIAL EVENTS AND FESTIVALS
Tours of the former Heineken brewery at Stadhouderskade 78 finish with three or four rounds of Heineken. The tours run at 9 a.m., 9.45 a.m., 10.30 a.m., 1 p.m., 1.45 p.m. and 2.30 p.m.). Tickets cost 2Dfl (£0.75; $1.10) which goes to UNICEF; they are on sale from 9 a.m. onwards, but often sell out quickly.

CHEAP EATERIES
Three-course meals for under 10Dfl (£3.50; $5.25)

Mensa de Weesper, Weesperstraat 5. University mensa offering cheap set menus Mon.–Fri. 5–7.15 p.m. Closed July–early Aug.

Atrium, Oudezijds Achterburgwal 237. University mensa. Open Mon.–Fri. noon–2 p.m. and 5–7 p.m. Closed July.

Three-course meals from 10–17Dfl (£3.50–6.00; $5.25–9.00)

De Keuken van 1870, Spuistraat 4 (tel. 624 8965). Opens at 11 a.m. Closed at weekends.

Vegetarish Eeethuis Sisters, Nes 102 (tel. 626 3970). Vegetarian restaurant. Open Mon.–Fri. noon–4 p.m. and 5–9.30 p.m.; weekends 2–9.30 p.m.

Egg Cream, Sint Jacobstraat 19. Vegetarian restaurant. Open daily 11 a.m.–8 p.m.

Old Nickel, Nieuwe Brugsteeg 11 (tel. 624 1912). Open from noon daily.

Rosmarijn, Haringpakkersteeg 6 (tel. 626 6377). Tourist Menu member. Open from 9 a.m. daily.

Scaramouche, Paleisstraat 15 (tel. 622 2043). Open from 9 a.m. Mon.–Sat.

Three-course meals from 17–23Dfl (£6–8; $9–12)

Rhapsody, Rembrandtplein 7 (tel. 626 2246). Tourist Menu member. Open from 11.30 a.m. daily.

Bojo, Lange Leidsewartstraat 51. Indonesian restaurant. Open Sun.–Thurs. 5 p.m.–2 a.m.; Fri.–Sat. 5 p.m.–5.30 a.m.

Oud Holland, Nieuwezijds Achterburgwal 105 (tel. 624 6848). Tourist Menu member. Open from noon Mon.–Sat.

De Rozenboom, Rozenboomsteeg 6 (tel. 622 5024). Tourist Menu member. Open from noon Mon.–Sat.

Royal Garden, Reguliersbreestraat 15–17 (tel. 627 6768). Chinese restaurant. Open from noon daily.

Three-course meals from 23–28Dfl (£8–10; $12–15)

De Vergulde Lantern, Haarlemmerstraat 43 (tel. 624 1952). Open daily from 9 a.m.

David en Goliath, Kalverstraat 92 (tel. 623 6736). Tourist Menu member. Open from 9.30 a.m. daily.

Bolhoed, Prinsengracht 60–62 (tel. 626 1803). Organic vegetarian and vegan restaurant. Open daily noon–10 p.m.

Kopenhagen, Rokin 84 (tel. 624 9376). Specializes in fish dishes. Open from noon Mon.–Sat.

SHOPPING
● Markets

Ten Katestraat, in Amsterdam Oud-West, out beyond the Vondel-park. Open Mon.–Sat. 9 a.m.–6 p.m.

Albert Cuypstraat, in the same part of town as the Heineken brewery. Open Mon.–Sat. 9 a.m.–6 p.m.

● Supermarkets

Albert Heijn, on the Nieuwemarkt

Mignon, at Leidsestraat 74–76

Big Banana Nightshop, near Mignon. Expensive, but open until 1 a.m. daily.

FURTHER INFORMATION
The brochure *Amsterdam*, available from the VVV Amsterdam
Tourist Office lists a selection of local restaurants, along with a
guide to prices in most of the establishments listed.

Delft

LOCAL SPECIALITIES

Delftse Poffer	a cake
Jan Hagel	biscuits
Delftse Roomboter	rum butter
Delftse Brouw	the local beer

CHEAP EATERIES
Three-course meals under 10Dfl (£3.50; $5.25)

Eettafel Tyche, Oude Delft 123 (tel. 12 21 23). Student mensa.
  Vegetarian options available. Open Sept.–May Mon.–Sat. 5.15–
  7.15 p.m.

Three-course meals from 10–17Dfl (£3.50–6.00; $5.25–9.00)

Ladera, Oosteinde 123 (tel. 12 59 50). Vegetarian dishes available.
  Open Mon.–Fri. until 8.30 p.m.
Peking, Brabantse Turfmarkt 78 (tel. 14 11 00). Chinese restaurant.
  Some vegetarian dishes. Open daily until 10 p.m.

Three-course meals from 17–23Dfl (£6–8; $9–12)

't Raedhuys, Markt 38–40 (tel. 12 51 15). Open daily except Thurs.
  until 9 p.m.
Stationsrestauratie, v. Leeuwenhoeksingel 43 (tel. 12 53 34).
  Vegetarian options available. Open daily until 7.30 p.m.
Onder Zeil, Oude Delft 92 (tel. 15 98 37). Vegetarian dishes
  available. Open Tues.–Sun. until 11 p.m.
Royal, Voldersgracht 9–10 (tel. 12 32 70). Open Mon.–Sat. until
  9 p.m.

Three-course meals from 23–28Dfl (£8–10; $12–15)

De Dis, Beestenmarkt 36 (tel. 13 17 82). Tourist Menu member. Vegetarian dishes available. Open daily except Wed. until 9.30 p.m.

India Garden, Kerkstraat 15 (tel. 12 51 17). Indian restaurant serving some vegetarian dishes. Open daily until 11 p.m.

San Marco, Brabantse Turfmarkt 23 (tel. 13 16 29). Italian restaurant. Vegetarian options available. Open daily until 10 p.m.

SHOPPING

A market takes place on the Markt every Saturday from early morning–5 p.m.

FURTHER INFORMATION

The local Tourist Office sells the brochure *Delft* which, as well as being an informative guide for sightseeing, lists a selection of local restaurants complete with details of average prices for a meal in all the listings (1994 price 3Dfl (£1.10; $1.60)).

The Hague

LOCAL SPECIALITIES

Haagse hopjes   a type of caramel

CHEAP EATERIES

As the youth hostel and many of the cheaper hotels are in Scheveningen, several restaurants in that part of town are included below. All others are in the central area of The Hague between the two main train stations and the Peace Palace. On the whole, cheap eateries are harder to find in The Hague than elsewhere in the country.

Three-course meals for under 14Dfl (£5; $7.50)

Lunchroom V & D, Spui 3 (tel. 311 8111). In the Voorm & Dreesmann department store. Closed Sun.

Three-course meals from 16–23Dfl (£6.00–9.50; $9.00–14.50)

De Mollige Haan, Strandweg 137–139, Scheveningen (tel. 355 2575).

Paviljoen Malieveld, Malieveld (tel. 363 9250). Specializes in pancakes.

King Do, Javastraat 13 (tel. 363 8579). Chinese restaurant. Closed Mon.

Lung Fung, Prinsengracht 2 (tel. 360 6357). Chinese restaurant. Closed Mon.

Rhodos, Buitenhof 36 (tel. 365 2731). Greek restaurant.

De 3e Kamer, Korte Houtstraat 4a (tel. 365 2164).

Panini, Gortstraat (tel. 365 1404). Italian restaurant.

Three-course meals from 20–28Dfl (£7–10; $10.50–15.00)

Keraton, Raamstraat 15 (tel. 364 4282). Indonesian restaurant.

De Dageraad, Hooikade 4 (tel. 364 5666). Vegetarian restaurant.

The Nutshell, Strandweg 183–187, Scheveningen (tel. 354 8032).

Pinelli, Dag. Groenmarkt 31 (tel. 365 6368). Italian restaurant.

SHOPPING
● **Market**
Markthof: indoor market at the junction of Spui and Gedempte Gracht. Open Mon. 11 a.m.–6 p.m.; Tues.–Sat. 9 a.m.–6 p.m.; late opening Thurs. until 9 p.m.

● **Supermarket**
In the Voorm & Dreesmann department store on Spui. Open Mon.–Fri. 9 a.m.–6 p.m. (late opening until 9 p.m. on Thurs.); Sat. 9 a.m.–5 p.m.

FURTHER INFORMATION
Local Tourist Offices sell the brochure *Tourist Information: The Hague* which includes a list of many local restaurants, including a guide to what you can expect to pay for a meal in individual establishments (1994 price 2.50Dfl (£0.90; $1.35)).

Rotterdam

CHEAP EATERIES
Three-course meals for under 14Dfl (£5; $7.50)

La Ruche (de Bijenkorf), Coolsingel 105 (tel. 411 7400). Open until 3 p.m. Mon.–Sat.

Three-course meals from 14–17Dfl (£5–6; $7.50–9.00)

De Eend, Mauritsweg 28 (tel. 41 29 80 80). Open Mon.–Fri. 4.30–
7.30 p.m.
La Place, Hoogstraat 185 (tel. 414 8844). In the Voorm & Dreesmann department store. Open Mon.–Sat. until 5.30 p.m.
King's Garden, Westersingel 1–3 (tel. 436 6633). Chinese
restaurant. Open daily until 10 p.m.

Three-course meals from 17–23Dfl (£6–8; $9–12)

Restauratie 'Het Station', Centraal station (platform 1) (tel. 414
9367). Open daily until 8.15 p.m.
Anak Amas, Meent 72a (tel. 414 8487). Indonesian restaurant.
Open Mon.–Sat. until 10 p.m.
Il Cappucino, Spaanse kade 12 (tel. 414 8986). Italian restaurant.
Open daily until 10.30 p.m.

Three-course meals from 23–28Dfl (£8–10; $12–15)

Katreya, Mauritsweg 52 (tel. 414 3734). Japanese restaurant. Open
until 10.15 p.m. Tues.–Sat.
Light of India, Goudesingel 256 (tel. 414 1777). Indian restaurant.
Open daily until 11 p.m.

SHOPPING
The Westend supermarket at Nieuwe Binnenweg 30a is open
Mon.–Sat. 8.30 a.m.–6 p.m. (Fri. until 9 p.m.).

FURTHER INFORMATION
The local Tourist Office sells the brochure *Welcome to Rotterdam Information Guide* which includes a selection of local restaurants complete with an indication of what you can expect to pay for a meal in
the different restaurants listed (1994 price 2.50Dfl (£0.90; $1.35)).

NORWAY

If your clothes have been getting a bit tight for you lately, a few days in Norway will help to restore your sylphlike figure. It's a very expensive country and you'll find yourself on a diet whether you like it or not! Eating on a limited budget is not easy – it's possible to pay a whopping 400kr (£36.80; $55) for a fixed-price meal, but don't let that put you off. Cheaper options do exist, as you'll find out in this chapter. Your best bet is to eat as much as possible at breakfast (*frokost*), which is a huge self-service meal, widely available and good value at around 50–60kr (£4.60–5.50; $6.90–8.25). You really can eat as much as you like, and can choose from smoked salmon, herring with onions, several cheeses, eggs, bread and plenty of coffee. Make the most of it, for after this you'll probably have to rely on picnic food, *kafeterias* (self-service cafés) where the cost of a meal is usually in the 50–80kr (£4.60–7.30; $6.90–11.00) price range; or *gatekjøkken* (street stalls). *Kafeterias* can be found in most department stores, large supermarkets and main railway stations.

To eat in restaurants in the evening, you should opt for the *koldtbord* (cold table), a Norwegian smörgåsbord from which you help yourself to as much as you like for 80–100kr (£7.30–9.20; $11.00–13.80). Fixed-price menus are also available, the best deals being at lunchtime and early evening, around 5 p.m. After that prices tend to rise. Look out for *dagens ret* (the daily special), which may consist of a main course plus bread and coffee, all for 60–70kr (£5.50–6.00; $8.25–9.00). Traditional Norwegian restaurants tend to be very expensive, with main courses from the *à la carte* menu usually starting around 80kr (£7.30; $11).

Open sandwiches (*smørbrød*) are a real feature of traditional Norwegian cuisine, along with all types of seafood, and meats like reindeer (*dyrestek*) and elk. *Smørbrød* are eaten at breakfast, lunch and supper, and can be bought from cafés and sandwich bars. The Norwegians eat a lot of cheese (*ost*), particularly *Jarlsberg* and *geitost* (a sweet, brown goats' cheese). Seafood specialities include: *nedlagt sild* (marinated herring); *gravet laks* (salmon marinated in salt, sugar, dill and cognac); *rakørret* (marinated trout), and *lutefisk*, which is dried cod marinated in potash and water. Some popular meat dishes are: *kjøttkaker* (meat balls in gravy); *fårikål* (mutton and cabbage stew); *fenalår* (smoked leg of mutton), *smalahoved* (boiled sheep's head), and *ryper* (ptarmigan braised in a thick, creamy sauce). Whale meat is still eaten here.

Vegetarians won't have a particularly easy time in Norway,

especially if they want to sample traditional cuisine. Cheese *smør-brød*, fruit and salads from the *koldtbord* are about all that is available. Specialist veggie joints tend to be worthy, rather than inventive, and there aren't that many of them around. The ethnic restaurants, particularly pizzerias, are often the best bet.

If you're putting together your own picnic, you should expect to pay 10kr (£0.90; $1.35) and upwards for a loaf of bread. Crispbreads (*flatbrød* and *knekkebrød*) are popular, as are *havrekjeks* (oatmeal biscuits) and *grahambrød*, a wholemeal bread. Waffles (*vafler*), while not a traditional treat, are also available everywhere. You're likely to be picnicking a lot in Norway, so it's as well that there are plenty of well-stocked supermarkets. Lavpris are a low-priced chain, and there are also discount supermarkets like REMA 1000 and Netto, which are open until 8 p.m. during the week. Other supermarket names to look for are the co-ops such as S-Lag, Tempus, Prix, Obs and Mega, which open Mon.–Fri., 9 a.m.–4 or 5 p.m.; Thurs. 9–6 or 8 p.m.; Sat. 9 a.m.–1 or 3 p.m. Kiosks selling food may stay open until 11 p.m., as well as at weekends. In summer, shops will close earlier than in the winter. Well-known brands of tinned and frozen food are Nora and Stabburet. Most Norwegians speak good English so shopping won't be a problem, but do try to learn a few key words of the language if you can.

If you want a hot snack, rather than a sandwich, during the day, street stalls sell hotdogs (*varm pølse*), pizza slices and chicken and chips. There are also some burger bars here such as the local Clockburger, but you'll find these are much more expensive than those at home. As an alternative to the *koldtbord* at night, opt for one of the growing number of ethnic restaurants; cheapest of which are the pizza joints. In summer you can also buy freshly cooked prawns virtually anywhere that fish and seafood is landed.

Those with a sweet tooth will be pleased to know that ice cream is very popular in Norway, and there are some other delicious desserts to try: *Tilsørte bondepiker* is made up of layers of stewed apples and toasted breadcrumbs, served with cream, while *multer* is sweet yellow cloudberries with cream and sugar. Less unusual, but still delicious, are *fløtelaper* (pancakes made with cream, eaten with sugar and jam), and *riskrem* (creamed rice pudding).

Norwegians drink a great deal of coffee, and while a cup in a café can cost anything from 8–15kr (£0.75–1.40; $1.10–2.10) you often get free refills. Tea is less commonly served and comes with lemon, unless you specifically request milk. A favourite soft drink is *Solo*, a fizzy orange, along with its non-fizzy cousin, *Sino*.

Strict alcohol laws and heavy taxes make drink expensive, and rigorous licensing laws limit the times when it may be bought. Beer is served all day and evening, but only in the afternoon on Sundays. It is lager-like and comes in three classes I, II and III – III being the strongest and most expensive. A glass of beer will set you back 35–45kr (£3.20–4.10; $4.80–6.20). Controls on the sale of spirits are even tighter than those governing beer: the hours are 3 p.m.–midnight, except on Sundays or public holidays. A traditional local brew is *aquavit*, which is made from potatoes and often drunk with beer. A brand called *Brennevin 60%* is one to be treated with care as it's 120% proof! Wines are very expensive in Norway, costing 30–40kr (£2.75–4.10; $4.10–6.20) per glass. A local drink worth trying is *St Halvard*, a liqueur which is similar to Benedictine. To buy alcohol to take away, you must go to a branch of Vinmonopolet, the government stores, which are open from 10 a.m.–5 p.m. weekdays (6 p.m. on Thurs.), and 9 a.m.–1 p.m. Saturday.

Bergen

CHEAP EATERIES
Two-course meals under 55kr (£5; $7.50)

Student Centre, Parkveien 1. No student ID required. Open Sept.–May.
Marken Spisen, Marken 9. Open Mon.–Fri. 11 a.m.–5 p.m.; Sat. 11 a.m.–3 p.m.

Two-course meals from 55–75kr (£5–7; $7.50–10.50)

Ola's Inn, Vaskerelvsmuget 1. Open Mon.–Fri. 10 a.m.–10 p.m.; Sat. 10.30 a.m.–5 p.m.
Kaffistova. Opposite Torget, on the second floor. Open Mon.–Fri. 10 a.m.–6 p.m.; Sat. 11.30 a.m.–3.30 p.m.
Spisestedet Kornelia, Fosswinckelsgate 8. Vegetarian restaurant. Open Mon.–Fri. 11.30 a.m.–7.30 p.m.; Sat. 12.30–5 p.m.; Sun. 2–6 p.m.
Ervingen, Strandkaien 2 (tel. 32 30 30). Open Mon.–Fri. until 8 p.m.; Sat. until 6 p.m.

Two-course meals from 75–110kr (£7–10; $10.50–15.00)

The Great India, Marken 26. Indian restaurant. Several vegetarian options. Open Mon.–Thurs. 3–11 p.m.; Fri.–Sun. 2–11 p.m.

Jeppes Kro & Pizzeria, Vågsalmenning 6. Open daily until midnight.

SHOPPING
● Market
Torget (by the harbour), Mon.–Sat. Fish and seafood predominate, but fresh fruit and vegetables are also available.

● Supermarkets

Mekka, Skostredet, Marken and Busstation
Laerøy Mat, Galleriet Shopping Centre
Epa, Kaigaten 5 (next to the bus station)
Opal, Dreggsalmenning 10–12
Rema 1000, Nedre Korskirkealmenning 2

Oslo

Most city-centre restaurants and cafeterias offer a lunchtime special (either a buffet or *dagens ret*), but if you want to see what is on offer at a number of establishments then it is worth heading for the Aker Brygge, Paléet or Oslo City shopping centres, where there are lots of eateries clustered close together.

CHEAP EATERIES
Two-course meals under 55kr (£5; $7.50)

Student Mensa, Karl Johans Gate 47. Student ID is rarely required. Open Mon.–Fri. 7 a.m.–6 p.m.
Nador, Dronningensgate 22. Moroccan restaurant offering a lunchtime buffet.
Nørrona Kafé, Grensen 19 (tel. 42 64 00). Self-service cafeteria. Open daily 11 a.m.–5 p.m. in summer; 8 a.m.–6 p.m. in winter.
Café Bacchus, Dronningensgate 27 (tel. 42 45 49). Open Mon.–Sat. 11–1 a.m.; Sun. 1 p.m.–midnight.

Two-course meals from 55–75kr (£5–7; $7.50–10.50)

Kafé Celsius, Rådhusgata 19 (tel. 42 45 39). Open Tues.–Wed. 11 a.m.–12.30 a.m.; Thurs.–Sat. 11 a.m.–3 a.m.; Sun. 1 p.m.–12.30 a.m.

Peppe's Pizza, Stortingsgata 4 (tel. 41 22 51). Open Mon.–Sat. 11 a.m.–11.30 p.m.; Sun. noon–11.30 p.m.

Kaffistova, Rosenkrantzgata 8 (tel. 42 99 74). Some vegetarian options. Open Mon.–Fri. 11 a.m.–8 p.m.; Sat.–Sun. 11 a.m.– 6 p.m.

Two-course meals from 75–110kr (£7–10; $10.50–15.00)

Charly's Potej Keller, SAS Scandinavia Hotel, St Olavsgate 33. Open daily 11.30 a.m.–1 a.m.

L'Opera, Rosenkrantzgate 13. Italian restaurant. Open Mon.–Sat. 2 p.m.–midnight; Sun. 2–11 p.m.

Taj Mahal Tandoori, Peder Claussøns Gate 3. Indian restaurant. Good choice of vegetarian dishes. Open daily 1–11 p.m.

Vegeta Vertshus, Munkedamsveien 3/b (tel. 83 42 32). Vegetarian restaurant with an all-you-can-eat buffet. Open daily 10 a.m.– 10 p.m.

SHOPPING
● Markets
On Jernbanetorget; Youngstorget; Grønlands Torg; and in the Basarhallene on Karl Johans Gate. All open Mon.–Sat. 7 a.m.– 2 p.m.

● Supermarkets

Rimi, Rosenkrantzgate 20. Open Mon.–Fri. 9 a.m.–5 p.m.; Sat. 9 a.m.–2 p.m. Also at Akersgate 16 (open Mon.–Wed. and Sat. 9 a.m.–6 p.m.; Thurs.–Fri. 9 a.m.–7 p.m.

Stabburet, Karl Johans Gate 6. Open Mon.–Fri. 8.30 a.m.– 5.30 p.m.; Sat. 9 a.m.–4 p.m.

Rema 1000, Holmesgata 7. Open Mon.–Wed. and Fri. 9 a.m.– 6 p.m.; Thurs. 9 a.m.–8 p.m.

Tempus, Youngsgata 11. Open Mon.–Fri. 8 a.m.–7 p.m.; Sat. 10 a.m.–6 p.m.

Jens Evensen, in the Grønland T-bana station. Open until 11 p.m.

Stavanger

CHEAP EATERIES
Two-course meals under 55kr (£5; $7.50)

Hong Kong Garden, Østervåg 9 (tel. 56 16 81). Chinese restaurant.
Mosvangen Youth Hostel, Henrik Ibsengate 21 (tel. 87 09 77).

Two-course meals from 55–75kr (£5–7; $7.50–10.50)

Dickens, Skagenkaien 6 (tel. 52 73 24). Open 11 a.m.–1 a.m.
Café Sting, Valberggata 3 (tel. 53 24 40). Open noon–4 a.m.
Breitorget Bistro, Breitorget (tel. 52 29 80). Open 10 a.m.–5 p.m.

Two-course meals from 75–110kr (£7–10; $10.50–15.00)

Go'mat hjørnet, Ø. Holmegate 20 (tel. 52 49 21). Open 9.30 a.m.–
4 p.m.
Patrioten Bistro, Hillevågsveien 100 (tel. 58 20 20). Open 11 a.m.–
11 p.m.

SHOPPING
● **Market**
On Torget, Mon.–Sat.

● **Supermarkets**
Torvets Kolonial is at Skagen 3 and there are several supermarkets
in the Arkaden shopping centre at Klubbgate 5. Opening hours
vary, but are generally Mon.–Wed. and Fri. 9 a.m.–5 p.m.; Thurs.
9 a.m.–8 p.m.; Sat. 9 a.m.–2 p.m.

POLAND

Despite the fact that food prices have risen sharply in Poland over the past few years the country still offers a very good range of cheap eating possibilities to travellers. Vegetarians will also appreciate the widespread availability of meat-free meals.

The cheapest option for a cooked meal in Poland is the self-service eatery known as a *bar mleczny* (milk bar). Although meat-based dishes are now more commonly found on milk bar menus than was previously the case, the thrust of milk bar cooking is still mainly towards meat-free dishes. Food is usually displayed in (heated) cabinets, so even if you cannot fathom out the menu you can always just point to what takes your fancy. A full meal of soup, main course and a sweet generally costs about £0.75–1.00 ($1.10–1.50); a bonus being that the quality of the food is usually fine, and in the best milk bars can be very good indeed.

A variation on the milk bar which you may see in some coastal towns such as Danzig (Gdańsk) is the *bar rybny* (fish bar) which provides light meals based around a fish main course for only slightly more than you would expect to pay in a milk bar. Again, the food on offer is generally perfectly acceptable, and sometimes very enjoyable.

A less appealing option for eating out is the snack bar; like the milk bar this is a self-service establishment, but with the emphasis on meat-based dishes, typically prepared with rather poor quality meat. A two-course meal consisting of soup and a main course normally costs about £0.90–1.20 ($1.35–1.80) in a snack bar. If you are looking for something more than the milk bar has to offer then you would really be far better heading for a local restaurant (*restauracja* or *jadłojajnia*) than a snack bar. Outside of Warsaw and Cracow the difference between buying a popular meat dish such as *bigos* in a snack bar or buying it in a decent city-centre restaurant is seldom more than £0.60 ($0.90).

Until 1989 all the country's restaurants were graded from *kat 1* down to *kat 4*; the lower two categories being on the whole rather unattractive places to eat. Nowadays, with the grading system in obvious disarray, there is no way to gain an impression of the likely standard of a restaurant short of having a look inside. Although the sizeable price increases of the last few years have made restaurant meals something of a luxury for many Poles, visitors will still find prices low. On average prices in Warsaw and Cracow are about 25 per cent higher than what you might expect to pay in the other main cities, but even in these two main tourist destinations there are plenty of attractively decorated restaurants serving decent three-course meals for about £2.75–3.75 ($4.10–5.60), and very fine restaurants serving up more expensive specialities such as roast duck for as little as £4.50 ($6.75).

Few Poles would dream of eating a main meal without a bowl of soup (*zupa*), and you would be wise to follow suit as the tremendous range of soups (from thick broths to light, subtly flavoured soups) is possibly the highpoint of the Polish cuisine. In addition to the likes of *zupa pomidorowa* (tomato) and *zupa jarzynowa* (vegetable), there is the light *zupa ogórkowa* (cucumber) and the exceptionally thick *krupnik* (barley, potatoes, carrots, celeriac and pieces of meat), plus the cold *chłodnik* (a sour milk and vegetable soup). The most famous of Polish soups is the spicy, beetroot based *barszcz*, often served *z pasztecikem* (with a little pastry).

The choice of starters depends very much upon the quality of the restaurant. At the top end of the scale (such as the ORBIS hotel restaurants) can be found delicacies such as *pasztet zają*ca (wild rabbit paté) and *szynka w galerecie* (jellied ham), but elsewhere you will most likely be offered a very basic choice of cold meat, salami and possibly some form of *śledź* (pickled herring).

Few nations eat more meat per head of population than the Poles, with pork (*wieprzowe*) and beef (*wołowe*) consumed in vast quantities. The meat dish you will see most frequently on restaurant menus is *kotlet schabowy* (pork cutlet). *Bigos* (cabbage and meat stew) and *pierogi* (dumplings filled with meat and mushrooms) are two national specialities which also feature prominently. If you want to try something really different you can sometimes find elk (*sarnina*) or wild boar (*dzik*) on the menus of the very best restaurants (particularly those in the ORBIS hotels), but be warned that these do not come cheap.

Chicken (*kurczak*) is far from uncommon in Poland, but specialities in the poultry line all revolve around duck (*kaczka*). Of these, it is always worth looking out for roast (*pieczen*) duck, often served with apples (*jabko*).

Fish dishes can be particularly good value for money as fish such as trout (*pastrąg*), carp (*karp*) and eel (*węgorz*) are usually sold at a fraction of the price you would pay in the UK. As a rough guide to prices, in a typical local restaurant you might expect to pay £1.50–3.00 ($2.25–4.50) for any of these.

Whatever your main course it will be served with vegetables, usually a salad, cabbage boiled or pickled (*sauerkraut*) or potatoes. The latter are rarely served in the form of chips, but you may come across *placki ziemniaczane* (potato pancakes), which are a Polish speciality, instead of the more common boiled or mashed potatoes.

The institution of the milk bar means that vegetarians can get by more easily in Poland than in all but a few other countries covered in this guide. However the heavily meat-orientated cuisine means that in all but the very best restaurants – where a selection of vegetarian dishes (*potrawy jarskie*) is usually included on the menu – things can be tricky for vegetarians restaurant-wise. You can try asking which dishes are made without meat (*bezmiesne*), but do not expect to find many (if any) meat-free selections available. Even if they are not on the menu there are, however, a couple of possibilities you might request before you are forced to fall back on the usual standbys like omelettes or pasta (*makaron*). *Pierogi ruskie* is a meat-free variation on the national speciality *pierogi* in which the dumplings are filled with cottage cheese, onion and various spices. Filled pancakes (*naleśki*) are another good option. These are often served as a main course, and one of the more common versions is *naleśki z serem* (with cottage cheese), though you might also request a pancake filled with various vegetables (*jarzyny/warzywa*) such as tomatoes (*pomidor*), onion (*ciebula*) and peas (*groch*) or mushrooms (*grzyby pieczarki*).

The choice of desserts in Polish restaurants is normally slim, though depending upon which time of year you are travelling, you may have the option of excellent dishes prepared with fresh fruits (*owoce*) like strawberries (*truskawki*), raspberries (*maliny*), blackcurrants (*czarne poreczki*), brambles (*czarne jagody borówki*) or plums (*śliwka*). Most popular of the year-round offerings are fruit compotes (*kompot*) or pancakes (*naleśki*) with jam.

A sweet tooth may easily be indulged in the cake shops (*cukiernia*) which are a feature of even the smallest towns. Polish favourites include *makowiec* (poppyseed cake) and *drożdówka* (sponge cake), not to mention *sernik* (cheesecake), the most popular of the lot. The quality is very good and prices are low – £0.20 ($0.30) will buy a sizeable cake or piece of cake. *Cukiernia* also sell ice cream (*lody*) which the Poles consume avidly throughout the year, though the quality of ice cream sold in a *cukiernia* is as variable as that sold from street booths.

The classic Polish street snack is *zapiekanki* (bread topped with melted cheese) which you can buy from street vendors throughout the country. Similarly widespread are stalls selling the Polish equivalent of a hotdog, and chips (*frytki*) are often available from the same outlets. In the coastal towns and in the Mazurian lake district there is also a good choice of takeaway fish snacks.

On one level, shopping is no great problem in Poland as there are always plenty of small general and specialist food shops (such as bakeries (*piekarnia*)) in the town centres, and shopping hours

are relatively long (typically Mon.–Fri. 8 a.m.–7 p.m.; Sat. 8 a.m.–
5 p.m.). However, language difficulties, coupled with the fact that
items are not always clearly priced, make supermarket (*samoobsłu-
gowe*) shopping a very attractive option. Names to look out for are
SuperSam, Spolem, Centrum and Dom Towarowy. Unfortunately
you cannot always be sure of finding a centrally located supermarket (the best options in Cracow and Poznan, for example, are
small mini-markets on the fringe of the historic centres). This relative scarcity of convenient supermarkets is mitigated to some extent
by the fact that it is usually easy to find markets operating
Mon.–Sat. in Polish towns, and there is no shortage of stalls selling
fresh fruit, dairy produce and bread in the immediate vicinity of
the main train stations in Warsaw, Cracow, Danzig and Breslau.
Wherever you do your shopping you will find prices for Polish-
produced foodstuffs low in comparison to the UK: yoghurt about
£0.15 ($0.22) for 250g; bread (*chleb*) around £0.20 ($0.30) for 500g.
You will, however, see a number of German products in Polish
shops nowadays, and prices for these are higher than what you
would pay in Germany.

Levels of alcohol consumption are comparatively high in Poland,
and, as you might expect, vodka accounts for a large percentage of
the alcohol consumed. However, whereas in the UK vodka comes
in one basic form, a whole range of different varieties are on sale
in Poland. If you would like a clear vodka similar to those sold in
Britain simply request *wodka* as the flavoured varieties are all
known by their particular names. Amongst the latter are the
famous *Zubrówka* (flavoured with bison grass), *Myśliwska* (made
with juniper berries), and the lemon vodka *Ctrynówka*. Apart from
vodka, the spirit you will see most of is the Polish brandy *winiak*.
Polish-produced spirits are very cheap: a large measure in a restaurant will typically cost from £0.60–1.00 ($0.90–1.50); a bottle
of one of the better-known clear vodkas such as *Polonez* only about
£2.50 ($3.75) in a local shop.

Although there is not a very wide choice of beers (*piwo*) in Poland
compared to that on offer in Germany or the Czech lands, at least
there is quite a diversity in taste amongst those available. The most
widely available beers are Lezajsk, Okocim, Tatra Pils and Piwo
Zywiecki (the latter two both brewed in Zywiec), but there are also
some fine local beers – such as Breslau's Wrocława and Poznan's
Lech and Ratusz – which are only available round about their town
of origin. In many restaurants and bars you will also have the
choice of Czech, German or Austrian beers (some establishments
do not offer Polish beers at all), but whereas a half-litre of Polish
beer would cost £0.50–1.00 ($0.75–1.50) you can reckon on pay-

ing £1.20–1.80 ($1.80–2.70) for a half-litre bottle of imported beer.

Only a tiny amount of wine is produced in Poland, so it is very rare to see anything other than imported wines in restaurants and shops. Wines from neighbouring Slovakia and the Czech Republic are your best bet if you want reasonable quality without paying dearly for the privilege.

Tea (*herbata*) and coffee (*kawa*) are roughly equal in popularity in Poland (tea being tops – but only just), and both are consumed in astonishing amounts. If you order tea you will normally be presented with a tea bag and hot water so you can make it as strong or as weak as you like, though you will have to request milk (*mleko*) if you want it. The same goes for coffee, which most Poles drink black; if you want white coffee you should request *kawa z mleckiem*.

Cracow

LOCAL SPECIALITIES

Karp w galerecie   jellied carp

CHEAP EATERIES
Two-course meals under £1.50 ($2.25)

Panie Stasi, ul. Mikołasjka 16 (in the courtyard) (tel. 21 50 84). Recommended dish: *pierogi* (dumplings filled with meat or vegetables). Opens at 12.45 p.m. and closes when the food runs out (about 4 p.m. usually).

Chimera Salad Bar, ul. św. Anny 3. Open daily 9 a.m.–10 p.m.

Uniwersytecki, ul. Piłsudskiego (junction with ul. Straszewskiego). Open Mon.–Fri. 6 a.m.–8 p.m.; Sat. 7 a.m.–4 p.m.; Sun. 7 a.m.–3 p.m.

PTTK Dom Turysty, Westerplatte 15–16. The self-service restaurant of the Dom Turysty is open to the public.

Two-course meals from £2.00–3.50 ($3.00–5.25)

Balaton, ul. Grodzka 37 (tel. 22 04 69). Hungarian restaurant. Recommended dishes: *zupa gulaszowa* (goulash soup), *placek ziemniaczany* (potato pancake stuffed with pork and vegetables) and *karp* (carp). Open daily 9 a.m.–10 p.m.

Zywiec, ul. Floriańska 10 (tel. 22 76 21). Recommended dishes:

barszcz (beetroot soup) and *bigos* (cabbage and meat stew).
Recommended drink: *Piwo Zywiecki* (Zywiec beer).
Bella Italia, ul. Grodzka 5. Italian dishes. Open daily noon–11 p.m.
Pod Sokokłem, ul. Piłsudskiego 27 (tel. 21 80 55). Recommended
dish: *kotlet schabowy* (pork cutlet). Open daily 10 a.m.–9 p.m.

Two-course meals from £3.00–4.50 ($4.50–6.75)

Starapolska, ul. Sienna 4 (tel. 21 88 93). Recommended dish: *kaczka*
(roast duck). Open daily 9 a.m.–11 p.m.

Two-course meals from £6.50–8.00 ($10–12)

Wierzynek, Rynek Główny 15 (tel. 22 98 96). Extensive menu,
available in English. Recommended dishes: venison and wild
boar.

SHOPPING
It is possible to pick up a whole range of foodstuffs from amongst
the market stalls outside the main train station.

● Supermarkets
There is no large supermarket in the historic centre. The best option
is the mini-market on the fringe of the historic centre at the junction of ul. Basztowa and ul. Długa which is open daily and keeps
long hours.

Danzig

LOCAL SPECIALITIES
Fish dishes, available in restaurants, *bar rybńy* (fish bars), or in street
snack form. And the five beers (*Gdańskie, Remus, Artus, Hewelius* and
Kaper) produced by the Gdansk Brewery. Incredibly, *Gdańskie* may
have to be re-named unless the local council abandons its demands
for large amounts of money in return for using the city's name.

SPECIAL EVENTS AND FESTIVALS
Provided that you book in advance (tel. 41 52 15), you can take a
tour of the Gdansk Brewery, which ends with some sampling of
the brewery's products.

CHEAP EATERIES
Two-course meals for under £1.50 ($2.25)

Bar Rybny Krewetka, ul. Elżbietańska 10. Open Mon.–Fri. 10 a.m.–
6 p.m.; Sat. noon–6 p.m.
Bar Mleczny Neptuny, ul. Długa 32–34. Good choice of meat-based
and vegetarian dishes. Open Mon.–Fri. 7 a.m.–7 p.m.; Sat.
9 a.m.–5 p.m.
Bar Mleczny Ruczaj, ul. Waly Jagiellońskie 8.

Two-course meals from £1.50–3.00 ($2.25–4.50)

Barstarówska, ul. św. Ducha 8–10 (tel. 31 03 13). Recommended
dishes: *zurek* (thick potato and sausage soup) and *kotlet schabowy*
(pork cutlet). Open daily 10 a.m.–10 p.m. in summer (closes at
8 p.m. the rest of the year).
Zolty Kur, Długi Targ 4. Recommended dishes: any of the chicken
(*kurczak*) dishes.
Tan Viet, ul. Podmłyńska 1–5. Chinese, Vietnamese and Polish
dishes. Open daily 11 a.m.–10 p.m.

Two-course meals from £4–6 ($6–9)

Tawerna, ul. Powroznica 19–20 (tel. 31 41 14). Excellent food.
Recommended dishes: *pstrąg* (trout) or *węgorz* (eel), though your
bill will be nearer £10 ($15) if you choose these rather than the
meat or poultry dishes on offer.

SHOPPING
There are markets opposite the main train station and around the
Jacek Tower, and a supermarket may be found in the shopping
complex off Targ Węglowy.

Warsaw

CHEAP EATERIES
Two-course meals for under £1.50 ($2.25)

Economistów, Nowy Świat 49. Recommended dishes: *barszcz*
(beetroot soup) and chicken (*kurczak*) dishes.

Pod Barbakanem, ul. Mostowa 27–29 (tel. 31 47 37). Recommended dishes: *pomidorowa z makaronem* (tomato soup with pasta) and *kurcza pieczone* (roast chicken, served with potatoes). Open Mon.–Fri. 8 a.m.–6 p.m.; weekends 9 a.m.–5 p.m.

Pod Samsonem, ul. Freta 3–5 (tel. 31 17 88). Good range of fish and vegetarian dishes. Recommended dish: *wêgorz* (eel). Open daily 10 a.m.–10 p.m.

Uniwersytecki, Krakowskie Przedmieście 16–18. Recommended dish: *bigos* (cabbage and meat stew). Open Mon.–Fri. 7 a.m.–8 p.m.; weekends 9–11 a.m.

Two-course meals from £2–3 ($3.00–4.50)

Pod Gołêbiama, ul. Piwna 4a (tel. 635 0156). Recommended dishes: *barszcz* (beetroot soup) and *kotlet schabowy* (pork cutlet). Open daily 10 a.m.–10 p.m.

Two-course meals from £2.50–4.00 ($3.75–6.00)

Restaurant Maryla, ul. Nowogrodzka 24–26 (tel. 21 02 71). Inside the Hotel Forum. Recommended dish: roast pork.

Zapieczek, ul. Piwna (junction with ul. Zapieczek) (tel. 31 56 93). Recommended dish: *pierogi* (dumplings filled with meat and mushrooms). Open Mon.–Sat. 11 a.m.–11 p.m.

Two-course meals from £4.00–5.50 ($6.00–8.25)

Bong Sen, ul. Poznanska 12 (tel. 21 27 13). Vietnamese restaurant. Open daily 11 a.m.–10 p.m.

Nowe Miasto, Rynek Nowego Miasta 13 (tel. 31 43 79). Vegetarian restaurant. English menu available. Open daily 10 a.m.–midnight.

Pekin, ul. Senatorska 27 (tel. 27 48 04). Chinese restaurant. Open daily noon–11 p.m.

Two-course meals from £6–8 ($9–12)

Bazyliszek, Rynek Starego Miasta 5 (tel. 31 18 41). Recommended dish: roast duck. Some vegetarian options. Open Mon.–Fri. noon–midnight; weekends noon–1 a.m.

Kamienne Schodki, Rynek Starego Miasto 25. Recommended dish: roast duck served with apples.

SHOPPING
● Markets
The Hala Mirowska market lies off Towarowa, near the junction with Wolska. There are other markets on ul. Polna and around the Palace of Culture.

● Supermarket
Spolem, on Marszalkowska, between the main train station and the Old Town.

PORTUGAL

By Western European standards eating out in a Portuguese restaurant (*restaurante*) is still a terrific bargain, especially if you choose to order the *ementa turistica* (a fixed-price meal of soup, main course and dessert) which most restaurants offer. In an average local restaurant this should cost in the region of 850–1,100$ (£3.40–4.40; $5.00–6.50). Eating *à la carte*, a three-course meal in a similar establishment would be likely to cost 1,000–1,500$ (£4–6; $6–9). Another good-value option can be the *prato do dia* (the dish of the day). As well as normal restaurants which serve up a cross-section of Portuguese cuisine there are specialist restaurants called *marisquerias* and *churrasquerias* which prepare seafood and chicken main courses respectively.

For quick or lighter meals and snacks head for one of the local cafés. Offerings here range from quite substantial fare such as *bifoque* (steak, chips and fried egg) down to what is normally a decent selection of sandwiches (*sandes*). Although some will be suitable for vegetarians this is certainly not the case with the *prego* (steak sandwich) that is so hugely popular with the Portuguese.

Two cheap eating options which can be overlooked as they are not available everywhere are pensions (*pensoes*) and student cafeterias (*cantinas*). Although pensions are found countrywide, outside the coastal tourist areas it is much rarer for guests to be offered meals. Wherever meals are available, these are usually very good value, often being cheaper even than an *ementa turistica*. In university cities such as Coimbra, student cafeterias sell meals for as little as 250–500$ (£1–2; $1.50–3.00). Usually any student ID is sufficient to gain entrance, though the *cantinas* in Lisbon have recently changed their policy and now admit only those holding cards issued locally.

Portuguese soups are usually thick and filling, though there are also some lighter soups such as *consommés*, and *gaspachos* (cold vegetable soups) which are found in the south of the country. Typical heavy soups are the cabbage and potato based *caldo verde* and the range of exceptionally thick soups called *açordas* whose main ingredient is bread. Along the coast there are a variety of soups prepared using seafood.

Portugal is justifiably renowned for the quality of its seafood. Cod (*bacalhau*) is the favourite fish of the Portuguese, and not surprisingly it features prominently on restaurant menus. The fish is served up in a bewildering variety of forms, but probably the most common is *meia-desfeita com Grão* (boiled cod served with chickpeas). Other popular saltwater fish include hake (*pescada*) and sole (*linguado*), along with the sardines (*sardinhas*) for which Portugal is famous. These have been canned and exported from the country for years, but here you also have the option of sampling them fresh. As with other saltwater fish it is normal just to fry or grill sardines, but they may also be prepared in a marinade (typically containing wine, garlic and olive oil), or in one of the fish stews (*caldeiradas*) which are a speciality of the country. These evolved in fishing communities as a means of utilizing whatever fish was available to make a filling meal, and so although they often contain just one variety of fish you can also find some which are combinations of different fish, the prime example of which is the *Caldeirada Rica*.

Lobster (*lagosta*) is expensive, but mussels (*mexilhões*), clams (*ameijoas*) and shrimps (*camaroes*) are more easily affordable. *Ameijoas na cataplana* is an unusual mixture of clams, ham and herbs that is a speciality of the Algarve. Octopus (*polvo*) and squid (*lulas*) are both widely eaten, with *lulas grelhada* (squid grilled and served whole) being a great delicacy.

Freshwater fish such as salmon (*salmão*), lampreys (*lampreias*), shad (*savel*) and trout (*truta*) are all relatively common; these are usually prepared in similar ways to saltwater fish (with the exception of the stews). Trout is probably the favourite with most Portuguese, though shad is a speciality of Oporto.

Portugal produces first-class pork and ham. Dishes such as *porco à alentejana* (roast pork with clams and herbs), *leitão* (roast suckling pig) and *presuntos* (dried ham) are all highly recommended. In contrast, beef, veal and mutton are generally of rather poor quality as prime grazing land is at a premium throughout much of the country. Lamb is a slightly better option. For something different you might want to try one of the dishes prepared from kid meat (*cabrito*).

Like the Spaniards, the Portuguese are avid consumers of sausages, the vast majority of which are made from pork. As a rule Portuguese sausages are highly seasoned and frequently include a fair amount of garlic.

Offal dishes are quite common in Portuguese cuisine. Oporto-style tripe (*tripas à moda do Porto*) is the classic in this field, though *iscas com elas* (pork liver and potatoes) is a speciality of the capital.

Spit-roasted and barbecued chicken (*frango assado* and *frango no churrasco* respectively) are both cheap and easy to find, either in restaurants or from takeaways. The hot *piri-piri* sauce is invariably offered as an accompaniment to these dishes. Turkey (*perú*) – usually prepared in a marinade to help tenderize the meat – is much more difficult to find.

Favourite Portuguese desserts include *pudim flan* (like crême caramel), *arroz doce* (rice pudding) and *mousse de chocolate* (chocolate mousse). There is also a wide selection of desserts based upon eggs and sugar (and sometimes nuts), examples of which are *toucinho de ceu* and *morgado*. Fresh fruit and nuts are very popular as desserts. Generally they are served up quite plainly, but an exception to the rule which is well worth looking out for is pears (*peras*) in port wine with raisins.

Though hardly rosy, the situation for vegetarians in Portugal is not as bleak as is sometimes made out (and certainly nowhere near as bad as it was only a relatively short time ago). In touristy areas the options for eating out have improved substantially over the last decade or so. Specialist vegetarian restaurants are still quite thin on the ground, but many restaurants have realized that offering even a limited selection of vegetarian dishes can be good for business.

There are street markets in most Portuguese towns, and invariably a range of small general and specialist shops in the centre where you can buy food, though centrally located supermarkets (*supermercados*) can be a bit more tricky to find. The main supermarket chains are Friac and Iriõ. Consequently, provided you remember that shopping hours are generally Mon.–Fri. 9 a.m.–1 p.m. and 3–6 p.m.; Sat. 9 a.m.–noon only, and that markets seldom operate beyond midday on Saturday either, you will have no trouble putting together a picnic. Prices for fresh fruit and vegetables, milk, bread and most other home-produced products are cheaper than in Britain, but imported foodstuffs can be expensive. Portuguese bread is rated as one of the best in Europe: the type which draws most plaudits is *Broa de Milho*, a traditional country loaf that is much more filling than ordinary white bread and has the added advantage of remaining fresh much longer.

If you like cakes (*bolos* or *pastéis*) then there are several places you can indulge yourself. Cafés invariably have a selection of cakes, though for what amounts to a negligible increase in price you can generally find a wider selection and better quality in a *casa de chã* (teahouse). Should you want to buy a cake for eating later you will seldom have to walk far in any town to find one of the local cake shops (*pastelerias*). Specialities include *queijadas de Sintra* (Sintra cheesecakes) which are now sold countrywide, and the various marzipan concoctions that are produced in the Algarve.

If you want a drink with your meal both restaurants and cafés serve alcohol. Cafés are cheaper than bars if you just want a drink, but provided you stick to domestic alcohol local bars will not break your budget as prices are low in comparison to Britain.

Wine (*vinho*) is by far the most popular alcoholic drink amongst the Portuguese, fittingly so, given that Portugal ranks as one of the great wine-producing nations. Much of Portugal's claim to fame in this field rests on the fortified wines port and madeira, both of which (port especially) have been exported from Portugal for centuries. However, Portugal also produces a fine selection of very palatable table wines. Within this category special mention must be made of the Dão region near Coimbra which is known for its consistently high-quality reds, and of the northern Vinho Verde region whose sparkling whites have been one of Portugal's great export successes of recent years. Buying a bottle of wine from a local store is very cheap: table wine costs as little as 350$ (£1.40; $2), and even port or madeira can be bought for about 1,200$ (£4.80; $7.20).

If wine drinkers are confronted with a wide choice of fine wines, beer (*cerveja*) drinkers are nowhere near as fortunate. As individual tastes vary there is little point in making subjective comment on the quality of Portuguese beers, but it is fair to say that if you like the first one you try you are unlikely to be disappointed thereafter; however if you do not like your first beer do not count on things improving. In short, Portuguese beers are all pretty similar in taste, with nothing like the diversity of beers found in Germany, Belgium, or even Britain. The label you are likely to see most often in Portugal is Sagres, which dominates the national market. Draught beer is normally sold by the half-litre (*uma caneca*). If you would prefer a smaller measure request *um fino* or *uma imperial*: depending upon the bar you will receive a third-litre or quarter-litre.

As is the case with imported beer, imported spirits are expensive, so it is advisable to buy domestic vodka (*vodka naçional*), *aguardente* (which is like brandy), *bagaceira* or *bagaço* (like gin), or one of the various liqueurs (*licor*), which are often fruit-based, though the aniseed-flavoured *Erva-Doce* is a notable exception.

Tea (*chã*) is a more popular drink than coffee (*café*), with the predominance of tea symbolized by the institution of the teahouse. Tea is normally taken without the addition of either sugar or milk. In contrast the Portuguese drink coffee in one of three main forms: *uma bica* (a small cup of strong, black coffee), *um garoto* (a small cup of strong, white coffee), *um galão* (a large cup of white coffee, often very weak).

Coimbra

For cheap meals there are plenty of options along Rua Direita, and also on the streets off Praça Comercio and Largo de Portagem, but best of all is probably the university quarter around Praça da República. The old courtyard of the university houses one of several student cafeterias (*cantinas*) where a full meal is available for about 250$ (£1.20; $1.80).

LOCAL SPECIALITIES

Leitão à Bairrada   roast suckling pig

CHEAP EATERIES
Two-course meals under 1,250$ (£5; $7.50)

Churrasqueria do Mondego, Rua Sargento Mór 25 (tel. 23355). Recommended dish: *frango no churrasco* (barbecued chicken). Open noon–3 p.m. and 6–10.30 p.m.
Restaurante Democratica, Travessa Rua Nova 5–7 (tel. 23784). Recommended dish: *espatadas de porco á Africana* (African-style pork kebabs). Open Mon.–Sat. noon–3 p.m. and 7–10 p.m.
Casino de Urca, Rua de Baixo (tel 81 30 59). Recommended dish: *espetada a casa* (kebab). Open noon–3 p.m. and 7 p.m.–midnight.

Two-course meals from 1,250–1,750$ (£5–7; $7.50–10.50)

Restaurante Adega Funchal, Rua das Azeiteiras 18 (tel. 24137). Recommended dishes: *chanfana carne de cabra regional* (goat broiled in red wine) and *escalopes de vitela com champignons* (tenderloin of veal with mushrooms). Open Sun.–Fri. 7 a.m.–2 a.m.
Restaurante Oberão, Rua Simão de Évora (tel. 24155). Recommended dishes: *codornizes no churrasco* (barbecued quail) and *chocos grelhados* (grilled cuttlefish).

Faro

Amongst the best places to look for inexpensive meals are the restaurants on Praça Ferreira de Almeida and along Rua Cruz de Mestras.

LOCAL SPECIALITIES

Ameijoas na cataplana   a dish combining cockles, ham and herbs
Porco à alentejana   roast pork with clams and herbs

The various marzipan-based cakes of the region are also worth trying.

CHEAP EATERIES
Two-course meals under 1,200$ (£5; $7.50)

Restaurante Snack-Bar Centenário, Largo Teneiro do Bispo 4—6 (tel. 82 33 43). Recommended dish: *pasteis de bacalhau* (cod fish-cakes). Open noon—11 p.m.

Restaurante Dois Irmãos, Largo Teneiro do Bispo 14 (tel. 82 33 37). Recommended dish: *arroz de polvo* (octopus and rice). Open noon—11 p.m.

Restaurante Peking, Av. República 168 (tel. 27051). Chinese restaurant. Open noon—3 p.m. and 7 p.m.—midnight.

Restaurante Chelsea, Rua D. Francisco Gomes 28 (tel. 82 84 95). Recommended dish: *camarões* (curried shrimps). Open 11 a.m.—3 p.m. and 6.30—11 p.m.

Two-course meals from 1,250—1,750$ (£5—7; $7.50—10.50)

Restaurante Fim do Mundo, Rua Vasco da Gama 53 (tel. 26299). Recommended dish: *perú* (roast turkey). Open Mon. noon—3 p.m.; Wed.—Sun. noon—3 p.m. and 5—10 p.m.

SHOPPING
● **Market**
On Praça Dr. Francisco Sa Carneiro. Open Mon.—Fri. 9 a.m.—1 p.m.

Lisbon

There is an enormous range of cheap eateries to choose from in the Portuguese capital. At lunchtime, in addition to the many restaurants offering inexpensive fixed-price menus (particularly in the Baixa) you have the option of eating in one of the many workers' cafeterias scattered throughout the city. For evening meals some of the best restaurants are in the Barrio Alto, but unfortunately this is not a safe area for anyone (but especially females) to walk around in at night.

LOCAL SPECIALITIES

Iscas com elas liver with potatoes
Meia-desfeita com grão boiled cod with chickpeas

CHEAP EATERIES
Two-course meals under 1,250$ (£5; $7.50)

Os Minhotos, Rua Remédios 31 (tel. 87 55 80). Recommended dishes: squid (*lulas*) and broiled cod (*bacalhau assado*). Open Mon.–Sat. 11 a.m.–4 p.m. and 7 p.m.–midnight.

Mestre André, Calcadinha de Santo Estevão 6 (tel. 87 14 87). Recommended dishes: *murcela frita* (spicy blood sausage) and *truta grelhada* (grilled trout). Open Mon.–Sat. noon–3 p.m. and 7–10.30 p.m.

O Caradinho, Rua de Santa Marta 4a.

Rio Coura, Rua do Limoeiro 30. Recommended dish: squid (*lulas*).

Adega Popular 33, Rua Conceição 33 (tel. 84 94 72). Recommended dish: *lulas grelhadas* (grilled squid). Open Mon.–Fri. 8 a.m.–9.30 p.m.

Casa de Pasto de Francisco Cardoso, Rua Século 244 (tel. 32 75 78). Open 8 a.m.–midnight.

Rei dos Frangos/Bom Jardim, Travessa de Bom Jardim. Chicken dishes.

Adega do Atum, Rua Bacalhoeiros 8D. Good choice of fish and seafood dishes. Recommended dish: *chocos assados con tinta* (squid boiled in its own ink). Open Mon.–Sat. 7 a.m.–midnight.

A Pérola do Bomjardim, Rua Cruz dos Poiais 95A (tel. 60 84 80). Open Mon.–Sat. 7 a.m.–midnight.

Celeiro, Rua 1 de Dezembro 65. Vegetarian restaurant under a healthfood store. Open Mon.–Fri. 9 a.m.–7 p.m.

Restaurante Bonjardim, Trav. de Santa Antão (tel. 342 7424). Recommended dishes: *frango no churrasco* (roast chicken) and *chouriço asado na brasa* (roast sausage). Open noon–3 p.m. and 6.30–10.30 p.m.

Two-course meals from 1,250–1,750$ (£5–7; $7.50–10.50)

Porto de Abrigo, Rua Remolares 16–18 (tel. 346 0873). Recommended dish: duck with rice and olives (*pato com arroz*). Open Mon.–Sat. noon–3 p.m. and 7–10 p.m.

Cervejeria da Trinidade, Rua Nova da Trinidada 20C (tel. 32 35 06). Open Tues.–Sun. 9 a.m.–2 a.m.

Bota Alta, Trav. Queimada 37 (tel. 342 7959). Recommended dishes: *caldo verde* (cabbage and potato soup) and *sopa alentejana* (garlic soup). Open Mon.–Fri. noon–2.30 p.m. and 7 p.m.–midnight.

Lua Nova, Trav. Queimada 4 (tel. 346 5792). Closed 1–15 July, otherwise open Mon.–Sat. 10 a.m.–10 p.m.

Two-course meals from 1,750–2,500$ (£7–10; $10.50–15.00)

Xêlê Bananas, Pr. Flores 29. Open Mon.–Fri. 12.30–3.30 p.m. and 7.30–11 p.m.; weekends 7.30–11 p.m.

Adega Belém, Rua de Belém 40 (tel. 363 9167). Open Wed.–Mon. 9 a.m.–midnight.

SHOPPING
● **Market**

'Mercado Ribeira', down by the Cais do Sodré train station on Av. 24 de Julho. Open Mon.–Sat. early morning–2 p.m.

● **Supermarkets**

Expresso supermarket on Rua Jardim do Regidor. Open Mon.–Fri. 8 a.m.–11 p.m.; Sat. 9 a.m.–11 p.m.; Sun. 9 a.m.–9 p.m.

For a wider choice head for the huge Supermarket Pão de Açucar in the Amoreiras Shopping Center de Lisboa on Av. Duarte Pacheco.

Oporto

Workers' cafeterias are common in the area to the west of Av. dos Aliados. There are plenty of cheap restaurants in the vicinity of the São Bento train station (the red-light district), and between the university (*universidade*) and the Hospital de Santo Antonio. Prices are only slightly higher in the restaurants down by the Douro.

LOCAL SPECIALITIES

Port wine	many of the Port houses give free tours followed by free drinks (details from the Tourist Office)

| *Tripas à moda do Porto* | Oporto-style tripe |
| *Savel fumado* | shad smoked over old wine barrels (spring only) |

CHEAP EATERIES
Two-course meals under 1,250$ (£5; $7.50)

Churrasqueria Moura, Rua do Almada 219–223 (tel. 200 5636). Chicken dishes. Recommended dish: *frango no churrasco* (roast chicken). Open Mon.–Sat. 11.30 a.m.–10 p.m.

Taberna Tipica, Rua Reboleira 12 (tel. 32 03 73). Recommended dish: *arroz de polvo* (octopus with rice). Open Thurs. 10.30 a.m.–3 p.m., Fri.–Sun. 10.30 a.m.–2 p.m. and 7 p.m.–midnight.

Casa Filha da Mãe Preta, Cais da Ribeira 40 (tel. 31 55 15). Recommended dish: *cavala frita com arroz e feijão* (fried mackerel with rice and beans). Open 11 a.m.–3 p.m. and 7–10.30 p.m. daily.

Brasa Churrasqueria, Praça de Batalha 117 (tel. 200 6785). Chicken dishes. Recommended dish: *frango no churrasquo* (barbecued chicken). Open Wed.–Mon. 9 a.m.–10 p.m.

Restaurant/Snack Bar Kinary, Rua Dom João IV 8.

Restaurante Boa Nova, Muro dos Bacalhoeiros 115 (tel. 26086), offers a fine variety of fish dishes. Recommended dish: *carapaus fritos* (fried whitefish). Open Mon.–Sat. 9 a.m.–midnight.

Taberna de Bebobos, Cais de Ribeira 21–25 (tel. 31 35 65). Recommended dishes: *sardinhas grelhadas* (grilled sardines) and *lulas ribeirinho* (braised squid). Open Mon.–Sat. noon–2.30 p.m. and 7–9.30 p.m.

Two-course meals from 1,250–1,750$ (£5–7; $7.50–10.50)

Taberna do Bebodos, Cais da Ribeira 21–25 (tel. 31 35 65). Recommended dish: *lulas ribeirinho* (braised squid). Open Mon.–Sat. noon–2.30 p.m. and 7–9.30 p.m.

Restaurante Abadia, Trav. Passos Manuel 22 (tel. 200 8757). Recommended dish: *bacalhau à gomes de sá* (speciality cod dish). Open noon–3 p.m. and 7–10 p.m.

SHOPPING
● Markets

Mercado de Bolhão, at the junction of Rua Formosa and Rua Sá de Bandeira. Open Mon.–Fri. 7 a.m.–5 p.m.; Sat. 7 a.m.–1 p.m.

Cais da Ribeira. A general market is open from 8 a.m.–8 p.m. daily, with food stalls mixed in amongst all the others.

ROMANIA

Independent travellers visiting Romania during the last years of the Ceauşescu regime were brought face-to-face with one of the harsher realities of Romanian life, with little food to buy in the shops (*alimentară*) or markets (*piaţa*), and a very limited choice of dishes in all but the most expensive restaurants. Since the revolution things have improved somewhat, with the result that you can normally pick up basics such as bread (*pîine*), milk (*lapte*), cheese (*brînză*) and yoghurt (*iaurt*) relatively easily in shops and supermarkets (*magazin universal*), though markets can be a better bet for fresh fruit and vegetables. However, at the time of writing some items were still in short supply and many restaurants were still offering only a few basic dishes, regardless of what their menu might say. Nor is it possible to say just where food might be difficult to come by: distribution seems to be a major problem, so you can find an abundance of food in some small towns and a relative dearth in larger centres not far away. Hopefully things will have improved by 1995, but as things stand it makes sense to take some canned goods with you into Romania just in case you really get stuck, and once there to stock up with food whenever you have the chance. You can expect to find a market operating Mon.–Sat. mornings at least in most towns of a reasonable size, and although shopping hours vary across the country you can generally count on local shops being open Mon.–Sat. 9 a.m.–5 p.m. (some shops in the capital also open on Sunday mornings). Visitors will find the prices of foodstuffs produced in Romania remarkably low, though anything imported from Western Europe will be costly.

The cheapest options for a cooked meal are *Autoservire* and *lacto-vegetarian* restaurants. The former (found in all Romanian towns) are self-service establishments in which you are virtually guaranteed unpalatable food in depressing surroundings. In contrast the food in *lacto-vegetarian* restaurants, whilst simple, tends to be quite acceptable. These are unfortunately much more difficult to find than *Autoservire*, but assuming you can find one, it will offer the best option for a quick cooked meal. Two courses in an *Autoservire* should cost about £0.50 ($0.75), in a *lacto-vegetarian* restaurant about £0.75 ($1.10). However, if you are in no hurry it would be foolish for non-vegetarians not to head for a local restaurant. Even allowing for the fact that there may still be items listed on the menu (*la listă*) which are unavailable, the quality of whatever food is on offer will on the whole be immeasurably better than what you could get in an *Autoservire*. In any case, eating out in a Romanian restaurant is cheap: a two-course meal in an average local restaurant will seldom cost more than £2 ($3), indeed, many charge a good deal less.

An even better option is one of the traditionally decorated establishments known as *Han*. These are also very cheap for visitors: a three-course meal in the famous *Hanul Manuc* in Bucharest only costs about £5 ($7.50). The real bonus is that they tend to offer a larger selection of dishes than ordinary restaurants, including national and regional specialities (*specialitățile regiunii*), and the food is very well prepared. It is worth paying just a little more to enjoy the best food on offer as Romanian cuisine has much to commend it. In addition to dishes such as the Moldavian speciality *rasol Moldovenesc cu hrean* (boiled beef, pork or chicken served with a sour cream and horseradish sauce) there are many mainstream dishes which show a clear Turkish influence. The cuisine of Transylvania is especially interesting due to the strong input from the region's ethnic Hungarian and German communities.

One of the finest aspects of Romanian cuisine are the soups (*supe*). Not only are there relatively straightforward soups such as *supă de zarzavat* (vegetable) and *supă de roşii* (tomato) but there is also a whole range of soups in which sour cream (*ciorbe*) is a major ingredient. Common examples of these include *ciorbă de cartofi* (potato), *ciorbă de miel* (lamb broth), and *ciorbă perişoare* (soup with meatballs) – a particular favourite. *Ciorbă de peşte* (fish soup) is also worth a try, if you are lucky enough to come across it.

For the most part salads (*salată*) are much the same as you would expect to see elsewhere, with the likes of *salată de roşii şi castraveţi* (tomato and cucumber) and *salată verde* (lettuce) being amongst the most common starters (*gustări*) or accompaniments to main courses. However, there is one real Romanian delicacy in this line – *salată de icre de crap* (carp roe salad).

Beef (*vacă*), pork (*porc*), ham (*sunca*) and lamb (*miel*) are the most common meats (*carne*), but occasionally you may also find goat (*ghiudem*). Pork and beef figure prominently in the many stews (*tocană*) which are found in Romanian cuisine. Salted and smoked pork or goat (*pastrama de porc* or *ghiudem*) are traditional specialities, while you will often see *şniţel pane* (pork cutlet), especially in Transylvania. Two other old favourites are *muşchi ciobanesc* (pork stuffed with ham, served with cheese, mayonnaise and cucumber) and *muşchi poiana* (beef filled with bacon, mushrooms and paprika).

There is no mistaking the Turkish influence in popular main courses such as *ghiveci cu carne* (meat and vegetable stew); *ardei umpluţi* (stuffed peppers); *samarle* (stuffed cabbage) and *musaka* (alternating layers of meat and vegetable).

Poultry (*pasăre*) and fish (*peşte*) are not nearly as important in Romanian cuisine as meat, though chicken (*pui*) appears on many menus and it is always worth watching out for trout (*păstrăv*) and carp (*crap*), as these are sold very cheaply in Romania.

Were it not for the difficulties regarding supplies of food the outlook for vegetarians in Romania would be reasonably bright as there are plenty of suitable dishes in Romanian cuisine. Amongst the more popular meat-free dishes are *ardei umpluţi* (stuffed peppers); *ouă umpluţe picante* (spicy filled eggs); *ouă umpluţe cu ciuperci* (eggs with a mushroom filling); *ghiveci* (fried mixed vegetables) and *ouă româneşti* (poached eggs). Even if none of these are listed on the menu you can try requesting one of them; failing that, to ascertain what might be suitable ask *este cu carne?* (is there meat in this?).

A number of the more popular desserts such as *baclava* and *cataif* are indigenous versions of the exceptionally sweet syrup-and-pastry combinations found in Turkey. Typically Romanian desserts include *clătite* (pancakes), *dulceaţă* (a small glass of jam) and *plăcintă* (pies filled with fruit or cheese).

The two main outlets for takeaway snacks (*gustări*) are street vendors and bakeries. Filled sandwiches (*sandvici* or *tartină*); brioches (*cozonac*); the long sausages called *patricieni*; spicy meatballs (*chiftele*) and meat- or cheese-filled pastries (*pateuri cu carne* or *cu brînză*) are all widely available.

For a cup of coffee (*cafea*) or tea (*ceai*), head for a *Cofetărie*; these coffee houses are easy to find in most town centres. Coffee is drunk Turkish-style (*cafea neagră*) – small cups of strong, black coffee with the remnants of the ground coffee at the bottom of the cup, to which Romanians usually add a fair amount of sugar. You should request your coffee *fără zahăr* if you do not want sugar, and *cu lapte* if you want it white. As an accompaniment to your coffee or tea, *cofetăries* sell most of the desserts mentioned above, and a variety of other cakes and pastries.

Most Romanian beer (*bere*) is of the light Pilsner type, though there are some dark beers (*bera neagra*) brewed around the country. Neither are held in very high regard outside Romania, but if you do find a Romanian beer you like you can drink it to your heart's content as prices are very low indeed. Draught beer is uncommon, so you are almost always sold beer by the (half-litre) bottle (*una sticlă*).

In contrast to the country's beers, Romanian wine has of late acquired a reasonable reputation abroad. Moldavia is the major wine-producing region, and amongst its better table wines are *Pinot Gris* and *Aligote*. If you stick to wines like these and others of similar quality you can enjoy a bottle with a meal for as little as £1.00–1.50 ($1.50–2.25).

The home distillation of all kinds of spirits is a popular pastime in Romania, but what you are most likely to see in bars and local shops are the plum brandy *ţuică* and Romanian rum (*rom*). Domestic spirits are dispensed in large measures and cost very little, but do not make the mistake of asking for an imported spirit as these sell at about three or four times the price you would expect to pay at home.

Braşov

CHEAP EATERIES
Two-course meals around £0.50 ($0.75)

Autoservire Poiana, blvd Gheorge Gheorghiu-Dej (under the Hotel Capitol).

Two-course meals around £0.80 ($1.20)

Lacto-Vegetarian Restaurant, Strada Gheorge Bariţui 1.

Two-course meals around £1 ($1.50)

Restaurant Pescarul, Str. Porta Schei (junction with Str. Ciucaŝ). Fish and seafood restaurant (if supplies permit).
Crama Postăvrul, Str. Republicii (across from the Hotel Postăvrul).

Two-course meals from £1.75–2.50 ($2.60–3.75)

Hotel Postăvrul, Str. Republicii.
Cetatea Braşov. Part of the citadel's restaurant complex. Open Wed.–Mon. 1–10 p.m.
Cerbul Carpaţin, Piaţa 23 August 12. Open from 10 a.m.–10 p.m.
Gustări, Piaţa Sfatului. Good choice of traditional dishes. Open daily 9 a.m.–9 p.m.

Two-course meals around £3–4 ($4.50–6.00)

Restaurant Chinezesc, Piata 23 August. English menu, with some
vegetarian options. Open Thurs.–Tues.

SHOPPING
There is a market by the Parc Central, just along from the ONT
office, and the UNIC supermarket is at Str. 7 Novembre 13.

Bucharest

CHEAP EATERIES
Two-course meals around £0.50–0.80 ($0.75–1.20)

Salon Spaniol, Calea Victoriei 116, Pizzeria.
Dorobanţi Autoservire, Strada Mihail Eminescu (beneath the Hotel
  Dorobanţi).
Select Autoservire, Aleea Alexandru 18.
Lacto Marna, Strada Buzeşti 3 (under the Hotel Marna). Closed
  Sun.
Lacto Rahova, Strada 30 Decembrie (at the junction with Calea
  Rahovie).

  Two-course meals from £2–3 ($3.00–4.50)

Restaurant Moldova, Strada Icoanei 2. Moldavian cuisine.
Restaurant Elegant-Efes, Blvd Margheru 24A (tel. 659 5430).
  Recommended dish: *pui* (roast chicken). Open daily 10 a.m.–
  3 p.m.
Snack Bar Negoiu. To the side of the Hotel Negoiu at Strada Ion
  Câmpineanu 16. Open Mon.–Sat. 8 a.m.–11 p.m.
Berlin Restaurant, Strada Constantin Mille 4.

  Two-course meals from £4–6 ($6–9)

Hanul Lui Manuc, Strada 30 Decembrie 62 (tel. 613 1415). Open
  daily 7 a.m.–midnight.

SHOPPING
There are markets on Piaţa Unirii, Piaţa Amzei and Piaţa Pintilie.

● Supermarkets

UNIC, at Piaţa Amzei 33.
Unirea, in the department store on Piaţa Unirii.

SERBIA

For a cooked meal the basic choice is between self-service eateries called *Expres Restoran* and restaurants with table service (*restoran*). Unless you are specifically looking for a quick meal it is advisable to eat in a *restoran*. This is not meant as a criticism of *Expres Restoran* food, which is usually well prepared, but whereas £1.50 ($2.25) will get you a two-course meal in an *Expres Restoran* in Belgrade, a *restoran* menu will offer a much wider range of options (including speciality dishes you will never see in an *Expres Restoran*) and you can choose a fine two-course meal for £2.50–4.00 ($3.75–6.00). Elsewhere in Serbia *restoran* meals are even cheaper, so if you are travelling around you can sample the fine Serbian cuisine very inexpensively indeed.

The dominant influence on Serbian cuisine has been that of the Turks who ruled over the country for centuries. Travelling in Kosovo you are far more likely to encounter Albanian cuisine, but this too reflects the influence of years of Turkish occupation. However, if you are travelling in the Vojvodina it is worth noting that Hungarian dishes predominate in parts of that region because of the large ethnic Hungarian communities.

Soups (*supa/juha*) such as *pasulj* (thick, bean soup), *juha od pvorča* (vegetable), *pileča juha* (chicken), and *govedja juha* (beef soup) – often made with egg (*govedja juha sa jajem*) – are mainstays of restaurant menus, but keep an eye out for *alaska čorba* (a spicy soup based on freshwater fish), a Serbian speciality.

For obvious reasons Dalmatian smoked ham (*prsut*) is not found on the hors d'oeuvres section (*predjela*) of Serbian menus at present; instead you may well find locally produced ham (*sunka*), which is much less expensive, and usually very good. That apart the standard offerings are salads (*salata*), best-known of which is the Serbian salad *Srpska salata* (peppers, onions, tomatoes, chilli, olive oil and vinegar); scrambled eggs (*kajgana*); grilled mushrooms (*gljive na žaru*); different types of paté (*pašteta*); and curd cheese (*kajmak*).

The Turkish influence on Serbian cuisine is particularly evident in the realm of meat (*meso*) entrées, where there is a selection of both spicy, grilled meat dishes and stuffed vegetables; slowly cooked stews and casseroles such as *djuveć* (lamb or pork casserole with rice and tomatoes) and *kapama* (lamb and onion stew with yoghurt); and *musaka* (a baked dish comprising alternate layers of meat and vegetable – typically aubergine). Most common amongst the stuffed vegetables are *sarma* (cabbage leaves) and *punjene paprika* (peppers), which are usually stuffed with minced meat, rice and tomatoes. Travelling around the country you cannot fail to notice the grilled meat dishes: *ražnjiči* (pieces of grilled meat on a skewer), *čevapčići* (small, spicy grilled meatballs or sausages on a skewer), and beefburger-like *pljeskavica*. All three often turn up in a *mešano meso* (mixed grill), along with a pork cutlet, liver and onions. One Serbian speciality which shows no signs of Turkish origin is *karadjordje va snicla* (breaded veal cutlet, rolled up and then filled with cheese). Although there are no real Serbian specialities featuring chicken (*piletina*), it is commonly found on restaurant menus.

In the capital's restaurants you may find fish (*riba*) such as *barbun* (red mullet) or bream (*zubatac*) on the menu, but on the whole freshwater fish, especially trout (*pastrmka*), is more predominant in Serbian cuisine.

The situation for vegetarians in Serbia is not easy, but it is possible to get by. As well as meat-free dishes like *gibanica* (cheese pie) and *zeljanica* (cheese pie with spinach) there is always the option of ordering larger portions of some of the starters listed above. The outlook for vegetarians improves dramatically the more they can communicate with restaurant staff (German can be useful) as the latter are usually eager to please. At a very basic level you can always request an omelette even if none figure on the menu; fillings include mushrooms (*gljive/pecurke/šampinjons*), tomatoes (*paradajz*), aubergine (*plavi paradajz*), peas (*grašak*), beans (*pasulj*) or cheese (*sir*). A more interesting option is a meat-free version of a traditional dish, as there are some excellent possibilities here, notably with the stuffed vegetables.

Ice cream (*sladoled*), fresh fruit (*voče*), stewed fruit (*kompot*), and *palačinke* (filled pancakes) all feature in the desserts section of Serbian menus, as does *baklava* (the most popular of a number of very sweet, syrup-drenched pastries that are a legacy of Turkish rule).

For a quick snack while you explore, the most widely available options are the *ražnjick*, *čevapčići* and *pljeskavica* mentioned above, and the flaky pastry *burek* (typically filled with cheese or meat) sold by street vendors all over Serbia. Less common is *kukuruz* (grilled corn on the cob). For something sweeter, ice-cream parlours (*slastičarvice*) usually offer a good range of pancakes, pastries and cakes (*torta*), as well as ice cream and yoghurt.

Shopping is seldom problematic in Serbian towns, and prices for home-produced foodstuffs are very low. Most towns have markets operating Mon.–Sat. where you can pick up fruit, vegetables, bread (*hleb*) and dairy products. There are always lots of small shops in town centres and conveniently located supermarkets in the main towns (the local Tourist Office will advise you on locations if need be). Normal shopping hours are Mon.–Fri. 8 a.m.–7 p.m., Sat. 8 a.m.–5 p.m., though many shops, particularly in smaller towns, are closed from noon–3 p.m.

The best Serbian wine (*vino*) comes from the north of the country, and just about anything from that region will be of a decent quality. Wines from elsewhere in Serbia are much more variable, though a widespread and very reliable option is the red *Vranac* from Montenegro. A bottle of Serbian (or Montenegrin) wine (*domaće vino*) costs only £1–2 ($1.50–3.00) in a restaurant, though imported wines can be much more expensive.

Beer (*pivo*) drinkers will also pay much more for imported brands than *domaće pivo*. The choice of beers in Serbia is not as good as you will find in Croatia or Slovenia, but Serbian beer does compare favourably with that found elsewhere in Southern Europe. The most highly rated of Serb beers, Apatinsko, comes from the Vojvodina. Another well-regarded beer you are likely to see as you travel around is the Montenegrin Nikšičko. A beer with a restaurant meal will cost £0.40–0.80 ($0.60–1.20); outside Belgrade it will invariably be much closer to the lower figure.

Spirits are inexpensive: typically about £2 ($3) per bottle in a shop; £0.25 ($0.37) for a measure in a bar. *Šljivovica* (plum brandy), *vinjak* (brandy) and the aniseed-flavoured *mastika* are the most popular spirits. More unusual is *travarica*, which is made from herbs and wild fruits.

Coffee (*kafa*) is normally taken Turkish-style: black, in small cups with the remnants of the ground coffee in the bottom. Similarly tea (*čaja*) invariably comes without milk. If you want milk request your tea or coffee *sa mlekom*.

Belgrade

CHEAP EATERIES
There are many fine restaurants along Skadarska in the Skadarlija district and on Ada Ciganlija which, although relatively expensive by local standards, offer excellent quality Serbian cuisine at affordable prices.
Two-course meals under £1.50 ($2.25)

Expres Restoran Luksor, Balkanska 7. Open daily 6 a.m.–10 p.m.
Kasina, Terazije 25. Open 7 a.m.–10 p.m.

208 · *Cheap Eats Guide to Europe*

Two-course meals from £1.50–2.50 ($2.25–3.75)

Pizzeria Atina, Terazije 28.
Cafe, 7 Jula 6. Open daily 7 a.m.–11 p.m.
London, Kneza Milosa (junction with Maršala Tita). Serbian dishes
and pizzas.
Kolarac, Kneza Mihaila 46. Open daily 8 a.m.–1 a.m.

Two-course meals from £3.50–5.00 ($5.25–7.50)

Dva Jelena, Skadarska 32. Open 9 a.m.–1 a.m.
Ima Dana, Skadarska 38. Open 9 a.m.–2 p.m.
Tri Šešira, Skadarska 29. Open daily 8 a.m.–1 p.m.

SHOPPING
The Zeleni Venac market is located at the upper end of Narodnog
Fronta.

● **Supermarkets**

Beogradjanka, downstairs in the department store at Masirikova 5.
Robna Kuća Beograd. Branches located downstairs in the depart-
ment store at Knez Mihailov 5 and in the underpass under Moše
Pijade.

SPAIN

Spanish restaurants (*restaurantes*) are classified from one- to five-forks, as are the specialist seafood restaurants known as *marisquerías*. Generally only the one- and two-fork establishments will be of interest to those travelling with limited funds. Whilst the difference in price between these two categories is relatively small, that between two-fork and three-fork restaurants is considerable. To keep costs down, rather than eating *à la carte* take advantage of fixed-price menus (*menú del dia*, *menú de la casa*, *cubierto* or *menú turistico*) or *platos combinados*. A typical fixed-price menu of two or three courses with wine or a beer will cost anything from 800–1,600ptas (£4–8; $6–12). In theory all restaurants should offer a fixed-price menu, but in practice more and more seem to be shirking that responsibility. Nevertheless, finding a two-course set menu for around 800–1,000 ptas (£4–5; $6.00–7.50) is still relatively easy in most of the main tourist destinations and, with a few exceptions, the set menu option will be available at the majority of local restaurants throughout the day. However, in some towns (notably Barcelona) fixed-price menus become very difficult to find after lunchtime. *Platos combinados* are available at many one- and two-fork restaurants, with prices ranging from 500–800ptas (£2.50–4.00; $3.75–6.00). As the name suggests, these are simply combinations of different foods. Amongst the more typical constituents of *platos combinados* are chicken, fried hake or squid, different types of omelette, fried egg, sausage, potato salad and chips. Those with large appetites may find *platos combinados* very poor value in comparison with a fixed-price menu as the former's portions tend to be on the small side.

Cheaper set menus can be found in *comedores*, where three courses will cost from 600–1,200ptas (£3–6; $4.50–9.00), with wine generally included in the price of the meal. The basic purpose of a *comedor* is to provide workers with filling meals during their lunch breaks, with the result that few remain open in the evening. *Comedores* are difficult to find in smaller Spanish towns, and the last decade or so has seen a marked fall in their numbers in the larger towns too. Those that do remain are seldom easy to spot, since *comedores* rarely have much in the way of signs advertising their presence and it is quite easy to walk right past them.

At the same time as the institution of the *comedor* has been suffering a decline there has been a growth in the number of *cafeterías*. Here the emphasis is on light meals and although *cafeterías* may occasionally offer a fixed-price menu it is likely that the most substantial meals available will be various *platos combinados*. It is cheaper to eat at the counter in a *cafetería* than at a table.

Tabernas, *bodegas*, *tascas* and *cervacerías* are different types of bar where you can sample the peculiarly Spanish phenomenon of *tapas*. These small servings of seafood or, to a lesser extent, meat, omelettes, cheeses and olives originated in Seville but are now found throughout the country (though Seville is reputed to remain the best place to sample *tapas* due to the vast choice available there). Customers simply choose the *tapa* of their choice from the trays on display at the bar. Prices per serving are usually in the 120–180ptas (£0.60–0.90; $0.90–1.35) range, but can be much higher for ham (several types of ham are regarded as delicacies). Although *tapas* are primarily intended to be hors d'oeuvres or tidbits to accompany a drink, those with light appetites can easily make a meal out of them by ordering them as *raciones* or *bocadillos*. A *racione* is simply a larger than normal serving of a *tapa*, while *bocadillos* are tapas served up in a French style baguette.

Wherever you travel in Spain you will notice that olive oil and garlic play an important role in many dishes. That apart, the difference in the various regional cuisines is so pronounced that it makes no sense to talk of a Spanish national cuisine. Even dishes such as *gazpacho* and *paella* which visitors may think of as typically Spanish are still much more prevalent in their regions of origin (whereas the *Wiener Schnitzel* is now a favourite throughout Austria and Germany). Possibly the only dishes which could be said to be truly Spanish are the meat and pulse stews (*cocido*, *olla*, *pote* and *escudella*), as these are found in all the different regional cuisines, albeit in many different forms. The following is a very basic guide to the various regional cuisines.

Seafood is particularly important in the cuisines found along the northern seaboard (Galicia, Cantabria, Asturias and the Basque Country), with cod (*bacalao*), bream (*besugo*), hake (*merluza*), sardines (*sardinas*), tuna (*bonita*), squid (*calamares*) and octopus (*pulpo*) all common ingredients. Often these are prepared simply by grilling or frying, but there are also speciality dishes such as Asturian *merluza a la sidra* (hake in cider) and the Basque *bacalao a la vizcaina* (cod with peppers and onions) or *bacalao/merluza al pil-pil* (cod or hake fried with garlic). There are also many speciality dishes in these cuisines which do not feature seafood, such as Galicia's *caldo gallego* (a filling dish of cabbage, potatoes and beans); *lacon con grelos* (salted ham with turnip tops) and *empanadas* (filled pies) and the most famous of all Asturian dishes *fabada* (a stew based on the white beans *fabes* – found only in that region). Asturias is also recognized as the largest salmon- (*salmon*) producing region in Spain.

The cuisines of the Ebro, Aragon and La Rioja are more inclined towards meat (*carne*) dishes (this is especially true of Aragon), but the defining characteristic of this group is the use of *chilindrónes* (sauces made from tomato, peppers and onions) in the preparation of lamb (*cordero*), pork (*cerdo*) and chicken (*pollos a la chilindrón*). The most famous dish to emerge from this area is the Aragonese favourite partridge (*perdiz*) with chocolate. The cooking of Navarre is quite diverse, with noticeable Basque, Aragonese and French influences, but it is particularly noted for *la trucha a la navarra* (fried trout with ham), a way of preparing the fish that is now imitated well beyond the borders of Navarre.

Catalan cooking offers an especially wide range of specialities: Gerona veal (*temera*); famous stews such as *habas a la catalana, escudella i carn d'olla* and the noodle based *fideos a la cazuela*; rice dishes like the popular *el rossejat*; rock fish and angler fish (and the soups made from them); and an extraordinary number of sausages, including the *butifarra* which plays the role in Catalan cuisine that the chorizo or morcilla plays in Spain as a whole.

If rice dishes are but one of many aspects of Catalan cooking they are the most notable feature of the cuisines of Alicante, Castellon, Murcia, Valencia and the Valencia Community. Foremost amongst these is *la paella* which originated near Valencia. There is no set recipe for this dish, but typical ingredients include chicken, pork, shellfish, eel, squid, beans, peas, artichokes, and peppers, plus the absolutely essential saffron. The fame of *la paella* tends to obscure the existence of other traditional rice dishes such as Valencia's *el arroz amb fessols i naps* (rice with beans and turnips) or Murcia's *arroz el caldero* (rice with a variety of fish), not to mention other dishes like Valencia's *el pato a la naranja* (duck with orange), Alicante's *bajoques farcides* (stuffed peppers) and Murcia's *el Pastel de Cierva* (meat pie).

Andalusian cooking has one of the best-documented histories in the Iberian peninsula. The real delicacies are hams (*jamon*) such as Granada's *Trevelez* and the celebrated *Jabugo* from Huelva, but the cuisine is dominated by seafood, much of which is prepared simply by deep frying (*pescaito frito* is said to be best in Cadiz and Malaga). Other specialities include Granada's stew *las habas a la granadina*, the city's famous omelette *la tortilla Sacromonte*, and Seville's tripe (*menudo gitano*). Andalusia is also the home of the world-renowned *gazpacho*. There are countless variations on this cold soup, but bread, olive oil, water, garlic and tomatoes are the basis of most versions.

The cuisines of the interior regions of Estremadura, Castile-León and Castile-La Mancha are characterized by the prevalence of roast meat and game dishes, and, certainly in the latter two regions, of stews. Although Estremaduran cooking is comparatively short on stews one of its great specialities is *caldereta extremeña* (lamb or kid stew). However, Estremadura is best known for its *Montchanez* ham, and for its pork which is acknowledged as the best in Spain. Castilian specialities include roast lamb (*cordero/lechazo*) and the celebrated *toston* (roast suckling pig). Despite being landlocked, Castile also offers the speciality cod and garlic dish *bacalao al ajo arriero*, whilst sea bream in breadcrumbs with parsley and lemon is a particular favourite in the capital (one of several Madrid specialities not found in Castilian cuisine as a whole).

Vegetarians reading the above may have begun to think they will be in for a hard time in Spain, and it has to be said that this is very much the case. Vegetarian restaurants are rare, even in the main tourist destinations, and the concept of vegetarianism is not really recognized in the country so there is little incentive for ordinary restaurants to include vegetarian options on their menus. The most readily available options are *tortilla francesa* (plain omelette) and *tortilla con champiñones* (mushroom omelette) which most chefs will prepare for you even if they are not on the menu. Thereafter how well you fare in Spanish restaurants depends very much upon your command of Spanish, as in some cases it is very easy for chefs to produce a vegetarian version of a traditional dish (for example *caldo gallego*, *paella*, and many of the other rice dishes).

As is the case with main courses there are great regional variations in sweets and desserts. Apart from fresh fruit, rice pudding and custard, there are no dishes which could be said to be truly national. Neither Galicia nor the Basque Country are particularly renowned for desserts, but Asturias is said to produce the best rice pudding in the country, and Cantabria the best custard. Aragon is noted for its pears in wine, but even more so for its chocolate-covered fruits. The Catalan favourite is custard (*crema cataluña*). Estremadura is famous for its fresh fruits, above all for cherries from the Jerte valley. The great Castilian speciality is marzipan-based confectionery, a legacy of the Moorish period. The Moorish influence is also clear in the sweets and desserts favoured in the regions of Valencia, Murcia, Alicante and Andalusia, epitomized by Alicante's *los turrones* (varieties of almond paste), though as regards names none displays its origins more clearly than Murcia's *pan de Alá* (Allah's bread).

Shopping for food is usually quite straightforward in Spain. Most of the larger towns have well-established markets operating Mon.–Sat. where you can buy fresh fruit, vegetables, meat, fish, bread and dairy products. There are always lots of small specialist and general stores in the town centres, and you should have no trouble finding a supermarket, if not in the historic centre of town then just 5–10 minutes walk away on the fringe of the historic centre. Supermarkets attached to El Corte Inglés department stores can be very good indeed, but unfortunately not all the main towns, far less smaller towns, have branches; however Spar supermarkets are a reliable, reasonably common alternative. Normal shopping hours are Mon.–Fri. 9 a.m.–1.30 p.m. and 5 p.m.–7.30 or 8 p.m.; Sat. 9 a.m.–noon. Stores like El Corte Inglés are generally open Mon.–Fri. 9 a.m.–8 p.m., Sat. 9 a.m.–5 p.m. Prices for fresh fruit and vegetables are noticeably lower than in the UK; other foodstuffs tend to cost slightly less.

Spain is one of the great wine (*vino*) producing nations of Europe, renowned for its sherry (*vino de Jerez*), of which there are ten different varieties. Sherry production centres on the Andalusian town of Jerez de la Frontera where many of the local *bodegas* offer free tours and sampling. Less well known outside the country but with a fine reputation within Spain itself are the dry, fragrant wines of Córdoba and the *moscatel* of Malaga. The tiny northern province of La Rioja is noted for the quality of its table wines (mostly reds and rosés). These sell particularly well in the Basque Country, but if they are not quite to your taste you can always try the Basques' own acidic white *txakoli*. Galicia is best known for the slightly sour *Ribeiro*, and the very high-quality white *Albariño*. Like the wines of Córdoba and Malaga, Catalan wines enjoy a much greater reputation within Spain than outside the country; the thick reds of *El Priorato* being especially well-regarded. Wine and fruit is the basis of *sangria*, a punch-like drink which over the years has become synonymous with Spain amongst British holidaymakers. Wines can be bought very cheaply: a decent table wine costs about 600ptas (£3; $4.50) in a restaurant, 300ptas (£1.50; $2.25) in a local store, and sherry sells for as little as 550ptas (£2.75; $4.10) in a shop.

Famous as Jerez de la Frontera is for its wine, the fact that the town is the centre of Spanish brandy (*coñac*) production is often overlooked. Another Spanish favourite is the aniseed-flavoured *anis*. Galicia has its own spirit, *orujo*, distilled from the remains of grapes used in the wine-making process. Although *orujo* is widely consumed on its own it is even more commonly drunk as *la queimada* (burnt with lemon, sugar and coffee).

There is not a great choice of beers in Spain. San Miguel is one name you will see all over the country. Others (often quite different in taste) such as Granada's Alhambra or Galicia's Estrella Galiza are more or less restricted to their place of origin.

Asturias differs from the rest of Spain in that apple cider (*sidra*) and not wine is the main drink of the region.

Coffee is invariably served espresso unless you specify that you want it white (*con leche*). Similarly you will normally have to request milk when ordering tea (*te*).

Barcelona

With the exception of Sundays and the holiday period in August when many restaurants are closed you will seldom have far to walk in the Catalan capital to find a decent restaurant serving reasonably priced food. There is an abundance of restaurants offering good value fixed-price menus for around 850−950ptas (£4.25−4.75; $6.40−7.10) in the Barri Gòtic. On the other side of the Ramblas there are plenty of similarly priced establishments around Tallers and Sitjas. Although there are some excellent exceptions to the rule, prices are generally higher in the Eixample. If your funds do not stretch beyond a set menu it should be noted that these are available in very few local restaurants of an evening.

LOCAL SPECIALITIES

Escudella i carn d'olla	a stew based on different meats, the famous Catalan sausage *butifarra*, chickpeas and a wide range of vegetables
Habas a la catalana	a stew based on broad beans, *butifarra* and a range of herbs
Butifarra con judias blancas	*butifarra* with white beans
Fideos a la cazuela	noodles with meat and *butifarra*

CHEAP EATERIES
Two-course meals under 1,000ptas (£5; $7.50)

Bar Cal Kiko, Pelau (corner of c/Cervantes). *Comedore* serving a cheap fixed menu from 1−4 p.m.

Restaurante Self-Naturista, Santa Anna 11−15 (tel. 318 2388). Self-service vegetarian cafeteria. Open Mon.−Sat. 11.30 a.m.−10 p.m.

Els Tre Ne Bots, Sant Pau 42. Varied selection of Catalan dishes.

Los Pergaminos, Ample 19 (tel. 302 2029). Open 1–5 p.m. and 8 p.m.–midnight.

Restaurante Biocenter, Pintor Fortuny 24 (tel. 302 3567). Vegetarian restaurant. Open Mon.–Sat. 1–4.30 p.m.

Restaurante Pas de Virreina, Torrijos 53 (tel. 237 5109). Recommended dish: *bistec amb patates* (grilled steak with potatoes). Open noon–5 p.m. and 8 p.m.–midnight. Closed July.

Bar-Restaurante Can Segarra, Ronda Sant Antoni 102 (2nd floor) (tel. 302 4422). Recommended dish: *gazpacho*. Open Fri.–Wed. 1–4 p.m. and 8–11 p.m. Closed Nov.

Restaurant Super Pollo a l'Ast, Sant Pau 100 (tel. 242 4479). Chicken dishes. Recommended dish: *pollo al ajillo* (chicken roasted with garlic). Open Wed.–Mon. 9 a.m.–11 p.m. Closed July.

Restaurante Bidasoa, Serra 21 (tel. 318 1063). Recommended dishes: any seafood. Open Tues.–Sun. 1–4 p.m. and 8–11 p.m.

Restaurante Egipte, Jerusalem 3 (tel. 317 7480). Open Mon.–Sat. 1–4 p.m. and 8–10.30 p.m. Closed Aug.

Restaurante El Cid, Princessa 11 (tel. 319 2825). Recommended dish: *paella con asparagós* (paella with asparagus), though this will take your bill into the next price category. Open Mon.–Sat. 8 a.m.–10 p.m.

Restaurante Cafeteria Nervion, Princessa 2 (tel. 315 2103). Open Mon.–Sat. 6–10 a.m. and 11 a.m.–10 p.m. Closed Aug.

Restaurante Riera, Joaquim Costa 30 (tel. 242 5058). Recommended dish: *paella*. Open Sun.–Thurs. 1–4 p.m. and 8.30–11 p.m.; Fri. 1–4 p.m. Closed Aug.

Pakistani El Gallo Kirko, Avinyo 19 (tel. 412 4838). Recommended dish: *couscous* (steamed wheat semolina). Open daily noon–midnight.

Two-course meals from 1,000–1,400ptas (£5–7; $7.50–10.50)

Govinda, Plaça Villa de Madrid 4 (tel. 318 7729). Vegetarian restaurant. Open Mon.–Sat. 1–4 p.m. and 8.30–11.45 p.m. Closed on national holidays and during festivals.

Al Primer Crit, Banys Vells 2 (tel. 319 9933). Recommended dish: *llom amb salsa d'ametlles* (beef in almond sauce). Open Tues.–Sun. 8.30 p.m.–midnight. Closed Aug.

Restaurant Les Corts Catalanes, Gran Via de les Corts Catalanes 603 (tel. 301 0376). Vegetarian restaurant. Recommended dish: *tarta de espinicas con guarnición* (savoury spinach flan). Open Mon.–Fri. 1–4.30 p.m. and 8–11.30 p.m.

Two-course meals from 1,400–2,000ptas (£7–10; $10.50–15.00)

Els Quatre Gats, Montsió 3–5 (tel. 302 4140). Open Mon.–Sat. 8 a.m.–2 a.m.; Sun. 5 p.m.–2 a.m.

Restaurant Pitarra, Avinyo 56 (tel. 301 1647). Recommended dishes: *paella* and *escalopines ternera* (veal). Open Mon.–Sat. 1–4 p.m. and 8–11.30 p.m. Closed Aug.

Buffet Comida, Gran Via de les Corts Catalanes 609 (tel. 301 3399). All-you-can-eat buffet. Mon.–Fri. 1,800ptas (£9; $13.50), weekends 2,000ptas (£10; $15). Open Mon.–Thurs. 1–3.30 p.m.; Fri.–Sun. 1–3.30 p.m. and 8.30–10.30 p.m.

SHOPPING
● **Market**
There is a covered market, Mercat Sant Josep ('La Boqueria') off the Ramblas at Rambla de Sant Josep 89 (Mon.–Sat. 8 a.m.–2.30 p.m. and 5–8 p.m.).

● **Supermarkets**

El Corte Inglés has branches on Plaça de Catalunya and near the Nou Camp stadium at the junction of Av. Diagonal and Via Carlos III (the latter is within easy walking distance of the youth hostel on Numancia).

Drugstore, Passeig de Gracia 71. Overpriced, but open round the clock.

Córdoba

With some notable exceptions the tourist-oriented restaurants around the Mezquita are expensive and not such good value as restaurants elsewhere in the city, including the rest of the old town.

LOCAL SPECIALITIES

Salmorejo	the local gazpacho (tomatoes, bread, olive oil, garlic and pepper)
Rabo de toro	oxtail stewed with tomato sauce
Manos de cerdo	pig's trotters
Esparragos en cazuela	scrambled asparagus
Montilla-Moriles	wines

CHEAP EATERIES
Two-course meals under 1,000ptas (£5; $7.50)

Taberna Santa Clara, Oslo 2.
Bar Cristobal, San Felipe.
Restaurante La-La-La, Cruz del Rastro 3 (tel. 47 15 30). Open Tues.–Sun. 9.30 a.m.–4.30 p.m. and 7 p.m.–12.30 a.m. (winter evenings 6–11 p.m.). Closed Mon.
Mesón-Restaurant El Tablón, Coregidor Luis de la Cerda 75 (tel. 47 60 61). Recommended dish: *gazpacho con guarnacion* (with a choice of garnishes). Open daily noon–4 p.m. and 7.30–11 p.m. (closes at 10.30 p.m. in winter).
Bar Restaurante Carmona, Menendez y Pelayo 3 (tel. 47 31 10). Open 9 a.m.–4 p.m. and 8.30–11 p.m.
Bodega Taberna Rafae, Deanes (junction with Buen Pastor). Recommended dish: *rabo de toro*. Open Wed.–Mon. 9.30 a.m.–10.30 p.m.

Two-course meals from 1,000–1,400ptas (£5–7; $7.50–10.50)

El Extremeño, Plaza Benavente 1 (tel. 47 83 14). Cordovan, Andalusian and Estremaduran dishes. Recommended dish: *rabo de toro*. Open 10 a.m.–midnight (11 a.m.–10 p.m. in winter).
Cafetín Halal, Rey Heredia 28 (tel. 47 76 30). Arabic restaurant. Recommended dish: *couscous* (steamed wheat semolina). Open noon–4.30 p.m. and 6.30–11.30 p.m.

Two-course meals from 1,400–2,000ptas (£7–10; $10.50–15.00)

El Churrasco, Romero 16. Recommended dishes: *salmorejo* and *churrasco* (grilled pork with pepper sauce).

SHOPPING
● **Supermarket**

Supermercado Gama, Medina Azahara 3. Open Mon.–Fri. 9 a.m.–1.30 p.m. and 5.30–8.30 p.m.; Sat. 8 a.m.–2 p.m.

Granada

You can find a reasonably priced restaurant almost anywhere in the centre of Granada, but the streets between Gran Vía de Colón and Plaza Santa Ana, Plaza del Carmen and Las Navas are better supplied with cheap eateries than other parts of the city centre.

LOCAL SPECIALITIES

Tortilla Sacromonte	an omelette with lambs' brains, lambs' or calves' testicles, and vegetables
Tortilla a la granadina	an omelette with lamb and chicken offal
Las habas a la granadina	beans, Trevelez ham and various herbs
Cazuela de fideos	a stew of cod, beans and noodles
Sesos a la Romana	fried calves' brains
Alhambra	the local beer

CHEAP EATERIES
Two-course meals under 1,000ptas (£5; $7.50)

Restaurante-Bar León, Pan 3 (tel. 22 51 43). Recommended dish: *chuleta de cerdo* (pork chop). Open Thurs.–Tues. 1–4 p.m. and 7.30–11.30 p.m. Closed mid-June to late July.

Gargantua, Placeta Sillería 7.

Restaurante-Café Boabdil, Hospital de Peregrinos 2 (tel. 22 81 36). Open daily except Tues. noon–11 p.m.

La Nueva Bodega, Cetti Merién 3 (tel. 22 59 34). Open noon–midnight.

Restaurante Vegetariano Raíces, Pablo Picasso 30 (tel. 12 01 03). Vegetarian restaurant. July–Sept. open daily 1.30–4 p.m. and Thurs.–Tues. 9–11.30 p.m.; Oct.–June open Thurs.–Tues. 1.30–4 p.m. and (except Sun.) 8.30–11 p.m.

Oriente y Occidente, La Cruz 2 (tel. 26 60 20). Vegetarian Indian cooking.

Bar Gambino, Plaza Mariana Pineda. Fine roast chicken dishes are sold in the *comedor* attached to the bar.

Ricnón de Pepe, Escudo de Carmen 17 (tel. 22 07 63). Recommended dish: *pollo al ajillo* (chicken in garlic sauce). Open noon–4 p.m. and 7.30–11 p.m.

Restaurante Pizzeria Lago di Como, Campo de Principe 8 (tel. 22 61 54). Open 1–3 p.m. and 9 p.m.–midnight.

Two-course meals from 1,000–1,400ptas (£5–7; $7.50–10.50)

El Ladrillo, Placeta de Fatima. Recommended dishes: any fresh seafood dish, though two people might be advised to try *barco*, a platter of mixed fried fish for two. Open 1–4 p.m. and 8 p.m.–midnight.

Restaurante Alcaicería, Oficios 6 (tel. 22 43 41). Recommended dishes: any *pollo* (chicken) dishes. Open 1–4 p.m. and 8–11.30 p.m.

SHOPPING
Archaeological excavations have recently displaced the main market from its traditional location on San Augustín to the nearby Plaza Romanilla. Once the dig has been completed the market will probably move back to its old location. For groceries, head for the store next to Galerías Preciados on Ribera del Genil. Open Mon.–Sat. 9.30 a.m.–1.30 p.m. and 5–8.30 p.m.

Madrid

The area roughly bounded by Puerta del Sol, Carrera de San Jerónimo, the Paseo del Prado and the Atocha station has probably the densest concentration of eating possibilities of any major European city: streets such as Victoria, Ventura de la Vega, Echegaray and Huertas being particularly well supplied with cheap eateries. There are also some fine restaurants on the way from Puerta del Sol to Plaza Mayor, though the restaurants on Plaza Mayor itself tend to be expensive. Gran Vía is increasingly dominated by fast-food outlets, with many of the surviving restaurants given over to foreign cooking. Chueca boasts a vast number of cheap establishments, but hard-drug users have moved in on this, the heart of the gay district, making it less than pleasant to walk around there at night. Restaurants in the Argüelles and Moncloa districts are far from the sights, but convenient if you are staying in the hostel on Santa Cruz de Marcenado.

LOCAL SPECIALITIES

El cocido	chickpea-based stew containing meat, sausage, black pudding and a variety of vegetables
Callos a la madrileña	tripe in tomato, onion and herb sauce
La sopa de ajo	garlic soup
Besugo	bream in breadcrumbs with parsley and lemon

CHEAP EATERIES
Two-course meals under 1,000ptas (£5; $7.50)

El Garrabatou, Echegaray 5. Recommended dish: *cebolla con atún* (onions filled with tuna). Open 11.30 a.m.–4 p.m. and 8.30–11.30 p.m.

Restaurante El Parque, Fernando El Católico 78 (tel. 243 3127). Open Mon.–Sat. 1–4.30 p.m. and 8.30–midnight, Sun. 1–4.30 p.m. only.

Restaurant del Estal, Rodríguez San Pedro 64 (tel. 243 3069). Recommended dish: *churrasco* (grilled steak) though this will take you into the next price range. Open Mon.– Sat. 1–4 p.m. and 8 p.m.–midnight.

Museo del Jamón, San Jerónimo 6 (tel. 521 0346). Ham-based dishes. Open Mon.–Sat. 9 a.m.–12.30 a.m.; Sun. 10 a.m.–12.30 a.m. The similarly priced restaurant upstairs opens at 1 p.m.

Bar Restaurante El Bierzo, Encomienda 19 (tel. 468 5403). Recommended dish: *salmón a la plancha* (griddled salmon).

Restaurante-Cafeteria El Valle, Fuencarral 8. Recommended dishes: *churrasco* (grilled steak) and *pulpo* (octopus).

La Granja Restaurante Vegetariano, San Andrés 11 (tel. 532 8793). Vegetarian restaurant. Recommended dish: *potaje* (vegetable stew).

Two-course meals from 1,000–1,400ptas (£5–7; $7.50–10.50)

La Gata Flora, Dos de Mayo 1 (junction with c/San Vicente Ferrer) (tel. 521 2020). Italian restaurant. Recommended dish: *cappelletti al pesto* (dumplings in basil sauce). Open Sun.–Thurs. 2–4 p.m. and 8 p.m.–midnight; Fri.–Sat. 8.30 p.m.–1 a.m.

El Granero de Lavapiés, Argumosa 10 (tel. 467 7611). Vegetarian restaurant. Recommended dishes: *filetes de arroz con salsa* (rice fillets with almond sauce) and *empanadillas vegetales* (vegetable turnovers). Open Sun.–Fri. 1–4 p.m. Closed Sat.

Restaurante Zara, Infantas 7. Recommended dish: *carne asada* (roast beef with black beans and rice). Open Mon.–Sat. 1–5 p.m. and 8–11.30 p.m. Chueca district.

Restaurante Rias Baixas, Amanuel 38 (tel. 248 5084). Galician cuisine. Recommended dish: *pulpo* (octopus). Ribeiro wine available. Open Tues.–Fri. 1–4 p.m. and 9 p.m.–1 a.m.; Sat. 1–4 p.m. and 8 p.m.–midnight.

Restaurante-Cafetería Sabatini, Bailén 15 (tel. 246 9240). Recom-

mended dishes: *paella* and *pollo al ajillo* (garlic chicken). Open
9 a.m.–1 a.m.
Restaurante El Cuchi, Cuchilleros 3 (tel. 266 4424). Mexican and
Spanish dishes. Open 1–4 p.m. and 8 p.m.–midnight.
Madrid 1600, Cava de San Miguel. Recommended dish: *cocido mad-
rileño* (Madrid stew). Open 1–4 p.m. and 8 p.m.–midnight.

Two-course meals from 1,400–2,000ptas (£7–10; $10.50–15.00)

Casa Portal, Olivar 3 (tel. 239 0739). Asturian cuisine. Recom-
mended dishes: *salmon* and *tortilla de angulas* (eel omelette).
Asturian cider (*sidra*) available. Open Thurs.–Sat. and
Mon.–Tues. noon till midnight; Sun. and Wed. noon–4 p.m.
only.
Edelweiss, Jovellanos 7 (tel. 521 0326). German and Central
European dishes. Open Mon.–Sat. 12.45–4 p.m. and
7 p.m.–midnight.
Casa Ciriaco, Mayor 84. Traditional local ham, chicken and bean
dishes. Open 1–4 p.m. and 8 p.m.–midnight.
La Ancha, Zorilla 7 (tel. 489 8174). Good range of fish dishes. Open
1.30–4 p.m. and 8.30–11 p.m.

SHOPPING
● **Markets**

Mercado San Miguel, just off Plaza Mayor. Open Mon.–Sat. 9 a.m.–
3 p.m. and 5.30–7.30 p.m.
Mercado de la Cebada, at the junction of Toledo and San Francisco.

● **Supermarkets**

El Corte Inglés – at Preciados 3 looking out onto Puerta del Sol and
at the junction of Princesa and Alberto Aguilera (the latter is
convenient if you are staying in the hostel on Santa Cruz de
Marcenado). Both stores open Mon.–Sat. 10 a.m.–9 p.m.; Sun.
noon–8 p.m.

Málaga

Some of the best deals are to be found in the small streets off Plaza
de la Constitución and those off Calle Granada. The number 11

bus from Paseo del Parque will take you to the beach at Pedregalejo where there is a string of moderately priced restaurants specializing in seafood dishes.

LOCAL SPECIALITIES

Pescaíto frito	deep-fried fish
El boquerón	young anchovies
Choto	goat cooked in vinegar, garlic, almonds and olive oil
Ajo blanco	the local gazpacho (olive oil, almonds, garlic, water and grapes)
Moscatel	wines

CHEAP EATERIES
Two-course meals under 1,000ptas (£5; $7.50)

La Cancela, Denis Belgrano 3 (tel. 22 31 25). Recommended dishes: *calamares a la Romana* (fried squid) and *pollo al jeréz* (chicken in sherry sauce). Open Thurs.–Tues. 1–4 p.m. and 8–11 p.m.

Bar Los Pueblos, Atarazanas. Recommended dishes: any of the stews.

El Tormes, San José 6 (tel. 222 2063). Open Tues.–Sun. 1–5 p.m. and 8–11 p.m.

Cafeteria Restaurante El Yardin, Cañon 1 (tel. 22 04 19). Open 9 a.m.–midnight.

La Tarantela, Granada 61 (tel. 222 2201). Recommended dish: *insalata mista* (mixed salad). Open noon–4 p.m. and 8.30 p.m.–midnight.

SHOPPING
● **Market**
Mercado Atarazanas on Atarazanas.

● **Supermarket**
El Corte Inglés supermarket at Avda Andalucía 4–6. Open Mon.–Sat. 10 a.m.–9 p.m.

Salamanca

There is an abundance of cheap eateries around the university, and down Rua Mayor.

LOCAL SPECIALITIES

chanfaina a highly spiced dish of rice, lamb, black pudding, sausage and assorted vegetables
jeta fried pigs lips – served as a *tapa*

CHEAP EATERIES
Two-course meals under 1,000ptas (£5; $7.50)

Restaurante El Bardo, Compañía 8 (tel. 21 90 89). Vegetarian options available. Open Nov.–Sept. Tues.–Sun. 11 a.m.–4 p.m. and 7 p.m.–midnight.
El Trigal, Libreros 20 (tel. 21 56 99). Vegetarian restaurant. Open daily 1–4 p.m. and 8.30–11 p.m.
Restaurante Roma, Ruiz Aguilera. Open daily noon–3.30 p.m. and 7.30–11 p.m.

Two-course meals from 1,000–1,400ptas (£5–7; $7.50–10.50)

Imbis, Rua Mayor 31. Open 8 a.m.–midnight.

SHOPPING
● **Market**
Plaza del Mercado. Open daily 8.30 a.m.–2 p.m.

● **Supermarket**
On Zamora. Open Mon.–Fri. 9.45 a.m.–1.45 p.m. and 5–8 p.m.; Sat. 10 a.m.–2 p.m.

San Sebastian

Local restaurant (*jatetxea*) prices are noticeably higher than is normal in the Basque Country or Spain as a whole, irrespective of whether you choose to order *à la carte* or go for a set menu. In effect this means the set menus in the 800–900ptas (£4.00–4.50; $6.00–6.75) range are much harder to find than normal. Take comfort in the fact that the high quality of Basque cooking means that even if you are forced to spend about 1,200ptas (£6; $9) on a set menu you are likely to get a very good meal for your money. Unfortunately for those who prefer to eat late very few restaurants offer their set menu in the evening. Many of the city's cheaper restaurants are congregated in Gros, the district at the foot of Monte

224 · *Cheap Eats Guide to Europe*

Ulia on the opposite side of the Urumea from the cathedral. Whichever part of town you are in, seafood is generally more expensive in the restaurants closest to the waterfront.

LOCAL SPECIALITIES

Bacalao a la vizcaina	cod, peppers and onions
Bacalao/merluza al pil-pil	cod or hake fried with garlic and oil
Angulas	elver dipped in boiling oil, served with garlic and pepper
El marmitako	tuna, fish and potato stew
Calamares en su tinta	squid in its own ink

CHEAP EATERIES
Two-course meals for under 1,000ptas (£5; $7.50)

La Barranquesa, Larramendi 21 (tel. 45 47 47). Recommended dishes: *calamares en su tinta, lengua en salsa* (cow's tongue with sauce) and *cabeza de cordero* (lamb's head). Open Mon.–Sat. 1.15–3.30 p.m. and 8.15–11 p.m.

Restaurante Bar La Maitia, Easo 31 (tel. 42 79 64). Recommended dishes: *salmon* and *trucha* (trout). Open 1–3.30 p.m. and 8.30–10 p.m.

Zurriola Jatetxea, Zabaleta 9. Open Mon.–Sat. 1–3.30 p.m.

Self-Service la Oka, San Martín 43 (tel. 46 38 84). Recommended dish: *pulpo a la plancha* (griddled octopus). Open Sun.–Thurs. 1–3.30 p.m.; Fri.–Sat. 1–3.30 p.m. and 8.30–11 p.m. Closed around Christmas and for a few weeks in June.

Bar Etxanis, Fermin Calbetón 24. Good range of omelettes. Open Thurs.–Tues. 10.30 a.m.–4 p.m. and 6.30 p.m.–midnight.

O Mamma Mia, San Bartolomé 18 (tel. 46 52 93). Italian restaurant. Open 1.30–4 p.m. and 8.30 p.m.–12.20 a.m.

Self-Service Aurrera, Urbieta 12 (tel. 42 31 82). Recommended dish: *pastel de merluza* (hake in puff pastry). Open daily 1–3.30 p.m., and on Fri. and Sat. from 8.30–11 p.m.

Two-course meals from 1,000–1,400ptas (£5–7; $7.50–10.50)

Bar Etxadi, Errega Katolikoen 9 (tel. 46 07 85). Recommended dishes: *anchoas al ajillo* and *gambas al ajillo* (respectively, anchovies and shrimps in garlic). Open Tues.–Sat. 1.30–3.30 p.m. and 9–11.30 p.m.

Morgan Jatetxea, Narrika 7 (tel. 42 46 61).

Two-course meals from 1,400–2,000ptas (£7–10; $10.50–15.00)

Bar Restaurant Alotza, Calbetón 7 (tel. 42 07 82). Open 1–
3.30 p.m. and 8–11.30 p.m.
Bar-Restaurante Txalupa, Fermin Calbetón 3. Open Wed.–Mon.
1–3.30 p.m. and 8–11.30 p.m.

SHOPPING
● **Markets**

Mercado de la Bretxa, at the junction of Boulevard Zumardia and
Narrika. Open Mon.–Sat. 8 a.m.–2 p.m. and 5–7 p.m.
Mercado San Martín, on San Martzial (times as above).

● **Supermarket**

Iñigo Saski at Iñigo 7 is a small store conveniently located in the
old city. Open Mon.–Fri. 9 a.m.–1.30 p.m. and 4.45–7.15 p.m.;
Sat. 9 a.m.–1.30 p.m.

Santiago de Compostela

The majority of the city's restaurants (in all price categories) are
along rua del Villar, Raíña and Franco.

LOCAL SPECIALITIES

Caldo gallego	a dish featuring cabbage, potatoes and beans
Lacón con grelos	salted ham with turnip tops
Empanadas	pies with a variety of fillings, typically tuna and tomato
Vieiras	scallops
Torta compostelana	almond pie
Estrella Galiza	the Galician beer
Ribeiro and *Albarino*	wines
Orujo	a Galician spirit, distilled from the remains of grapes used in the wine-making process
La queimada	*orujo* burnt with lemon, sugar and coffee

CHEAP EATERIES
Two-course meals under 1,000ptas (£5; $7.50)

O' Sotano, Franco 8 (tel. 56 50 24). Open 11 a.m.–4.30 p.m. and 9.30–11.30 p.m.

El Asesino, Plaza Universidad 16. Check the street numbers, the restaurant has no sign.

Bar Rois, Raíña 12 (tel. 58 24 44). Special fixed-price menu for students. Open 9 a.m.–midnight.

Casa Manolo, Traviesa 27 (tel. 58 29 50). Open Tues.–Sun. 1–4 p.m. and 8 p.m.–midnight.

Café-Bar El Metro, Nova 12. Recommended dishes: *pollo al grillo* (grilled chicken), *callos* (tripe) and *salmón a la plancha* (griddled salmon). Open 1–5 p.m. and 8 p.m.–midnight. Closed during Holy Week and at Christmas.

Mesón Candilexas, Cardenal Paya 13. Recommended dish: *merluza a la romana* (fried hake).

Restaurante Abella, Franco 28 (tel. 58 29 81). Recommended dish: *churrasco* (roast beef). Recommended drink: *Ribeiro* wine. Open 9.30 a.m.–4 p.m. and 6–11.30 p.m.

Two-course meals from 1,000–1,400ptas (£5–7; $7.50–10.50)

Mesón-Restaurant O Papa Upa, Raíña 18 (tel. 56 65 98). Recommended dish: *paella*. Open Tues.–Sun. 1–4 p.m. and 7 p.m.–midnight; Mon. 1–4 p.m.

Restaurante San Jaime, Raíña 4 (tel. 58 31 34). Recommended dishes: *caldo gallego*, *merluza* (hake) or *ternera asada* (roast veal).

SHOPPING
● **Supermarket**

Supermercados Lorenzo Froiz, Pr. do Toural 2. Open Mon.–Fri. 9.15 a.m.–2.15 p.m. and 4.45–9 p.m.; Sat. 9.15 a.m.–2.15 p.m. and 5.30–8.30 p.m.

● **Market**
Along the street from Plaza San Felix towards the Convento de San Augustin. Open Mon.–Sat. 7 a.m.–3 p.m.

Seville

Restaurants in the Barrio Santa Cruz cater to a clientele composed mainly of tourists. As a result, many of the restaurants in this part of town are overpriced and poor value compared to those elsewhere in the city, including the adjoining Centro district where there are many fine options around Sierpes and San Eloy. Across the river there are some very good restaurants in the Barrio de Triana – an area also known for its high quality *tapas* bars. *Tapas* originated in Seville, and the city is still reputed to be the best place to sample them due to the particularly wide choice available here.

LOCAL SPECIALITIES

El cocido a la sevillana	a stew containing meat fried with eggs
Ternera a la sevillana	larded veal with wine, almonds and olives
Menudo gitano	tripe
Heuvos a la flamenca	a baked dish of eggs, potatoes, various vegetables, ham and sausage
Pato	duck, with olives
Cruz Campo	the local beer
Aljarafe	wines

CHEAP EATERIES
Two-course meals for under 1,000ptas (£5; $7.50)

Mesón La Barca, Santander 6. Recommended dish: *estafado de venado* (venison with red wine, garlic and vegetables) – this will take you into the 850–1,250ptas price range. Open Sun.–Fri. 11 a.m.–midnight.

Restaurante El Baratillo, Pavia 12 (tel. 422 9651). Open Mon.–Fri. 1–10 p.m.; Sat. noon–5 p.m.

Buffet Libre, Mateus Gago. Self-service buffet of *paella* and seafood.

La Bodeguita de Pollos, Azofaifo 9 (tel. 421 3044). Chicken dishes. Open 1–4.30 p.m. and 7–11 p.m.

Pizzeria Renato, Pavia 17 (tel. 421 0077). Italian cuisine. Recommended dish: *lasagna al horno*. Open Thurs.–Tues. 1.15–3.45 p.m. and 8.30–11.45 p.m. (Sat. 8.45 p.m.–midnight).

Restaurante Chino Palacio Imperial, Marques de las Paradas 55 (tel. 421 8816). Chinese restaurant. Recommended dish: *arroz frito de tres delicias* (fried rice with ham, eggs, peas and carrots). Open daily 11.30 a.m.–4.30 p.m. and 7.30 p.m.–midnight.

Two-course meals from 1,000–1,400ptas (£5–7; $7.50–10.50)

Jalea Real, Sor Angela de la Cruz 37 (tel. 421 6103). Vegetarian restaurant. Recommended dishes: *gazpacho* and *panqueques de champiñones* (mushroom pancakes). Open Tues.–Fri. 1.30–5 p.m. and 8.30–11.30 p.m.; Sat. 1.30–4.30 p.m.

Bar-Mesón El Serranito, Antonia Díaz 11 (tel. 421 1243). Open Mon.–Sat. noon–4.30 p.m. and 8 p.m.–midnight.

Casa Diego, Plaza Curtidores 7 (tel. 441 5883). Recommended dishes: *sopa de picadillo* (bread-and-egg soup) and *brochetas* (breaded strips of meat or fish). Open Mon.–Fri. 1–4 p.m. and 8.30–11.30 p.m. (Nov.–Mar.: until 11 p.m. only); Sat. 1–4 p.m.

El Puerto, Betis (tel. 427 1725). Recommended dish: *boquerones fritos* (fried baby anchovies). Open Tues.–Sun. 1–4 p.m. and 8.30 p.m.–midnight.

Two-course meals from 1,400–2,000ptas (£7–10; $10.50–15.00)

El Mesón, Dos de Mayo 26 (tel. 421 3075). Specializes in bull meat. Recommended dishes: *estofado de toro* (stew), *cola de toro* (tail) or simple steaks. Eating at the bar cuts the bill by about 16%. Open daily 12.30–4.30 p.m. and 8.30 p.m.–midnight, except Sun. during the main season and Mon. during the off-season (Oct.–Mar.).

Casa Manolo, San Jorge 16 (tel. 433 4792). Recommended dish: *pescado frito* (mixed fried fish). Open Tues.–Sun. 9 a.m.–midnight.

Cervacería Giralda, Mateos Gago 1 (tel. 422 7435). Recommended dish: *champiñones a la plancha* (mushrooms griddled in olive oil and garlic). Open daily 1–4.30 p.m. and 8 p.m.–midnight.

SHOPPING
● **Markets**

On Pastor y Landero, close to the bullring. Open Mon.–Sat. 9 a.m.– 2 p.m.

Mercadillo de la Encarnación on Plaza de la Encarnación. Open Mon.–Sat. 9 a.m.–2 p.m.

● **Supermarket**

El Corte Inglés, Plaza del Duque de la Victoria 10. Open Mon.–Sat. 10 a.m.–9 p.m.

Supermarcado Antonio de Pablo, Av. República Argentina 12–13.

% Día, San Juan de Avila. Open Mon.–Thurs. 9.30 a.m.–2 p.m. and 6–9 p.m.; Fri.–Sat. 9 a.m.–2.30 p.m. and 5.30–9 p.m.

Toledo

On average, restaurant prices are higher than is usual for Spain. The difference is most noticeable if you eat *à la carte*, but even the set menus cost that little bit extra.

LOCAL SPECIALITIES

Perdiz   partridge, stewed with bay leaf, pepper and garlic
Cuchifrito lamb with egg, tomatoes, saffron and white wine

Red wines from Mentrida.

CHEAP EATERIES
Two-course meals under 1,000ptas (£5; $7.50)

Bar-Restaurante Bisagra, Real del Arrabal 14 (tel. 22 06 93). Open Sun.–Fri. 1–4 p.m. and 8–11.30 p.m.
Arrabal, across the street from the Bisagra, above.
Bar Ludena, Plaza Magdalena 10. Inexpensive fixed-price menu.
Restaurante-Bar Mariano, Paseo de Merchan (tel. 21 13 34). Open 1.30–3.45 p.m. and 8.15–10.45 p.m.
Cafeteria Fuensalida-Manila, Plaza de Conde 2 (tel. 22 20 88). Open 8 a.m.–11 p.m.

Two-course meals from 1,000–1,400ptas (£5–7; $7.50–10.50)

Restaurante La Cubana, Paseo Rosa 2 (tel. 22 00 88). Recommended dishes: *gazpacho* and *pollo al ajillo* (chicken in garlic sauce).

SHOPPING
● **Market**

Plaza Mayor, Wed.–Mon. 8.30 a.m.–2 p.m.
Paseo del Carmen, Tues. 8.30 a.m.–2 p.m.

● **Supermarket**
There is no large supermarket in the old town, but along the way from Zocodóver to the cathedral there is a well-stocked mini-market on the left-hand side of the street. The Frutería-Pan just

inside the Puerta de Bisagra on Real de Arrabal stocks most of the essentials.

València

Restaurants around Plaza del Ayuntamiento and Plaza Zaragoza are by and large overpriced, and poor in quality compared to restaurants in the old town (c/Roteros is a particularly good place for cheap eating).

LOCAL SPECIALITIES

La paella	rice and saffron with a combination of chicken, pork, shellfish, eel, squid, beans, peas, artichokes and peppers
Arroz amb fessols i naps	rice with beans and turnips
El pato a la naranja	duck with orange
Anguila or *salmonete al ali-ipebre*	eel or red mullet in a garlic, paprika and olive oil sauce
Horchata	a sweet, non-alcoholic drink made from earth almonds

CHEAP EATERIES
Two-course meals under 1,000ptas (£5; $7.50)

Restaurante La Utielana, Pl. Picadero Dos Aguas 3 (tel. 352 9414). Recommended dishes: *paella* and *gambas a la plancha* (griddled shrimps). Open Mon.–Fri. 1.15–4 p.m. and 9–11 p.m.; Sat. 1.15–4 p.m. Closed Aug.

Comidas Eliseo, Conde de Montornes 9 (tel. 392 3358). Open Mon.–Sat. 1–4 p.m. and 8–11 p.m.

La Lluna, Sant Ramón (tel. 392 2146). Vegetarian restaurant. Open Mon.–Sat. 1.15–3.45 p.m. and 8.15–11.30 p.m.

Café Valiente, Xátiva 8 (tel. 351 2117). Recommended dish: *paella* (only available 1–4 p.m.). Open Mon.–Sat. 1–4 p.m. and 7–10 p.m.; Sun. 1–5 p.m.

Café Xátiva, Xátiva 14 (tel. 394 1964). Open 9 a.m.–11 p.m.

Comidas Esma, Zurradore 5 (tel. 331 6352). Recommended dish: *emperador* (swordfish). Open Mon.–Fri. 1–3.30 p.m. and 8.30–11.30 p.m.; Sat. 1–3.30 p.m. Closed mid-Aug.–mid-Sept.

Centro Aragones, Don Juan d'Austria 18 (2nd floor) (tel. 351

Recommended dish: *paella*. Open Mon.–Sat. 1.30–4 p.m.
Bar Pilar, Mora Zeit. Recommended dish: *mejillones* (mussels).

SHOPPING
● **Market**

Mercat Central, Pl. Mercat. Open Mon.–Thurs. 7 a.m.–2 p.m.; Fri.
7 a.m.–2 p.m. and 5–8.30 p.m.; Sat. 7 a.m.–3 p.m.

● **Supermarket**

El Corte Inglés, Pintor Sorolla 26.

SWEDEN

Sweden is one of the most expensive countries in Europe, and eating out on a limited budget is far from easy. The cheapest meals are usually to be found in cafeterias (often within department stores), pizzerias, or vegetarian or ethnic restaurants, but even in these you can expect to pay at least 45kr (£3.75; $5.75) for a couple of courses. Traditional Swedish cooking (*husmanskost*) is more expensive, with 85kr (£7.15; $10.75) being the very least you can expect to pay for a two-course *à la carte* meal, though upwards of 120kr (£10; $15) would be the norm. Unless you are prepared to splash out now and again the only realistic option for sampling something of the Swedish cuisine is the *dagens rätt* which most restaurants (especially those in town centres) offer from roughly 11 a.m.–2 p.m. A fairly typical *dagens rätt* will comprise a choice of a meat or fish entrée, a salad, bread or crispbread, plus tea, coffee, a soft drink, or, very occasionally, *lättol* (see below). Prices for *dagens rätt* vary, but normally you can expect to pay something in the region of 50–70kr (£4.20–5.90; $6.30–8.80).

Swedish cuisine revolves mainly around meat and fish dishes. Amongst the former *lövbiff* (slices of fried beef with onions), *bruna bönor* (brown beans and bacon), *sjömansbiff* (beef, potato and onions stewed with beer), *köttbullar* (meatballs served with a brown sauce and cranberries) and *pytt i panna* (cubes of meat and fried potato served up with a fried egg) are the dishes you will most often find on a *dagens rätt*. *Renstek* (roast reindeer), *älg* (elk) and *björnstek* (roast bear) are specialities that have to be ordered *à la carte*, and, as you might imagine, these are prohibitively expensive. The same is true of one of the country's greatest fish delicacies: *kräftor* (freshwater crayfish). More affordable options are *strömming* (Baltic herring), *sill* (herring) and *äl* (eel); *sillbricka* (an all-embracing term for a number of pickled herring dishes) and *torsk* (cod) are sufficiently cheap as to feature regularly on *dagens rätt*. Vegetarians are quite well catered for in Sweden. Most of the main towns have a selection of vegetarian restaurants, which, as mentioned above, can be amongst the cheapest places to eat in town. A further bonus is that ordinary restaurants tend to make some provision for vegetarians on their menus, and often on their *dagens rätt* as well (look for the *vegetarisk rätt*).

One great Swedish tradition is the institution of the *smörgåsbord*. Traditionally a *smörgåsbordet* was a table from which guests simply ate as much as they liked from a wide selection of delicacies and more mundane offerings. In recent times, with the exception of the southern region of Skane, there has been something of a decline in the number of restaurants offering a *smörgåsbord*, but with a bit of effort you can usually find one (restaurants often advertise this and other special offers next to the entertainments section in Swedish newspapers). It is rare to find a *smörgåsbord* on offer for less than 100kr (£8.40; $12.60), so unless you have a very peculiar constitution which allows you to gorge yourself and then eat nothing for ages it is not suited to those on a tight budget, though it can be a rare treat if you have the money to spare. Standard offerings include boiled ham, slices of beef, a variety of fish (particularly pickled herring), salad, potatoes, vegetables and cheese, with a fruit salad or pastry to finish off, to which might be added the likes of smoked salmon or smoked reindeer.

A Swedish breakfast (*frukost*) is usually an all-you-can-eat affair as well, though the ingredients are a good deal less exotic than those which make up a *smörgåsbord*. The basics are usually cereals, salami, boiled eggs, bread, jam, juice, milk and *filmjolk* (thick, sour milk), though you may well find cold meats, paté and (pickled) herring on offer as well. Breakfast is included in the overnight price at hotels, and is available at most hostels at a cost of 40–50kr (£3.35–4.20; $5.00–6.30), about the same as you would pay in a local restaurant.

Takeaway snacks such as burgers, kebabs, hot dogs and pieces of pizza or chicken are all pricey: typically 25kr (£2.10; $3.20) and upwards – about the same as you would pay for one of the large open sandwiches known as a *smögåsar* in a local *konditori* (coffee shop).

From the above it should be clear to anyone travelling on a tight budget that trips to local markets and supermarkets (Åhlens, Konsum and Domus are the main chains) will be a priority. Although the prices for some articles will stun you, not everything is as dear as you might expect. Fresh fruits such as apples, bananas and kiwi fruits are only slightly more expensive than at home. Yoghurt and milk are dearer, but not any more so than in countries such as Belgium or Italy. A very good choice if you can develop a taste for it is the highly nutritious *filmjölk* (see above) which is cheaper to buy than both milk and yoghurt. Packets of muesli are reasonably priced, but of those canned foods which don't require cooking the only things that are good value are mussels (*blåumusslor*) and mackerel (*makrill*). Bread (*bröd*) is very expensive, with prices for a loaf starting at about 15kr (£1.25; $1.90). White bread is a poor option compared to the heavier brown loaves, for not only are the latter more nutritious but they also keep for several days whereas white bread goes stale very quickly (it is worth noting that supermarkets often sell off unsold bread at half-price on the day after it was baked). The outlook improves considerably if you have a camping stove or access to cooking facilities: rice, pasta, potatoes, onions and tinned tomatoes are all good basic ingredients from which to put together a decent, filling meal reasonably cheaply. Shopping hours are generally Mon.–Fri. 9 a.m.–6 p.m., Sat. 9 a.m.–1 p.m. (though some large stores also open on Sun. afternoon).

If you like a drink you might want to consider bringing some with you because alcohol is very expensive to buy in a restaurant or a bar, and there are also some annoying restrictions put in the way of buying it. Beer (*öl*) is classified according to its alcohol content: *starköl* (class III); *folköl* (class II); and *lattöl* (class I). The latter two are freely available in restaurants and bars at around 25–35kr (£2.10–3.00; $3.20–4.50) for a half-litre, or in supermarkets, where a half-litre usually costs about 11–14kr (£0.90–1.15; $1.35–1.75). One of the kinder things that has been said about *lattöl* is that it resembles British alcohol-free lager; *folköl* is only a little stronger. The one class of beer that has what most British visitors would regard as a decent alcohol content is *starköl*, which costs around 40–50kr (£3.35–4.20; $5–6) per half-litre in most bars and restaurants. However, because of Sweden's strict laws regarding the sale of 'strong' alcohol, *starköl* is not sold in supermarkets and can only be bought in takeaway form from one of the state-run off-licences known as a *Systemsbolaget*, where a third-litre bottle typically costs around 13kr (£1.10; $1.65). With wine (*vin*) costing at least 110kr (£9.25; $13.80) a bottle in a restaurant, wine drinkers are also likely to end up looking for the nearest *Systemsbolaget*, as is anyone looking for a bottle of the Swede's favourite spirit, *aquavit*. The opening hours of *Systemsbolaget* are restricted to Mon.–Fri. 9 a.m.–6 p.m., the only variation from these hours being that they close on the day preceding a public holiday. No alcohol is sold to those aged under 20, and you may be asked to show your passport.

Tea (*te*) and coffee (*kaffe*) both cost around 10–15kr (£0.85–1.25; $1.25–1.90) per cup, though coffee drinkers sometimes get the bonus of free refills.

Gothenburg (Göteborg)

There is no particularly cheap area to eat within the city centre, but Haga Nygatan and the surrounding streets offer a wider choice

of eateries in all price categories than is usual. Restaurants on
Avenyn tend to be overpriced compared to their counterparts elsewhere in the centre, though this is less noticeable at lunchtime
when most restaurants serve a lunchtime *dagens rätt* in the 50–
70kr (£4.20–5.90; $6.30–8.80) price range.

CHEAP EATERIES
Two-course meals under 60kr (£5; $7.50)

Kåren, Götabergsgatan 17. Student canteen. Student ID sometimes
   requested. Open Mon.–Fri. 11 a.m.–2 p.m.
Plankan, Vasaplatsen 3 (tel. 11 63 02). Open Mon.–Thurs.
   10.30 a.m.–1 a.m.; Fri. 10.30 a.m.–2 a.m.; Sat. 1 p.m.–2 a.m.;
   Sun. 1 p.m.–1 a.m.
Norrlands Café, Västra Hamngatan 20. Vegetarian options available.
   Open Mon.–Thurs. 9 a.m.–11 p.m.; Fri. 9 a.m.–2 a.m.; Sat.
   11 a.m.–2 a.m.; Sun. noon–9 a.m.
Kungstorgcaféet, Kungstorget. Open Mon.–Fri. 6 a.m.–5 p.m.; Sat.
   6 a.m.–2.30 p.m.
Krakow, Karl Gustavsgatan 28. Polish restaurant.
Gyllene Prag, Sveagatan 25. Czech cuisine.
Malaysia Saté Restaurant, Östra Hamngatan 19. Malaysian and
   other Far Eastern dishes.
Solrosen, Kaponjärgatan 4a. Vegetarian restaurant with vegan
   options. Open Mon.–Sat. until 11 p.m.; Sun. until 8 p.m.

Two-course meals from 60–85kr (£5–7; $7.50–10.50)

Hos Pelle, Djupedalsgatan 12.
Hemma Hos, Haga Nygatan 12.
Taj India, Odinsgatan 6. Indian restaurant. Vegetarian dishes
   available. Open Tues.–Sun. until 11 p.m.

SHOPPING
● **Markets**
The Saluhallen and Grönsakhallen markets are side-by-side, just
off Kungsportstorget. Both open Mon.–Fri. 9 a.m.–6 p.m.; Sat.
8 a.m.–1 p.m.

● **Supermarkets**

Domus, at Kungsportstorget 28 and on Avenyn.
Åhléns, at Ostrahamngatan 18.
Bilhälls, at Stigbergstorget 6.

FURTHER INFORMATION

The newspaper *City Nytt* contains a lot of useful information on eating out in Gothenburg.

Kiruna

CHEAP EATERIES
Two-course meals for under 60kr (£5; $7.50)

Mat & Mums, in the Simhall on Bergmästaregatan. The *dagens rätt* (available Mon.–Fri. until 2 p.m.) includes an all-you-can-eat salad. Open Mon.–Fri. 10 a.m.–10 p.m.; Sat. noon–10 p.m.; Sun. noon–8 p.m.

SHOPPING
The ICA Toppen supermarket is at Greningsgatan 9; the ICA Signalen at Österleden Lombolo; and there is an OBS Interior at Österleden 12. The ICA shops are open daily, OBS Interior Mon.–Sat. only.

Stockholm

With many restaurants in central Stockholm offering a lunchtime *dagens rätt* in the 50–70kr (£4.20–5.90; $6.30–8.80) price range it does not make too much difference whether you eat in the modern city centre, Gamla Stan or Södermlm in the middle of the day, but you can usually count on paying a lot more for an evening meal in a Gamla Stan restaurant than you would elsewhere.

CHEAP EATERIES
Two-course meals under 60kr (£5; $7.50)

Herman's Lilla Gröna. Vegetarian restaurant with four branches at: Katarina Bangata 17 (tel. 640 3010); Fjällgatan 23a (tel. 643 9480); Stora Nygatan 11; and Regeringsgatan 91. All open Mon.–Fri. 11 a.m.–8 p.m.; Sat. noon–9 p.m. (8 p.m. in winter); Sun. 1–8 p.m.
Kafé 44, Tjärhovsgatan 44 (tel. 644 5312). Vegetarian options available. Open Mon.–Fri. 9 a.m.–7 p.m.

La Bamba, Kungsgatan 15 (tel. 20 00 23). Open Mon.–Thurs.
11 a.m.–midnight; Fri.–Sat. 11 a.m.–midnight; Sun. 11 a.m.–
11 p.m.

Daily News Café, Kungsträgården (by the Sverigehuset). Lunches
served 11.30 a.m.–3 p.m.

Sergels Pärla Pizzeria, Sergels Torg (underground arcade). Pizza and
pasta dishes. Open daily 11 a.m.–9 p.m.

Soldaten Svejk, Östgötagatan 15. Czech and Swedish dishes. Cheap
lunchtime meals, and special evening offers Mon.–Tues.

Ersta Café, Erstagatan 1. Open until 5 p.m.

Lilla Budapest, Götgatan 27. Hungarian restaurant.

Fisherman's Inn, Stora Nygatan 25. Seafood restaurant.

Two-course meals from 60–85kr (£5–7; $7.50–10.50)

Örtagården, Östermalmshallen, Östermalmstorget. Vegetarian
restaurant with an all-you-can-eat buffet available.

Jerusalem Kebabn, Hornsgatan 92. Middle Eastern cuisine. Plenty
of vegetarian options.

Österns Pärla, Götgatan 62. Far Eastern cuisine. Good value three-
course set lunches.

Two-course meals from 85–120kr (£7–10; $10.50–15.00)

Dragon Palace, Kornhamnstorg 55. Chinese restaurant. Plenty of
vegetarian dishes available.

Bistro Rubi, Österlångatan. French restaurant.

SHOPPING
● Markets
On Hötorget (off Vasagatan) and Östermalmstorg. Both open
Mon.–Fri. 9.30 a.m.–6 p.m.; Sat. 9.30 a.m.–2 p.m.

● Supermarkets

Åhléns, in the department store at the junction of Klarabergsgatan
and Drottninggatan. Open Mon.–Fri. 9.30 a.m.–9 p.m., Sat.
9.30 a.m.–8 p.m., Sun. noon–8 p.m.

Servus, at the train station end of T-Centralen. Open Mon.–Sat.
7 a.m.–11 p.m.; Sun. 9 a.m.–11 p.m.

Konsum: branches throughout the city – call 7435000 to find the
location of the closest. Open Mon.–Thurs. 7.45 a.m.–5 p.m.; Fri.
7.45 a.m.–3 p.m.

Uppsala

CHEAP EATERIES
Two-course meals under 60kr (£5; $7.50)

Café Ubbo. Student canteen located in the Student Union premises, across from the main university building.

Vegetariana, Östra Ågatan 11. Vegetarian restaurant. Open Mon.–Fri. 11 a.m.–2 p.m.; Sat. noon–2 p.m.

Delikatess Hörnan, Sysslomansgatan 7. Open Mon.–Sat. 11 a.m.–10 p.m.; Sun. 3–10 p.m.

Barowiak, off Nedre Slotsgatan, just below the castle. Good choice of vegetarian dishes.

SHOPPING
The Saluhallen market is at St Erik's Torg. Open Mon.–Fri. 9.30 a.m.–6 p.m.; Sat. 9.30 a.m.–3 p.m.

SWITZERLAND

Amongst budget travellers there is a widely held assumption that Switzerland is a very expensive place to dine out, and since you will seldom be able to eat a three-course meal with table service for under 20SFr (£9.30; $14) if you order *à la carte* it has to be conceded that on one level at least Swiss restaurants are amongst the most expensive covered in this guide (dearer in fact than all but their Scandinavian counterparts). However, before even starting to consider possibilities for cheaper restaurant meals or other types of eateries it should be pointed out that in one way Swiss restaurants do offer very good value for money. Put quite simply, if you do pay the equivalent of £10 for a meal in Switzerland you are virtually assured good service and a well-prepared meal with generous helpings of all the courses; the same cannot be guaranteed in superficially cheaper countries such as Italy or the UK.

More affordable options than eating *à la carte* in restaurants are the three-course fixed-price menu (*mittagsmenu*) or the speciality dish of the day (*plat du jour*) that most restaurants in the towns and cities offer to attract lunchtime custom from the local workforce. Typically the *plat du jour* sells at around 12SFr (£5.60; $8.40). Set menus vary in price, with 15−20SFr (£7.00−9.30; $10.50−14.00) being about the least you can expect to pay, but happily there is usually no shortage of restaurants offering a set menu in that price range. In station restaurants you can be virtually assured of being offered a set menu. As similar establishments at home are often heavily criticized, many travellers overlook station restaurants elsewhere: this would be a mistake in Switzerland as here they are of a high standard. As a rough guide to how much you can save by opting for a set menu, you might reasonably expect to pay 25−40SFr (£11.60−18.60; $17.40−28.00) for a three-course *à la carte* meal in a restaurant offering a fixed-price menu in the 15−20SFr (£7.00−9.30; $10.50−14.00) range.

For a cheaper cooked meal you might try the Manora or Mövenpick chains, or the cafeterias within the larger Co-op and Migros supermarkets, where you can get a two-course meal for 9−12SFr (£4.20−5.60; $6.25−8.40). Some of these also do three-course fixed price menus in the same price range. All these establishments are self-service, but the quality of the food on offer is good. With the exception of the student mensas to be found in university cities such as Geneva, Fribourg, Berne and Zurich, no other Swiss restaurants offer such low-priced, high-quality meals.

A noticeable characteristic of Swiss cuisine is that the dishes tend to be very filling. It would, however, be a mistake to assume that Swiss cooking is stodgy and uninteresting. Not only is there an abundance of different recipes for a great variety of meats, fish and vegetables, but the widespread use of herbs provides a zest often missing in northern European cuisines.

Swiss soups are usually thick meat and vegetable combinations like the celebrated *Berner Märitsuppe* that is a speciality of the capital. If you want to try something a bit different there are various fish soups on offer throughout the country, or the cheese soups (*kässuppe*) of central Switzerland.

The classic Swiss entrée is dried beef (*viande sechée* or *Bundnerfleisch*) which is served in very thin slices with the preferred local accompaniments. Mushrooms are also very popular as a starter – often served on toast. The majority of Swiss entrées are substantial hot dishes such as the courgette flan that is a speciality of Vaud, or the small potato croquettes (*gnocchi*) that are popular everywhere.

All the usual types of meat are widely available in Switzerland. Stews are particularly popular though none really ranks as a speciality dish. *Berner Platte* (a selection of cold meats and sausages) and Geneva's fricassée of pork do fall into that category, but the greatest meat dish of all is generally held to be sliced veal Zurich-style. Sausages play an important role in Swiss cuisine, and despite what some guidebooks would have you believe, French- and Italian-speaking Swiss are just as fond of sausages as the German speakers. Few nationalities are as keen on tripe as the Swiss, but the Ticinese show a passion for it which is remarkable even by Swiss standards. Chicken is nearly always available on restaurant menus, but with the exception of some of the western cantons it is fair to say that it plays nowhere near as important a role in the national cuisine as meat, or indeed fish.

One of the highlights of Swiss cuisine is the talent they have developed for preparing freshwater fish, most vividly displayed in the cooking of perch, which never fails to draw plaudits from the world's gourmets. Trout and salmon feature regularly on restaurant menus, but for a real treat there are more unusual fish such as the fera, bondelle, coregonus and dace.

Apart from the above categories there are three Swiss specialities: *rösti*, the simple entrée of fried grated potato with various accompaniments, and *fondue* and *raclette*, the famous cheese dishes. *Emmental* and *Gruyère* cheese is the basis of the thick fondue mixture into which you dip small pieces of bread with the aid of a fork. *Raclette* is prepared by heating half a cheese (almost always the mild *Bagnes* or *Conches*) in front of a fire or a grill, scraping off the melted cheese and then serving it with the preferred local accompaniments.

Switzerland is undoubtedly one of the best countries for vegetarian travellers. Most of the larger urban centres have vegetarian restaurants and the extremely helpful Tourist Offices can usually point you in the right direction. Even in ordinary restaurants there are no great problems as there are rarely any language difficulties and the concept of vegetarianism is understood. Staff may well alert you to regional specialities which are suitable for vegetarians, such as Geneva's *cardoons au gratin*, or will offer to make a vegetarian version of a traditional dish if there are no veggie options on the menu.

Fruit and nut tarts predominate in the realm of desserts. Zurich's vicarage gateau and Geneva's pear flan are but two examples, but the one which is most often held up as the best of all is the Engadine walnut tart (*Tuorta de Nusch Engiadinaisa*). For something a bit lighter you could try one of the many sponge cakes, pastries, or gingerbread – a Swiss favourite.

These desserts may all be purchased either in a *pâtisserie*, or in a *café* with tea or coffee. The oatflake, fruit and nut combination known as *Birchermüesli* is a favourite with the Swiss as an accompaniment to the important ritual of afternoon tea.

Switzerland is famous for its cheese. Most first-time visitors are likely to be familiar with such names as *Gruyère*, *Emmental* and *Tilsit*. In addition to these better-known cheeses, there is the creamy *Vacherin*; the Parmesan-like *Sbrinz*; the previously mentioned *Bagnes* and *Conches*; and *Schabzieger*, which is prepared with herbs.

Swiss chocolate enjoys similar renown, and names such as Nestlé, Lindt, Suchard and Toblerone will be immediately recognizable to most visitors. Sadly, constant indulgence can be a costly affair, with a typical 100g bar of chocolate costing about 1.50SFr (£0.70; $1).

Food prices in Swiss shops are not always as high as you might imagine. Fresh fruit is roughly similar in price to what you would pay at home: apples and bananas both sell at around 2.60SFr (£1.20; $1.80) per kilo, the equivalent of £0.55 ($0.82) per pound. Similarly, Swiss yoghurt costs about 0.85SFr (£0.40; $0.60) for a 180g pot; at the time of writing a similar amount of Britain's leading yoghurt brands cost about £0.35 ($0.53), but they fall far short of the quality you will find in Switzerland. Milk and cheese are both more expensive than at home, typically retailing at 1.85SFr (£0.86; $1.30) per litre and 2SFr (£0.93; $1.40) per 100g respectively; bread usually costs about 1.90SFr (£0.88; $1.32) for a 500g white loaf. There are many different varieties of wholemeal-type loaves which are only marginally more expensive, and, even leaving aside the nutritional argument, these are better value in as much as they are more filling. It is always worth keeping an eye out for the previous day's bread being sold off at about half-price (another bonus of wholemeal bread is that it remains fresh for several days, whereas day-old white bread will be stale). As usual, supermarkets are most convenient places to shop and Switzerland has two exceptionally good chains: Migros and the Co-op, both with branches in virtually every town (the Co-op also have mini-markets in many villages). The standard of both Co-op and Migros supermarkets is so high that there is no point in recommending one over the other, but one advantage the Co-op stores do have is that they sell alcohol, whereas Migros do not as a matter of company policy. Normal shopping hours are Mon. 2–6.30 p.m.; Tues.–Fri. 8.30 a.m.– 6.30 p.m.; Sat. 8.30 a.m.–3 or 5 p.m.

Switzerland produces some very palatable red and white wines, and if you stick to buying a bottle from a local store they can be sampled relatively cheaply as prices are normally in the 7–12SFr (£3.25–5.60; $4.90–8.40) region. However, buying a similar bottle in a restaurant will cost 20–35SFr (£9.30–16.30; $14.00–24.50). Wines are produced all over the country, but there are four main centres of production: Vaud, Valais, Neuchâtel and Ticino.

The latter is the only part of the country without a strong beer-drinking tradition. Swiss beers may not be as highly regarded as their Belgian or German counterparts but there are plenty of good quality beers available. No brewery dominates the national market, but one brand you will see more often than most is Feldschlößen. In most places you will have the choice of at least one beer brewed in the town, or at least in the region. Compared to the UK, carry-outs are cheap with a half-litre bottle of beer generally costing about 1.30SFr (£0.60; $0.90) (not including deposit) in a local store, though prices are noticeably higher in a restaurant: typically 2.70SFr (£1.25; $1.90) for the standard third-litre measure of draught beer, or 3.50SFr (£1.60; $2.40) for a small quarter-litre bottle.

Swiss spirits are most often based on fruit, as is the case with *kirsch*, which is distilled from cherries. A measure of a Swiss-produced spirit in a restaurant will usually cost 4–6SFr (£1.85– 2.80; $2.80–4.20). Imported spirits such as whisky are normally twice as expensive.

If you are one of those people who think you cannot do without tea or coffee Swiss prices may just force you to contemplate abstinence: 2.20–2.50SFr (£1.00–1.15; $1.50–1.75) for a small glass of tea or a cup of coffee is the norm in Swiss cafés.

Basle

LOCAL SPECIALITIES

Basle soup	made with beef stock, onions, red wine, flour, bread and Gruyère
Basle-style salmon cherry cake	
Baselbieter Weine	wines produced in the vicinity of the city
Warteck and *Ueli*	local brands of beer

CHEAP EATERIES
Two-course meals under 11SFr (£5; $7.50)

Migros Restaurants. Attached to the supermarkets on Claraplatz and Sternengasse.
Co-op Restaurants. Attached to the supermarkets on Claraplatz and Aeschengraben.

Two-course meals from 11–16,50SFr (£5–7; $7.50–10.50)

Börse, Marktgasse 4 (tel. 261 8733). Open daily until 11 p.m. (except Apr.–Oct.: closed Sun.)
Brauner Mutz, Barfüsserplatz 10 (tel. 261 3369). Recommended dish: any fish dish. Open daily until 11.15 p.m. (except 1 July–15 Aug.: closed Sun.).
Gifthüttli, Schneidergasse 11 (tel. 261 1656). Open Mon.–Sat. until 1.30 a.m.
Spaghetti Factory Paradise, Falknerstraße 31 (tel. 261 3443). Open daily until 11.30 p.m. (Fri. and Sat. until 12.30 a.m.).
Jeffery's Indian Restaurant, Centralbahnstraße 17 (tel. 272 1040). Open Mon.–Sat. noon–1.30 p.m. and 6–11.30 p.m.
Wirtshaus zum Schnabel, Trillengasslein 2 (tel. 261 4909). Open Mon.–Sat. until 11 p.m. Closed on public holidays.

Two-course meals from 16,50–22SFr (£7–10; $10.50–15.00)

Basilisk (Hotel Basilisk), Klingentalstraße 1 (tel. 681 4666). Open daily until 10 p.m.
Chez Alain and Old Red Ox Bar (Hotel Helvetia), Küchengasse 13 (tel. 272 0688). Chez Alain open daily until 11 p.m.; Red Ox Bar open Mon.–Fri. until 6 p.m.

Brasserie Gambrinus, Falknerstraße 35 (tel. 272 2112). Recommended drink: *Warteck* beer. Open daily until 11.30 p.m.

SHOPPING
● **Market**
At Marktplatz, open Mon. 6 a.m.–6.30 p.m.; Wed. and Fri. 6 a.m.–1.30 p.m.

● **Supermarkets**

Migros, Sternengasse 17, at the junction of Freie Straße and Eisengasse, and on Claraplatz.
Co-op on Aeschengraben and on Claraplatz.

FURTHER INFORMATION
The local Tourist Offices distribute the *Basel Hotel and Restaurant Guide* which lists many local restaurants and gives an idea as to what you can expect to pay for a meal in the different establishments.

Berne

LOCAL SPECIALITIES

Berner Märitsuppe	a thick soup containing knuckle of pork, smoked bacon and a variety of vegetables and herbs
Berner Platte	a cold dish of different meats, sausage and vegetables
Felsenau and *Gurten Brau*	locally brewed beers
Toblerone	chocolate

CHEAP EATERIES
Two-course meals for under 11SFr (£5; $7.50)

Mensa der Universität, Gesellschaftstraße 2. Open Mon.–Thurs. 11.30 a.m.–1.45 p.m. and 5.45–7.30 p.m.; Fri. 11.30 a.m.–1.45 p.m.
Restaurant Manora, Bubenberg Platz 5a (tel. 22 37 55). Open Mon.–Sat. 7 a.m.–10.45 p.m.; Sun 9 a.m.–10.45 p.m.
Ryfflihof, Genfergasse 5. *Co-op* self-service restaurant attached to the supermarket. Open Mon. 11 a.m.–6.15 p.m.; Tues.–Fri.

8 a.m.−6.15 p.m. (Thurs. until 8.45 p.m.); Sat. 8 a.m.−4 p.m.
Migros Restaurant, Zeughausgasse 31. Open Mon.−Fri. 8.30 a.m.−
7.30 p.m. (until 9.30 p.m. on Thurs.); Sat. 8 a.m.−4 p.m.

Two-course meals from 11−16,50SFr (£5−7; $7.50−10.50)

Teestübli, Postgasse 49 (tel. 22 64 84). Vegetarian restaurant. Open
Tues.−Sun. 9 a.m.−11 p.m.
Landhaus, Altenbergstraße 6 (tel. 41 41 66). Open Mon.−Sat.
11 a.m.−11.30 p.m. (Wed. until 12.30 a.m.).

Two-course meals from 16,50−22SFr (£7−10; $10.50−15.00)

Klötzlikeller, Gerichtigkeitgasse 62 (tel. 22 74 56). Open Tues.−Sat.
Kornhauskeller, Kornhausplatz 18 (tel. 22 11 33). Open Tues.−Sun.

SHOPPING
● **Markets**

Barenplatz: open daily from May−Oct.; at other times open Tues.
and Sat. only.
Bundesplatz: fruit and vegetable market open Tues. and Sat.
throughout the year.
Munstergasse: meat market open Tues. and Sat. throughout the
year.

● **Supermarkets**

Ryfflihof (Co-op), enter from Neuengasse or Aarbergergasse
Migros, enter from Marktgasse or Zeughausgasse
Denner Superdiscount, in the Kaiserhaus Passage between
Marktgasse and Amthausgasse

Geneva

LOCAL SPECIALITIES

fricassee of pork
fricassee of chicken
Cardoons au gratin   cardoons in cheese
pear flan

CHEAP EATERIES
Two-course meals under 11SFr (£5; $7.50)

Co-op Restaurants, attached to the three supermarkets listed below.

Migros Restaurants, attached to the three supermarkets listed below.

Restaurant Manora (Placette), rue de Cornavin 6 (tel. 731 3146/7400). Open Mon.–Sat. 7 a.m.–9 p.m.; Sun. 9 a.m.– 9 p.m.

Le Zofage, rue des Voisins 6. A university mensa open to non-students. Open Sun.–Fri. noon–2 p.m. and 6–8 p.m.

L'Age d'Or, rue de Cornavin 11 (tel. 731 3093). Pizzeria. Open Mon.–Sat. 7 p.m.–1 a.m.

Two-course meals from 11–16,50SFr (£5–7; $7.50–10.50)

Café du Rond-Point, Rond-Point de Plainpalais 2. Open daily 6 a.m.–midnight.

Two-course meals from 16,50–22SFr (£7–10; $10.50–15.00)

Dent de Lion, rue des Eaux-Vives 25 (tel. 736 7298). Vegetarian restaurant. Open Mon.–Fri. 10 a.m.–2.30 p.m. and 6–10 p.m. No alcohol.

Les Cinq Saveurs, rue du Prieuré 22 (tel. 31 78 70). Mainly vegetarian dishes in the evening; completely vegetarian at lunchtime. Recommended dish: *paella aux cinq couleurs* (a vegetarian *paella*). Open Mon.–Fri. noon–2 p.m. and 6– 9.30 p.m.

Relais de la Poste, rue de Lausanne 27 (tel. 732 8438). Closed Sat. evening and Sun.

Le Coq Rouge (Hôtel d'Allèves), rue du Cendrier 16 (tel. 732 7730).

Brasserie Hollandaise, place de la Poste 3 (tel. 311 3606). Closed Sun. and public holidays.

Les Armures, rue du Puits-St-Pierre 1. Open Mon.–Fri. 8 a.m.– midnight; Sat.–Sun. 11 a.m.–midnight.

Au Carnivore, place du Bourg-de-Four 30 (tel. 311 8758). Open daily 11 a.m.–11 p.m.

Au Pied du Cochon, place du Bourg-de-Four 4 (tel. 20 47 97). Open daily 10 a.m.–midnight.

SHOPPING
● **Supermarkets**

Co-op: rue du Commerce 5; rue de la Terrassière 35; and at rue de Montbrillant 90.

Migros: rue de la Terrassière 29; rue de Lausanne 18–20; and at rue des Pâquis 41.

FURTHER INFORMATION
The *Restaurants* guide available from the local Tourist Office lists a selection of the city's restaurants (including the usual price for a meal at some of the establishments listed). The Tourist Office may also have a copy of *Dinerscope*, a small booklet listing a number of restaurants in the cantons of Genève and Vaud (again with average prices given for some of the listings).

Lausanne

LOCAL SPECIALITIES

courgette flan with mint
rabbit livers in puff pastry
trout or char with green grapes

Papet Vaudois	leek, onion and potato stew
Boxer	local beer

Wines from the canton of Vaud (see **Further Information** below)

CHEAP EATERIES
Two-course meals under 11SFr (£5; $7.50)

Co-op Restaurant Le Gourmet, Au Centre, rue St-Laurent. Open Mon.–Fri. 8.30 a.m.–6.45 p.m., Sat. 8 a.m.–5 p.m.

Restaurant Innovation, rue du Pont. In the department store.

Migros Restaurant, Metropole 2000, rue des Terreaux.

Restaurant Placette, rue St-Laurent. In the department store.

Manora Sainf, place St-François 17 (tel. 20 92 93). Open Mon.–Sat. 7 a.m.–10.30 p.m.; Sun. 9 a.m.–10.30 p.m.

Two-course meals from 11–16,50SFr (£5–7; $7.50–10.50)

La Locanda, place de la Riponne 4 (tel. 23 20 30). Meals served 11.30 a.m.–2 p.m. and 6.15–10 p.m.

Au Couscous, rue St-Pierre 2 (tel. 312 2017). Tunisian and Middle Eastern food, plus a large selection of vegetarian dishes (including a vegetarian set menu). Open daily 6 a.m.–1 a.m. (Fri.–Sat. until 2 a.m.).

Du Cygne, rue du Maupas 2 (tel. 312 2180). Open Mon.–Sat. Meals served 11.30 a.m.–2 p.m. and 5.30–11 p.m.

Ticino, place de la Gare 12 (tel. 20 32 04). Good choice of cantonal dishes. Open Mon.–Sat. Meals served 11 a.m.–2 p.m. and 5.30–11.30 p.m.

Two-course meals from 16,50–22SFr (£7–10; $10.50–15.00)

Café Romand, place St-François 2 (tel. 312 6375). Range of cantonal specialities. Recommended dish: *papet Vaudois*. Open Mon.–Sat. 11 a.m.–11 p.m.

Pinte Besson, rue de l'Ale 4 (tel. 312 7227). Open Mon.–Sat. 7 a.m.–midnight.

SHOPPING
● **Markets**

Every Wed. and Sat. on pl. de la Palud, pl. de la Riponne and pl. St-François. Open 7.30 a.m.–12.30 p.m.

● **Supermarkets**

Migros, branches in Metropole 2000 Centre Commercial on rue des Terreaux, and on rue du Petit Chêne.

Co-op, branch in the Au Centre complex on rue St-Laurent.

Innovation, in the department store on rue du Pont.

FURTHER INFORMATION

Dinerscope is a brochure available from the local Tourist Office which lists a selection of restaurants in the cantons of Vaud and Genève, and gives the average prices for some of the listings. The Tourist Office also distributes the *Guide du Vignoble Vaudois* – an informative booklet on the different wines of the canton (like *Dinerscope*, this is printed in French).

Lucerne

LOCAL SPECIALITIES

Kässuppe	cheese soup
Lent vegetable soup	
dace	
Lucerne vol-au-vent	pastry filled with meat, sausage, fruit, mushrooms and onions
gingerbread	
Eichhof	local beer

CHEAP EATERIES
Two-course meals under 11SFr (£5; $7.50)

Migros Restaurant. Next to the Migros supermarket on Hertenstein-straße. Open Mon.–Sat. 6.30 a.m.–6.30 p.m.
Co-op Restaurant. In the supermarket on Zürichstraße.
EPA Restaurant. In the supermarket on Mühleplatz/Rössligasse.

Two-course meals from 11–16,50SFr (£5–7; $7.50–10.50)

Tearoom Roxy, Mühleplatz 4 (tel. 51 53 97). Open Mon.–Fri. 8.30 a.m.–7 p.m., Sat. 8.30 a.m.–5 p.m.
Waldstatter Hof, Zentralstraße 4 (tel. 23 54 93). Good range of vegetarian options. Open daily 6.30 a.m.–8.30 p.m.
Kesselturm, Franziskanerplatz 9 (tel. 23 08 98).
Karibia, Pilatusplatz (tel. 23 61 10). Plenty of vegetarian options. Recommended dish: seafood buffet. Open Tues.–Sat. 7 a.m.–midnight; Sun.–Mon. 10 a.m.–midnight.

Two-course meals 16,50–22SFr (£7–10; $10.50–15.00)

Wirsthaus Zum Eugel, Pfistergasse 31. Open Mon. 5 p.m.–midnight; Tues.–Fri. 9 a.m.–midnight; Sat. 9 a.m.–10 p.m.
Fire Pub, Hirschengraben 19 (tel. 23 55 49). Vegetarian dishes available.
Schiff, unter der Egg 8 (tel. 51 38 51). Speciality fish dishes, and traditional Swiss and cantonal food.
Walliser Spycher Le Mazot, Eisegasse 15. Open Mon.–Fri. 4 p.m.–12.30 a.m.; Sat. 11.15 a.m.–12.30 a.m.

SHOPPING

Stalls selling fresh food are dotted throughout the Old Town from Mon.–Sat., particularly along the banks of the river.

● **Supermarkets**

Migros, Hertensteinstraße 44. Open Mon.–Sat. 8 a.m.–6.30 p.m. (Thurs. until 9 p.m.).
Co-op, Zürichstraße. Same hours as Migros.
EPA, Mühleplatz (junction with Rössligasse). Open Mon.–Fri. 8 a.m.–6.30 p.m. (Thurs. until 9 p.m.); Sat. 8 a.m.–4 p.m.

Zürich

LOCAL SPECIALITIES

Zurich-style sliced veal
calves' livers skewered and grilled
vicarage gateau   a fruit and nut tart
Löwenbrau and *Hürlimann*   beers

CHEAP EATERIES
Two-course meals under 11SFr (£5; $7.50)

Mensa der Universität Zurich and Mensa Polyterrasse. At Ramistraße 71 and 101 respectively. Student ID required. Open Mon.–Thurs. 11.15 a.m.–1.30 p.m. and 5.30–7.30 p.m.; Fri. 11.15 a.m.–1.30 p.m. and 5.30–7.15 p.m.; Sat. 11.30 a.m.–1 p.m. (except mid-July–mid-Sept when the mensas open only for lunch).
Migros Restaurants. In the supermarkets listed below.
Co-op Restaurant. Attached to the supermarket listed below.

Two-course meals from 11–16,50SFr (£5–7; $7.50–10.50)

Restaurant 1001, Niederdorfstraße 4. Turkish food. Open daily 11 a.m.–midnight.
Café Marion, Mühlegasse 22. Open Mon.–Fri. 6.30 a.m.–7 p.m.; Sat. 8 a.m.–6 p.m.; Sun. 9 a.m.–6 p.m.
Rheinfelder Bierhalle, Niederdorfstraße 76. Open daily 9 a.m.–midnight.

Cafeteria Freischütz, Freischützgasse 1. Open daily 9 a.m.–7 p.m.

Two-course meals from 16,50–22SFr (£7–10; $10.50–15.00)

Zeughauskeller, Bahnhofstraße 28a (tel. 211 2690). Open 11.30 a.m.–9.30 p.m.
Vier Linden, Gemeindestraße 48. Vegetarian restaurant. Open Mon.–Fri. 6 a.m.–9 p.m.
Hiltl Vegi, Sihlstraße 28 (tel. 221 3870/3871). Vegetarian establishment offering two different restaurants: Vegetini on the ground floor, Vegitable above. After 6 p.m. Vegitable offers an Indian buffet from which you can eat as much as you like. Both restaurants are open Mon.–Sat. 6.30 a.m.–9 p.m., and Sun. 9 a.m.–9 p.m.

SHOPPING
● **Supermarkets**

Co-op, just over the River Limmat from the main train station.
Migros, on Bahnhofstraße, and at the Morgental stop of tram 7 (convenient if you are staying in the youth hostel).

TURKEY

Turkey's cuisine is rated as one of the best in the world, and the good news for travellers is that sampling its delights costs precious little. Apart from the coastal resorts where restaurants are (relatively) overpriced, a three-course meal in a typical local restaurant is unlikely to cost more than £4 ($6), and will normally be a good deal cheaper.

The two most notable features of Turkish cuisine are the prevalence of slow-roasting and slow-stewing as ways of preparing meat, and the use of yoghurt in the preparation of many dishes.

There are quite a few options open to you if you are looking for a sit-down meal. Restaurants divide into several categories: a *restoran* serves Turkish and foreign food and alcohol; an *içkili lokanta* serves Turkish food and alcohol; and a *lokanta* serves Turkish food without alcohol. *Kebapçi*, *köfteci* and *pideci* or *pide salonu* are establishments specializing in kebabs, *kofte* and *pide* respectively (see below). A further option is a *meyhane* where, although eating is of secondary importance to drinking, you can also get good quality food (women should note that no self-respecting Turkish woman would go into a *meyhane*).

The Turks are particularly partial to soups (*çorba*). Typical favourites include *tavuk suyu* (chicken), *ezo gelin* (red lentil and rice), *kirmizi mercimek* (red lentil) and *işkembe* (tripe). A real speciality is *tarhana çorbasi* (dried yoghurt soup).

Turkish hors d'oeuvres (*meze*) are very highly rated. Salads are common, none more so than the one prepared from tomatoes, cucumbers, onion, parsley and peppers called *çoban salatasi*. There is also a range of purées such as the famous *humus* made from chickpeas. Very different in style are *arnavut ciğeri* (Albanian-style lamb's liver) and *Çerkez tavuğu* (Circassian chicken). Included amongst the hors d'oeuvres are the many stuffed vegetables (*dolma*) for which Turkey is renowned. Fairly common examples are *lahana dolmasi* (cabbage leaves), *kiymali yaprak* (vine leaves) and *kiymali domates* (tomatoes). The most celebrated of these dishes is *iman bayildi* (aubergine stuffed with onion, garlic and tomatoes).

Lamb (*kuzu*) is by far the most commonly eaten meat (*et*) in Turkey, though you will never have much trouble finding beef (*sığır*) should you so wish. The Islamic religion prohibits the consumption of pork and related products.

Lamb is the basis of most of the range of *kebaps* – the dish visitors associate more than any other with Turkey (the *doner kebap* in particular). The most popular kebab is the *şiş kebapi* (lamb pieces skewered and grilled), while the *doner kebap*, *Iskender kebap* and the spicy *Adana kebap* are the most frequently seen of the countless other variations. Similarly there are many different ways of preparing the small meatballs called *köfte*. Stews and casseroles such as *soğanli yahni* (lamb and onion stew) and *güveç* (slowly casseroled lamb) are a very important part of Turkish cuisine, and you are almost guaranteed to find at least one on most restaurant menus. *Musakka* is a dish of alternate layers of meat and vegetable — usually aubergine (*patlıcan* musakka). A mixed grill (*karışık izgara*) can be especially good value, though the squeamish might not fancy the fact that offal such as tripe (*işkembe*), heart (*yürek*) and lambs' testicles (*billur* or *koç yumurtasi*) are often included in this dish.

Both chicken (*piliç*) and fish (*balık*) dishes are more expensive on average than meat dishes. The former are relatively scarce in Turkish cuisine, but there is an excellent choice of fish dishes. As well as sardines (*sardalya*), mackerel (*uskumru* or *kolyoz*) and freshwater trout (*alabalık*) there are more unusual options such as bluefish (*lüfer*), grouper (*lagos*), red mullet (*barbunya* or *tekir*) and swordfish (*kılıç*). Mussels (*midye*), shrimps (*karides*) and squid (*kalamar*) are amongst the most popular seafoods. Seafood is normally prepared quite simply: fish by frying, grilling or baking; shellfish by frying or boiling. A notable exception is *midye dolmasi* (mussels stuffed with pine nuts, rice, onions and currants). Even if you do not want to pay a little extra for a seafood entrée consider buying some of the above in snack form if you are near the coast; a few stuffed mussels, for example, or a fish sandwich.

It is often stated that vegetarians will be faced with a struggle in Turkey, yet there are plenty of traditional dishes which are meat-free, including some of the many stuffed vegetables and pilaffs (*pilav* – dishes based on rice or cracked wheat (*bulgur*)). *Etli mi*? (does this have meat in it?) is a useful basic phrase, but really the more effort you make to learn a few key phrases the more you will get out of your trip as regards enjoying the cuisine. Useful standbys which chefs will generally put together on request are *mücver* (courgette fritters), *menemen* (Turkish scrambled eggs) and omelettes.

For dessert the usual choices are rice pudding (*sütlaç*), the very thick chocolate pudding called *supangile*, or one of the intensely sweet syrup-drenched pastries such as the classic *baklava*, *tulumbu tatlısı* and *tel kadayif*. One highly unusual dessert which is well worth looking out for is *tavukgöğsü* (milk and chicken breast pastry). The most famous Turkish sweet of all is of course Turkish Delight (*lokum*), though the real thing is far removed from what appears in Britain. *Lokum* is not something you would expect to find in a restaurant, but rather on market stalls or in pâtisseries (*pastanes*) where you can also buy *baklava* and similar products.

Both snacks and light meals are readily available in Turkey. Popular takeaway snacks include *sandviç* (sandwiches), *lahmacun* (a small, Arab-style pizza) and *börek* (a cheese- or mince-filled pastry), all of which can be bought from a *Bufé*, or from street vendors (you can also buy *börek* in small general food stores). *Pide* is flat bread with a topping of egg (*yumurtali*), cheese (*peynirli*), mince (*kiymali*) or sausage (*sucuklu*) and these you will find in *pideci* or *pide salonu*.

With cheap restaurant meals and inexpensive street snacks so widely available there is no pressing need to buy food from shops or markets, yet there are plenty of food shops and the quality is excellent. The local market or bazaar is your best option as these are always teeming with fresh and dried fruit, vegetables and dairy produce. Supermarkets are not particularly common, but there is no shortage of small general and more specialized food stores, so all in all shopping is a simple matter in Turkey. Prices for foodstuffs produced in the country are usually very low, but you can expect to pay Western European prices for imported products.

The national drink is tea (*çay*), which is served without milk, and with several lumps of sugar to add if you so wish. The cups are small, though you can request a *duble çay* if you would like a larger measure. The offering of tea is a traditional part of Turkish hospitality, and something you are likely to encounter many times during a visit.

Turkish coffee (*kahve*) is also served in small cups, again without milk, but in contrast to tea it is normal to specify whether you want your coffee without sugar (*sade*), with a little sugar (*orta şekerli*), or with lots of sugar (*çok şekerli*). Be sure not to drink too fast as the remnants of the finely ground unfiltered coffee gather in the bottom of the cup.

Ayran is a popular cold drink of diluted yoghurt with salt which is available in almost any eatery, as well as from shops and street vendors. Another favourite which you will see if you are travelling in autumn or winter is the mildly alcoholic millet-based *boza*.

Alcohol is freely available in all but a few parts of Turkey. The Turkish favourite is the aniseed-flavoured *raki* (similar to the Greek *ouzo*). In a bar or restaurant you can expect to pay anything from £0.40−1.00 ($0.60−1.50) for a measure of *raki*, but you can buy a 70cl bottle in a local shop for about £2.50 ($3.75). Imported spirits are expensive − usually at least three times the price you would pay in the UK.

Turkey also produces a number of very palatable red and white wines (*ŝarap*). *Yakut* and *Kavaklidere* stand out amongst the reds, whilst *Villa Doluca* and *Ĉankaya* are to the fore amongs the whites. A bottle of any of these would cost about £1.00–1.50 ($1.50–2.25), in a local shop, or £2.50–3.50 ($3.75–5.25) in a restaurant.

Beer (*bira*) drinkers are not exactly spoiled for choice in Turkey as there are only two main brands: *Efes Pilsen* and *Tuborg* (the latter also produce the beer marketed under the name *Venus*), but at least these are quite distinct in taste. It is some consolation to know that if you like either of these then you are certain to see them in most places you will visit. Buying a half-litre bottle in a bar or a restaurant typically costs from £0.50–1.00 ($0.75–1.50).

The water is safe to drink almost anywhere in Turkey, but even the locals tend to drink either *memba suyu* (still mineral water) or *maden suyu* (carbonated mineral water), both of which are widely available and cost pennies to buy.

Ankara

CHEAP EATERIES
The greatest concentration of cheap restaurants is in the central Ulus district, but if you happen to be in Kızılay there are a number of possibilities near the junction of Karanfil Sok and Ziya Gökalp Cad. Restaurants in the latter area are more expensive on average than in Ulus, but even here a couple of courses and a drink should leave you with change from £3.50 ($5.25).
Three-course meals from £1.50–2.00 ($2.25–3.00)

Tandir Kebap, Sanayi Cad.
Uludağ Kebapcisi, Denizciler Cad 51 (tel. 312 4565).
Ĉiçek Lokantası, Ĉankırı Cad 12/A.
Uğrak Piknik and Lokantası, Ĉankırı Cad. Restaurant with adjoining cafeteria. Eating in the restaurant may just push the bill into the £2–3 price range.
Haci Mehmet Özlek, Sanayi Cad 7.

Three-course meals from £2–3 ($3.00–4.50)

Cihan Kebap, Selanik Cad 3/B.
Kebapistan, Karanfil Sok (junction with Yüksel Cad).

Three-course meals around £4.50 ($6.75)

Yeni Karpiç Restaurant. In the shopping plaza across from the Atatürk statue. Recommended dish: *bonfile* (steak, with peppers).
Spaghetti House, Selanik Cad 65. Pasta dishes predominate.

SHOPPING
There is a market to the right off Hisarparki Cad as you walk from
Ulus Meydani.

Antalya

Antalya's burgeoning tourist trade has resulted in higher than average prices in local restaurants. That said, unless you head for an
obviously expensive restaurant it is highly unlikely that you will
pay more than £4–5 ($6.00–7.50) for a three-course meal with a
drink. Along Cumhuriyet Caddesi there is a good choice of restaurants catering for both tourists and locals. The concentration
of restaurants along Eski Sebzeciler ıçi Sok near the junction of
Cumhuriyet Caddesi and Atatürk Caddesi are more tourist-
orientated.

LOCAL SPECIALITIES

Tandir kebap   mutton roasted in a clay pot

CHEAP EATERIES
Three-course meals for under £2.50 ($3.75)

Saray Lokantası. In an alley off Müftüler Cad. Recommended dish:
   piliç (roast chicken).

   Three-course meals from £2.50–3.50 ($3.75–5.25)

Gaziantep I & II. Two restaurants (200m apart) accessible through
   the passageway on İsmet Paşa Cad opposite the PTT office.
   Recommended dish: *Adana kebap*.
Kadir Usta'nin Döner Kebapi, Esli Sebzeciler ıçi Sok. Very good for
   vegetarian dishes.

   Three-course meals from £4–5 ($6.00–7.50)

Develiler Kebapçisi, Kenan Evren Bulvari 68/C.

Three-course meals around £5.50 ($8.25)

Hisar Restaurant. Overlooking the old port on the castle ramparts. Recommended dishes: any of the fish (*balik*) dishes.

Bodrum

Average prices in all types of eatery are probably the highest in Turkey. There are no particular concentrations of relatively inexpensive restaurants, but the choice is a bit wider than usual along Cevat Šâkir Cad, and as a rule you can find cheaper meals in the establishments set back from the water.

LOCAL SPECIALITIES
Seafood: especially *kalamar* (squid) and *ahtopod* (octopus).

CHEAP EATERIES
Three-course meals under £1.75 ($2.60)

Uslu Büfe, Neyzen Tevfik. Few places are cheaper than this establishment.
Uğrak Lokantası, Cevat Šâkir Cad. Cheap by local standards. Recommended dishes: the puddings *sutlac* (rice pudding) and *supangile* (chocolate pudding).
Karaca, Cevat Šâkir Cad.
Čakir Ali, Cevat Šâkir Cad (near the Adliye Camii). Mainly *kebap* and *pide*.
Kumbahçe Köftecisi, Cumhuriyet Cad.

Three-course meals around £2.50 ($3.75)

Sakkali Ali Doksan Restaurant, Eski Kasaphone Sok 53. Open Mon.–Sat. 9 a.m.–9.30 p.m.

Three-course meals around £5.00–7.50 ($7.50–11.00)

Orhan's No. 7, Eski Banki Sok 7. Excellent seafood. Recommended dish: octopus.

SHOPPING
The main market is close to the bus station (*otogar*), but Cevat
Ŝâkir Cad is also a good place to pick up fruit, vegetables and dairy
produce from street vendors.

Istanbul

Options for eating out are strictly limited in the Sultanahmet district, particularly in the evenings. Around lunchtime there are a
number of small hole-in-the-wall type establishments where you
can get an inexpensive light meal, but these are invariably closed
in the evening. Restaurants in this area are all too often overpriced,
and poor value for money, including the much vaunted Pudding
Shop. Although many of the best restaurants are on the opposite
side of the Golden Horn in Tepebaşi, Beyoğlu and Taksim, there
are plenty of good places to eat in Eminönü and Sirkeci, and in
Kumpapi.

LOCAL SPECIALITIES
Fish dishes. For fishy snacks a host of vendors down by the Galata
Bridge sell sandwiches containing freshly grilled anchovies (*hamsi*),
mackerel (*uskumru*) or sardines (*sardalya*).

CHEAP EATERIES
Three-course meals from £2.50–4.00 ($3.75–6.00)

Sultanahmet Köftecısı, Divan Yolu 12 (tel. 511 3960). Open daily
11 a.m.–midnight.
Vitamin Restaurant, Divan Yolu 16 (tel. 526 5086). Recommended
dishes: *mercimek çorbasi* (lentil soup) and *patlican dolmasi* (stuffed
aubergine). Open daily 7 a.m.–midnight.
Karadeniz Restaurant. One of a number of seafood restaurants
under the Galata Bridge. Fresh fish dishes around £2.75 ($4.15).
Hasir I, Kalyoncu Kulluğu Cad 94/1, Tarlabaşi Bulvari, Beyoğlu.
Good selection of vegetarian dishes.
Han Restaurant, Kartçinar Sok 16, Karaköy (tel. 152 5452). Open
11 a.m.–2 p.m. and 7.30–10.30 p.m.
Altin Sofrasi, Süleymaniye Cad 33 (tel. 522 5518).
Doy-Doy, Şifa Örücüler Sokak 13 (tel. 517 1588).
Istanbul Restaurant, Gedikpaşa Cad 24 (tel. 522 9458). Open daily
6 a.m.–11 p.m.

Kimene Restaurant, Çiçek Pasaji, Sahne Sok, Tepebaşi (tel. 244 1266). One of a number of restaurants along Çiçek Pasaji. Open daily noon till midnight.

Three-course meals from £4–6 ($6–9)

Gölçek, Ördekli Bakkal Sok 1, Kumkapi (tel. 519 4033). Seafood restaurant. Recommended dish: *karides güvec* (shrimp casserole).
Ayazpaşa Restaurant, Inönü Cad 77/1, Taksim (enter from Miralay Šefik Bey Sok) (tel. 143 4892). Russian food. Recommended dish: *borscht* (beetroot soup).
Altiu Kupa, Yerebatan Cad 6 (tel. 519 4770).
Hacı Abdullah, Sakizağaci Cad 19, Istiklâl Cad, Beyoğlu (tel. 244 8561). Recommended dish: marinated artichokes (June only). Open daily 11 a.m.–10 p.m. Unlicensed.
Yeni Rejans, Ikuvi Geçidi 15, Istiklâl Cad (down the alleyway at no. 244), Tünel, Beyoğlu (tel. 244 1610). Russian food. Recommended dishes: *borscht* (beetroot soup) and beef stroganoff. Recommended drink: lemon vodka (distilled on the premises). Open daily noon–3 p.m. and 7–10 p.m.

Three-course meals from £4–6 ($6–9)

Krependeki Imroz, Meyhaneler Sok, Tepebaşi (tel. 249 9073).

SHOPPING
There are markets on Hasircilar Cad in Eminönü, near the Egyptian Bazaar (Mısır Carşısı), and on Meşrutiyet Cad in Tepebaşi, close to the British Embassy.

İzmir

Considering İzmir is Turkey's third city there is a relative shortage of possibilities for eating out in all price categories. The best selection of cheap eateries is to be found in the bazaar, or along the stretch of Anafartalar Cad closest to the bazaar, but few of these remain open after 7.30 p.m. For evening eating there is a concentration of restaurants around the Basmane train station, and another group of restaurants along Atatürk Cad (Birinci Kordon). Although restaurants in the latter area are generally more expensive than those around the train station or the bazaar they are still easily affordable.

LOCAL SPECIALITIES
Midye (mussels) are available in restaurants or from street vendors fried (*midye tavasi*) or stuffed with rice, currants and pine nuts (*midye dolmasi*).

CHEAP EATERIES
Three-course meals from £1.50–2.50 ($2.25–3.75)

Ömür, Anafartalar Cad 794.
Cankay Côrba Salonu, Gazi Bulvarı (junction with 1370 Sok).
Şark Lokantasi, Anafartalar Cad. Open 7 a.m.–9 p.m.
Urfa Lokantasi, Anafartalar Cad (opposite the police station).
   Specializes in dishes from Eastern Turkey. Open twenty-four hours.
İnci Et Lokantası, 1369 Sok 51/A (tel. 19 89 91). Open 10 a.m.–midnight.
Câgdas, Anafartalar Cad 606.

Three-course meals from £2.50–3.50 ($3.75–5.25)

Halikarnass Balik Lokantası. Fish restaurant in the bazaar at the intersection of 870 Sok, 871 Sok and 873 Sok. Unlicensed. Closes at 7.30 p.m.
Öz Ezo Gelin, Anafartalar Cad (junction with 848 Sok). Closes at 9 p.m.
Bolulú Hasan Usta, 853 Sok 13/B. Recommended dishes: any of the puddings. Open until 8 p.m.

SHOPPING
The bazaar is off Anafartalar Cad by the Kemeralti Camii, about 300m from Konak Meydanı.

Selçuk

CHEAP EATERIES
Although prices in local restaurants are slightly inflated by the tourist trade most still offer good value for money. A succession of fine restaurants line the pedestrianized Cengiz Topel Cad.

Bayrakli Pide Salonu. At the upper end of Cengiz Topel Cad. The fare on offer goes well beyond *pide*. Three-course meal around £2.20 ($3.30). Open 7 a.m.–midnight.

Efes. Beside the Bayrakli Pide Salonu. Similar in price.

Gözde. A short distance along Cengiz Topel Cad from the Otel Aksoy. Recommended dishes: *karışık izgara* (mixed grill) or any of the fish dishes. Three-course meal £2.75–3.50 ($4.15–5.25).

UNITED KINGDOM

The numerous fast-food chains that have popped up all over the UK, combined with the success of all manner of ethnic restaurants, means that eating well on a budget is fairly easy wherever you go. Just avoid obvious tourist traps which are sure to rip you off – and, in big cities at least, eat your main meal at lunchtime along with the office workers.

Restaurants and hotels are the most expensive places to eat; the snootier establishments can easily charge £30 ($45) per head for two courses. French restaurants in particular are often greatly overpriced in the UK, and unfortunately places specializing in British cuisine can also be very expensive. Cheaper restaurants do exist though and along with popular continental-style bistros, brasseries and trattorias, can provide two-course meals for around £10 ($15) per head. Cafés and tea rooms are often good bets for light meals and snacks during the day, as well as department stores and some retailing chains which have in-store cafeterias serving food of the pie-beans-and-chips or baked potato variety. A cup of coffee in a café can cost anything from £0.50–1.20 ($0.75–1.80) and a main course should be around £4 ($6).

The traditional British fast food, fish and chips, is still popular, but many outlets have disappeared and been replaced by burger bars, pizza and kebab joints, and baked potato chains. Fast food is always cheaper if you take it away rather than sit down and eat it. In all the major cities there are also plenty of sandwich bars which sell many types of sandwiches and filled rolls, and often hot soup and cakes as well.

Perhaps the best place to find good food at low prices, however, is in a pub. Soup, sandwiches and hot meals like chicken and chips, curry, lasagne, steak pie, salads and the ubiquitous 'ploughman's lunch' (bread, butter, cheese, pickle and tomato), are always on offer and can be particularly good value at lunchtime. While 'pub-grub' was once chiefly known for being cheap and filling, but rather stodgy and unimaginative, things are changing and many places now offer excellent food and a wide choice, including vegetarian options. A main dish in a pub shouldn't set you back more than £4 ($6) and can often be as low as £2.50 ($3.75). On the subject of pubs you'll find that beer costs around £1.50 ($2.25) a pint, while a glass of wine will cost from £1.20–1.60 ($1.80–2.40), depending on where you buy it. Pubs in England and Wales open between 12.30–2.30 p.m. and 5.30–10.30 or 11 p.m. In Scotland opening hours are more relaxed and pubs often open all day. Don't forget wine bars, which can sometimes be very pretentious, but often provide the best value on wine, and certainly offer more choice than anywhere else. They may also sell food, generally of the quiche and paté variety, and although pricier than pubs, can still be worth exploring.

British food has been the butt of many jokes over the years; it has been dismissed as stodgy and fatty, the vegetables as bland and overcooked. This was fair comment at one time, but over the past ten years or so things have changed, and a greater interest in healthy eating has resulted in much lighter versions of traditional dishes, and crisper vegetables and salads. There is enormous variety, too, since ethnic dishes, often slightly adapted for the British palate, have become as common as fish and chips. In fact pizzas, pasta dishes and curries are generally easier to find, and certainly cheaper, than many traditional British dishes.

Perhaps the best-known part of the British diet is the 'great British breakfast', a large plateful of fried bacon, egg, sausage and often bread, black pudding (oatmeal mixed with blood and seasoning), tomatoes and mushrooms, followed by toast and marmalade, and washed down with tea. As more and more people have sedentary jobs and little time in the morning, breakfast in the average household is more likely to consist of tea and toast, or cereal, but traditional breakfasts are still available in hotels, bed and breakfasts, and transport cafés.

For many people today lunch is a light meal, usually a bowl of soup, or sandwiches. Almost anything can go into a sandwich, from cold meats, hard-boiled egg or cheese, to smoked salmon, salad or paté. Soups are also an excellent way of filling up, particularly on a cold day. Vegetable, tomato, mushroom, lentil and potato and leek are perhaps the most common, but vegetarians should always check whether a meat stock has been used.

The midday meal, eaten between noon and 2 p.m., was once the main meal of the day for working class people (who called it dinner) but today most people take a smaller 'lunch' at midday and dinner in the evening. On Sundays, however, lots of people in England still eat the traditional 'Sunday lunch' of roast beef, Yorkshire pudding, roast potatoes and gravy. Roast meats are something that Britain as a whole tends to do well, the most popular being beef, lamb, chicken and pork. They're usually served with potatoes and vegetables, such as carrots, greens or peas. Potatoes are a staple item in the British diet and can be cooked in a number of ways: roasted, boiled, mashed with milk and butter, baked, sautéed or fried (chips). They're also used in many soups, stews and casseroles.

In addition to roast meats, traditional main courses are pies, stews and casseroles made with different varieties and cuts of meat. Some of the best-known entrées include steak and kidney pie (stewed steak and kidney in rich gravy with a pastry topping); steak and kidney pudding (the same but cooked for longer and with a suet crust); meat casseroles, stews or hot-pots with dumplings (small fluffy balls of suet); sausage and mash (sausages with mashed potatoes) and of course fish and chips, which should be sprinkled with salt and vinegar, and the fish fried in a crispy batter. There are many regional and national variations on these dishes.

Filling pies and puddings are the traditional desserts, although today you are more likely to see ice cream or cheesecake on the menu. Fruit pies, such as apple, are popular everywhere, as are fruit crumbles (stewed fruit covered with a crunchy topping), and both are traditionally served hot with custard. Bread-and-butter pudding, Bakewell tart (a rich almond and jam tart), fruit fools (fruit and cream mixed to a mousse), and steamed sponge puddings are also worth looking out for.

Afternoon tea is a British tradition that is enjoying something of a revival and should be tried at least once. Eaten at around 4 p.m. it consists of delicate sandwiches followed by scones and jam, and cakes such as Victoria sponge, washed down with tea. It is not only delicious but excellent value. Even top hotels may only charge around £8 ($12) for a huge satisfying tea. A variation on this is the cream tea, which consists of scones, jam and thick clotted cream, the best examples of which are found in the West Country.

When it comes to drinks you will find beer served in pubs everywhere. Brewed from hops and malt it is served at room temperature and comes in many types from bitter to dark stout and brown ale. Local and regional brewers still produce their own distinctive varieties and the taste can vary considerably. Well-known brands are Courage, Charringtons, Tennents and Theakstons. England and Wales are particularly proud of their 'real ales', which are brewed in the old-fashioned way. Lager, served chilled, is lighter than beer and has become very popular in recent years. Guinness (a stout) is available everywhere, but is predominantly an Irish drink and tastes much better there than anywhere else. The most popular spirits are gin, whisky, rum and vodka, and these too are available everywhere, although you will find a greater choice of whiskies in Scotland, its land of origin. Cider is another traditional brew made from apples and particularly popular in areas like the West Country; well-known brands include Bulmers, Strongbow and Taunton. The national hot drink is of course tea, which is drunk strong with milk, or sometimes lemon. Indian teas are the most popular, although Chinese ones are available, and you will often be able to choose from a wide range, such as strong Assam, delicate Darjeeling or smoky Lapsang Souchong. However, coffee is now extremely popular and is drunk either black or white (with milk), or as frothy Italian cappuccino.

While you won't notice huge differences in the food available throughout the UK, there are plenty of regional and national variations on basic dishes. In England, counties famous for their apples make Dorset apple cake, Somerset cider cake or preserves like Kentish apple chutney. The West Country also produces scrumpy, a rough cider that should only be drunk by the uninitiated in moderation. Other regional dishes are: Cornish pasties (meat, diced potato, onion and sometimes swede folded in pastry); Cumberland sausage (a thick pork sausage); Lancashire hot-pot; shepherd's pie (minced meat and onion topped with a layer of mashed potatoes); and pan haggerty (a potato and cheese casserole from the North). Coastal areas also have many varieties of smoked fish and fish pies. Yorkshire pudding, (made from a flour, egg and milk batter) used to be eaten by itself before the meat course, with a rich gravy poured on top, and is still available like this in the north of England.

Scotland has its own traditional dishes such as *haggis* (sheep's offal, mixed with oatmeal and herbs and spices, and served with mashed potatoes and swede – 'neeps' – sounds awful but tastes delicious); *stovies* (mashed potatoes mixed with onions and mince); oatcakes; and Scotch broth, a thick meat-and-vegetable soup. It's also noted for top quality venison, Aberdeen Angus beef, fish (such as Arbroath smokies and fresh salmon), and shellfish. Whisky is of course the national spirit and comes in many varieties, the main difference being between blended types and the more expensive malts, which are ten or twelve years old before they are drunk. Malt whiskies vary considerably in taste, from rich and smooth to smoky, depending on local conditions.

Wales is famous for its leeks (try the cheesy leek tarts). The most unusual of the Welsh dishes must be laver bread, a black seaweed often fried with oatmeal for breakfast. Also look out for: *cawl* (a thick soup made with meat, root vegetables and leeks); griddle-cooked Welsh cakes; *bara brith* (a speckled bread); *teisen lap* (shallow fruit cake); Anglesey cake and *punchnep*, a mixture of fried root vegetables. Welsh lamb, fish (particularly salmon and trout) and shellfish (such as Penclawdd cockles) are also well worth trying.

When in Northern Ireland look out for fresh seafood, particularly salmon and oysters, and meats like ham, bacon and lamb. Many areas will serve smoked fish patés and you may also see eels from Lough Neagh. Some traditional breads to look for are potato bread (made with soda and buttermilk rather than yeast), and *bannocks* and *bambracks*, made with fruit and spices. Potatoes are cooked in a variety of ways, one of these being *champ* (mashed potatoes mixed with chopped spring onions, milk and butter). The national drink, Guinness, is available everywhere and may also be used in stews to give a rich flavour to the meat.

Britain is noted for its hard cheeses, with over a hundred varieties to try. Some well-known ones are Cheddar, Caerphilly, Cheshire, Lancashire, Double Gloucester and Stilton, but there are plenty of others to sample. Look out for Lanark Blue (a Scottish cheese similar to Roquefort), *Teifi* (a Welsh Gouda-like cheese) and Cornish Yarg, a mild cheese coated with nettles.

Although British cookery is traditionally based on meat and fish, being a vegetarian here isn't difficult and is improving all the time. There are quite a number of vegetarian restaurants throughout the UK, particularly in England, and the majority of places will offer a veggie choice on the menu – although this is often rather unimaginative. The many ethnic eateries, especially Indian and Italian places, are also safe bets.

If you want to put together your own picnic, supermarket chains to look out for are the Co-op, Sainsbury, Safeway, Asda, and Tesco. Marks & Spencer have excellent food halls (though not cheap), and you can also buy provisions from other department stores like Littlewoods. Expect to pay around £0.50–0.75 ($0.75–1.10) for a loaf of bread. Many towns (particularly in England) will have an open-air market at least once a week, and you'll be able to buy cheap fruit and vegetables. Shops are generally open Mon.–Sat. from 9 a.m.–5.30 p.m., although supermarkets tend to stay open until 6 p.m. (8 p.m. on Thursdays). They will also open on Sundays in Scotland.

Bath

LOCAL SPECIALITIES
The Bath Bun. You can buy ones made to the authentic recipe at Mountstevens Bakers in Westgate Street.

CHEAP EATERIES
Two-course meals under £5 ($7.50)

The Crystal Palace, 11 Abbey Green. Open daily noon–2.30 p.m. and 6–8.30 p.m.

Alexander's Brasserie, 12 George Street (tel. 484 191). Open Mon.–Sat. 8 a.m.–6 p.m.

Scoffs, Monmouth Street (junction with Westgate Street). Open Mon.–Sat. 9 a.m.–5 p.m.

Demuth's, 2 North Parade Passage (tel. 446 059). Vegetarian restaurant. Open Mon.–Sat. 9.30 a.m.–6 p.m.; Sun. 10 a.m.–5 p.m.

Two-course meals from £5–7 ($7.50–10.50)

The Bear, 8 Wellsway (tel. 425 795). Open daily noon–2.30 p.m. and 6.30–9 p.m.

The Canary, 3 Queen Street (tel. 424 846). Recommended dish: Somerset rabbit. Open Mon.–Sat. 9 a.m.–9 p.m.

Pasta Galore, 31 Barton Street (tel. 463 861). Italian restaurant. Open Mon.–Wed. noon–2.30 p.m. and 6–10.30 p.m.; Thurs.–Sat. noon–2.30 p.m. and 6–11 p.m.; Sun. 6–10.30 p.m.

Two-course meals from £7–10 ($10.50–15.00)

The Walrus & Carpenter, 25 Barton Street (tel. 314 864). Some vegetarian options. Open Mon.–Sat. noon–2.30 p.m. and 6–11 p.m.; Sun. 6–11 p.m.

The Boatman, Bath Boating Station, Forester Road (tel. 469 342). Vegetarian dishes available. Open Mon.–Fri. 7–10 p.m.; weekends noon–2 p.m. and 7–10 p.m.

Peking, 1–2 New Street, Kingsmead Square (tel. 466 377). Chinese restaurant. Open daily noon–2 p.m. and 6–11.15 p.m.

Jamuna, 9–10 High Street (tel. 464 631). Indian restaurant. Open Mon.–Fri. noon–2.30 p.m. and 6 p.m.–midnight; weekends noon till midnight.

SHOPPING
● Market
Guildhall Market. Between the High Street and High Parade. Open Mon.–Sat. 9.30 a.m.–5.30 p.m.

● Supermarkets

Sainsbury's, Green Park Station (tel. 444 737)
Waitrose, The Podium, Northgate Street (tel. 481 347)
Somerfield, Marchant's Passage, Southgate (tel. 462 868).
Marks & Spencer, Stall Street.

Belfast

LOCAL SPECIALITIES

Hilden   a local real ale

CHEAP EATERIES

In contrast to most places in the United Kingdom, many people in Belfast still eat a traditional high tea (consisting of a light cooked meal with bread, scones, cakes and tea or coffee) at around 6 p.m. As many hotels and restaurants cater for this demand it can be a good time to find a reasonably priced meal: look out for signs advertising an Ulster Fry (usually fish, or bacon, sausages and eggs, served with chips).

Two-course meals under £5 ($7.50)

The Lamplighter, 115A Ormeau Road. Run on a non-profit-making basis. Open Mon.–Sat. 10 a.m.–9 p.m.

Spice of Life, 62 Lower Donegall Street (tel. 332 744). Vegetarian restaurant. Recommended dish: hummus (served with salad). Open Mon.–Wed. 10 a.m.–4 p.m.; Thurs.–Fri. 10 a.m.–11 p.m.

Bob Cratchit's, Russell Court, 38 Lisburn Road (tel. 332 526). Open Mon.–Sat. noon–7 p.m.; Sun. 12.30–2 p.m.

Cloisters, 1 Elmwood Avenue (tel. 245 133). University refectory. Advance booking advised. Open Mon.–Sat. 9 a.m.–9 p.m.

Two-course meals from £5–7 ($7.50–10.50)

Ashoka, 363–365 Lisburn Road (tel. 660 362). Indian restaurant. Open Mon.–Fri. noon–2 p.m. and 5.30–11.30 p.m.; Sat. 5.30–11.30 p.m.; Sun. 5.30–10.30 p.m.

Front Page, 106 Donegall Street (tel. 324 269). Serves fish and vegetarian dishes. Open Mon.–Sat. noon–9.30 p.m.

Fat Harry's, 91 Castle Street (tel. 232 226). Specializes in steaks and grills. Open Mon. 11.30 a.m.–5 p.m.; Tues.–Sat. noon–9 p.m.

Two-course meals from £7–10 ($10.50–15.00)

Strand, 12 Stranmillis Road (tel. 682 266). Vegetarian options available. Open Mon.–Sat. noon–11 p.m.; Sun. noon–10 p.m.

Saints & Scholars, 3 University Street (tel. 325 137). Plenty of vegetarian options. Open Mon.–Sat. noon–11 p.m.; Sun. noon–2.30 p.m. and 5.30–9.30 p.m.

Manor House, 47 Donegall Pass (tel. 238 755). Chinese restaurant. Open daily noon till midnight.

SHOPPING
● **Market**
St George's Market, East Bridge Street. Open Tues. and Fri. 7 a.m.– 3 p.m.

Cambridge

SPECIAL EVENTS AND FESTIVALS
Cambridge hosts a beer festival every June.

CHEAP EATERIES
Hills Road and Mills Road are particularly good places to look for cheap restaurants.
Two-course meals under £5 ($7.50)

Corner House Restaurant, 9 King Street. Open Mon.–Fri. 11.30 a.m.–2.30 p.m. and 5–9.30 p.m.; weekends 11.30 a.m.– 9.30 p.m.
Mr Chips, 78 King Street. Recommended dish: cod and chips. Open Mon.–Thurs. 11.30 a.m.–midnight; Fri.–Sat. 11.30 a.m.– 12.30 a.m.; Sun. 5.30 p.m.–midnight.
Varsity Restaurant, 35 St Andrews Street (tel. 356 060). Open Mon.–Sat. 11.30 a.m.–11 p.m.
Rajbelash, 36–38 Hills Road (tel. 354 679). Indian restaurant. Open daily noon–2.30 p.m. and 6 p.m.–midnight.
Belinda's, 15 Trinity Street (tel. 356 845). Open Mon.–Sat. 8.30 a.m.–6.30 p.m.; Sun. 9 a.m.–6 p.m.

Two-course meals from £5–7 ($7.50–10.50)

The Little Rose Restaurant, 37 Trumpington Street (tel. 62433). Open Mon.–Sat. 11.30 a.m.–2.30 p.m. and 5.30–11 p.m.; Sun. 11.30 a.m.–11 p.m.
The Boathouse, Chesterton Road (tel. 460 905). Vegetarian options available. Open Mon.–Sat. 11 a.m.–11 p.m., Sun. noon–3 p.m. and 7–10.30 p.m.
Eraina Taverna, 2 Free School Lane (tel. 68786). Greek, English,

and Indian dishes. Open Mon.–Fri. noon–2.30 p.m. and 5.30–
11.30 p.m.; Sat. noon–11.30 p.m.; Sun. noon–11 p.m.
Browns Restaurant, 23 Trumpington Street (tel. 461 655). Open
Mon.–Sat. 11 a.m.–11.30 p.m.; Sun. noon–11.30 p.m.

Two-course meals from £7–10 ($10.50–15.00)

Pasta Galore, 5 Jordans Yard (tel. 324 351). Italian dishes. Open
Mon.–Thurs. 10 a.m.–10.30 p.m.; Fri.–Sat. 10 a.m.–11 p.m.;
Sun. noon–2.30 p.m.
Myttons, Jesus Lane (tel. 324 033). Some vegetarian options. Open
Mon.–Sat. 11 a.m.–11 p.m.; Sun. 11 a.m.–4 p.m.
Restaurant Angeline, 8 Market Passage (tel. 60305). Open
Mon.–Sat. noon–2.30 p.m. and 6–11 p.m.; Sun. noon–2.30 p.m.

SHOPPING
● **Market**
Market Square, Mon.–Sat. 8 a.m.–5 p.m.

● **Supermarkets**

Sainsburys, 44 Sydney Street. Open Mon.–Wed. 8.30 a.m.–7 p.m.;
Thurs.–Fri. 8.30 a.m.–8 p.m.; Sat. 8.30 a.m.–5 p.m.
Marks & Spencer, 8 Sydney Street (Market Square). Open
Mon.–Tues. 9.30 a.m.–5.30 p.m.; Wed. 9 a.m.–8 p.m.; Thurs.
9 a.m.–6 p.m.; Fri. 8.30 a.m.–7.30 p.m.; Sat. 8.30 a.m.–6 p.m.
Co-op, Grafton Centre, Burleigh Street.

Cardiff

CHEAP EATERIES
Two-course meals under £5 ($7.50)

Crumbs, 33 David Morgan Arcade (tel. 395 007). Vegetarian restaurant. Open Mon.–Fri. 9.30 a.m.–3 p.m.; Sat. 9.30 a.m.–4 p.m.
Celtic Cauldron, 47–48 Castle Arcade (tel. 387 185). Welsh and
vegetarian dishes. Open Mon.–Sat. 10 a.m.–6 p.m.
Philharmonic, St Mary Street. Pub lunches and suppers.

Two-course meals from £5–7 ($7.50–10.50)

Sandy's Restaurant, St Mary Street (tel. 232 161). Open Mon.–Sat. 11 a.m.–11 p.m., Sun. noon–9 p.m.

Indo Cymru Restaurant, 173 Cowbridge Road East (tel. 344 770). Indian restaurant. Open Mon.–Thurs. noon–2.30 p.m. and 6 p.m.–2 a.m.; Fri.–Sat. noon–2.30 p.m. and 6 p.m.–3 a.m.; Sun. 6 p.m.–1 a.m.

Two-course meals from £7–10 ($10.50–15.00)

Ristorante Topo Gigio, 12 Church Street (tel. 344 794). Italian restaurant. Open Mon.–Sat. noon–11.30 p.m.; Sun. noon–11 p.m.

The Market Tavern, Trinity Street (tel. 224 482). Vegetarian dishes available. Open Mon.–Sat. 6–10.30 p.m.

SHOPPING
● **Market**
Cardiff Central Market, St Mary Street. Open Mon.–Sat.

● **Supermarkets**
Marks & Spencer and Littlewoods both have branches in Queen Street.

Edinburgh

There is no shortage of pubs serving bar meals in central Edinburgh, but the choice is widest along Rose Street, and in the part of town around the Edinburgh University buildings on George Square. Whilst vegetarians are generally well catered for in local pubs and restaurants, the latter area is particularly good for vegetarian meals. Close by, Nicolson Street, Clerk Street and South Clerk Street contain a number of decent cafeterias serving basic Scottish and English dishes at reasonable prices.

CHEAP EATERIES
Two-course meals under £5 ($7.50)

Teviot Restaurant, Teviot Row Students' Union. Student ID may be requested. Open Oct.–June Mon.–Fri. 8.30 a.m.–6.45 p.m.; weekends 12.30–6.30 p.m.

Seeds Café, 53 West Nicolson Street (tel. 667 8673). Vegetarian meals. During the Festival: open Mon.–Sat. 11 a.m.–11 p.m.;

Sun. 11 a.m.–8 p.m. At other times open Mon.–Sat. 10 a.m.–
9 p.m.; Sun. noon–8 p.m.

Braidwoods, 50 West Port (tel. 228 4543). Bar meals served daily
noon–7 p.m. Vegetarian options available.

The Corner Stone Café, St John's Church, Princes Street (West
End) (tel. 228 8722). Vegetarian meals served Mon.–Sat.
noon–4.30 p.m.

Greyfriars Bobby, 34 Candlemaker Row (tel. 225 8328). Bar meals
served daily noon–8 p.m. Vegetarian options available. Special
£2.25 ($3.40) dish-of-the-day for ISIC card holders.

The Last Drop, 74 Grassmarket (tel. 225 4851). Bar meals served
daily noon–6.30 p.m. Vegetarian dishes available.

Two-course meals from £5–7 ($7.50–10.50)

Carters Bar, 185 Morrison Street (tel. 228 9032). Bar meals served
noon–3.30 p.m. and 5.30–10 p.m. daily. Vegetarian options
available. Recommended drink: Belhaven St Andrew's Ale.

Parrots, 3–5 Viewforth (tel. 229 3252). Vegetarian options available. Recommended dishes: aubergine and mushroom mous-
saka, and plum pudding with brandy. Open Sun.–Thurs.
6–10.30 p.m.; Fri.–Sat. 5–10.30 p.m.

Kalpna, 2 St Patrick's Square (tel. 667 9890). Indian vegetarian
dishes. Open Mon.–Fri. noon–2 p.m. and 5.30–11 p.m.

Le Sept, 7 Old Fishmarket Close (tel. 225 5428). French restaurant.
Vegetarian dishes available. Open daily noon–2.15 p.m. and
6–10 p.m.

Shezan Tandoori, 25 Union Street (tel. 557 5098). Indian
restaurant. Some vegetarian dishes. Open daily.

Two-course meals from £7–10 ($10.50–15.00)

Black Bo's, 57 Blackfriars Street (tel. 557 6136). Vegetarian
restaurant.

Bell's Diner, 7 St Stephen Street (tel. 225 8116). Open Sun.–Fri.
6–10.30 p.m.; Sat. noon–10.30 p.m.

The Caprice Restaurant, 327 Leith Walk (tel. 554 1279). Italian
cuisine.

SHOPPING
● **Supermarkets**

Scotmid Co-op, 52 Nicolson Street.
Wm Low, 94 Nicolson Street.

Marks & Spencer, 53 Princes Street.
Littlewoods, 91 Princes Street.

Glasgow

CHEAP EATERIES

For a particularly wide choice of cheap eateries, head for the Byers Road and the streets just off it (an area popular with local students).
Two-course meals under £5 ($7.50)

Strathclyde University Students' Union, John Street. Open Mon.–Fri. 8.30–10.30 a.m. and noon–2.30 p.m.

Magnus Dining Room, Glasgow University Refectory, Hillhead Street. Open Mon.–Thurs. 8.30 a.m.–6.10 p.m.; Fri. 8.30 a.m.–3.30 p.m.

The Bay Tree Vegetarian Café, 403 Great Western Road. Vegetarian restaurant with vegan options. Recommended dish: hummus. Open Tues.–Sun. 10 a.m.–9 p.m.

Nico's, 375 Sauchiehall Street. Open Mon.–Fri. 8 a.m.–midnight; Sat. 10 a.m.–midnight; Sun. noon till midnight.

The Grosvenor Café, 35 Ashton Lane. Open Mon.–Fri. 9 a.m.–7 p.m.; Sat. 9 a.m.–6 p.m.

Granary Restaurant, 82 Howard Street (tel. 226 3770). Vegetarian restaurant. Open Mon.–Sat. 8.30 a.m.–6 p.m.; Sun. 11 a.m.–5 p.m.

Two-course meals from £5–7 ($7.50–10.50)

Koh-I-Nor, 235 North Street (tel. 221 1555). Indian restaurant. Open daily noon till midnight.

O'Sole Mio, 32 Bath Street (tel. 331 1397). Italian restaurant. Open Mon.–Thurs. noon–2.30 p.m. and 5 p.m.–midnight; Fri. and Sat. noon–2.30 p.m. and 5 p.m.–1 a.m.; Sun. 5 p.m.–midnight.

The Vegetarian Ashoka, 141 Elderslie Street (tel. 248 4407). Vegetarian Indian dishes. Open Mon.–Sat. noon–2 p.m. and 5–11.30 p.m.

Fire Station Restaurant, 33 Ingram Street (tel. 552 2929). Open Mon.–Thurs. noon–2.30 p.m. and 5 p.m.–midnight; Fri. noon–2.30 p.m. and 5 p.m.–12.30 a.m.; Sat. noon–1 a.m.; Sun. noon–11.30 p.m.

Two-course meals from £7–10 ($10.50–15.00)

Café Gandolfi, 64 Albion Street (tel. 552 6813). Vegetarian options available. Open Mon.–Sat. 9 a.m.–11.30 p.m.

The Belfry, 652 Argyll Street (tel. 221 0630). Open Mon.–Fri. noon–2.30 p.m. and 6–11.30 p.m.; Sat. 6–11 p.m.

Colonial India Restaurant, 25 High Street (tel. 552 1923). Indian restaurant. Open Sun.–-Thurs. noon–11 p.m.; Fri.–Sat. noon till midnight.

SHOPPING
● Market
The Barras, open every Sat. and Sun. from 9 a.m.–5 p.m.

● Supermarkets

Marks & Spencer, 2 Argyll Street (tel. 552 4546) and 172 Sauchie-hall Street (tel. 332 6097).

Gateway, by the St Enoch Shopping Centre.

Littlewoods, Argyll Street.

Inverness

CHEAP EATERIES
Two-course meals under £5 ($7.50)

Allander Garden Restaurant, Arnotts, 7–17 Union Street (tel. 236 661). Department store restaurant. Open Mon.–Sat. 9 a.m.–5.15 p.m.

Gunsmiths, 30 Union Street (tel. 710 519). Open Mon.–Wed. 11 a.m.–11 p.m.; Thurs.–Fri. 11 a.m.–1 a.m.; Sat. 11 a.m.–11.45 p.m.; Sun. 6.30–11 p.m.

Lauders, Church Street. Bar meals.

Two-course meals from £5–7 ($7.50–10.50)

The Copper Kettle, 50 Baron Taylor's Street (tel. 233 307). Open Mon.–Sat. 10 a.m.–7 p.m.

Nico's, Glen Mhor Hotel, 9–12 Ness Bank (tel. 234 308). Open daily noon–2.15 p.m. and 5–10 p.m.

Two-course meals from £7–10 ($10.50–15.00)

Dickens International Restaurant, 77–79 Church Street (tel. 713 111). Vegetarian dishes available. Open Mon.–Sat. noon–2 p.m. and 5.30–11 p.m.; Sun. 12.30–2.30 p.m. and 5.30–11 p.m.

Inverness Steakhouse, Bank Street (tel. 236 577). Open Mon.–Sat. 10 a.m.–11 p.m.; Sun. noon–2.30 p.m. and 5–11 p.m.

Brookes Wine Bar and Restaurant, 75 Castle Street (tel. 225 662). Open Mon.–Wed. 11 a.m.–11 p.m.; Thurs.–Fri. 11 a.m.–1 a.m.; Sat. 11 a.m.–11.45 p.m.

SHOPPING
● **Supermarkets**

Safeway, Rose Street.
W M Low, King Street.
Co-op, Church Street.

The Lake District

The Lake District is simply teeming with tea shops, pubs and (rather expensive) restaurants. Check the prices on the menu before you order anything as this is a very touristy area (particularly Windermere) and sometimes food costs more than you might expect. There are plenty of local specialities to try, including fish dishes such as Solway Firth salmon, Morecambe Bay shrimps or char, an unusual fish from the deepest lakes such as Windermere. There's also the famous Cumberland sausage, which is traditionally eaten with red cabbage or apple sauce, and Cumberland ham, still cured in the region. Sheep are reared all over this area and lamb and mutton are therefore used in many dishes. Those with a sweet tooth will find plenty to enjoy. A traditional afternoon tea might consist of scones with Cumberland Rum Butter (brown sugar, rum, nutmeg and cinnamon beaten into butter), Borrowdale Tea Bread and Grasmere Gingerbread. Wherever you go you will also find Kendal Mint Cake, a hard sugary slab, flavoured with mint and eaten by walkers everywhere. Local cheeses are Cumberland farmhouse and Calthwaite cheese, try them with the delicious local bread.

SHOPPING
There aren't many supermarkets in this area so stock up at small grocer's shops in the villages and towns.

Ambleside

CHEAP EATERIES
Two-course meals under £5 ($7.50)

Chesters, Kirkstone Gallery, Skelwith Bridge (tel. 332 553).
Vegetarian dishes available. Open daily noon–2 p.m.
Wilf's Café, 3–4 Cheapside (tel. 33660). Some vegetarian options.
Open Thurs.–Tues. 9 a.m.–4.30 p.m.

Two-course meals from £7–10 ($10.50–15.00)

The Harvest, Compston Road (tel. 33151). Vegetarian restaurant.
Open Apr.–Oct. Mon.–Fri. 5–9.30 p.m.; weekends
noon–2.30 p.m. and 5–9.30 p.m.; Nov.–Mar. weekends
noon–2.30 p.m. and 5–9.30 p.m. only.

FURTHER INFORMATION
Ambleside tourist information office is in Church Street (tel. 0966
32582). Open daily 9 a.m.–6 p.m. in season; from Nov.–Mar. open
Fri. 1–4 p.m. and Sat. 10 a.m.–4 p.m.

Grasmere

CHEAP EATERIES
Two-course meals under £5 ($7.50)

Baldry's, Red Lion Square (tel. 09665 301). Some vegetarian
options. Recommended dish: Cumberland Rum Nicky (a pie
filled with eggs, roast ginger and dates, and flavoured with rum).
Open Easter–Nov. 9.30 a.m.–6 p.m. daily; hours variable at
other times of year.

Two-course meals from £5–7 ($7.50–10.50)

The Rowan Tree, Langdale Road (tel. 09665 528). Open Easter–
July Mon. and Wed.–Sun. 9.30 a.m.–8 p.m.; Aug.–Oct.
9.30 a.m.–8 p.m. daily.
Traveller's Rest, just outside the village (tel. 09665 604). Open daily
noon–3 p.m. and 6–9.45 p.m.

Kendal

CHEAP EATERIES
Two-course meals under £5 ($7.50)

Nutters Coffee House, Yard 11, Stramongate (tel. 725 135). Some vegetarian options. Open Mon.–Sat. 8.30 a.m.–6.30 p.m.

Plough Inn, Selside (tel. 83687). Open daily noon–2 p.m. and 7–9 p.m.

Waterside Wholefoods, Kent View (tel. 729 743). Plenty of vegetarian dishes. Open Mon.–Sat. 11.45 a.m.–2 p.m.

Pizza Margherita, 181 Highgate (tel. 731 303). Open Sun.–Wed. 6–10 p.m.; Thurs.–Sat. noon–2 p.m. and 6–10 p.m.

Two-course meals from £7–10 ($10.50–15.00)

Moon, 129 Highgate (tel. 729 254). Open Sun.–Wed. 6–10 p.m.; Thurs.–Sat. noon–2 p.m. and 6–10 p.m.

Keswick

CHEAP EATERIES
Two-course meals under £5 ($7.50)

The Wild Strawberry, 54 Main Street (tel. 74399). Open Mon. and Thurs.–Sat. 10 a.m.–4.45 p.m.; Sun. noon–4.45 p.m.

Two-course meals from £5–7 ($7.50–10.50)

Maysons, 33 Lake Road (tel. 74104). July–Oct. open daily 10.30 a.m.–9 p.m.; Nov.–June. 10.30 a.m.–4 p.m.

Kirkby Lonsdale

CHEAP EATERIES
Two-course meals under £5 ($7.50)

Verdant, 36 Main Street (tel. 71595). Vegetarian café. Open daily 9 a.m.–5.30 p.m.

Two-course meals from £5–7 ($7.50–10.50)

Snooty Fox, Main Street (tel. 71308). Open daily noon–2.30 p.m.
   and 7–10 p.m.
The Sun, Market Street (tel. 71965). Open daily 11 a.m.–2 p.m.
   and 6–10 p.m.

Windermere

CHEAP EATERIES
Two-course meals under £5 ($7.50)

Coffee Pot, 15 Main Road. Recommended dishes: shepherd's pie
   and apple pie with cream. Open Mon.–Sat. 9.30 a.m.–6.30 p.m.

Liverpool

The largest concentration of restaurants (in all price categories) is
in the Bold Street and Hardman Street area; alongside Albert Dock;
and down Nelson Street (the main thoroughfare of Liverpool's
Chinatown).

CHEAP EATERIES
Two-course meals under £5 ($7.50)

Everyman Bistro, 9–11 Hope Street (tel. 708 9545). Plenty of vegetarian options available. Open Mon.–Sat. noon till midnight.
Kirkland's, 13 Hardman Street (tel. 707 0132). Vegetarian dishes
   available. Recommended dish: vegetable lasagne. Open
   Mon.–Fri. 11 a.m.–7 p.m.
Ma Bo, 16 Nelson Street (tel. 709 4551). Chinese restaurant
   specializing in chicken dishes. Open daily noon till midnight.
Greenbank, 332–338 Smithdown Road (tel. 734 2378). Vegetarian
   restaurant. Open Tues.–Sat. 11 a.m.–3 p.m. and
   5 p.m.–midnight; Sun. 5 p.m.–midnight.

Two-course meals from £5–7 ($7.50–10.50)

Casa Italia, 36–40 Stanley Street (tel. 236 4004). Italian restaurant. Open Mon.–Sat. noon–2.30 p.m. and 5.30–10 p.m.

Golden Phoenix, 58 Hanover Street (tel. 709 1332). Chinese restaurant. Open Mon.–Thurs. 11.30 a.m.–11 p.m.; Fri.–Sat. 11.30 a.m.–11.30 p.m.; Sun. 5–11 p.m.

Eureka, 7 Myrtle Parade (tel. 709 7225). Greek restaurant offering some vegetarian dishes. Open Mon.–Wed. 10 a.m.–8 p.m.; Thurs. 10 a.m.–9 p.m.; Fri. 10 a.m.–10 p.m.; Sat. 11 a.m.–10 p.m.

Two-course meals from £7–10 ($10.50–15.00)

Mayflower, 48 Duke Street (tel. 709 6339). Open daily noon–4 a.m.

Valparaiso, 4 Hardman Street (tel. 708 6036). Chilean restaurant. Open Tues.–Fri. noon–2.30 p.m. and 5.30–10.30 p.m.; Sat. 5.30–10.30 p.m.

L'Oriel, Oriel Chambers, Water Street (tel. 236 5025). Open Mon.–Fri. noon–2.30 p.m. and 7–10.30 p.m.; Sat. 7–10.30 p.m.

SHOPPING

There is a food market in St John's Market in the city centre and a Kwik Save supermarket on Hanover Street.

London

Contrary to most people's assumptions, it is possible to eat cheaply in London, even in the centre of the city. Although Russell Square and Victoria are poor areas for good value cheap eating, Soho, Piccadilly and Chinatown are good districts to look for meals under £5 ($7.50), or in the £5–7 ($7.50–10.50) price range, while the slightly more expensive Covent Garden quarter offers plenty of choice in the £5–10 ($7.50–15.00) range. Out from the centre, there are affordable eateries even in upmarket districts such as Kensington. Ethnic restaurants abound – particularly Chinese (not surprisingly, there is a large concentration of these in Chinatown), and those offering the cuisines of the Indian subcontinent. The latter have an especially high reputation, though this is due more to a number of highly rated establishments in the central districts mentioned above than to the overall quality of such eateries, which are packed together around the likes of Brick Lane (in E2) or Drummond Street (NW1). The quality of the restaurants in these parts of the city varies enormously, and the districts themselves are quite depressing.

LOCAL SPECIALITIES

Pie 'n' mash   meat pie, mashed potatoes and liquor (a parsley sauce)

faggots   savoury pork rissoles

jellied eels

roast chestnuts   a winter street snack

CHEAP EATERIES
Two-course meals under £5 ($7.50)

Leadenhall Wine Bar & Restaurant, Leadenhall Market (tel. 623 1818). Underground: Bank. Open Mon.–Fri. 11.30 a.m.– 8.30 p.m.

Pollo, 20 Old Compton Street (tel. 734 5917). Underground: Leicester Square or Piccadilly Circus. Italian restaurant. Open Mon.–Sat. 11.30 a.m.–11.30 p.m.

The Stockpot, 18 Old Compton Street (tel. 287 1066). Underground: Leicester Square or Piccadilly Circus. Recommended dish: apple crumble with custard. Open Mon.–Sat. 8 a.m.– 11.30 p.m.; Sun. noon–11.30 p.m.

The Wren at St James's, 35 Jermyn Street (tel. 437 9419). Underground: Piccadilly Circus or Green Park. Vegetarian and wholefood dishes. Open Mon.–Sat. 8 a.m.–7 p.m.; Sun. 10 a.m.– 4 p.m.

Wong Kei, 41–43 Wardour Street (tel. 437 3071). Underground: Leicester Square. Chinese restaurant. Recommended dish: roast pork with egg rice. Open daily noon–11.30 p.m.

Food for Thought, 31 Neal Street (tel. 836 0239). Underground: Covent Garden. Vegetarian restaurant. Open Mon.–Sat. 8 a.m.– 7 p.m.

Piazza, Cecil Street (junction with St Martin's Lane) (tel. 623 6296). Underground: Covent Garden. Open Mon.–Sat. 8 a.m.–midnight; Sun. 9 a.m.–11.30 p.m.

Spicy Bites, 24 Short's Gardens (tel. 379 1179). Recommended dish: green chicken curry. Underground: Tottenham Court Road or Leicester Square. Open Mon.–Sat. 11.30 a.m.–5 p.m.

Two-course meals from £5–7 ($7.50–10.50)

The East-West Restaurant, 188 Old Street (tel. 608 0300). Underground: Old Street. Macrobiotic restaurant. Recommended dishes: hummus and tofu cheesecake. Open Mon.–Fri. 11 a.m.– 8.30 p.m.; weekends 11 a.m.–3 p.m.

Ludgate, 9–11 New Bridge Street (tel. 583 0670). Underground: Blackfriars. Italian dishes predominate. Recommended dish: veal milanese with vegetables. Open Mon.–Fri. 6 a.m.–6 p.m.

Rasa Sayang, 10 Frith Street (tel. 734 8720). Underground: Leicester Square. Indonesian restaurant. Recommended dish: *kado kado* (vegetables in a spicy peanut sauce). Open Mon.–Fri. noon–2.45 p.m. and 6–11.30 p.m.; Sat. 6–11.30 p.m.; Sun. 1– 10 p.m.

Soho, 11–13 Frith Street (tel. 494 3491). Underground: Leicester Square. Recommended dish: grilled chicken with dijon mustard and sage vinaigrette. Open Mon.–Fri. 8 a.m.–1 a.m.; Sat. 11 a.m.–1 a.m.

Chuen Cheng Ku, 17 Wardour Street (tel. 437 1398). Underground: Leicester Square. Chinese restaurant. Recommended dish: Ho-fun noodles with beef. Open daily 11 a.m.–midnight.

Bhatti, 37 Great Queen Street (tel. 831 0817). Underground: Covent Garden. Highly rated Indian restaurant. Open daily noon–2.45 p.m. and 5.45–11.30 p.m.

Diana's Diner, 39 Endell Street (tel. 240 0272). Underground: Covent Garden. Open Mon.–Sat. 7 a.m.–7 p.m.; Sun. 8 a.m.– 5 p.m.

Cosmoba, 9 Cosmo Place (tel. 837 0904). Underground: Russell Square. Italian restaurant. Open Mon.–Sat. 11.30 a.m.–3 p.m. and 5.30–11 p.m.

Two-course meals from £7–10 ($10.50–15.00)

Ye Olde Cheshire Cheese, Wine Office Court, 145 Fleet Street (tel. 353 6170). Underground: Blackfriars. Recommended dishes: steak and kidney pie, and pork rolls with apple. Open daily 11.30 a.m.–11.30 p.m.

Café Pasta, 2–4 Garrick Street (tel. 497 2779). Underground: Covent Garden. Italian dishes. Open Mon.–Sat. 9.30 a.m.– 11.30 p.m.; Sun. 9.30 a.m.–11 p.m.

La Toscana Trattoria, 33 Southampton Street. Underground: Covent Garden. Italian restaurant. Open Mon.–Fri. 7.30 a.m.– 3 p.m. and 5.30–11.15 p.m.; Sat. noon–11.15 p.m.

Bar Escoba, 102 Old Brompton Road (tel. 373 2403). Underground: South Kensington. Spanish restaurant. Recommended dish: grilled chicken breast with lemon and chili sauce. Open Mon.–Sat. noon–11 p.m.; Sun. noon–10.30 p.m.

Il Falconiere, 84 Old Brompton Road (tel. 589 2401). Underground: South Kensington. Italian restaurant. Recommended dish: veal with mushrooms, cream and brandy sauce. Open Mon.–Sat. noon–2.45 p.m. and 6–11.45 p.m.

Star of India, 134 Old Brompton Road (tel. 373 2901). Underground: South Kensington. Indian restaurant with a good choice of vegetarian dishes. Recommended dish: lamb *tikka*. Open daily noon–3.30 p.m. and 6–11.30 p.m.

Tomyum, 233b Earl's Court Road (tel. 244 6060). Underground: Earl's Court. Thai restaurant. Recommended dishes: beef with basil, and roast duck curry with pineapple and tomato in red curry paste. Open daily 6.30–11 p.m.

SHOPPING
● **Markets**

Jubilee Market Hall, Covent Garden. Underground: Covent Garden. Open Mon. 6 a.m.–5 p.m.; Tues.–Sun. 9 a.m.–5 p.m.

Leadenhall Market, Gracechurch Street. Underground: Bank. Open Mon.–Fri. 9 a.m.–5 p.m.

Leather Lane. Underground: Chancery Lane. Open Mon.–Fri. 10 a.m.–2.30 p.m.

Lower Marsh. Underground: Waterloo. Open Mon.–Fri. 10 a.m.– 3 p.m.

Wentworth Street. Underground: Aldgate. Open Mon.–Fri. 10.30 a.m.–2.30 p.m.

Shepherds Bush. Underground: Shepherds Bush. Open Mon.–Sat. 9 a.m.–5 p.m.

Strutton Ground. Underground: St James's Park. Open Mon.–Fri. 11.30 a.m.–3 p.m.

Whitecross Street. Underground: Old Street. Open Mon.–Fri. 8 a.m.–3 p.m.

● **Supermarkets**

Safeway: branches on King's Road (Underground: Sloane Square); on Edgware Road (Underground: Edgware Road); and in the Brunswick Shopping Centre (Underground: Russell Square).

Sainsbury: branches in Victoria Road (Underground: Victoria) and Cromwell Road (Underground: Gloucester Road).

Tesco: branch on Bedford Street, off the Strand (Underground: Embankment).

Marks & Spencer: branches on Oxford Street (Underground: Marble Arch); on Poland Street (Underground: Oxford Circus);

and on Kensington High Street (Underground: High Street Kensington).

Harrod's: on Brompton Road (Underground: Knightsbridge). A stunning variety of food, but very expensive.

Fortnum & Mason: on Piccadilly (Underground: Piccadilly). A splendid and very pricey food hall.

FURTHER INFORMATION
Time Out, available from newsagents all over the city, can be a useful source of information on cheap eating possibilities.

Manchester

The biggest concentration of cheap eateries in the city centre is in the Chinatown area around Portland Street. Slightly further afield, Oxford Road and the streets just off it offer a wide selection of restaurants.

CHEAP EATERIES
Two-course meals under £5 ($7.50)

Cornerhouse Café, 70 Oxford Street (2nd floor). Vegetarian dishes predominate. Open daily noon–2 p.m. and 5–7 p.m.

Viceroy of India, 63 Whitworth Street (tel. 236 6268). Indian restaurant. Some vegetarian dishes. Open daily for lunch and dinner.

Amigos, 14 Oxford Road (tel. 236 8438). Mexican restaurant. Vegetarian options available. Open Mon.–Sun. 11.30 a.m.–11.30 p.m.

Lass O'Gowrie, 36 Charles Street (tel. 273 6932). Bar meals, with some vegetarian dishes. Open Mon.–Fri. 11.30 a.m.–11 p.m.; Sat. 11.30 a.m.–3 p.m. and 6.15–11 p.m.; Sun. noon–3 p.m. and 7–10.30 p.m.

Two-course meals from £5–7 ($7.50–10.50)

Bouzouki By Night, 88 Princess Street (tel. 236 9282). Greek restaurant. Open Mon.–Sat. 8 p.m.–2 a.m.

Siam Orchid, 54 Portland Street (tel. 236 1388). Thai restaurant. Open daily for lunch and dinner.

Golden Rice Bowl, 33a Cross Street (tel. 832 9033). Chinese

restaurant. Some vegetarian options. Open Sun.—Thurs. noon till midnight; Fri.–Sat. noon–1 a.m.

Ashoka, Basil House, 105–107 Portland Street (tel. 228 7550). Indian restaurant. Open Mon.–Sat. noon–2.30 p.m. and 6–11.30 p.m.; Sun. 6–11.30 p.m.

Two-course meals from £7–10 ($10.50–15.00)

The Armenian Taverna, 5 Princess Street (tel. 834 9025). Armenian cuisine. Open daily for dinner, and Mon.–Fri. for lunch.

Bella Pasta, 92–96 Deansgate (tel. 832 4332). Italian restaurant. Open Sun.—Thurs. 10 a.m.–11 p.m.; Fri.–Sat. 10 a.m.–midnight.

The Pleasure Restaurant, 58–60 George Street (1st floor) (tel. 237 9272). Chinese restaurant. Vegetarian dishes available. Open daily noon–11.30 p.m.

SHOPPING
● **Markets**
On Church Street, and in the Arndale Centre on the High Street.

● **Supermarkets**

Safeways, St Mary's Gate.
Marks & Spencer, Corporation Street.
Littlewoods, Market Street.
Kendals, Deansgate.

Oxford

LOCAL SPECIALITIES

Oxford marmalade
Oxford sausages — made from pork or veal, flavoured with sage
Oxford collops — mutton or veal cooked with herbs, and often with claret

CHEAP EATERIES
Two-course meals under £5 ($7.50)

The Nosebag, 6–8 St Michael's Street (tel. 721033). Vegetarian and wholefood meals. Open Mon. 9.30 a.m.–5.30 p.m.; Tues.–Sun. 9.30 a.m.–9 p.m. (Fri.–Sat. until 10.30 p.m.

The Bear, Alfred Street (tel. 244680). Pub meals served daily noon–2 p.m. and 6–8.30 p.m.

The Bulldog, 108 St Aldate's (tel. 250201). Open Mon.–Thurs. 11 a.m.–11 p.m.; Fri.–Sat. 11 a.m.–3.30 p.m. and 4.30–11.30 p.m.; Sun. noon–3 p.m. and 7–10.30 p.m.

Polash Tandoori Restaurant, 25 Park End Street. Indian restaurant with some vegetarian options. Open Mon.–Thurs. noon–2.30 p.m. and 6–11.30 p.m.; Fri.–Sat. noon–2.30 p.m. and 6 p.m.–midnight; Sun. noon–11.30 p.m.

Littlewoods, 52–53 Cornmarket Street (tel. 244781). Self-service restaurant. Open Mon.–Sat. 9 a.m.–5 p.m.

Two-course meals from £5–7 ($7.50–10.50)

Shuman's Den II, 67–69 George Street (tel. 792919). Asian dishes. Open Mon.–Sat. 11.30 a.m.–2 a.m.

Bella Pasta, 14–16 George Street (tel. 791032). Italian dishes. Open daily 10 a.m.–11.30 p.m.

The Turf Tavern, Bath Place (tel. 243235). Bar meals (including vegetarian dishes) served daily noon–2.30 p.m. and 6–9 p.m.

Gate of India, 135 High Street (1st floor) (tel. 242062). Indian cuisine. Open daily noon–2.30 p.m. and 6–11.30 p.m.

Two-course meals from £7–10 ($10.50–15.00)

Browns Restaurant & Wine Bar, 5–9 Woodstock Road (tel. 511995). Open Mon.–Sat. 11 a.m.–11.30 p.m.; Sun. noon–11.30 p.m.

Munchy Munchy, 6 Park End Street (tel. 245710). Indonesian and Malaysian dishes. Vegetarian options always available. Open Tues.–Sat. noon–2 p.m. and 5.30–10 p.m.

Elizabeth Restaurant, 84 St Aldate's (tel. 242230). Open Tues.–Sat. 12.30–2.30 p.m. and 6.30–11 p.m.; Sun. 12.30–2.30 p.m. and 7–10.30 p.m.

Pasta Galore, 103 Cowley Road (tel. 722955). Italian dishes. Open Mon.–Thurs. 10 a.m.–2.30 p.m. and 6–10.30 p.m.; Fri.–Sat. 10 a.m.–2.30 p.m. and 6–11 p.m.

SHOPPING
● Market

The covered market between Market Street and Carfax is open Mon.–Sat. 8 a.m.–5.30 p.m.

● **Supermarkets**

Sainsbury's, Westgate Shopping Centre.
Co-op Food Hall, Cornmarket Street.

Stratford Upon Avon

Few English towns are as dominated by tourism as Stratford-Upon-Avon. One consequence of this is that, whilst there is no shortage of restaurants, many are overpriced when compared to eateries elsewhere in the country. On the whole, pub and cafeteria meals offer the best value for money.

CHEAP EATERIES
Two-course meals under £5 ($7.50)

Café Natural, Greenhill Street (tel. 415741). Vegetarian café. Open Mon.–Sat. 9 a.m.–5 p.m.
Elizabeth the Chef, Henley Street. Open Mon.–Sat. 9.30 a.m.–5 p.m.; Sun. 10 a.m.–5 p.m.
Dirty Duck Pub, Southern Lane. Open daily 11 a.m.–11.30 p.m.
Jaquenetta's Courtyard Café, The Minories (tel. 294471).

Two-course meals from £5–7 ($7.50–10.50)

Vintner Bistro & Café Bar, 5 Sheep Street (tel. 297 259). Recommended dish: ham salad. Open Mon.–Sat. 10.30 a.m.–11 p.m.; Sun. 10.30 a.m.–10.30 p.m.
Hussain's Indian Cuisine, 6a Chapel Street. Indian restaurant. Open Mon.–Thurs. noon–2 p.m. and 5.15–11.45 p.m.; Fri.–Sat. noon–2 p.m. and 5 p.m.–midnight; Sun. 12.30–2.30 p.m. and 5.30–11.45 p.m.
Garrick, 25 High Street (tel. 292 186). Pub meals served Mon.–Fri. noon–2 p.m. and 5–7 p.m.; Sat. noon–2 p.m. and 5–8 p.m.; Sun. noon–2 p.m.

Two-course meals from £7–10 ($7.50–15.00)

Sir Toby's, 8 Church Street (tel. 68822). At least one vegetarian dish available. Open Tues.–Sat. 5.30–9.30 p.m.

Slug and Lettuce, 38 Guild Street (tel. 299 700). Open daily
  noon–2 p.m. and 5.30–9 p.m.
Loose Box, 18 High Street (tel. 204 999). Open daily.

SHOPPING
● **Market**
There is an open-air market in town every Friday.

● **Supermarkets**

Gateway, 1 Fountain Way.
Safeway, 8 Greenhill Street.
Marks & Spencer, Bridge Street.

York

LOCAL SPECIALITIES

Yorkshire pudding   batter pudding served on its own with gravy
                     or with roast beef and vegetables

CHEAP EATERIES
Two-course meals under £5 ($7.50)

St William's Restaurant, 3 College Street. Open daily 10 a.m.–
  5 p.m.
Gillygate Vegetarian Restaurant, Millers Yard (off Gillygate). Some
  vegan options. Student discount. Open Mon.–Sat. 10 a.m.–
  4.30 p.m.
Hole in the Wall, High Petergate (tel. 634 468). Open Mon.–Fri.
  noon–8 p.m.; Sat.–Sun. noon–6 p.m.
Tap and Spile, Monkgate (tel. 656 158). Bar meals served daily
  11.30 a.m.–2 p.m.
Cockatoo Crêperie, 34 Fossgate (tel. 633 351). Vegetarian options
  available. Open Tues.–Sat. noon–2 p.m. and 6–10.30 p.m.; Sun.
  6–10 p.m.

Two-course meals from £5–7 ($7.50–10.50)

La Romantica, 14 Goodramgate. Italian dishes. Open Mon.–Sat.
  noon–2.30 p.m. and 5.30–11.30 p.m.; Sun. 5.30–11.30 p.m.

Oscar's Wine Bar & Bistro, Little Stonegate. Open daily 11 a.m.–10 p.m.

The Blake Head, 104 Micklegate (tel. 623 767). Vegetarian restaurant with vegan options. Open Mon.–Thurs. 9.30 a.m.–6 p.m.; Fri.–Sat. 9.30 a.m.–6 p.m. and 6.30–9.30 p.m.

Four Seasons Restaurant, 45 Goodramgate (tel. 633 787). Some vegetarian and vegan dishes available. Open daily 10 a.m.–10 p.m.

Two-course meals from £7–10 ($10.50–15.00)

Taj Mahal, 7 King's Staith. Indian restaurant. Open daily noon–2.30 p.m. and 5.30 p.m.–midnight.

Russells Restaurants, 34 Stonegate (tel. 641 432) and 26 Coppergate (tel. 644 330). Both open daily 10 a.m.–10 p.m.

Kites Restaurant, 13 Grape Lane (tel. 641 750). Thai, French and vegetarian dishes. Open Mon.–Fri. 7–10.30 p.m.; Sat. noon–1.45 p.m. and 7–10.30 p.m.

SHOPPING
● **Market**

York Market, Jubbergate. Open Mon.–Sat. 8 a.m.–5 p.m.

● **Supermarkets**

Tesco, Tadcaster Road.
Sainsburys, Foss Islands Road.
Marks & Spencer, Piccadilly.
Presto, Rougier Street.
Grandways, Bootham.

INDEX

Hitch-hiker's Guide to Europe 1995

Ken Welsh and Katie Wood

16th edition – updated by the author of the bestselling
Europe by Train

Hitchhiker's Guide to Europe 1995 covers:

- Western Europe • Eastern Europe
- British Isles • Scandinavia
- Iceland • Turkey
- North Africa • Middle East

Packed with inside info on:

- Hitching tactics • Emergency hints
- Sex and drugs on the road • What to see
- Survival basics • How to rough it
- Black markets • Languages
- Routes • Where to eat and sleep
- Travel philosophy

All this and more in a book aimed at people who know what cheap *really* means!

'Practically researched . . . colossal fun to read'   *Observer*

'Any freak who can't use this book and save money should give up hitching and get a job'   Pete the Bear, Glasgow

ISBN 0 00 638378 5

HarperCollins Paperbacks – Non-Fiction

HarperCollins is a leading publisher of paperback non-fiction.
Below are some recent titles.

- [ ] EUROPE BY TRAIN 1995 Katie Wood & George McDonald £8.99
- [ ] 1995 GLOBETROTTER'S BIBLE Katie Wood £6.99
- [ ] CHEAP SLEEP GUIDE TO EUROPE 1995 Katie Wood £8.99
- [ ] CHEAP EATS GUIDE TO EUROPE 1995 Katie Wood   £6.99
- [ ] HITCHHIKER'S GUIDE TO EUROPE 1995 Ken Welsh & Katie Wood £6.99
- [ ] FAMILY WELCOME GUIDE 1995 Jill Foster & Malcolm Hamer £8.99

These books are available from your local bookseller or can be ordered
direct from the publishers.
To order direct just tick the titles you want and fill in the form below:

Name: _____

Address: _____

_____

Postcode: _____

Send to: HarperCollins Mail Order, Dept 8, HarperCollins*Publishers*,
Westerhill Road, Bishopbriggs, Glasgow G64 2QT.
Please enclose a cheque or postal order or your authority to debit your
Visa/Access account –

Credit card no: _____

Expiry date: _____

Signature: _____

– to the value of the cover price plus:
UK & BFPO: Add £1.00 for the first and 25p for each additional book
ordered.
Overseas orders including Eire, please add £2.95 service charge.
Books will be sent by surface mail but quotes for airmail despatches will
be given on request.
24 HOUR TELEPHONE ORDERING SERVICE FOR
ACCESS/VISA CARDHOLDERS –
TEL: GLASGOW 041-772 2281 or LONDON 081-307 4052